JUDAH MAGNES

UNIVERSITY OF NEBRASKA PRESS   LINCOLN

Judah Magnes

The Prophetic Politics of a Religious Binationalist

DAVID BARAK-GORODETSKY

TRANSLATED BY MERAV DATAN

THE JEWISH PUBLICATION SOCIETY   PHILADELPHIA

© 2021 by David Barak-Gorodetsky

Originally published as *Yirmiyahu be-tzion: Dat u-politika be-olamo shel Yehuda Leib Magnes* [Jeremiah in Zion: The Religion and Politics of Judah Leib Magnes] in 2018 by the Publishing House of the Ben-Gurion Research Institute for the Study of Israel and Zionism, the Ben-Gurion University of the Negev.

Acknowledgments for the use of copyrighted material appear on pages xvii–xviii, which constitute an extension of the copyright page.

All rights reserved. Published by the University of Nebraska Press as a Jewish Publication Society book. Manufactured in the United States of America.

Library of Congress Cataloging-in-Publication Data
Names: Barak-Gorodetsky, David,
author. | Datan, Merav, translator.
Title: Judah Magnes: the prophetic politics of a religious binationalist / David Barak-Gorodetsky; translated by Merav Datan.
Other titles: Yirmeyahu be-Tsiyon English.
Description: Philadelphia: Jewish Publication Society; Lincoln: University of Nebraska Press, 2021. |
Includes bibliographical references and index.
Identifiers: LCCN 2021007258
ISBN 9780827615168 (paperback)
ISBN 9780827618824 (epub)
ISBN 9780827618831 (pdf)
Subjects: LCSH: Magnes, J. L. (Judah Leon), 1877–1948. | Berit shalom (Organization: Palestine) | Rabbis—Palestine—Biography. | Reform Judaism—Palestine. | Reform Zionism. |
Political theology. | Palestine—Biography.
Classification: LCC DS151.M225 B3713 2021 |
DDC 956.94/04092 [B]—dc23
LC record available at https://lccn.loc.gov/2021007258

Set in Lyon by Laura Buis.
Designed by N. Putens.

To my wife and children
Anat, Shalem, and Ilay

CONTENTS

Preface *ix*

Acknowledgments *xvii*

Introduction *xix*

PART 1. "MENDING THE WORLD":
RELIGIOUS AND POLITICAL FOUNDATIONS

1. The Importance of Being Earnest *3*
2. "Palestine or Death" *21*
3. Prophetic Socialism and the Social Gospel *39*
4. The Religious Mission of Pacifism *51*

PART 2. "FOR THE SAKE OF ZION":
PROMOTING BINATIONALISM IN PALESTINE

5. The High Holy Days in Jerusalem *77*
6. Hebrew University and Brit Shalom *93*

7. The Prophetic Model *107*

8. Nationalism and Binationalism *125*

9. Binationalism as Theological Politics *147*

10. Magnes and the Theopolitics of Buber *167*

11. Faith and Skepticism in the Binational Cause *181*

PART 3. "THE ECLIPSE OF GOD":
WAR, HOLOCAUST, AND THE FOUNDING OF THE STATE

12. Existential Theology and Moral Politics *201*

13. Religion Overrides Nationalism *221*

14. The Sacred Land and the Negation of the State *233*

15. The Confederation Plan between Hope and Despair *253*

Conclusion *261*

Notes *269*

Bibliography *305*

Index *321*

PREFACE

In his novel *Shira*, Israeli Nobel laureate S. Y. Agnon describes Judah Leib Magnes without actually naming him: "All eyes were on the president of the university, who had begun his speech. He had been a Reform rabbi in his youth and had been forced to leave his post because he was a Zionist. Although he retained some of the mannerisms of the Reform rabbinate, which are considered ridiculous in this country, his height, style, and dignity led even the cynics in the hall to listen to what he had to say."[1]

Agnon's backhanded compliment captures how Magnes was perceived in the Yishuv (the prestate Jewish community of Israel): some measure of respect for his personality and sacrifice in immigrating to Palestine—a rare move among Zionist American leaders, which alongside him only Henrietta Szold, founder of Hadassah, had taken—mixed with reservations about his political activity and lack of understanding as to its origins.

Magnes was and remained a foreigner in Jewish Palestine. His culture, customs, and beliefs were unfamiliar, completely detached from the daily and spiritual life of the Yishuv. So too was his style of dress, which was elegant and meticulous even when he visited kibbutzim (agricultural cooperatives) and rural settlements in the heat of summer. So too was the slightly clumsy Hebrew he spoke, with its traces of an undefinable accent; and so too was the baseball game he organized on every Fourth of July—the American day of independence and the day preceding his own birthday.

In Palestine, to reinforce his university status but also to play down his religious identity, Magnes opted for the title "Dr." over "Rabbi." At the same time, Magnes's religious perspective was the cornerstone and principal pillar of his political outlook. Even when he withdrew from the Reform movement and adopted more Conservative views, Magnes was, and remained, at the core of his identity, a Reform rabbi. Yet Reform Judaism, at the time mostly alienated from Zionism, had no formal presence in the Yishuv, and did not resonate with the local Jewish populace, few of whom were from America or Western Europe. Instead, Magnes's Reform Judaism was taken as evidence that he lacked authentic Jewish roots. This perception struck at the heart of Magnes's complex internal religious world, which combined American Reform liberalism with Conservatism, an openly prophetic ethos with a torturous personal quest, and pragmatic rationalism with religious sensitivity that encompassed clandestine worship among the Hasidic communities of New York and Jerusalem. Yet, as this work hopes to demonstrate, Magnes was a deeply religious man, forever questioning the ways of God in the world.

Because of its individualistic American tendencies, Magnes's religious worldview also conflicted with the collective ethos of the traditional East European Judaism that shaped the outlook of the Yishuv's political leaders—even those presumably liberated from it. He was a hero and, perhaps, victim of the sociopolitical American ethos of the prophetic preacher-revolutionary who brings the name of the Lord to a wayward people and returns them to the path of the righteous.

Magnes believed in subordinating politics to morality and divine justice. As this book documents, he knew that binationalism was probably a lost cause, a battle similar to that of Don Quixote. A year before the 1929 riots in Palestine, which motivated him to engage openly in political activism, Magnes predicted the futility of the political process he was planning to initiate, quipping that his decision to join the Palestine movement would eventually prove itself to be "illusory and almost barren."[2]

Like a prophet unable to suppress his prophecy, Magnes could not resist what he saw as a religious calling to take political action, even against all odds. This was the secret of his political determination and the source of attraction behind his idealistic stance, as well as the core reason his plans failed to materialize. Although Magnes, like the Jewish philosopher Martin Buber, regarded the moral, prophetic outlook as the true and far-sighted form of realism, ultimately a lack of willingness on the part of a majority of Palestine's Arabs and leaders to agree to the preconditions necessary for political cooperation with the Jewish Yishuv, whether through partition or binationalism, eluded him. This is illustrated, for example, by his meeting with the Palestinian Christian intellectual Khalil al-Sakakini at the Shepherd Hotel in Jerusalem during World War II. Magnes was convinced that the Christians in Palestine were leaning toward political extremism because they were an unrepresented minority that feared the Muslim majority; otherwise, they would cooperate with the Yishuv and accept binationalism. "Let us speak openly, Doctor," responded al-Sakakini, and told him a tale involving a donkey. A man who was riding his donkey saw another man walking and invited him to ride together. The second man climbed on the donkey and commented, "How fast your donkey is!" They rode on, and the stranger observed, "How fast our donkey is!" The donkey's owner then said, "Get down!" and the other man asked "Why?" The owner replied, "I'm afraid that soon you'll say 'How fast my donkey is!'"[3] In other words, Magnes failed to grasp that the Arab position stemmed from fears about losing ownership over land they considered their own.

Magnes never held an official Yishuv position of the sort that necessitated political effort to achieve and therefore demanded compromise, and he did not have to deal with the practical responsibility of a public post. Members of the Yishuv's political leadership—in particular the future first prime minister of Israel, David Ben-Gurion, and future first president, Chaim Weizmann, whose views were closer to those of Magnes—regarded his prophetic politics as overly conciliatory and as a dangerous formula for conducting negotiations in the Middle Eastern setting. Even Magnes's colleagues from the Central European circle at the Hebrew University, who openly backed his proposed solutions and took part in his political efforts, ultimately came to view him as an American troubadour and relic of nineteenth-century idealism in the midst of ever-changing twentieth-century politics. And thus, as he had feared, his American voice remained the only one in favor of binationalism, a lone voice in the desert.

That conclusion, however, also points to a major oversight in accounts to date of Magnes's story. The members of Brit Shalom, and later Ichud—the two leading organizations promoting binationalism in the Yishuv—participated in Magnes's political plans and generally shared his view of the moral demands incumbent upon Zionism, as well as some sources of influence (such as the Cultural Zionism formulator, Ahad Ha'am). But Magnes differed from them, both in terms of his simple and direct American pragmatism, as compared with their dialectical European roots, and even more so in terms of the religious fervor that drove his political activity. They repeatedly claimed that Magnes had restored their faith in politics. But at the moment of truth, Magnes—the tireless religious seeker and servant of God in his own eyes—cast his lot entirely with the moral compass of idealism, while they retreated to a more complex stance that enabled them to survive the complete upheaval resulting from the creation of the State of Israel. Compared with them, Magnes's achievements and the historical memory of his activity seem frozen in time, in 1948, with his passing in the United States shortly after the founding of Israel.

"There are some Jews who object to the Jewish State for religious or for political reasons," he wrote in 1942. "I am not among them. They say that Judaism is a religion and that religion has nothing to do with politics. I also say that Judaism is a religion but that religion has everything to do with politics."[4] These remarks provide a good starting point for this book's proposed quest: the religious and political identity of Judah Leib Magnes in the Land of Israel.

First, though, I wish to add a personal note about the study before you. By its very nature, a book, especially one based on academic research, is an ongoing journey of many years. During those years, an author's perspective might change in significant ways. Such was my journey.

It was as an undergraduate student in the Jewish History Department at Haifa University that I first began to research the figure of Magnes. At the time I had been planning to explore other aspects of my personal and collective Jewish identity—Greek and Turkish Jewry and the political aspects of the Sabbatean movement—but I took the good advice of Professor Mina Rozen: either pick a different subject, or register for courses in Ladino, Turkish, and Greek. A research paper I completed for a course on U.S. Jewry taught by Professor Zohar Segev, who in time became one of my dissertation advisers, opened a gateway to a new world of research and thought surrounding Jewish history, politics, and religion. The language was more accessible, too, and my hope was that this research could have an impact on current events.

The first factor motivating me to explore the figure of Judah Leib Magnes was his religious search, which paralleled my own journey through the complexities of Jewish identity. The choice of Haifa University was the eventual outcome of seven years of quest, and occasional discovery, across a broad spectrum of Jewish communities within and outside Israel. Seeking to ground my personal religious quest in an academic environment, I entered the undergraduate program in Jewish thought and from there continued directly to doctoral studies in Jewish history. The transition from Jewish philosophy to Jewish history allowed me to integrate religious and theological themes with actual, and often political, historical developments. Thus there emerged the specific interface of approaches and directions of query that characterize this study.

At the time I also saw myself as more closely aligned with Magnes's political outlook. I was living in Haifa, a city that prides itself on Jewish-Arab coexistence, and had close ties with political circles that were calling for the inclusion of binationalism on Israel's agenda. My academic interest in Magnes was therefore a natural extension of my political views. His proposal seemed to me to offer a way to combine a liberal religious doctrine encompassing prophetic elements with the particular politics of the hour and the situation in my divided country. I must admit that over time—indeed, as a direct result of closely examining the figure of Magnes—I developed doubts about his political path. It is my hope that the reader will be able to discern the two perspectives presented here—that which sees Magnes's moral force and idealistic charm, alongside that which recognizes the danger inherent in liberal religious ideology encountering the political arena, with all of the latter's real-world constraints.

After finishing my doctorate, I set out on another journey—Reform rabbinical studies at the Hebrew Union College-Jewish Institute of Religion in Jerusalem. These studies, and my consequent work as a community rabbi, have given me insights into the rabbinic dimension of Magnes's identity. At the same time, I realize my study might generate doubts as to the esteem in which Magnes is held in Reform circles. As the book illustrates, Magnes was conservatively inclined in his religious outlook, and the possibility that he could be remembered today as a cofounder of Conservative Judaism is not inconceivable. The fact that he was not among the movement's founders in practice was the result of personal circumstances yet to be elucidated through scholarship. Furthermore, Magnes was quite critical of the American Reform movement at the time, and some of his criticism might find an echo today. I have refrained, to the best of my ability and knowledge, from moderating this criticism, yet I have also tried to avoid overemphasizing it.

Let me also address the historiographic context in which this book appears. I consider myself part of a wide circle of historians who seek to reintroduce into the academic and public discourse the question of religion's place in the Zionist story. In Magnes's context, the absence of religion from the story is especially puzzling: How did it happen that even within American Jewish historiography, it is not seen as self-evident that there would be a correlation between the religious and political outlooks of an ordained Reform rabbi? The answer, in my view, rests on the extent of religiosity inherent in American Jewish liberal religious identity. This study reveals the deeper religious roots of Magnes's thinking, and these in turn make it possible to identify the missing piece of Magnes's theopolitical puzzle.

Above all, I have endeavored to construct a worthy monument to the figure of Magnes within collective Israeli and American Jewish memory. On more than one occasion I have asked myself: Am I being faithful to the true figure of Magnes, or deviating from it? This process necessitated extensive self-examination along personal, historiographic, and public dimensions.

One aspect of being true to the figure of Magnes was the publication of this book in Hebrew before English. This English version was translated from the Hebrew edition published in 2018 by the Publishing House of the Ben-Gurion Research Institute for the Study of Israel & Zionism, The Ben-Gurion University of the Negev. It has now been edited, expanded, and updated to be salient for an English readership, with its title adjusted as well. Current academic practice encourages the publication of studies on Israel in English first, but in my view that would have been inapt here. Magnes wanted his voice to be heard in Zion, and given his Ahad Ha'am–like commitment to the Hebrew language as the cornerstone of Jewish cultural renewal, I believe Magnes himself would have wanted it this way.

"In this book, David Barak-Gorodetsky offers fascinating new perspective on Judah L. Magnes. Part Jeremiah, part Gandhi, and part Sisyphus, Magnes was an American in Palestine, a religious man in a political world, and an idealist among pragmatists. Barak-Gorodetsky's superb excavation of Magnes's roots in American theology opens our eyes to a much fuller portrait than has been offered before. One grasps Magnes's animating sensibilities, as well as the discomfort he felt and generated in his transplanted home in Jerusalem. But generating discomfort was one of his goals, as he challenged the verities of Zionism with his prophetic voice, pointing to a different, moral standard as the ideal axis around which the national movement should revolve. A pathbreaking biography of an ever-intriguing and enigmatic figure."
—DAVID N. MYERS, professor and Sady and Ludwig Kahn Chair in Jewish History, University of California, Los Angeles

"One might imagine that nothing novel could be written about Judah Magnes, but this highly original, sophisticated, and brilliantly insightful portrait of Magnes against the backdrop of his times allows Magnes to come alive anew as a man of great religious conviction, shedding crucial new light on Magnes and highlighting his significance for our moment. I enthusiastically recommend this book to anyone interested in Magnes, the history of Zionism and the Yishuv, and modern Jewish intellectual and religious history."
—RABBI DAVID ELLENSON, chancellor emeritus, Hebrew Union College—Jewish Institute of Religion

"With this compelling biography, David Barak-Gorodetsky offers important revision to our understanding of Judah Magnes, rightly centering his religious fervor and idealism at the core of his politics."
—PAMELA S. NADELL, author of *America's Jewish Women: A History from Colonial Times to Today*

PRAISE FOR THE HEBREW VERSION

"A solid work of intellectual history, devoted above all to understanding Judah Magnes as he understood himself, sympathetic but honest, and attentive to the weaknesses as well as the strengths of his thinking."
—ALLAN ARKUSH, *Jewish Review of Books*

ACKNOWLEDGMENTS

Many have helped me along this fascinating journey, through advice, guidance, and grants that enabled me to complete the research, and I am deeply grateful to all.

The book is based on a doctoral dissertation completed in the Department of Jewish History at Haifa University under the supervision of Zohar Segev from that department and Shalom Ratzabi from Tel Aviv University. It was a tremendous privilege for me to have both of them as mentors and I benefited greatly from their vast knowledge and insights. Special thanks are due to Professor Segev, whose door was always open for consultation or conversation, and whose persistence helped me secure the funding necessary to complete this study.

I also wish to thank the Graduate Studies Authority at Haifa University for the grants I received during the course of my studies, especially the President's Scholarship. Additional thanks are due to Gur Alroey, who took me on as an instructor at the Ruderman Program for American Jewish Studies, and to Cedric Cohen-Skalli, who lent an ear whenever I had an intellectual question or quandary.

I am also grateful to the personnel of the various archives on which I relied, without whom the work of a historian could never be completed.

I specifically wish to thank the staff of the American Jewish Archives in Cincinnati, and in particular Gary Zola and Dana Herman.

Additionally I thank the Publishing House of the Ben-Gurion Research Institute for the Study of Israel & Zionism, The Ben-Gurion University of the Negev, which published the original version of this book in Hebrew in 2018.

The publication of this book subsequently in English was made possible thanks to the generous assistance of the Israel Movement for Progressive Judaism (IMPJ). Special thanks are due to Rabbi Gilad Kariv, executive director of the IMPJ, for his assistance in obtaining this funding and his support for the ongoing research. Many thanks are also due to Ofer Shiff, who opened the gates of the Ben-Gurion Research Institute for the Study of Israel & Zionism to me and received me as a research fellow at the Laboratory for the Study of Israel and the Jewish People. In addition, I would like to thank the devoted translator of this work, Merav Datan, who worked diligently and swiftly to produce the best translation possible.

I would especially like to thank my editor on behalf of The Jewish Publication Society, Joy Weinberg, whose meticulous reviews and creative suggestions were essential in transforming the book for an English-speaking audience. Additional much-deserved thanks to Rabbi Barry Schwartz, director of The Jewish Publication Society, for approaching me to suggest the publication of this book with JPS and for his patience and professionalism in the production process. I also wish to thank the University of Nebraska Press for being a publication partner for this volume.

Finally, I must admit that this book would never have seen the light of day without the daily assistance, encouragement, and support of my beloved wife, Anat, or without the patience of my children, Shalem and Ilay, who were born during the course of this research. To them, above all, my thanks and my love.

INTRODUCTION

The political theorist Hannah Arendt would eulogize Judah Leib Magnes as "the conscience of the Jewish People."[1] To philosopher Samuel Hugo Bergman, who worked alongside Magnes, he was "one of the crucial figures in the development of Jewish religious thought and life in our time, especially in Israel." Bergman ranked Magnes among the German Jewish philosophers and theologians Hermann Cohen and Franz Rosenzweig, Martin Buber, Zionist ideologue and agriculturist Aaron David Gordon, and the first chief rabbi of prestate Israel, Rabbi Abraham Isaac Kook.[2]

Magnes was a Reform rabbi, American Zionist leader, and, in time, the first chancellor of the Hebrew University of Jerusalem.[3] Most of his political activity related to the concept of binationalism and the bodies that sought to advance it at the time, in particular Brit Shalom (though he was not a member), founded in 1926, and the association Ichud, which he helped establish in the summer of 1942.

This book aims to uncover the connection between Magnes's political activity and his religious outlook. It explains how, because of its religious as well as political American foundations, Magnes's outlook is unique among the views of his partners in the struggle for binationalism, including Buber, Bergman, educator Ernst Simon, and other West European intellectuals. One may view Magnes's experience as a unique attempt to reproduce the religious politics of the American Reform movement in the Zionist arena of Jewish Palestine in a way that links American federative concepts with Jewish moral principles.

This book also delves into Magnes's political motivation and subsequent modus operandi. As we shall see, a main driver behind Magnes's political activity was his identification with the figure of the prophet (especially Jeremiah) who calls on his people to repent morally, and Magnes's corresponding efforts to realize the ethical monotheism and biblical prophecy that characterized the Reform movement generally and the American stream specifically. This model of motivation is characterized by loneliness, which, despite his partnership with the Central European circles of Brit Shalom and Ichud, corresponded with Magnes's status as an American immigrant in Jerusalem. The model also embodies a pattern of abstention from political activity (like the prophet who seeks to suppress his prophetic vision) followed by immersion in political activity against all odds. For Magnes this meant losing his status in established institutions—first the Reform movement, then the Zionist movement and American Judaism generally, and later the Hebrew University and Jewish Palestine as a whole.

Notably, Magnes was not a methodical thinker, and he never proposed an interpretation of Judaism in the form of an orderly doctrine. He did not engage in systematic scholarly writing; nor was he an active partner in the academic discourse of his time. While his administrative role at the Hebrew University brought him into regular contact with prominent figures in the scholarly discourse of the day—members of Central European intellectual circles that shaped the character of the Hebrew University—and even though he too had earned his doctorate in Europe, Magnes never earned the esteem of most members of these circles as an intellectual of equal stature. At the same time, Magnes's lack of orderliness and consistency in his espoused positions attest to the centrality of the religious dimension in his outlook, which manifested in both ups and downs: messianic zeal and self-conviction alongside crises of faith and a sense that God had been eclipsed.

To what extent was Magnes's religious view a personal one related to the question of faith between man and God, and to what extent was it a systematic religious worldview, or theology, from which one can derive a political system as well? This book addresses these questions through multiple lenses: the extent to which and manner in which his experiential religious view motivated him to engage in political activity; the patterns of action that followed; and this author's efforts to characterize his (not always coherently framed) religious perspective as a political theology in which a political outlook and plan—in this case, binationalism—followed logically from his religious position. As we shall see, in Magnes's case the religious and political approaches were deeply intertwined.

This book therefore focuses on assessing the interconnectedness between Magnes's religious worldview and its evolution, on the one hand, and his political outlook and activity, on the other. Drawing on his publications, journals, and correspondence, it surveys the range of conceptual thought that shaped Magnes's world along these two main axes (religious and political), its theopolitical aspects in particular,[4] as well as links to Magnes's ideological environment. It demonstrates how Magnes's views on fundamental questions of religion, first and foremost the question of faith and the vindication of God's goodness and omnipotence even in the face of evil (theodicy), developed hand in hand with fundamentally American political precepts based on pragmatism and federalism.

The juxtaposition between the religious and the political is further examined in relation to key moments in Magnes's political career: his strong opposition to World War I after the United States entered the war (1917), the publication of his piece *Like All the Nations?* after the Western Wall riots (1929),[5] and his political activity in the Yishuv during the

1930s and 1940s, particularly his testimony before the Anglo-American Committee of Inquiry on Palestine (1946). Thus one might regard this study as a religious-political biography of Magnes: first establishing the centrality of the religious dimension in his thinking and then examining his political work from this perspective.

A Brief Biography

Judah Leon Magnes was born in Oakland, California, in 1878. In time he changed his middle name to Leib, in memory of his grandfather, who came from a Hasidic community in Poland. He acquired full mastery of the German language thanks to his mother, who was of German heritage. As a child he attended Jewish schools in the San Francisco Bay area, and by age eight he delivered his first sermon at a synagogue.

In 1896, as a rabbinical student at the Hebrew Union College in Cincinnati, a year before the First Zionist Congress, Magnes wrote an article, "Palestine—or Death," criticizing the Reform movement for its position that "America is our Palestine, and Washington is Jerusalem." In October 1901, while in Berlin pursuing a doctorate (which he eventually completed in Heidelberg), Magnes established the Zionist student union Agudah Leumit (the "National Association") and wrote to his parents that Zionism was his life's plan (*Lebensprogramm*).[6]

In August 1904, after completing his doctorate and moving to New York, Magnes served as a rabbi for three Reform congregations, regularly clashing with their lay leaders. Magnes viewed the alternative stream of Judaism proposed by Jewish scholar and educator Solomon Schechter, which came to be known as Conservative Judaism, as an opportunity to vitalize liberal Judaism in the United States. On the eve of Passover 1910, while delivering a sermon at New York's Temple Emanu-El under the heading "Reform Judaism: Plans for Reconstruction," Magnes called on the congregation to dissociate officially from the Reform movement and identify itself as an "unofficial Reform congregation." By identifying as such, he argued, the congregation would bridge the gap between itself and traditional Jewish identity, which he believed was being best carried into modernity through the initiatives of Schechter and Zecharias Frankel, founder of the Jewish Theological Seminary in Breslau. At the same time, Magnes was among the initiators, founders, and leaders of the Kehillah (1909 to 1922), the first umbrella organization uniting all the Jewish congregations in New York.[7]

Magnes's activities during World War I combined pacifism with socialism. He was among the founders of the People's Council of America for Democracy and Peace (the umbrella organization of antiwar movements), and among the speakers at the organization's founding conference on May 30, 1917.[8] His socialist outlook and stated pacifism brought Magnes in close contact with other social and religious circles in American society, in particular the Social Gospel, a religious social reform movement that had emerged in the United States in the late nineteenth century.[9] In the Jewish world, on the other hand, his radical position drove him to the margins of American Jewish discourse: American Jews saw his opposition to the war as threatening the patriotic image they were determined to advance. He was removed from leadership positions, and in 1922 he immigrated to Palestine. A year later he was elected to supervise the establishment of the Hebrew University of Jerusalem, and then to head it.

Magnes's involvement in founding and overseeing the Hebrew University was the crowning glory of his activity in Palestine during the 1920s, as well as the basis for his authority among the public. Magnes saw the Hebrew University as the cultural center for the Jewish people with a unique and vital role to play: to build a moral society in the spirit of the prophets of Israel. During this period Magnes refrained from open political activity.

He became publicly active in Palestine as a direct consequence of the August 1929 Western Wall riots (a series of demonstrations and riots that erupted when a long-running dispute between Muslims and Jews over access to the Western Wall in Jerusalem escalated into violence).

During the first decade of his political activism in the Yishuv (1929–1938), Magnes was involved in several initiatives to reach agreement between Jews and Arabs in Palestine. He espoused parity and binationalism, and opposed the idea of a national Jewish state.

The second decade of his political activism (1939–1948) was marked by World War II and the fate of European Jews, the Biltmore Program (May 1942)—which, for the first time, set the establishment of a Jewish state upon conclusion of the war as the central aim of Zionism—and later the United Nations Partition Plan for Palestine, which recommended the establishment of separate Jewish and Arab states in Palestine and the termination of the British Mandate. He established the association Ichud following the announcement of the Biltmore Program; and in March 1946 (alongside Buber) delivered testimony before the Anglo-American Committee of Inquiry on Ichud's behalf, opposing partition and proposing a phased outline for binationalism. In May 1948, on the verge of Israel's independence, Magnes met with President Harry Truman and Secretary of State George Marshall in what would be a last-minute failed effort to promote a binational alternative. A few months after Israel attained statehood, Magnes passed away in the United States.[10]

Historiography

One of the salient points that emerges from the historiography on Magnes to date is the complexity of his character. The historian of American Judaism Jonathan Sarna portrays Magnes as having "chameleon-like qualities," being "at one and the same time, trained in the Classical Reform tradition, enchanted by Orthodoxy, related to New York's best Jewish families, and sympathetic both to Zionism and to Socialism."[11] "The more books I read about him," writes the Israeli novelist Hadara Lazar, "in the many journals and letters he wrote, the more I felt that I actually do not know who J. L. Magnes [was]."[12] Gershom Scholem, a scholar of Jewish mysticism and contemporary of Magnes, said of him that he was the most complex figure he had ever met.[13] Many scholars who addressed his complexity have situated Magnes along some sort of axis of internal tension—such as East versus West or tradition versus progress (David Myers)—or between priest and prophet (Arthur Goren).[14]

Interestingly, the research on Magnes over the past twenty years can also be distinguished by the geographical location of the scholar. North American scholars tend to highlight the American dimension to Magnes's work, framing it as "an attempt to Americanize the Yishuv."[15] Among Israeli scholars, there have emerged two major, discernible lines of thought: the first, a right-wing critique of Magnes's political activity, and the second, a part of the leftist historiography of the Zionist enterprise, which explores historical alternatives to Zionism's course of development before Israel's independence and regards Magnes as a case study.[16] To date the rich body of research on binationalism in the Zionist Jewish context has largely focused on the Central European circle with which Magnes had contact, without close examination of all the American, religious, and political factors unique to his perspective. Otherwise put, the research to date has lacked a comprehensive conceptual study on the American aspects of the Jewish perspective on binationalism, of which Magnes was the main representative. This book aims to fill that gap.

Furthermore, it endeavors to illuminate other broad fields of study, most significantly the importance of the religious dimension in the Zionist enterprise, a subject receiving renewed attention in our times.

Political Theology: A Conceptual Framework

The separation of church and state is considered one of the hallmark principles of modernity. Many view a relationship between religion and politics as an anachronism, as a dangerous form of excess from the Middle Ages.[17] The Jewish scholar and sociologist of religion Jacob Taubes, in contrast, points out that theology emerged as an issue within political theory, and that the term itself first appeared in Plato's dialogues. For the ancient Greek philosopher Plato, the subject of religion is intertwined with political thought, because the philosopher's political concern for the community is what informs theoretical disciplines, including theology. Even the theology of the Divine as an absolute "other"—which aims to be apolitical—is not devoid of political implications. Taubes goes on to argue that just as there is no theology without political implications, there is also no political theory devoid of theological premises.[18]

Haim Rechnitzer, who has examined the writings of twentieth-century political philosopher Leo Strauss, who in turn draws on Plato and Enlightenment philosopher Baruch Spinoza, proposes a functional definition of political theology. Theopolitical thought, according to Rechnitzer, is characterized by the meaning and validity it grants ideology and political thought through religious language and theological models. In other words, political theology is a historiosophic discourse that uses religious concepts to interpret the course of history. This interpretation, along with other factors, facilitates the delineation of political policy. A change in the political position of someone who adheres to a political theology must therefore, according to Rechnitzer, be based on a religious worldview and on reasoning that uses theological language.[19]

Scholars William Cavanaugh and Peter Scott propose a conceptual framework for the analysis of political theology that defines theology as a "discourse about God, and human persons as they relate to God," and politics as "the use of structural power to organize a society or community of people." Following these broad definitions, political theology is defined as "the analysis and critique of political arrangements . . . from the perspective of differing interpretations of God's ways with the world." On the basis of this definition, Cavanaugh and Scott point to three possible approaches to theopolitical analysis. The first presumes that politics is a "given" and is conducted in an autonomous, secular space. According to this approach, politics and theology are two distinct and separate spheres of activity: politics refers to public authority, while theology deals with religious experience and the "semiprivate associations of religious believers." Admittedly, political theology might link religious beliefs to political issues, but it should not dismiss the autonomy of these two systems. The second approach, which may be termed "critical theology,"[20] views theology as a tool for critical political analysis. Theology is seen as "superstructure to the material politico-economic base" and it "reflects and reinforces just or unjust political arrangements." Here the role of political theology is to expose the manner in which theological discourse replicates and preserves social inequality (traditionally constructed in terms of gender, race, or economic status) and to propose an alternative and more just theology. The third approach regards theology and politics as essentially similar spheres of activity, as both are engaged in creating metaphysical images around which society and community organize. Since theology is inseparably intertwined into every activity and form of political organization, the task of political theology is to expose the "false" theologies underpinning supposedly secular politics while promoting "the true politics implicit in a true theology" in a constructive, rather than critical, manner.[21]

These three approaches overlap to some extent with Magnes's politico-religious conception. The first approach, which distinguishes between politics and theology, is largely reflected in the politico-theological outlook of American Reform Judaism. Reform Judaism in the United States developed in parallel to American Protestantism, and among the many influences by the latter on the former was drawing a distinction between the state/public sphere and the private sphere, and in viewing religion as a private, or at most communal, matter without concrete political implications. This was the conceptual foundation on which Magnes was raised, and his views on Zionism and its proper implementation in Palestine were perpetually in tension with this foundation.

The second approach, "critical theology," is compatible with the religious socialism and pacifism characteristic of Magnes's activities during World War I and prior to his emigration to Palestine. In the 1930s and 1940s Magnes also attempted to expose the deceptive political theologies of political Zionism, which he viewed as false messianism and a moral and political failing that could not be reconciled with Judaism.

The third approach, which points to the similarities between theology and politics, corresponds with Magnes's political theology during the period of his political efforts to promote binationalism in Palestine. He sought to promote a politics based directly on his religious worldview, regardless of the fact that the political environment—the Yishuv—was not particularly receptive to religious arguments regarding political matters.

Structure of the Book

This survey of Magnes's thought and work over the course of five decades, from 1896 to 1948, is organized into three parts, corresponding with the main developmental phases of Magnes's religious and political perspectives within the various spheres of his activity.

Part 1, "'Mending the World': Religious and Political Foundations," reviews the development of Magnes's views in the United States and the roots of his ideological and religious thought. The first chapter traces the evolution of Magnes's worldview during his youth and early days of activism in the American Jewish arena, taking into account the prevalent ideological trends of the time. Chapter 2 examines the development of Magnes's Zionist outlook, with attention to the cultural Zionism of Ahad Ha'am and its importance for American Zionism. Chapter 3 explores the many influences shaping Magnes's religious socialism: Reform Judaism, Hermann Cohen, the Social Gospel movement, and the radical Jewish socialist circles in New York with which Magnes interacted during the early twentieth century. The fourth chapter weighs Magnes's pacifism as a religious pacifism with traditional, textual, and historical characteristics, and in particular the Reform influences on his radical stance.

Part 2, "'For the Sake of Zion': Promoting Binationalism in Palestine," examines Magnes's political activity and thought during the 1920s and 1930s, after his 1922 immigration to Palestine. Chapter 5 presents his basic religious worldview; the importance he attributed to the fundamental questions of religious faith—whether God exists and how to vindicate God in the face of evil; and the impact these questions had on the entire range of his activities, including his political activism in the Yishuv. Chapter 6 assesses religious and political aspects of Magnes's efforts in founding the Hebrew University and interacting with the Central European circle of Brit Shalom intellectuals concentrated there. Chapter 7 analyzes how Magnes's identification with the image of the prophet, specifically Jeremiah, sheds light on his political modus operandi; and how Magnes applied his interpretation of Karl Barth's dialectical theology to his political activism and to Zionism more generally, in the context of actualizing a religious ideal in the material world. Chapter 8 examines Magnes's complex attitude toward nationalism in general and Jewish nationalism in particular. Chapter 9 discusses the evolution of Magnes's position on binationalism as a theopolitical stance (a political position fundamentally grounded in a religious perspective) against this background of his 1929 political plan for a binational state and its reception in the Yishuv. Chapter 10 compares the political theologies of Magnes and Buber, who also advocated binationalism, paying special attention to the differences between the American and European foundations of their respective outlooks. Chapter 11 studies Magnes's binationalism through the reality of his political activity during the 1930s.

Part 3, "'The Eclipse of God': War, Holocaust, and the Founding of the State," looks at the development of Magnes's religious and political views during the 1940s. Chapter 12 explores Magnes's political motivation in the context of his concept of God and enduring struggles of faith. Chapter 13 reflects on Magnes's inclination, on the eve of Israel's statehood, to return to religious study at the expense of Jewish nationalism. Chapter 14 surveys Magnes's political action during this decade, particularly his joint testimony with Martin Buber before the Anglo-American Committee on behalf of Ichud in March 1946. Chapter

15 discusses Magnes's relationship with the Jewish philosopher and political theorist Hannah Arendt: their mutual influence on one another in relation to the confederation solution—a binational political model for Palestine rooted in American political foundations. The conclusion integrates the many facets of Magnes's religion and politics as revealed in this book.

Magnes was a multifaceted figure, epitomizing the complexity of the juxtaposition of politics and religion in the Jewish response to modernity. During the span of his lifetime and journey from America to Zion, lofty ideas clashed with bitter realities to transform modern Jewish existence at an unprecedented scale. Following this journey offers a unique perspective on the innate tensions of modern Jewish realities, applicable then and today.

JUDAH MAGNES

PART 1

"Mending the World"

Religious and Political Foundations

1

The Importance of Being Earnest

Magnes's roots, which trace back to the Western liberalism of California, were a formative element of his identity. His birthplace, Oakland, was the first setting of the University of California—the Athens of the West at the time. This was an environment of optimism, adventure, and liberal aspiration. American novelist Gertrude Stein, too, had grown up in Oakland before leaving for Harvard and later immigrating to Paris, where she was at the center of literary and artistic avant-garde circles. Both Magnes and Stein grew up in traditional Jewish homes, and studied together under Rachel Frank, who, though not certified as a rabbi, led prayer services and delivered sermons throughout the West Coast. Both Magnes and Stein would later regard their California youths as a key factor in shaping their lives and inspiring their pursuit of individual liberty and intellectual integrity.[1] Magnes's friend and first biographer, Norman Bentwich, wrote of Magnes's ties to California: "From his earliest years he had the independence natural to the pioneer state that California still was in those days."[2]

Alongside the liberalism attributable to his California roots, Magnes also showed early signs of gravitas. To paraphrase playwright Oscar Wilde, he always knew the importance of earnestness.[3] In his earliest sermons, which were published in the local press, one finds evidence of both his rhetorical skill and his preoccupation with weighty issues, as illustrated by his commentary on Proverbs 10:7 ("The memory of the righteous is a blessing; but the name of the wicked shall perish") in a sermon delivered at age eight.[4] Later, in his essay "Palestine—or Death" (1896), Magnes would also praise the great earnestness of his parents' generation and their observance of religious practice, qualities and practices he believed the current generation lacked. Although he was not calling for a return to the isolation that characterized the previous Jewish generation, he viewed this loss of earnestness—which to him was a direct outcome of intellectualism, liberalism, and freedom—as the heavy price American Jews had paid for their successful integration into society.

Influence of Jacob Voorsanger

One of the figures that most influenced Magnes during his youth was Jacob Voorsanger. In 1886 Voorsanger was appointed as assistant to the rabbi of Temple Emanu-El in San Francisco. While he was never ordained as a rabbi—his formal education had concluded with graduation from a Jewish high school—he nonetheless inherited the title of "serving rabbi" three years later and maintained this position until his death in 1908. Voorsanger belonged to the radical second generation of Reform rabbis, alongside such figures as Emil Hirsch from Chicago and Kaufmann Kohler from New York (who would later become president of Hebrew Union College in Cincinnati). They opposed the direction in which Isaac Mayer Wise, Reform's quintessential founding father, had been taking the U.S. Reform movement: seeking compromise with Orthodox Judaism and unity among American Jewry. Voorsanger and his colleagues advocated a liberal theology characteristic of the Progressive Era. They believed that science had unlimited potential and the world was in a constant process of improvement. They aspired to create a synthesis between Judaism and scientific development that would ensure daily religious ritual was conducted in a dignified manner, without any residual elements from the premodern past. Voorsanger advocated use of *The Union Prayer Book* compiled by Kohler, which contained primarily English liturgical texts and lacked any reference to sacrificial offerings or genuine messianic aspiration. He strongly opposed the legalism of Orthodox Jewry and did not consider himself bound by the halakhah (body of Jewish law, spanning all spheres of life) pertaining to the Sabbath and kashrut (dietary laws). He led prayer services without the customary head covering and officiated at intermarriages.[5]

Voorsanger, like the prominent Reform rabbis of his time, was opposed to Zionism, which he saw as "one of the wildest of all wild dreams." In his view, the Zionist vision was impractical and a Jewish state antithetical to the mission of the Jewish people. "We refuse," he wrote, "to believe that the divine intention is the degradation of the Jew from his present lofty position as a world-teacher to again become the neighbor of mongrel tribes, on the very edge of civilization." At the heart of his resistance to Zionism was also his love for his new country. California, according to Voorsanger—a land of lush valleys filled with wheat, grains, and luscious apples; mountains from which floodwaters flew, nourishing and rejuvenating the valleys; and previously unseen flowers carpeting the hillsides—was the land "on which the Almighty poured out all the blessings left over from the sixth day of creation . . . a gorgeous *edition de luxe* of Palestine of old" as described in the holy texts.[6]

After Magnes completed rabbinical training at Hebrew Union College in Cincinnati in 1900, Voorsanger began raising funds for him to travel to Germany for doctoral studies, and invited him to deliver a sermon at Temple Emanu-El in San Francisco. In introducing Magnes, Voorsanger commented: "Never have I felt so happy or so proud as I do in making way for this lad, whom I sent away with a benediction and who now comes back a rabbi in Israel."[7] With respect to the first three rabbis to have come from California, Voorsanger observed that although a rabbi's birthplace is not determinative, "many of us entertain a justifiable pride in 'our boys'. . . . They all have the 'Frisco grit, the patience and endurance of scholars, and the pride of men who, in common language, mean business." He added that "in former years it was dinned into our ears that that it is was impossible to make a Rabbi out of a 'native.' Now the pleasant duty devolves upon us to din into the ears of our friends that the 'native' makes a better rabbi for America than the foreigner, and that his abilities, religiousness, and his devotion are up to the standard any Jewish congregation has the right to demand."[8]

Voorsanger was underscoring the unique character of the American West as well as one of Magnes's key characteristics—his being native born. The implications were twofold: inwardly Magnes had to demonstrate to the Jewish community that as an American-born rabbi he had a sufficiently solid grasp of Judaism, while outwardly, in the eyes of the American public generally, he represented the arrival of the "new American Jew"—a genuine, original product of American liberalism.

An act of nature, however, led to a rift between Magnes and Voorsanger. Following the catastrophic 1906 San Francisco earthquake, the National Conference of Jewish Charities sent Magnes from New York to San Francisco to assess the damage to the city's Jewish community. In their report, Magnes and his colleague disputed Voorsanger's claim that ten thousand of the city's Jews were homeless and needed immediate assistance. From their visits to camps established by the Red Cross, the two envoys estimated that only two thousand or so Jews were homeless and in need of aid.[9]

Voorsanger's influence over Magnes, at least until the incident described above, should not be underestimated. Although Voorsanger was a fierce advocate of Americanization, next to Magnes—the American "native" with his German and Hasidic heritage—he allowed himself to remove his public mask and reveal his bond with tradition. "I know something of the Cincinnati atmosphere, or rather the lack of it," he wrote to Magnes during the latter's studies at Hebrew Union College.

"You need the mellowing influence of the European universities and the steadying process of some old Yeshiba [religious college]."

Voorsanger, like Magnes, was critical of the college for being academically weak at that time, training rabbis but not scholars. He regarded Magnes as the link to "the genuine, not the counterfeit spirit of Judaism" and, despite his aversion to Zionism, welcomed Magnes's participation in the Zionist congresses and encouraged him to serve as a Zionist leader. He genuinely supported Magnes's intention "to regenerate Israel, to resuscitate its soul, to restore its honor, to rejuvenate its inheritance."[10]

A Reform Foundation

Magnes began his studies at Hebrew Union College in the autumn of 1894. The president at the time was the prominent Reform rabbi Isaac Mayer Wise, regarded as the movement's founder in the United States. However, at the time, the college was not officially affiliated with Reform Judaism: Wise insisted that because the seminary provided classical Jewish studies and focused on original sources such as Hebrew Scripture and the Talmud, its graduates should be able to serve any congregation of any affiliation in the United States. Even Orthodox rabbi Sabato Morais of Mikveh Israel Synagogue, who was no friend of Reform Judaism, considered the college "deserving of the support of all Israelites."[11] Wise's efforts to make the rabbinic curriculum comprehensive in nature are further evidenced by its inclusion of Hebrew studies, which were not customary in the Reform movement at the time, and its exclusion of critical biblical commentary that would anger the Orthodox. Nonetheless, the curriculum clearly leaned toward the Reform agenda, incorporating Jewish philosophy and history, as well as general academic studies in conjunction with the University of Cincinnati.[12]

Magnes was highly critical of the college and its program of studies. It particularly upset him that the seminary ordained "preachers rather than theologians." Even the Hebrew lessons, he argued, were aimed at enabling students to read Hebrew during a sermon rather than delve into the true meaning of Jewish texts. His independent nature led to friction with the seminary's administration, at times over relatively minor issues—such as his refusal to sign a declaration stating that he would not cheat on exams, because he regarded it as patronizing.[13] Other times, however, this friction stemmed from knowledge gaps regarding religion and tradition. During the course of his rabbinical studies, Magnes had occasion to deliver a lecture on Rosh Hashanah and Yom Kippur before a literary group of young Jewish women. Yet, he discovered, as he later wrote to his parents, that "I'll have to look up things as I know nothing about them myself." After this incident, Magnes began attending Orthodox prayer services twice a week. Increasingly drawn to Jewish tradition, he began openly criticizing Reform Judaism. "It is a sad, undeniable fact," he wrote, that Reform Jews "have far less religion than our Christian neighbors." He feared that "amalgamation" with Christianity would ultimately lead to the disappearance of Judaism, and he praised the "earnest" and "authentic" nature of Orthodox Jews. Reform Jews, he argued, don masks in order to be accepted into local society and be considered liberal, but toward this end they sacrifice their dignity as Jews.[14]

In his rabbinical dissertation, Magnes explored the main philosophical treatise of the early medieval Jewish philosopher Rabbi Sa'adia Gaon (882–942), *The Book of Beliefs and Opinions*. He stressed the centrality of ethics in Gaon's philosophy, essentially arguing that the book had "import for ethics." His analysis built on the work of Isaac Mayer Wise, who, in an effort to demonstrate the early roots of Reform Judaism, had underscored the importance of Rabbi Sa'adia Gaon as the first Jewish philosopher who sought to integrate Hebrew Scripture with philosophy and logic. The approach propounded by Wise and, later, Magnes was at odds with that of most scholars of Rabbi Sa'adia Gaon at the time (and to date), who argued that although religion and logic complement one another in Gaon's work, this was not because Gaon had adopted an ethical philosophy or placed ethics at the heart of his philosophy.[15]

Religious Conservatism

During the course of his studies in Germany, Magnes had his first real encounter with both European Jewry and the antisemitism that was then emerging among German students, hand-in-hand with the rise of German nationalism and the migration of East European Jews to Germany.[16] There he was also exposed to the works of Zecharias Frankel, founder of the Jewish Theological Seminary in Breslau, and the German Jewish scholar Leopold Zunz. As a result, his Conservative views grew stronger and his opposition to Reform Judaism increased. "Too much milk and water and not enough strength," he described one Reform Purim service in which he participated in Germany. Magnes also criticized German Reform Judaism for being overly focused on appearances and lacking authenticity.[17] Later he would voice a similar critique of Reform Judaism in the United States.

While in Germany, Magnes sought the company of Jews from Eastern Europe, although it appears that he had limited contact with them. He had romantic notions about East European Jewish culture and tradition as the most authentic Judaism. Drawn to the rich tradition of East European Jewry, he immersed himself in studying Yiddish literature, folklore, poetry, and proverbs. To enhance his knowledge of East European Jewry, Magnes planned to travel to Poland and Galicia in 1902 together with fellow student Max Schlesinger, later vice-chancellor of the Hebrew University of Jerusalem. "I put great hopes on this tour," he wrote. "We mean to devote all our powers to the service of the Jewish people. How can we expect any good result, if we do not know our Jews?" This particular plan never materialized, after novelist Karl Emil Franzos, who had initially inspired their quest, eventually persuaded them to abandon their travel plans so that they could avoid disillusionment and continue to "cling to [their] present ideas about the Ostjuden."[18]

Eventually, Magnes sought out his own roots in Eastern Europe. During a 1922 trip he came across several local Jews who claimed, without any basis, to know the burial spot of his grandfather and requested financial compensation or donations. In his travel diary, Magnes wrote:

> While he [the rabbi] was reading [the congregation's registry], I had glimpses through some of the many windows of the large room. Directly in the shadow opposite was the door of the old Schul. Then through another window to the north, lay the stream, 100 feet away; across the stream the little houses of Widoma, and beyond Widoma across the stream, the trees and the dark, bent, crowded gravestones of the cemetery.... This was the heart of the visit, and although all the rest was interesting, those moments in the Rabbi's room had a grace of their own, and I should have been satisfied to be lifted away from the old world of my ancestors back to my own world far away.[19]

This experience shattered Magnes's romantic view of East European Jewry, if only temporarily. Later, Magnes would argue that Palestine was situated at the crossroads between East and West, and that it was the role of Jews to return and mediate between the two.

Within Orthodox circles Magnes found the spiritual power and vitality he regarded as lacking in the Reform movement. The Orthodox synagogues of Berlin inspired in him a "feeling called religious ... [which] a modern man cannot duplicate."[20] This impression resonated with Magnes's vivid memories of the Hasidic hymns to which he had been exposed as a child in his father's home. In his heart of hearts, according to his first biographer, Norman Bentwich, Magnes felt close to Hasidic Jews even though he was unable to share in their mystical beliefs.

His long acquaintance with Martin Buber also had Hasidic undertones. In a letter he wrote to Buber in February 1948, Magnes recalled the first time he had seen Buber: at the University of Berlin during the 1900–1901 academic year, strolling like a righteous man followed by a group of Hasidic congregants.[21] Another episode illustrating Magnes's attraction to the Hasidic world is described by the composer Ernest Bloch. In a letter to his mother dated April 5, 1918, six months after having immigrated to the United States, Bloch described an encounter with Magnes as possibly the most unusual event of his life. Magnes, wanting Bloch to hear ancient Hebrew hymns, had arranged for both of them to participate in morning prayer services at a Hasidic synagogue in New York's Lower East Side during the Passover holiday. For Bloch this was a formative experience that, in his words, split his life into two. In his letter to his mother, he wrote that his own music sounded small and pathetic compared with what he had heard, and that all the kings of the land—rulers of empires, financial monarchs, or aristocrats in their own eyes—seemed vulgar compared with the ancient people he had met.

Bloch's comments also suggest that during this period Magnes was regularly attending prayer services at the same Hasidic synagogue.[22] Magnes's affinity for Orthodox worship was evident as well during his later years, when, according to Bentwich, he would participate in the prayer services of a small and devout congregation of ultra-Orthodox Jews who assembled in a private home.[23]

Relationship with Solomon Schechter

Magnes's work in New York during the early twentieth century, until the United States entered World War I, was shaped by his relationship with Solomon Schechter. A charismatic figure regarded at the time as the most prominent English-speaking Jewish scholar, Schechter had been invited to the United States from Cambridge, England, in April 1902, in order to head the Jewish Theological Seminary. He aimed to help the seminary attain the status of a European academic institution for Jewish research (Wissenschaft des Judentums), albeit with less of a focus on biblical scholarship, while at the same time fighting assimilationist trends in American society.[24]

Schechter accepted Magnes into his intellectual circle, which included founder of Hadassah Henrietta Szold, future founder of Reconstructionist Judaism Mordecai Kaplan, and scholar and educator Israel Friedlander, among others. According to historian Evyatar Friesel, the circle that formed around Schechter, which included Magnes, underwent a process of religious evolution that took it beyond Reform Judaism to what would in time be known as the Conservative movement. Schechter admired Magnes's intellectual abilities, and the two developed a strong relationship, meeting regularly for dinner and visiting bookstores together. Occasionally Schechter also invited him to deliver lectures on Jewish philosophy for the Jewish Theological Seminary students. On October 19, 1908, Schechter, alongside Joseph Silverman, the head rabbi at New York's Temple Emanu-El, where Magnes also served at the time, performed the marriage ceremony for Magnes and his bride, Beatrice (née Lowenstein).

For Magnes, Schechter represented a model that integrated modernity with a more substantial and Romanticist sense of tradition. At a dinner in honor of Schechter, Magnes commented that he felt like a lost child returned to his father's home. Magnes's religious views, he would later declare in his farewell speech at Temple Emanu-El, were closely aligned with the "positive-historical Judaism" of Zecharias Frankel, which accepted historical research and biblical criticism yet maintained traditional and nationalistic aspects of Judaism, and with Schechter's approach of promoting Judaism based on the collective will of *klal Yisra'el* (the collective Jewish people). These two thinkers justified a sense of traditionalism that would echo throughout Magnes's thought and reinforce his Zionism. Further, Bentwich claims that Schechter's influence would eventually lead to Magnes's resignation as rabbi at Temple Emanu-El (for more on this, see below).[25]

These claims, in combination with the speech by Magnes cited below, form a complex picture of his religious outlook. As we will see, after arriving in Palestine in the 1920s, Magnes would combine Conservative religious elements stemming from his continuous religious quest, which also entailed criticism of the Reform movement for its lack of religious passion, with adoption of the Reform movement's Mission Theology and all of its political implications, which he would put to the test of political actualization in Palestine.

Joining and Resigning from Temple Emanu-El

During the early twentieth century, the Reform synagogue Temple Emanu-El in New York was among the wealthiest and most influential in the United States. Its regular congregants included the banker and philanthropist Jacob Schiff; the Guggenheim family; Felix Warburg, a banker, Jewish leader, and later one of the most consistent supporters of Magnes's political activity in Palestine; and Louis Marshall, a lawyer and Jewish community leader who would in time become Magnes's brother-in-law.[26]

In 1906 the congregation was seeking a second rabbi to serve alongside Rabbi Silverman. The search was extended after Stephen Wise, later the rabbi of the Free Synagogue in New York and founder of the Jewish Institute of Religion, declined the offer (he objected to the requirement that he be subordinate to the Board of Trustees and subject to its authority). Despite their reservations about Magnes's Zionism and political activism, the synagogue's trustees were impressed by his character and hoped that he would draw young people back to the synagogue and enhance its influence among immigrants. By this time, Magnes had held a pulpit at Temple Israel in New York, from 1904 to 1906. His post had generally proven unsuccessful; he clashed with the leadership while trying to effect changes in adapting a more conservative stance and liturgy and endorsing Zionism, and left.

Magnes did proceed to serve as a second rabbi at Temple Emanu-El for a few years, from 1906 to 1910, but he never found his place in this congregation either. Given his more conservative religious inclinations, it upset him that the untrained cantor sang almost exclusively in English and that the congregants stood during the *Shema* prayer rather than the *Barchu*—and, even worse, while reciting the *Mourner's Kaddish*. Magnes referred to the practice of standing during the *Mourner's Kaddish* as "a neurotic, backboneless, simpering, ecclesiastical abomination" in which the congregation is "dependent on the dead for life; poor synagogue, if death be its only sustainer."[27] He was also critical of his congregants' wealth and lavish lifestyles, which contrasted with the poverty of the immigrants who traveled uptown to hear his sermons. He wrote in his diary: "I hate many of them, and yet as a good pastor I must call on them. At times, I would speak words of fire about their sins. . . . Can I serve two masters? The plain people, the young men and women, mostly of Russian descent, in whom some Jewish life is still left, and on the other hand the rich Jews, who would buy the soul of their servants for coin?"[28] Magnes's critique of Reform Judaism was consistent with the socialist perspective he was beginning to develop at the time.

From his pulpit at Temple Emanu-El, Magnes tried to promote the various issues in which he was then engaged: the Conservative Judaism championed by Schechter, the cultural Zionism of Ahad Ha'am, and the preservation of Yiddish culture. But these combined efforts to counter-reform the Reform synagogue amounted to a threefold head-on attack on the liberal and universalist tenets of Reform Judaism and its sociological goals of further integration into American society: thus resistance to his plans only increased. After the Temple Emanu-El Board demanded that he provide a detailed explanation of his plans for counter-reform of the synagogue, tensions reached a boiling point.

Finally responding to the board's demand that he explain his intentions, on April 24, 1910, the eve of Passover, Magnes delivered a sermon under the heading "Reformed Judaism—Plans for Reconstruction." In this seminal address, which would spark debate and reactions throughout the American Jewish world (via various periodicals), Magnes presented the congregation with his religious doctrine.

This sermon would later be understood as important in terms of form as well as substance. Scholars would point to striking similarities in style between the sermon and what was known as the "jeremiad sermon," a form developed by the early Puritans in New England that later spread across the United States. The general format of the latter comprised an opening statement describing the congregation's declining spiritual commitment, followed by an explanation of the consequent dangers facing the congregation, and concluding with a view to its dramatic redemption.²⁹

First Magnes quoted a passage from the Song of Songs (2:12) to illustrate the springtime revival of Passover: "For, lo, the winter is past, the rain is over and gone; the flowers appear on the earth; the time of the singing of birds has come, and the voice of the turtledove is heard in our land." He juxtaposed this with the bleak winter afflicting the childless congregation of Temple Emanu-El:

> Our young men and women are completely ignorant of Judaism. How, then, can they be loyal to it? ... When they think of it, it is only with a sense of the burden that it imposes upon them. It is for them a misfortune because it restricts their social activity. They approach Judaism by asking "What will the *goyim* [gentiles] say?," to which the answer is, "They say, and with truth, that our younger Jews and Jewesses are ignorant of Judaism, that they have cheapened themselves insofar as their religion is concerned, that they have lost their moral tone, that they have no self-respect, no pride of birth, no traditions, no hopes for their people."

He added: "Your sons and your daughters, many of them, are marrying outside of their people. They are rearing their children with all modern accomplishments, but with no religion. Their homes are bare of piety and of the spirit of prayer.... Are you satisfied with this result of your Reform Judaism?"³⁰

Magnes imputed the moral and spiritual state of the congregation to its having lost contact with tradition. He attributed the dire condition of U.S. Jewry more generally to two main factors: the Jewish education system and intergenerational change. According to him, even though most Jewish students attended separate, exclusively Jewish schools, and despite the existence of Sunday schools, Judaism meant nothing to them. They were not adopting a Jewish worldview of life and did not look at the world through Jewish eyes. Unlike their parents' generation,

Jewish young people were not being brought into contact "with Jewish ideas of life, with Jewish symbols, ceremonies, observances, traditions." Reform Judaism, added Magnes, addressing parents in the congregation, "has become so petrified that it is impervious to new life.... You are eager to buy for them [your children] all the outward graces your money can secure. But how unwilling and undesirous you are that they secure for themselves the inward grace of Judaism."[31]

From the very outset, this sermon reveals many aspects of Magnes's self-perception and worldview. In historical terms he saw himself as the instigator of a counterreform within Reform Judaism. His focus on the issue of Jewish education was consistent with his efforts within the Kehillah, where Jewish education played a central role and Magnes served on the education committee (more on this to come). His fierce criticism of the material wealth of his congregation corresponded with his socialist leanings.

The main solution Magnes proposed to address Temple Emanu-El's problems essentially embodied the seeds of the Conservative movement: Magnes called on the congregation to dissociate itself from official Reform Judaism and identify as part of unofficial Reform Judaism, which had yet to organize itself but represented, in Magnes's words, "the Judaism of the large majority of the Jews." Doing so would bridge the gap between Reform Judaism and traditional Jewish identity. Unofficial Reform Jews, among whom Magnes counted himself, were "less observant of Jewish religious practices than ... the Orthodox, but ... in far greater sympathy with Jewish traditions than are the officially Reformed." By leaving the Reform movement, he argued, Temple Emanu-El and like-minded congregations would be expressing their willingness to evolve and adapt themselves to a changing environment, thereby becoming "increasingly Jewish." The founding principle of the new movement was an intimate relationship with the sources of Judaism, which he identified as "first, the living Jewish people; second, the Torah (that is, the literature) of this people, its history, its language, its land; third, its living traditions, customs, observances, its aspirations."[32]

In this definition, one can discern Solomon Schechter's fingerprint, specifically in Magnes's emphasis on the dual foundation of the Jewish people (*klal Yisra'el*[33]) and the Torah in the development of Jewish identity and Jewish community. Magnes's inclusion of the Hebrew language among the sources of Jewish identity is indicative of his strong reservations about the exclusion of Hebrew from the Reform prayer book and his identification with Ahad Ha'am's cultural Zionism, centered on a revival of the Hebrew language. His redefinition of American Jewish identity also embodies Magnes's Zionist outlook, in which the "land of the Jewish People" constitutes one of the authoritative sources of Judaism.

This position starkly contradicted the principles of the 1885 Pittsburgh Platform—the platform of Reform Judaism at the time—and particularly its fifth paragraph, which rejected a return to Palestine. Such overt Zionism would have met with objection in a community with classic Reform foundations such as Temple Emanu-El, and a rift was therefore inevitable.

In retrospect, this was probably the first attempt to establish a Conservative congregation. On April 31 Magnes's sermon was published in the conservative-leaning Jewish publication *American Hebrew*, triggering mixed responses across a range of Jewish newspapers as well as letters directly to Magnes himself. Meanwhile, after convening to discuss Magnes's recommendations, the Temple Emanu-El Board informed him that they had rejected his proposed changes. In his response, which he also published as an open letter, Magnes announced that he was turning down the opportunity to be reappointed as a rabbi at Temple Emanu-El. In a subsequent interview with *American Hebrew* he expressed regret that the congregation was unable to direct its attention to the sources of Judaism, and added that he had plans, yet to be finalized, for future work with the Jewish community in New York, after returning from a planned trip to Palestine with his wife.³⁴ An additional attempt to serve as a pulpit rabbi at New York's Congregation B'nai Jeshurun was also short lived, and followed the patterns of his previous clashes with congregation lay leadership. Magnes was installed as rabbi on March 30, 1911, and by February 1912 had submitted his resignation.

Schechter, in an ensuing interview published in the weekly London *Jewish Chronicle*, described Magnes's resignation from his Temple Emanu-El post as "one of the finest sacrifices for a cause that Judaism has ever seen." Magnes, Schechter continued, "is a man of conspicuous ability and earnestness. He is modest, and has never worked for Dr. Magnes [that is, for himself]." He added that Magnes "has the power of . . . leadership, and he will lead a movement—a decidedly Conservative movement." Schechter considered Magnes suited to the role because he had supporters on both sides—the Reform side and the Conservative-Orthodox side.³⁵ Yet Schechter's immediate hopes in this regard met with disappointment. Some three more years would pass before an organization of Conservative congregations—the United Synagogue of America—was established in February 1913.

As to why Magnes did not lead the "decidedly Conservative movement" as Schechter had imagined, there are a number of plausible explanations. First, taking on the role of a leader of equal or subordinate status to Schechter would have been out of character for Magnes. A key factor in the consolidation of the Conservative movement was the charismatic aspect of Schechter's relationship with his students. Schechter's personality and unmediated leadership style elicited in the students a strong sense of group identity and common goals, enabling them to overcome their diverse range of opinions and work together to form a united Conservative movement.³⁶ A charismatic leader in his own right, Magnes likely lacked the self-effacement necessary to submit to the charisma of another. Second, after resigning from his rabbinical post at Temple Emanu-El, Magnes began a process of radicalization that reinforced his ties to socialist and pacifist elements within and outside of the Jewish community, and thereby reduced his interest in engaging in official Jewish community matters. On August 30, 1915, he wrote to his brother-in-law Louis Marshall, "Very often I feel that the breaking point with myself has come, and I can think of nothing more liberating than escaping the burden of endeavoring seriously to participate in 'leadership' in Jewish life. . . . How long, however, the grind can last, Heaven only knows."[37]

Leading the Kehillah

Toward the end of the first decade of the twentieth century, a large-scale initiative was undertaken to unite the ethnic Jewish communities of New York into one organization—the Kehillah (community). Driving this initiative were the internal tensions among the Jews of New York: between the long-standing, well-to-do residents of German descent and the East European immigrants who had arrived in large numbers, sparking antisemitic reactions among the American public. In September 1908 the New York City police commissioner Theodore A. Bingham spuriously asserted that Jews were responsible for half the crime in the city. Communal Jewish interest in striking a balance between the Jewish elite's efforts to defy but also silence his and others' such claims and the Jewish immigrants' popular protests in response to the remarks led to a collective realization that the needs of the hour demanded coordination and organization.

Magnes played a key role in founding the Kehillah, as both sides—longtime residents and immigrants—viewed him as a mediating agent. At the time he was still serving as a rabbi at Temple Emanu-El, having also married into one of the most respected dynasties in the community, the Lowenstein family. Established residents therefore saw him as one of their own, able to promote their interests. At the same time, the immigrants appreciated the uncondescending way in which he encouraged them to preserve their Jewish identity, as well as his socialist inclinations. Accordingly, Magnes was chosen to head the Kehillah.

The Kehillah existed for slightly more than a decade, from 1909 to 1922. At its peak it comprised more than two hundred diverse Jewish organizations, including both Orthodox and liberal synagogues, labor unions, charities, educational institutions, and Zionist organizations.[38] Magnes's eventual resignation from the post in the early 1920s would signal the organization's dissolution.[39]

Certain aspects of Magnes's activity in the Kehillah shed light on his character and on his social and political activism more generally. His role as mediator reflects the internal tension in his identity between his affinity for Reform ideas and his efforts to adapt Judaism to modernism, on the one hand, and a more conservative religious outlook combined with support for the immigrants' socialist ideas, on the other. Moreover, Magnes's effort appears to foreshadow his binational outlook and reflect its concrete foundations. The Kehillah strove to bridge two identity groups by means of an administrative body and the mechanisms of committees and procedures. Tensions between the groups were resolved in accordance with the ethos of bipartisanship and pragmatism characteristic of American progressiveness.[40]

At the same time, Magnes's experience on the Kehillah Education Committee reflected the difficulty of implementing this practical approach within the Jewish community. In the Labor Relations Committee, for example, the underlying ethos of the Kehillah bore fruit and galvanized a variety of actors to promote labor justice, but in the Education Committee, which naturally addressed more ideological issues, such as the nature of Jewish identity and continuity, Magnes was unable to overcome religious tensions concerning the makeup of Jewish education in America. His self-perception as neutral bridge builder could not stand up to Orthodoxy—as would later be the case with a more political form of collective Jewish adherence in Palestine—namely Zionism.

2

"Palestine or Death"

In January 1896, while a rabbinical student at Hebrew Union College in Cincinnati, Magnes published his first article on Zionism, "Palestine—or Death." From the American Jewish perspective—which Magnes regarded as subject to the control of the "Reform Church" (i.e., the Reform movement)—the return to Palestine and establishment of a Jewish state seemed neither possible nor desirable. Magnes argued that the American freedom that U.S. Jews so welcomed had led them to embrace liberalism, and because of their love for the American homeland, they would not return to Palestine, even if they could. Magnes bluntly tackled the matter: "I am as good an American as any of you. If it came to a choice between Palestine and America, I believe I should stay here."

Nevertheless, he regarded the establishment of a Jewish "Church and State" in Palestine as "the only salvation of our present-day Judaism." In his eyes, Zionism was the essential and sole solution to American Jewry's loss of affinity for the Jewish religion. Magnes, with implied reference to Felix Adler's New York Society for Ethical Culture,[1] asserted that trends toward integration would lead to Jewish assimilation into Christian society to the extent that Judaism might disappear. "For who is so blind as not to see the results of amalgamations, unions and Universal

Religions," he exclaimed. "The Jews will be absorbed on account of their fewness in number." The only way to prevent Jewry's assimilation was to seize the opportunity presented by the collapse of the Ottoman government. "What better can we do," he concluded, "than to take advantage of the imminent downfall of the ruler of Palestine and talk of a return to the land of our fathers?"[2]

From a historical perspective, this text may be seen as the first indication of the importance Magnes attributed to Zionism as a means of reviving the spirit of Judaism in the United States. While in this article, one of his earliest pieces of writing, Magnes presented Zionism as the only solution to the decline of American Judaism, he would later come to argue that Zionism also encouraged and enabled Jewish revival in the United States itself.

Magnes's outlook as presented here is consistent with his overall view regarding the nature and direction of influence between Judaism and Zionism. He viewed Zionism as a tool in the service of Judaism, and not the other way around. It is helpful to examine this outlook in the context of the Reform critique of Zionism, which was then informed by Reform Judaism's universalist perspective.

Reform Universalism

The Classical Reform theology predating World War I looked at Jewish existence through the egalitarian worldview of the Enlightenment, which rejected "chauvinist" nationalism as too self-centered and a threat to world peace. This universalist approach was the initial, fundamental source of tension between Reform Judaism and Zionism. Even before a consolidated Reform universalist ideology took shape, there was a discernable American Jewish trend toward invoking all-American values in order to overcome antisemitism and prejudice.[3] Eventually the universalist outlook crystallized into a genuine Reform ideology focused on Jewish integration into American society, with the shedding of all characteristics that might indicate difference or foreignness. The main figure responsible for transforming this universalist approach into a systematic historiosophic outlook was Rabbi David Einhorn, the Reform movement's foremost ideologue at the time. He believed that the pure humanist, universalist core of Judaism predated the Jewish people—its roots dated back to the early days of humanity. This belief, which gained ground to the extent that it informed the 1885 Pittsburgh Platform, is particularly evident in the fifth of the Platform's eight principles: "We recognize, in the modern era of universal culture of heart and intellect, the approaching of the realization of Israel's great Messianic hope for the establishment of the kingdom of truth, justice, and peace among all men."[4] Modern universalism, accordingly, was seen as the fulfillment of messianic aspirations.

Notably, Reform Judaism and Zionism shared the same aspiration for normalization: both sought to understand the unique character of Jewish existence while at the same time striving to integrate it into modern culture. And Reform Judaism had no conflict with Zionism in terms of the existence of a Jewish collective as the embodiment of Judaism through the ages. But there was an inherent tension between Reform's universalism and Zionism's nationalism. Reform Judaism regarded the Jewish people as a congregation of believers rather than as a national ethnic group, whereas Zionism saw the Jewish people as a national ethnic group that had created a religion but was not defined by it.

Furthermore, Zionism and Reform Judaism espoused divergent perspectives regarding the key to Jewish continuity in past, present, and future. Zionism stressed national cohesion, while Reform Judaism emphasized monotheism and the universalist concepts deriving from it. Essentially, Reform leaders viewed Judaism's universalist element—and not its national element—as the creative and dynamic force that had enabled it to develop and to cope with the cultures surrounding it without being assimilated into them or losing Judaism's physical and spiritual uniqueness.[5]

Against this background, there emerged a resistance to Zionism within Reform Jewry. The early Reform leaders—nearly all of them antinationalist liberals—called for the revocation (rather than merely the suspension) of religious laws relating to a national presence in Palestine. They also removed all references to the Diaspora and the return to Zion from Reform prayer books, since, they believed, the national or nationalist phase of Judaism was just temporary—one intended to prepare the Jewish people for its role in the service of all humanity. The Pittsburgh Platform's fifth principle includes the statement, "We consider ourselves no longer a nation, but a religious community, and therefore expect neither a return to Palestine, nor a sacrificial worship under the sons of Aaron, nor the restoration of any of the laws concerning the Jewish state."[6] Reform's confrontation with Zionist supporters who did not share such universalist enthusiasm was thereby inevitable.[7]

The Reform movement was not monolithic, however. By the first decade of the twentieth century, evident differences had emerged between Zionists and non-Zionists among the students and teachers at the Reform rabbinical seminary and the Reform movement's Central Conference of American Rabbis. Historian Michael Meyer points out that although at the time "the majority on both sides of the two movements seemed to be moral enemies," this was actually when the foundation for ideological rapprochement between Zionism and Reform Judaism was established.[8] Historian Jonathan Sarna would name Magnes among the Reform movement's "converts" to Zionism, alongside co-founder of The Jewish Publication Society Bernard Felsenthal, Columbia University professor Richard Gottheil, and American southerner Rabbi Max Heller.[9]

Indeed, Magnes's Zionism was a constant source of tension between him and the movement's institutions and congregations that he served. In promoting a Zionist agenda, Magnes criticized Reform Judaism for its opposition to Zionism. At the same time, Magnes remained fundamentally faithful to Reform Judaism's Mission Theology doctrine, which ascribes utmost importance to Israel's mission among the nations. This tension between the universalism of Reform Judaism and the nationalism of Zionism lay at the heart of Magnes's political outlook, and his later support of binationalism became the means to its resolution.

The Consolidation of Magnes's Zionist Outlook

Magnes began his doctoral studies at the University of Berlin in 1900. Since the university did not offer a degree in Jewish studies, he decided to specialize in philosophy, which had sparked his interest during his previous studies in Cincinnati. He ended up taking only one course in philosophy, however, while devoting the rest of his time to studying Christian theology and the Arabic language, in preparation for reading medieval Jewish texts.

In the summer of 1902, Magnes transferred to the University of Heidelberg, where he enrolled in the Department of Linguistic Studies. He appears to have been driven to complete his studies as soon as possible so as to resume his Zionist activity in the United States; additionally, the family of Max Schlesinger, his close friend from Berlin who would later serve as a rabbi in New York, resided in Heidelberg.[10]

Magnes's Zionist identity took shape during his doctoral studies in Germany, and in particular during his time in Berlin. The young Magnes was greatly influenced by the city's vibrant Jewish culture, which was fueled by both Zionism and socialism. Europe around the turn of the century was engulfed by neoromantic and even neo-mystical ideologies alongside political dissatisfaction and socialist revolutionism.[11] The Zionist discourse was similarly influenced by these trends.

In October 1901 Magnes, with Arthur Biram (later the founder of the Hebrew Reali School in Haifa), Max Schlesinger, Orientalist Gotthold Weil, and others, co-founded a Zionist student union at the Jewish studies institute they attended, Lehranstalt für die Wissenschaft des Judentums, also known as die Hochschule. He subsequently wrote to his parents that Zionism was his "life's plan" (*Lebensprogramm*). "Since I became a Zionist," he explained, "my view of life has changed, my view as to my calling has changed, my hopes and my prayers have changed."[12]

In a special issue of the American Zionist journal *The Maccabean*, published in August 1904 and dedicated to the memory of Theodor Herzl, Magnes chose to describe the influence of the man known as the "founding father" of Zionism on Jewish students in Germany. Before Herzl's appearance on the stage of Jewish history, the rise of antisemitism and the exclusion of Jewish students from general student unions had led to "a most unfortunate outcome—the loss of Jewish self-respect." Jewish students who continued to hold onto the "pathetic" position that they were Germans of the Mosaic faith had refused to take part in activities of a Jewish nature. Thanks to Herzl's influence, however, Jewish student unions had begun adopting explicitly Jewish names; Germany's Jewish student union, Verein Jüdischer Studenten, was one such example. The key to Herzl's success in this regard, Magnes avows, was Herzl's promotion of the ideal of Jewish nationalism.

At the time, therefore, Magnes had a positive attitude toward Jewish nationalism, even in the political version identified with Herzl, because of its contribution to promoting Jewish self-respect among young Jews in Europe.[13]

Ahad Ha'am and Zionism as the Key to American Jewish Renewal

Ahad Ha'am's cultural Zionism, also known as spiritual Zionism, is generally regarded as the counterposition to the political Zionism promoted by Herzl. Ahad Ha'am explained the essence of this concept in his article "The State of Jews and the 'Jewish Problem,'" published after the First Zionist Congress in Basel in 1897. Ahad Ha'am's basic premise was that since political Zionism was incapable of solving the "physical problem" of the Jews, Zionism should focus on the spiritual and cultural issue of renewing the Jewish "spirit of the nation." In his view, the establishment through political manipulation of a state that lacked a spiritual foundation was destined to fail, because a political concept that did not derive from national culture was liable to engender aspirations for political power among the Jewish people in a manner that severed the people from their historical roots. Accordingly, Ahad Ha'am sought to establish not only a "state of Jews" but a genuine "Jewish state."[14]

Ahad Ha'am had a formative influence on the development of the Zionist movement in the United States, which extended beyond Zionist circles to American Jewry as a whole.[15] American Zionists tended to share Ahad Ha'am's concerns about the possibility of assimilation into the non-Jewish environment driven by modernism and the spread of the modern concept of nationalism. Ahad Ha'am sought to preserve the collective Jewish identity of Europe, in light of the dangers it faced following the destruction of the ghetto walls and the end of Jewish seclusion. He was convinced that Judaism could undergo modernization without losing its uniqueness because the Jewish national spirit was based on moral foundations consistent with those of modernism. Likewise, American Jewry also faced threats to its continuing existence as a distinct entity, as a result of trends toward integration or radical universalism, such as that of Felix Adler. The moral outlook of Reform Judaism generally, and in the United States specifically, was also close to that of Ahad Ha'am.[16] Thus, even though Ahad Ha'am's position triggered resistance because it prioritized the national spirit (*Volksgeist*) over the Jewish religion in its concept of Jewish revival, American Zionists with a background in Reform Judaism, such as Magnes and Stephen Wise, were able to find echoes of Reform Judaism's principle of ethical monotheism in his writings.

Yet even when American Zionists supported Ahad Ha'am's theories, they would adapt them to the American Jewish arena. Ahad Ha'am was pessimistic about the future of Judaism in the Diaspora. Admittedly, his repudiation of the Diaspora, a position based on his analysis of the state of Jewry in Russia and his debate with historian and influential writer Simon Dubnow on this matter,[17] was not as explicit as that of the political Zionists. Yet even though he spoke of a national center that would serve diaspora Jewry as a cultural center for emulation and Jewish creativity, in effect he rejected the possibility of Judaism existing in the Diaspora. By contrast, Ahad Ha'am's American Zionist supporters, who were not at all interested in rejecting the Diaspora, had a fundamentally different outlook. Most of them, including Magnes, supported a model that would allow for the concurrent existence of Jewish cultural centers in Palestine and in the Diaspora. Some even went further. "America," wrote scholar and founding president of Young Judea Israel Friedlander in 1907, "is destined to become in the near future the leading Jewish center of the Diaspora.... It is the duty of American Jewry to live up to the great obligation placed upon it by history."[18]

In a lecture titled "The Harmonious Jew" delivered at Temple Emanu-El in early 1907, Magnes presented Ahad Ha'am as a remedy for the illnesses afflicting Reform Judaism. Ahad Ha'am, he added, was the prototype of the Jew who knows how to merge modernity with tradition—the "first modern Jew who has seen the great light in the distance. He is the first harmonious modern Jew."[19] Magnes continued:

> The Reform movement is not able to make the Jewish soul harmonious with its life, does not help to bridge over the chasm with the past and present. It was said of us that we had a mission. The Reform Jews have not been missionaries of the world; all the theological movements of the 19th Century have been from non-Jews....[20] This mission has given us no fire in the soul, no idealism in the mind, no sacrifice in the person.... [Ahad Ha'am is] the first harmonious modern Jew. For him the basis of Jewish life is the actual feeling of the Jewish national spirit. Upon that basis we can have a new people that will contribute to the culture of the world.[21]

Thus, in Magnes's eyes Ahad Ha'am had achieved the ideal of merging the Jewish tradition and national spirit with modernism. Magnes saw in Ahad Ha'am's teachings an opportunity for the renewal of Reform Judaism, whose Mission Theology doctrine he believed lacked the vitality necessary to generate "new values" and a new religious philosophy.[22] In his view, such a philosophy had to bridge the vast divide between the past and present and overcome the crises in Jewish spirituality and Jewry's sense of belonging induced by modernism.

That said, as previously noted in the context of American Zionism generally, and as I shall discuss in the context of Buber and the Central

European circles of Brit Shalom, Magnes had reservations about Ahad Ha'am's dismissal of the religious factor. He believed that religion had a central role in the spiritual process necessary for Jewish renewal and in providing justification for the Jewish national cause.

A Jewish Spiritual Center

Magnes's notes for a lecture titled "A Jewish Spiritual Culture," possibly delivered in 1911, summarize his religious outlook at the time as it correlated with his stance on Zionism. After first addressing the question of spiritual culture itself, he then linked it with religion:

> *A spiritual culture.* A seeking of God. A feeling of his presence, of his proximity despite his beyondness, of his governing of our lives, are the manifestations of culture to that effect. A culture not of philosophic aphorisms, while yet having a philosophy and a scientific basis: but a culture of life, an unconscious, natural religious culture; not always a word God on our lips; but with Him himself in our hearts.[23]

This portion of his lecture notes raises a number of theological issues. First is the question of proximity to or distance from God and the search for God, which would continue to preoccupy Magnes and possibly constitute the central religious theme of his life. Second is his reservation about philosophy as a tool for drawing closer to God. In a note from October 1947 Magnes wrote that philosophy includes epistemology, but religion does not. In religion, "there is a recognition of God. 'Recognition' in the sense of knowing, knowledge, direct access to the object. And object and subject are not separate, as in philosophy. Those who recognize facts, reality, the moment, the world, morality, personality, people, suffering... also recognize God. Not as an absolute that cannot be recognized." Maimonides, continued Magnes, was a philosopher rather than a man of religion, because he had stripped God of any title and made Him an abstract concept.[24]

Also of note is Magnes's sense of an inner connection with God that does not manifest in explicit speech. His statement is reminiscent of Hasidic perspectives, which ascribe more importance to one's inner relationship with God than to overt action and speech.[25] Notably, for Magnes the "culture of life" was neither secularized nor separable from religion; it was a "natural religious culture." Magnes did not seek to abandon scientific religious study or philosophical methodology, but rather to juxtapose them with what he termed a natural and unconscious "culture of life," which he extended to Judaism in the search to define a "Jewish spiritual culture":

> *A Jewish Spiritual Culture.* For me one that is like all culture, the bringing of men to a realization of the spiritual world. Why then recognize the "non-religion" Zionists; because that too is religious which doesn't always carry this name. A Jewish spiritual culture to bring Jews to a Jewish concept of God. Now this does not mean that because you subscribe to a Jewish creed, you, the philosopher, are therefore knowing God. Or because you shout that Judaism is ethical monotheism, or that we have a religious mission to the world, that: you have the Jewish God in your hearts (i.e., the Jewish conception of this spiritual actuality surrounding us). On the contrary, those who do the shouting are like the barkers at the amusement gardens. You could think they were the whole show, whereas they are but menials of-others who do the acting and the reaping of the reward.[26]

Magnes described the universality of Jewish spiritual culture, which in his view derived from the general spiritual culture to which he aspired. He then drew political conclusions that reflected his attitude toward Zionism.

Magnes also saw religious elements in the seemingly secular Zionist enterprise. He explained his support for nonreligious Zionists in Palestine by pointing out that "that too is religious which doesn't always carry this name." Later on, in relation to the supposedly secular Jewish socialists whom he admired (see chapter 3), Magnes would reassert this position, differentiating—in German historian of religion Rudolf Otto's terms—between the authentically experienced "numinous" (the unstructured emotional sensation of divinity) and "formally demonstrated" religious thought and practice.[27]

This approach is consistent with his general conception of a true spiritual culture, where the religious bond is innate and not always apparent. It also has conceptual similarities to the views of the forefather of religious Zionism, Rabbi Abraham Isaac Kook, regarding the hidden holiness of the secular Zionist enterprise.[28]

Building on the remarks cited above, Magnes went on in his speech notes to criticize the Reform movement in both ideological and practical terms. Regarding two of the movement's main ideological principles—ethical monotheism and Mission Theology—Magnes pointed to the gap that existed, in his view, between overt expressions of faith and the innate bond with God, which is supposed to be at the foundation of faith but is, in fact, absent. This critique did not necessarily refer to Reform ideology per se, but to the manner of its implementation, which subdued the expression of religious sentiment for the sake of uniformity and conformity to the American environment.

In addition to his criticism of the Reform movement, Magnes offers a practical vision of the gradual, natural, almost organic development of Jewish life, which, he professes, ultimately leads to the Jewish conception of God. The development of a Jewish spiritual culture—the ideal as Magnes presents it—was therefore an outcome of the gradual emergence of a more Jewish life, with Jewish institutions, holidays, and content. Magnes wrote in his diary:

> I believe that Jewish spiritual culture is more than a doctrine and a shout. It is a Jewish life with many phases leading to the Jewish conception of God. But this life must be full and natural. In other words our homes must be made Jewish, we must have Jewish institutions

and celebrations, a Jewish content to our lives. Can this be done here? God grant that we may be able to preserve much, aye all of what we have. But it is because I believe that a full Jew, with all the cultural aspects of a Jew, speaking a Jewish tongue, fighting Jewish struggles, on Jewish soil, in a Jewish atmosphere can better comprehend what the Jewish conception of God is, that I believe in Zionism.[29]

Magnes saw Zionism as a means to living a full Jewish life that ultimately leads to the Jewish conception of God—which for him was both the ideal and the objective. Although Magnes believed that in the United States one could preserve the Jewish life that already existed, he considered it impossible to fully realize the ideal in America. The opportunity offered to Jews in the United States was to become as fully Jewish as possible within the context of the inevitable modernization of American life. However, it was necessary to establish a fuller Jewish existence, within a reality entirely characterized by daily Jewish life, by all aspects of Jewish culture, including the Jewish language and "Jewish soil." The full and complete realization of Jewish existence would only be possible in Palestine.

That Magnes's faith in Zionism stemmed from his desire to promote the ideal of the Jewish conception and recognition of God can be seen as the first indicator for assessing Magnes's Zionism as a political theology—that is, a political outlook derived from a religious position and religious motive: namely, the aspiration to fully actualize Judaism.

The Zionist vision Magnes upheld did not look to the past. "Not because he will understand our past better," Magnes explained in his speech notes, "will [the American Jew] be able to preserve the good and beautiful in the old spirit better, but because also he will be able to create new Jewish cultural values in the future, new Jewish ways for the soul to see God, new ways that shall be modern as well as old, that I believe in Zionism."[30] To Magnes, Zionism had the potential to promote the modernization of Jewish culture, thereby making it possible to create new cultural Jewish values in the future. Modernism, in his view, did not give rise to the distancing from God that he attributed to the Reform movement; rather, it offered the soul new ways of seeing God.

Magnes's perspectives on "Jewish spiritual culture" contain striking similarities to Ahad Ha'am's concept of cultural Zionism. The very discussion of "Jewish spiritual culture" resonates with the ideas of Ahad Ha'am. The argument for the organic development of a full Jewish life is also very similar to Ahad Ha'am's conception of cultural Zionism, which views a gradual process of "natural development" as the key to establishing a full Jewish life—which, after the spiritual conditions are met, will lead to the establishment of a state.[31]

Yet, one must distinguish between the two men's goals in relation to this cultural development. Magnes's ultimate goal was religious—to reach a complete understanding of the Jewish concept of God. Ahad Ha'am's goal, on the other hand, was the revival of the Jewish national spirit. For Ahad Ha'am, the Jewish national spirit preceded the Jewish religion, whose development under conditions of exile, in his view, had suffocated its national foundation.[32] The two also differed in their conceptions of diaspora Jewry, specifically American Jewry. Magnes believed that Jewish life in America could continue to flourish side by side with a Jewish center in the Land of Israel. Ahad Ha'am, in the pessimistic spirit of East European Zionism, perceived a center in Palestine as the linchpin of Jewish continuity, and did not pin any hopes on a flourishing diaspora Jewry.

Cultural Pluralism and the Controversy over *The Melting Pot*

Israel Zangwill's play *The Melting Pot*, which opened in Washington DC in 1908 and debuted on Broadway a year later, sparked a controversy in the Jewish community over intermarriage and the future of Judaism in America.

In the play, a Russian Jew who has fled to safety in the United States after his family is killed in a pogrom falls in love with a Christian woman of Russian heritage. In time he discovers that her father had been responsible for the death of his parents. Eventually the father seeks forgiveness, and the couple is married, thereby ostensibly validating the status of the United States as a place where various ethnicities merge together.[33]

"Ethnologically the Jew is doomed to extinction in America and this perhaps is the real message that lies at the heart of Israel Zangwill's great play," concluded a front-page review in *American Israelite*, the main journal of the Reform movement at the time, voicing the concerns of the American Jewish public.[34] More conservative figures had harsh criticism for Zangwill specifically. Schechter, for example, called Zangwill "a corrupting and false prophet who committed villainy against Israel," and called for a campaign against him.[35]

In retrospect, the play catalyzed the articulation of one of the most influential concepts in Judaism and American Zionism at the time. Philosopher Horace Kallen coined the term "cultural pluralism" in his article "Democracy versus the Melting Pot," published in the progressive magazine *The Nation* in February 1915, also in response to Zangwill's play. Kallen was not deterred by the possibility of Jewish assimilation implied in the play but rather by what he considered the flawed way in which the play addresses cultural diversity in the United States.[36] He invoked the metaphor of an orchestra: "The 'American civilization' may come to mean . . . a multiplicity in a unity, an orchestration of mankind. As in an orchestra, every type of instrument has its specific timbre and tonality, founded in its substance and form; as every type has its appropriate theme and melody in the whole symphony, so in society each ethnic group is the natural instrument, its spirit and culture are its theme and melody, and the harmony and dissonances and discords of them all make the symphony of civilization."[37] The concept of cultural pluralism gained widespread support within and beyond Jewish circles because it provided potential validation for American ethnic diversity, although at the same time there also emerged concerns that it could lead to social fragmentation.[38]

On October 9, 1909, following the Broadway premiere, Magnes delivered a sermon from the Emanu-El pulpit criticizing Zangwill for endangering the future of American Jewry in the name of Zionism. This "backward" type of Zionism, Magnes asserted, which claims that "anti-Semitism or the fires of hate on the one hand, and America or the fires of love on the other, make it impossible for Jews to exist in the diaspora," does not benefit Judaism.[39] Such remarks convey Magnes's opposition to the repudiation of the Diaspora, which he termed Zionism's "Despair theory."[40] In his sermon, Magnes rejected Zangwill's call to choose between Zionism and assimilation, offering another alternative instead. Although it may not be stated explicitly, he claimed, "The young hero puts the alternative: America or Zion. This alternative, however, is by no means necessary. For myself I would say: America and Zion—America for the thousands who can live as Jews here, Zion for the thousands who must live as Jews there."

Early in the sermon Magnes sought to resolve the dilemma between America and Zion in practical terms, with the United States as the land of choice for its Jews and Palestine as a refuge for those facing persecution in Europe. He then proposed a more complex position, which envisioned the possibility of mutual influence between Zionism and American Jewry. Zionism, he advanced, was a tool that served the "national life"—a concept that in itself testifies to the influence of Ahad Ha'am not only in Palestine but also in the Diaspora. Magnes continued:

> Zionism is the desire not so much for the mere preservation of Jewish religion and Jewish nationality. These can and will be preserved here. Zionism is rather the desire for the live and unhampered and harmonious further development of Jewish nationality and Jewish religion. Zion is the complement to, the fulfillment of America, not its alternative. Zion is the foundation stone and the capstone of the whole structure. It is our duty and our privilege to preserve and develop Judaism in America to the utmost of our powers. The difficulties are great. That does not excuse our ceasing to try. What we cannot do

here, Zion will help us do—revive and develop our national life and make it fuller and finer than it ever was."⁴¹

In concluding the sermon, Magnes proposed his own version of the orchestra metaphor: The metaphor of a symphony or orchestra essentially borrowed from Zangwill's play, whose hero, David, was engaged in writing "the Great American Symphony."⁴² But Zangwill's symphony, according to Magnes, would be "a vast monotone.... The symphony of America must be written by the various nationalities which keep their individual and characteristic note, and which sound this note in harmony with their sister nationalities. Then it will be a symphony of color, of picturesqueness, of character, of distinction—not the harmony of the Melting Pot, but rather the harmony of sturdiness and loyalty and joyous struggle."⁴³ The vision Magnes proposed for American society was one of harmony stemming not from uniformity but from difference. In this state of harmony, not only was Zionism not a threat to Jewish integration into American society; Zionism reinforced the Nietzschean vitality and organic life of American Jewry.

In sum, Magnes supported making cultural pluralism the foundation of American Zionism. Indeed, Kallen defined Zionism in terms of cultural pluralism, and its role according to this view was to ensure the preservation and cultivation of the unique Jewish melody so that it could integrate into and contribute to the inclusive American harmony. One might therefore view Magnes, and later Jewish Supreme Court justice Louis Brandeis—who became the main spokesperson of the American Zionist position that Zionism is not in conflict with American identity but rather strengthens it—as sharing Kallen's position.⁴⁴

Despite the practical difficulties, Magnes ultimately adopted the view that Zionism was able to serve the development and continuity of American Jewry. As he elucidated: "Zion is the complement to, the fulfillment of America, not its alternative.... What we cannot do here, Zion will help us do."⁴⁵

Religious Worldviews Shaping Political Outlooks

Magnes's political outlook was also religiously motivated, as he believed that Zionism could help American Jews revive Jewish life in the United States. In his view, the effort to cultivate a revival of Judaism within the framework of the American Reform movement in the absence of a collective Jewish environment that was possible only in Palestine had ended in failure and resulted in spiritual decline and further alienation from tradition.

Magnes was not the only American Zionist whose religious worldview played a key part in shaping his Zionist outlook. Two other prominent figures in this regard were Stephen Wise and Abba Hillel Silver, who, in addition to being Zionist leaders, held rabbinical positions. Wise, who did not officially belong to the Reform movement—he founded an independent synagogue that allowed him the freedom to preach as he saw fit—thought of Zionism as a natural extension of Jewish history, and therefore as an inseparable part of his Jewish worldview.[46] Silver, who, like Wise, saw his role as a Reform rabbi as "the basis and framework for all [my] other activities," may be viewed as both a Zionist leader and a Jewish preacher who advocated progress and was committed to a universalist, prophetic sense of destiny.[47]

Magnes's position, however, was more "religious" in terms of its explicit link to his own faith and to faith generally—a link that Wise and Silver usually refrained from making in their public statements and private journals—and in terms of his closer association with the Conservative movement and even with Orthodoxy.

Addressing the Jewish-Arab Problem

The irony entailed in the title of Magnes's seminal Zionist article, "Palestine—or Death," albeit when observed anachronistically from the present, begs a question: At that time, what were Magnes's views on Jewish-Arab relations? Considering his preoccupation with the

Jewish-Arab problem later in life (discussed starting in chapter 6), there is a striking lack of attention to this issue in Magnes's early Zionist thinking. Admittedly, the Zionist movement at the time tended to ignore the Arab issue in general.[48] But, Ahad Ha'am, of whom Magnes considered himself a disciple and whose writings he read,[49] had recognized the Arab problem as early as 1891, in his article "Truth from Eretz Israel." Moreover, Magnes visited Palestine in 1907 and 1912 and therefore had firsthand knowledge of the situation there. Why, therefore, did he not address the question of Jewish-Arab relations in Palestine at that time?[50]

In my view, his lack of attention reflected the fact that at the time Magnes regarded Zionism primarily as a tool for the renewal of Jewish life in the United States. As such, the urgency of this issue overrode the discussion of other problems. Following World War I and the Balfour Declaration, Magnes developed an aversion to nationalism and its inherent dangers. After he immigrated to Palestine, his aversion to nationalism compelled his focus on the political situation there and the Zionist approach to the presence of Arabs in the Land of Israel.

The early Zionism of Magnes is thus best understood as emanating from religious and spiritual considerations and ideals. It serves, as he explicitly points out, to promote the better understanding and realization of a "Jewish conception of God," the cornerstone of his "belief" in Zionism. Eventually, in 1922, when Magnes moved to Palestine and experienced the Jewish-Arab question firsthand, he would come to readjust his Zionism to incorporate a solution to that problem—namely binationalism. This solution would also integrate his religious-socialist views and the devout pacifism that emerged in the eventful and turbulent "teens" (1910s)—which turned the tables on the world at large, and on the optimistic theology of Magnes and other religious thinkers, in Judaism and beyond.

3

Prophetic Socialism and the Social Gospel

During World War I, following his resignation from Temple Emanu-El, Magnes would become increasingly radicalized. Combining socialism with pacifism, he would establish and cement relations with radical American Jewish socialists and leaders of the Social Gospel movement, which sprang up in the United States in the early twentieth century with the aim of integrating social justice into American Protestant thought and practice. He would also champion Eugene Debs, the Socialist candidate for the U.S. presidency, in five election campaigns between 1900 and 1920.

Characterizing Magnes as a radical, however, would produce an incomplete picture, as other factors, of a religious nature, drew him to both socialism and pacifism. Magnes's religious socialism combined a moral Reform Jewish outlook, linked to Hermann Cohen's ethical socialism, which perceived socialism as a manifestation of ethical imperatives, with the views of the Social Gospel movement and its essentially Christian conceptualization of the "societal sin" of economic inequality and with the Jewish socialism of the Lower East Side, which focused on the masses of Jewish workers and harbored an explicitly secular worldview. Following his immigration to Palestine, his outlook would be further shaped by the religious socialism of members of the Central European circles of Brit Shalom.

Magnes and Radical American Jewish Socialism

The historiography of American Jewry tends to overlook its past ties to socialism. This is largely due to the incongruence between socialism and the prevailing Jewish American ethos, which holds that one should simultaneously be fully Jewish and fully American. Many historians of U.S. Jewry have regarded the American Jewish labor movement as a fleeting phenomenon that served mainly as an agent of Americanization, after which it dissipated—an inaccurate view that fails to appreciate the essence of Jewish socialism. American Jewish socialists did not regard the United States as a land of gold and limitless opportunity but as a country divided between the promised vision of democracy and the reality of economic exploitation that characterized most immigrants' daily struggle for subsistence. They did not seek to adapt themselves to existing society; instead, they wanted to build a new society.[1]

According to this conceptualization, suggested by historian Tony Michels, the development of American Jewish socialism was not, as many claim, the product of socialist ideas imported by Jewish intellectuals from Russia. Rather, it was the outcome of a multiphased process, beginning with the encounter between these intellectuals and non-Jewish German socialists who settled in the Lower East Side in the 1880s. The German socialists provided Jewish immigrants with financial assistance and ideological guidance, and helped them develop and spread organizational models. In time, the German socialists also encouraged these Jewish intellectuals to form trade unions of Jewish Yiddish-speaking workers, which required the German socialists to learn Yiddish.

These observations complement the historical claim that New York played a key role in developing the Jewish labor movement in the Soviet Union. The use of Yiddish to encourage unionization among Jewish workers in New York was a source of inspiration for Jewish revolutionaries in Vilnius as early as 1893, when they began using newspapers, posters, and publications in Yiddish from New York and London. Additional Jewish groups began to form in Poland, Lithuania, and Russia, and in 1897 they formed the Bund, the secular Jewish socialist party in the Russian Empire. Following the failed Russian revolution of 1905, thousands of Bund supporters, including socialist Zionists as well as Bolsheviks, started arriving in New York and infusing new energy and new ideas into the American Jewish labor movement.[2] The relationship between Jewish socialism in the United States and in Europe was therefore one of mutual influence.

The rise of socialism during this period coincided with the early phase of Magnes's community work and political career in the United States. From the very beginning of his career in New York he was drawn to Yiddish-speaking socialists, in particular to Chaim Zhitlovsky, one of the prominent American Jewish socialist leaders in the city.[3] In a June 1906 letter Magnes wrote, "Any one who has eyes to see can know of the great change Dr. Schitlovksy has brought about in the spiritual make-up of the community of Russian Jews in this country. His true Jewish heart, his inexorable logic, his artistic and dignified eloquence have carried conviction with them and have given a Jewish color to the life especially of our radical Jews."[4] In other words, Magnes viewed American Jewish socialism as a phenomenon of spiritual value—one that could preserve the bond to tradition among socialist Jews while also contributing to the renewal of Jewish life as a whole.

During World War I, Magnes developed strong ties with Morris Hillquit, a prominent American Jewish socialist and consistent opponent of the war. Hillquit, alongside Magnes and others, helped found the People's Council of America for Democracy and Peace, committed to calling a halt to the Great War and promoting a peace settlement that could bring about a world of equals. A secular Jew, Hillquit did not draw on Jewish concepts in discussing socialism, but at the same time did not deny that his Jewish identity influenced his views.[5] In late 1917, Hillquit ran for mayor of New York. Many of his supporters, including Magnes and the Yiddish poet Abraham Leissin, believed his opposition to the war was motivated by core Jewish values—and because Magnes viewed Hillquit's socialist pacifism as fundamentally Jewish in nature, he enthusiastically supported the latter's mayoral candidacy. At a dinner for election campaign activists in October 1917, Magnes avowed: "Since the outbreak of the war my affection for the Jewish people has been deepened immeasurably. This hatred of all the arts of soldiering, this repugnance to war, this abhorrence of blood spilling, that has characterized the Jewish masses is nothing more or less than a continuance of the great Jewish tradition which exalted the spiritual life."[6] Thus Magnes considered pacifism a natural extension of Jewish tradition, a popular Jewish phenomenon that represented the socialist Jewish masses. This outlook corresponded closely with his romantic view of Jewish tradition, which, as we saw, grew stronger following his exposure to Yiddish culture and Eastern European Jewry during his studies in Berlin.

On July 23, 1918, Magnes sent Hillquit a proposal outlining what he thought the Socialist Party platform should address in preparation for the upcoming congressional election. Magnes's proposal included five elements: support for any initiative that would promote and expedite a democratic peace agreement based on the principles of understanding and reconciliation between the warring parties; freedom for the Socialist Party and labor groups in the United States to forge ties with other workers' associations and socialist parties, including in enemy countries; reinstatement of the freedoms of protest, expression, press, and assembly as they existed before the war; the continued fight against war profiteering; and the establishment of a league of nations whose authority would be based solely on economic power.[7] In light of the need to appeal to the general public, rather than solely the Jewish sector, and given the official separation between church and state in the United States, there were no religious facets to the proposal.

The Prophetic Socialism of Magnes

The driving force behind religious Jewish socialism during the years before and immediately after the war, until his assassination in May 1919, was the European socialist thinker Gustav Landauer. In his 1911 book *For Socialism*, Landauer called for an internal revolution of the human spirit, which would bring about the social revolution.[8] Landauer's socialist worldview was grounded in neo-Kantian philosophy and the ethical socialism of Hermann Cohen. According to Cohen, the concepts of humanism and socialism were intertwined in the form of moral imperatives that rationality imposed on the individual and society. As such, ethical socialism conflicted with Marxism because it presented moral choice as an alternative to Marxist determinism: the progression of socialism was thereby *not* the product of the inevitable historical, materialistic process Marxists claimed. Moreover, religious socialism waged war on sociologist Max Weber's concept of realpolitik, which differentiated between human morality and political morality. It advocated instead the realization of God's kingdom here and now through a gradual process—not a revolution—and on the basis of internal change within the individual and society.[9]

The philosopher Martin Buber, strongly influenced by Landauer's outlook, integrated the latter's theory into his own ideas about religious socialism, which were based on his conception of Jewish humanism.[10] Later, Buber would become one of the pillars of the religious socialist movement emerging in Europe after World War I, alongside Christian philosophers and theologians Paul Tillich and Swiss Reformed theologian Leonhard Ragaz. Religious socialists objected to modern society's extreme polarization between the sacred and the profane—in their view, a division without any ontological basis, as all of creation is potentially sacred. Accordingly, the sanctification of what exists required that religious belief express itself in political and public spheres as well. In this spirit, Buber wrote, "In all the domains in which we are immersed, we cannot work but for the sake of the Kingdom of Heaven.... Heaven forbid that we ... exclude politics from the domain of things that need to be sanctified."[11]

How does Magnes fit into this picture of religious socialism during and after World War I? Jewish philosopher Hugo Bergman writes that Magnes found support for his views in Ragaz's argument that "to believe in God is easy. But to believe that one day this world will be God's world; to believe this in a faith so firm and resolute as to mold one's own life according to it—this requires faithfulness until death."[12]

In terms of its spirit, religious socialism did not differ greatly from the theology of the Social Gospel movement, from which Magnes drew his inspiration. Some of its intellectual aspects were distinctly European, while the Social Gospel movement was the product of fundamentally American thought, but the two had common roots in the moral theology of nineteenth-century liberal Protestantism, which held that morality, which manifests as action on behalf of the Kingdom of Heaven on earth, is a core element of religion.[13] In essence, then, although Magnes's rhetoric drew on socialist theory, it was grounded in a Jewish ethos.

The Social Gospel and Prophetic Judaism

Specifically, the universal morality of the prophets led Magnes from pacifism to radical socialism. He embraced Prophetic Judaism, which combined universal values with the social justice characteristic of American Reform Jewish thought.

Similarly, the Social Gospel movement, a fundamentally American Protestant movement dating to the late nineteenth century and peaking in activity and influence during World War I, also integrated particular religious as well as universal values. Its leading figure, the German Baptist minister Walter Rauschenbusch, had worked with temporary-housing residents in poor New York neighborhoods; his exposure to the city's slums drove him to develop an urban social action plan based on Christian principles.[14]

Influenced by the American concept of progress and attuned to developments in the Protestant Social Gospel movement, Reform rabbis began to engage in diverse political and communal activity. In the name of Judaism, they opposed the social injustices of child labor, the twelve-hour workday, and appalling working conditions, and lent their support to workers' associations. In place of the teachings of Jesus and the Gospel of his disciples, the Reform rabbis drew on the prophets Amos, Isaiah, and Micah.[15] In 1918 the Central Conference of American Rabbis (the principal organization of Reform rabbis) adopted a fourteen-point social action plan that called for an eight-hour workday, a fair minimum wage for all workers, and a more equitable distribution of industrial profits overall.[16]

Magnes additionally had close ties to the Social Gospel movement leader Norman Thomas, a Presbyterian minister and later a Socialist candidate for the U.S. presidency. Thomas had also cofounded the People's Council of America for Democracy and Peace, and the two men worked together to support Hillquit's mayoral candidacy. Later they corresponded about the possible publication of Magnes's articles in the magazine *The World Tomorrow*, which Thomas had helped found and served as editor. All such activities had to be conducted under a cloak of secrecy for fear of repercussions by the Postmaster General, who, by the power of the 1917 Espionage Act, had the authority to prevent the circulation of mail publications that might undermine U.S. military efforts or support the enemy. In June 1918, Thomas asked Magnes to write a review of the book *The End of the War*, a critique of American imperialism by the progressive writer Walter Weyl, "making such comments thereon as you think it safe to print these days"; Thomas suggested that he use a pseudonym if necessary (a suggestion to which Magnes did not respond). Thomas also requested that Magnes write about the emergence of liberal ideas in Germany, to which Magnes replied that he could not do so because he was prevented from receiving material published in Germany, probably also on account of the Espionage Act.[17]

While nothing came to pass with regard to Magnes contributing to *The World Tomorrow*, the generally like-minded Jewish and Presbyterian faith leaders would maintain a correspondence until Magnes's final days.[18]

On Religion and Socialism

On January 16, 1919, Magnes delivered a lecture to the Jewish Labor Congress addressing the correlation between Judaism and socialism. Pointing out parallels between the socialist ideal and the religious Jewish ideal, he added that alongside the conceptual congruence he saw between socialism and Judaism, he was aware that the rise of socialism might in fact alienate the Jewish masses from their Jewish heritage. At the outset of his speech Magnes therefore addressed the young socialist secular Jews in the audience:

> Just as the Jewish labor movement gives itself to the labor and radical forces of the world, so must it pour its spirit and its strength upon the living Jewish people. The living Jewish people needs the organized Jewish workers, Jewish life needs the freedom of spirit, of outlook, that zeal for justice and righteousness which organized Jewish labor can give it. . . . Jewish life needs the clear, direct, keen minds of the thinkers, the idealism, the vision of the poets, the singers, the enthusiasts, of the organized Jewish labor movement. Jewish life needs both the vigorous nationalism, and the generous, far-seeing internationalism, of the organized Jewish labor movement. Jewish life needs the organized Jewish workers in order that Jewish life may become thoroughly democratic, broad minded, undogmatic, unprejudiced.[19]

In reflecting Magnes's attempt to bridge between socialism and Jewish belongingness, his remarks highlight the tension between universalism and particularism (between "generous internationalism" and "vigorous nationalism") that permeated his thinking. His juxtaposition of the universal elements of socialism with the uniqueness of nationalism demarcated his position on a widely debated issue in socialist circles during the turbulent years following World War I—that is, the role of nationalism in the socialist revolution, manifested also in the equally contentious internal Jewish debate between socialist Zionism and the non-Zionist "Bund" (Jewish labor socialist organization and political party in Europe). The religious potential of socialism, according to Magnes, lay in its contribution to the establishment of a life of justice and equality "upon this earth":

> Jewish life needs that sense of reality which the organized Jewish laborers can give it, and which brings it home to us that it is in this world, the world we live in, that justice and righteousness and peace and love must be pursued, and that the kingdom of heaven is to be established here and now upon this earth, among living, breathing men and women. From among the Jewish working masses must come positive contributions to the culture, the national life, the language, the literature, the spiritual ideals and aspirations of the whole Jewish people.[20]

Magnes's call to establish the kingdom of heaven here and now on earth corresponded with the theological progression of religious socialism after World War I, which emphasized social action in this world. He supplemented this by calling on Jewish "religionists" to play their part in establishing a new partnership with "the Jewish working masses." The latter, Magnes held, were not responsible for having "lost religion," because this loss had resulted from critical historical thought emblematic of the sad state of Judaism, rather than from the masses' lack of spirituality. "The Jewish religionists," Magnes insisted, "must realize that many of the best among the Jewish people, as among all peoples, have lost religion; and these, to use the words of a great thinker of this war, [British philosopher] Bertrand Russell, have lost it because 'their minds were active, not because their spirit was dead.'"[21] If the Jewish religion wishes to fulfill its function in the world, Magnes continued, "it must enter into the arena of the living Jewish people and there fight out its battle with all kinds of Jews, whatever be their social, their political, their spiritual outlook."[22]

Magnes's remarks indirectly hint at the pervasive religious crisis the Western world was experiencing after World War I: the scale and brutality of the bloodshed had put into question the theological belief in modernity as the harbinger of a messianic age of peace. To him, this crisis required Judaism to seek life: to rid itself of Jewish separatism and engage actively in the vibrant arena of ideas of the living Jewish people—which included socialism not explicitly inspired by Jewish thought.

Note here Magnes's acceptance of the supposed loss of religion among the Jewish masses following the war. He finds an explanation in the intellectual thought of the time—that religiosity as a sense of divinely inspired purpose could also be manifested outside of formal religious institutions. He also experienced his own sense of individual religious alienation—a concern triggered by the war that would preoccupy Magnes to the end of his days. For Magnes, as we shall explore in chapter 5, religiousness was expressed as a personal search for a sense of faith that did not depend on an explicit religious affiliation. Likewise, he perceived the Jewish socialism of the masses (often authentically secular) as emanating from the same religious quest.

In a lecture delivered on May 31, 1919, marking the launch of the Liberation Fund of Po'alei Zion (Workers of Zion) in New York, Magnes again posited that the Jew who behaves religiously need not necessarily be identified as "religious." He aimed to reestablish the connection between the Jewish socialist masses and the sources of Judaism by demonstrating that Jewish socialism could be seen as religiously inspired even without exhibiting explicitly Jewish manifestations. This same outlook had served him in his attempt to reconcile the secular nature of Zionism with the religious value he attributed to it, by perceiving secular Zionism as implicitly religious. Moreover, his remarks ascribed religious legitimacy to the Zionist Jewish workers' movement in its own right. Whether or not Po'alei Zion "call their devoted work by the name of religion," Magnes insisted, their contribution "will be material for the Jewish religion of tomorrow." In his view, the Jewish workers' movement had a religious role: paving the way to a future that would combine the more earthly values of socialism with Jewish tradition, Torah, values, and even mysticism. Tomorrow's religion would combine socialism and class struggle with "the continued study of the Torah and of our tradition by the traditionally religious ... which is to be woven into the new religion, the religion of tomorrow." The same principle applied also to Zionism, in that "the enriched culture of tomorrow may overcome, if it be possible at all, the contradistinction between religion and radicalism, between religion and nationalism."[23]

Notably, despite the optimistic pathos and aspiration for harmony stemming from his adherence to Ahad Ha'am's cultural Zionism, Magnes still qualified his remarks regarding the likelihood of combining religion with radicalism or religion with nationalism. His attempt to resolve the tension between religion and nationalism would preoccupy Magnes for the rest of his life.

By 1919 Magnes already sensed that the antireligious foundations of the radical socialist circles in which he participated were incompatible with the utopian vision he presented. In May 1927, having formed a more sober view of socialism after the Bolshevik revolution, Magnes retreated somewhat from the view that socialism was fully compatible with Jewish principles and that Jewish socialists personified living Jewish culture. He wrote in his journal: "The Jewish 'socialist' idea cannot be so thoroughly absorbed in materialist things and thoughts as is the materialist socialism of the day. It cannot be so concerned with absolute equality of possessions. Rather, it is in the Jewish nature to say: neither riches nor poverty; enough for life and education."[24]

In short, Magnes's socialism at the time was complex, embodying a multitude of influences, from Hermann Cohen's morally inspired ethical socialism to the Social Gospel movement's emphasis on the sins of the current social order to the popular class struggle espoused by the radical Jewish socialist circles with which Magnes maintained ties in New York. A salient component was his belief that radical socialism embodies an innate religious spark.

His attitude toward Jewish socialism reflected his religious and historical outlook. Indeed, Magnes attempted to "Judaize" the political phenomena that emerged as a result of modernization and the dissolution of traditional religious structures, and to form a bridge between these movements and conceptions he regarded as fundamentally and inherently Jewish. In this sense his attitude toward socialism was similar to his attitude toward Zionism: he saw elements of the sacred in both, even though their overt manifestations lacked any religious dimension. To Magnes, both causes embodied the potential for Judaism's future development based on "the living Jewish people."

Later, however, when he would discover that both socialism and Zionism operated in accordance with values and interests that were ultimately irreconcilable with his Jewish worldview, he would retract his support for their organized representative bodies.

4

The Religious Mission of Pacifism

On June 5, 1929, on the other side of a journal entry titled "Pacifism," Magnes quoted the English novelist and poet Thomas Hardy's poem "Christmas 1924," which harshly criticized religion's enabler role in the war effort.[1] More than a decade after World War I and shortly before Magnes became politically active in Palestine in the aftermath of the 1929 riots (when disputes between Arabs and Jews on prayer arrangements at the Western Wall escalated into nationwide violence) his diary recollection merged the then unprecedented brutality of World War I, on the one hand, with the failure of religion to prevent the war or at least to limit its duration, on the other.

The American Socialist Party and the People's Council

Socialism and pacifism were intertwined in the United States. By 1916, the American Socialist Party had adopted a policy of opposition to the war, and, in the spring of 1917, when the United States joined the war effort, the party, comprising some 70,000 registered members, was the largest organized body opposed to the war. The party's candidate for the U.S. presidency, Eugene Debs, had received roughly 6 percent of the popular vote in the 1912 elections, and a notable number of Socialist

51

Party candidates had been elected as mayors and members of municipal councils. Nonetheless, the American Socialist Party's antiwar stance subjected the party to intense pressure based on the Espionage Act of June 1917, which made it a felony to "willfully obstruct the recruiting or enlistment service of the United States," and would ultimately lead to the party's decline as an influential body in the American political arena.[2]

Meanwhile, and by contrast, with the outbreak of World War I, the European socialist parties effectually abandoned the principles of class solidarity in favor of nationalism and support for the war. Their conduct generated ideological confusion among American socialists.

The various founders of the People's Council of America for Democracy and Peace, the umbrella organization of movements opposed to the war, were associated with a diverse range of circles—socialists, radicals, liberals, and pacifists. People's Council co-founder Magnes delivered the opening address at the council's inaugural conference on May 30, 1917, and he repeated this speech the following day before an audience of thousands at Madison Square Garden, under heavy police supervision.[3] "We have come in the midst of war," commenced Magnes, "to aid the cause of peace. We have come from all parts of our loved country to re-dedicate ourselves to the cause of democracy and international brotherhood. We come here because we love America and because we want America to assume leadership in bringing about a speedy and universal and democratic peace such as will endure for a long time to come."[4]

Throughout the speech Magnes refrained from quoting Jewish texts or otherwise hinting at his role as a rabbi. Rather, he aggrandized the "new and democratic Russia," whose "revolutionary democracy is dominated by men and women who are the creators and heirs of a rare revolutionary tradition permeated with a deep love of humanity, liberty, and justice." Aiming to convince the U.S. government to accept the peace terms suggested by Russia, which included a request for American financial aid, his speech ended with a plea that "our voices, the voices of many peoples, might be heard, and that America might justify the world's high hopes of her, by commanding peace forthwith as easily now she might. The president's peace aims can now be achieved without the killing of more millions. But the killing of more millions can never achieve the peace aims."[5]

The Quakers as Model

Within the American pacifist tradition, the Quakers (Society of Friends) had played a key part in keeping the concept of pacifism alive, from colonial times to the Civil War and beyond. Although during World War I the U.S. pacifist movement came to include multiple Christian denominations and multiple religions, as well as objectors driven by humanitarian reasons, it retained the religious conceptual foundations of Quakerism.[6]

Magnes had a special admiration for the Quakers. Toward the end of the war he resided in Chappaqua, New York, which had been founded as a Quaker community. He maintained close ties with Quakers who were active in the antiwar effort and sent his children to a Quaker school.[7] He later claimed that "the Quakers, and they alone of all the religious communities of America, preserved their sweetness of spirit during the war and were ready to bring comfort and healing to all sufferers, to friend and foe alike." After the war he thought about establishing a Jewish school that would be "something like the Friends School" and wrote in his journal that he wanted "to make Jew and pacifist identical," just as "Quakers and pacifist" were "identical."[8]

After he immigrated to Palestine, however, Magnes would conclude that pacifism was unrealistic in the Yishuv (Jewish Palestine). "I have no illusions," he said, "about the Jews here becoming a Quaker community. That would be too good to be true."[9]

Christian Churches and Pacifism

In March 1918 Magnes had a brief correspondence with John D. Rockefeller Jr., the youngest son of oil tycoon John D. Rockefeller. Rockefeller

Religious Mission of Pacifism

Jr. sent Magnes a booklet he had authored, *The Christian Church—What of Its Future?*, which argued that although the church had failed to prevent the war, the continuing Christian faith of individuals had been reflected in acts of courage both on the battlefield and among starving civilians behind enemy lines. In light of this, Rockefeller proposed the establishment of a "Church of the Living God," a democratic, egalitarian, and nondenominational church with love for God the only precondition for membership—as in the early days of Christianity. This church would embody practical religion, rather than the theoretical religion of theologians, and would address all of life's problems—of society and morality, industry and business, civics and education. Accordingly, its clerics would be trained not only at seminaries but by life itself. Incorporating as well the thinking of the "great movements"—possibly hinting to the Progressive movement and even socialism—the church would be "literally establishing the Kingdom of God on Earth."[10]

Rockefeller's view reflected the mood of the time: the need to address the failure of religion during World War I. Alternative visions were emerging, among them of a renewed religion that would struggle for its place in conceptual, social, and democratic arenas. Focusing mainly on God's everyday presence and the realization of God's Kingdom on Earth, rather than on eschatologically prone theoretical theology, this new religious vision aimed to restrain the messianic-nationalistic theopolitical trends contributing to World War I—trends that had not only sanctified nationalism but, in the spirit of German philosopher Nietzsche, had glorified man, which presumably had led man to try to take the place of God.

In many respects these views aligned with those of Magnes. At the same time, perhaps because of his socialist opposition to capitalists, Magnes was critical of Rockefeller's practical proposal of uniting the various church denominations into larger and grander structures. Magnes replied to Rockefeller, "I think the crux of the whole matter is in the assertion that the Church must be 'literally establishing the Kingdom of God on earth.' But I think also that the Church must be larger than buildings, or even ecclesiastic organisations, however imposing. The Church must be coincident with people themselves." Rockefeller's response was laconic, and their communication came to an end.[11]

Magnes was brutally frank in his criticism of churches for the support and religious justification they granted the American administration after the United States joined the war effort. Speaking before the World Peace Fellowship in Washington DC in November 1921, he railed: "But when the crash comes, together with the next war, our imperialist rulers will take courage. They know they will be able to count upon most of the peace societies and churches now forwarding peace resolutions to Washington. For they are bone of one bone, flesh of the same imperialism. When the next war comes, abundant religious sanction will again be given it."[12] Presenting then his own view of the appropriate relationship between church and state, he concluded by referring to the prophecy of Isaiah:

> Is the church the slave of the state, and is religion but the handmaiden of politics? . . . If the churches and the peace societies and others were to endorse such a declaration [i.e., "No More War—International Movement of England"], the next war, for America at least, would be infinitely longer in coming. There might then be some reality to that prophecy of Isaiah that "Nations shall beat their swords into plowshares and their spears into pruning hooks. Nation shall not lift up sword against nation, neither shall they learn war anymore" [Isa. 2:4].[13]

Magnes wanted the religious establishment to be an independent body operating on the basis of religious considerations in accordance with God's will as he understood it, and willing to take a stand that opposed the political establishment, whatever the cost.

Moral Politics

From the outset, Magnes's political activity, in the Jewish world as well as the political arena generally, was characterized by his identification with the figure of the prophet. It manifested in his withdrawal from the Reform movement, his fierce opposition to the war, and later in his struggle against the Zionist establishment in Jewish Palestine. Although his writings indicate that he recognized the disparity between historical reality and the prophet Isaiah's vision, he still believed that religious leaders had a duty to position themselves at the moral, rather than the practical, end of the spectrum.

Magnes's inclination toward prophetic politics brought him into conflict with more realistically oriented contemporaries. His main dispute in this regard was with Rabbi Stephen Wise, who had initially opposed the war but became a supporter when the United States joined the effort. The two harbored a long-standing rivalry in Jewish and Zionist affairs, and occasionally exchanged accusations in speeches and Jewish media outlets. In a September 1917 sermon, Wise accused Magnes of "aiding the cause of peace for the sake of Pax Germanica,"[14] effectively claiming that the latter's pacifism was motivated by pro-German sentiments and aimed at keeping the United States from curtailing German war gains. Magnes did not respond publicly to Wise's accusations, but his journal entry from October 2, 1917 (discussed later in this chapter), which addressed "preachers of the 'mission' [that had] ... become high priests of the patriotic cult," was probably a private counterblow aimed at Wise. In a March 8, 1918, article in the *New York Times*, Wise made similar allegations of pro-German sympathies, this time aimed at Israel Friedlander, then appointed by the Red Cross as representative to Russia on behalf of the American Jewish Joint Distribution Committee (JDC). Responding at a JDC meeting that addressed the allegations, Magnes lambasted Wise— "Jewish history is replete with tragedies that have come over the Jewish people because of the activity of Jewish *mosrim* [informers on the Jewish people]"—effectively accusing him of betraying the Jewish people.[15]

Preferring Christian to Jewish Allies in Pacifism

Magnes's views on the war struck a chord in like-minded Christian pacifist circles. His thinking tended to be similar to that of pacifist and socialist Christian figures, from whom he drew inspiration and with whom he found a common language. Besides his friendship with the Presbyterian minister and Socialist Party presidential candidate Norman Thomas (see chapter 3), Magnes also maintained close ties with John Haynes Holmes, a Protestant minister who visited Palestine in 1929 and wrote about Magnes for the American Christian press in the 1930s, equating him in detail with the prophetic image of Jeremiah of old (see chapter 7).

The closeness Magnes felt with Christian leaders whose religious outlook on pacifism resonated with his own was likely rooted in his own Reform upbringing. In the Christian Social Gospel Magnes found the willingness to translate into action the Reform ideals of mission and justice, which in his view the Reform movement had failed to actualize.

At the same time, Magnes did not consciously address aspects of syncretism or systematically examine similarities and differences between Judaism and Christianity in terms of resistance to war. Rather, he saw himself as representing what he considered an authentic Jewish pacifist position—faithfully representing Judaism within the general pacifist camp. As part of this camp, he lent his voice to criticism of the Christian church establishment for granting religious legitimacy to the war and thereby placing itself in the service of nationalism.

The bond he felt with Christian pacifists underscores his estrangement from the Reform movement. In a March 1911 letter to then CCAR president, Rabbi Max Heller, after Magnes had resigned from Temple Emanu-El, he wrote:

> You will pardon me if I say that I feel very much estranged from my colleagues of the so-called 'Reform' wing of Judaism. I have but very little bitterness towards them and not very much interest in what they are doing or not doing. Inasmuch as I am not a reader of the Jewish papers, I hardly get to know what my former colleagues are thinking about. There are, I know, many disadvantages in this method, yet I feel

that it enables me to preserve my equanimity, and, as a consequence, to be in better trim to do the little constructive work I am capable of.[16]

The Gotthard Deutsch Affair

Nevertheless, there were certain figures in the Reform movement with whom Magnes could have identified.[17] One such notable person was Professor Gotthard Deutsch of Hebrew Union College (HUC) in Cincinnati.

America's entry into the war on April 6, 1917, and the country's general mobilization for the war effort had led to a sharp rise in American nationalism. Calls for ideological conformity increased, and tolerance for the minority opinion opposing the war waned. Government censorship prevented dissemination by mail of periodicals expressing dissenting views, and minorities, especially those of German heritage but Jews as well, found themselves under attack because, presumably, they were secretly supporting the enemy.[18]

Late 1917 saw a formative event in terms of the Reform position on the war. Deutsch, a professor of Jewish history and philosophy at HUC and one of its senior faculty members, was, like many other faculty members, of Central European heritage, born in a family belonging to the German minority in Moravia. In December 1916, a few months before the United States entered the war, Deutsch published in *HUC Monthly* the article "Justice to the Enemy," an apologia in response to an argument in the Jewish press claiming that Germany was responsible for "the setting back of the ideals for life of mankind, to which every true Jew is wedded." Deutsch contrarily expressed distinctly pro-German sentiments. "The present German empire," he claimed, "never had any law discriminating against the Jews, [and] most German states had given to the Jews in 1848, full civic and political equality. . . . All this is not said as an apology for Germany," he concluded. "It is said in vindication of the self respect which every Jew owes to himself."[19]

At the time, he, alongside Herbert Bigelow, a progressive pastor affiliated with the People's Church of Cincinnati, was involved in founding a local chapter of the People's Council of America for Democracy and Peace—of which Magnes was one of the leaders. In a letter of June 5, 1917, to Jewish labor arbitration champion Jacob Billikopf, Deutsch expressed reservations about the efforts to assist Jewish war refugees in Europe, arguing that Magnes's brave stance for the sake of peace was more significant than the financial sacrifices offered by the likes of Louis Marshall and philanthropist Julius Rosenwald.[20]

In November 1917, while Deutsch was testifying in a Cincinnati court on behalf of an acquaintance applying for citizenship, the judge asked him which side he hoped would win the war—Germany or the United States. When Deutsch refused to answer, arguing that the question was inappropriate for the court, he was disqualified as a witness. The incident sparked criticism and outrage in the local general press. Reverend Madison C. Peters of New York, a supporter of the war effort, came to Cincinnati to deliver a speech, later published in the *Cincinnati Enquirer*, maligning Deutsch, "personally a lovely old man," as one of those "exceptional Jews today [who] are so loud in their traitorous activities that the American can't hear the patriotic Jew."[21]

Deutsch's position at HUC became the subject of three stormy meetings of the Board of Governors, during one of which the board's president, Edward Heinsheimer, actually collapsed and died. During the first meeting, on November 27, 1917, a statement from Deutsch was presented in which he explicitly declared he wished the United States to win the war. Meanwhile, prominent rabbis, such as Emil Hirsch from Chicago, sent letters of support to the Board of Governors, arguing that Deutsch should be allowed to keep his position at the college. Finally, on December 26, it was determined, by a slight majority, not to terminate Deutsch's employment at HUC, but to "censor" him instead.[22] Later in the meeting, the college unanimously decided to issue this public statement:

> The Hebrew Union College was founded to have the young men whom it educates for the ministry preach and teach Reform Judaism and promulgate American ideas and ideals. Loyalty and patriotism have characterized the institution since its establishment. This Is Our Country. We know no other fatherland than the land in which we live, and no other flag than the flag which floats over it. Our county is at war, and all of its citizens must be not passively, but actively loyal and patriotic. No one who does not subscribe to these sentiments is welcome within the walls of the College.[23]

The Gotthard Deutsch affair reflects the tension to which Reform Judaism was subject during the war as well as the practical position it eventually adopted to resolve this tension. On the one hand, the German roots of the movement and its prominent U.S. leaders meant that it had ideological ties to German culture as a whole, beyond the scope of Reform ideology per se. On the other hand, the movement had to take an unequivocal stance in favor of national loyalty to America, particularly after the latter entered the war, even if this sometimes required great effort, as illustrated by the Deutsch affair.

Thus we can appreciate just how radical Magnes's uncompromising opposition to the war was in the eyes of the American Reform movement from which he had emerged, and in the eyes of the American Jewish public in general. Magnes's only letter to Deutsch, dated June 14, 1916, was a message of congratulation on the occasion of events marking Deutsch's twenty-fifth anniversary as a faculty member. He expressed gratitude to his teacher for the privilege of having studied with him but did not mention the war or Deutsch's opposition to it. It remains unknown whether Magnes was aware of the affair. Magnes himself only began to actively oppose the war after the United States joined the effort.[24]

Reform Pacifism and Mission Theology

Magnes's pacifism rested on Jewish texts that advocated peace; the Jewish pacifism that had evolved in reaction to the historical experience of being a persecuted people; and, more recently, Reform Judaism's Mission Theology. In 1869, a nationwide conference of Reform rabbis, held in Philadelphia, had issued a Declaration of Principles embracing Mission Theology. Its second article avowed: "We look upon the destruction of the second Jewish commonwealth not as a punishment for the sinfulness of Israel, but as a result of the divine purpose revealed to Abraham, which, as has become ever clearer in the course of the world's history, consists in the dispersion of the Jews to all parts of the earth, for the realization of their high-priestly mission, to lead the nations to the true knowledge and worship of God."[25] Reform leaders of the time thus regarded Jewish life in the Diaspora as a means to the realization of Israel's universal mission among the nations: to spread the gospel of ethical monotheism. Sixteen years later, the Reform movement's seminal 1885 Pittsburgh Platform again championed Mission Theology. Its first article proclaimed: "We hold that Judaism presents the highest conception of the God-idea as taught in our Holy Scriptures and developed and spiritualized by the Jewish teachers. . . . We maintain that Judaism preserved and defended . . . this God-idea as the central religious truth for the human race." The second article added the missionizing imperative: "We recognize in the Bible the record of the consecration of the Jewish people to its mission as the priest of the one God."[26] Together, the two Pittsburgh Platform articles embodied the crux of Mission Theology: Judaism represented the ultimate monotheistic truth preserved throughout the generations, and the Jewish people had been charged with the mission to spread its teachings among the nations. Was this mission synonymous with pacifism? A heated debate ensued.

The War Debate in *HUC Monthly*

A review of the wartime issues of *HUC Monthly*, the journal of the Reform rabbinical seminary in Cincinnati in which articles by faculty members appeared alongside those of rabbinical students, reveals important trends both at the ideological level and in terms of the movement's political pragmatism. Its editorial board was largely composed of seminarians and, among them, when the monthly journal was still an annual publication titled *Cincinnatian*, was Magnes. Yet Magnes frequently complained about faculty "censorship," and eventually resigned from the editorial board.[27]

The war that broke out in Europe did not receive attention in the journal until April 1915, when there appeared "The Assurance of Peace—the Moral Nature of Man," rabbinical student Jacob I. Meyer's overtly pacifist critique of the war. "Ultimately," Meyer propounded, "no arguments as to the folly, the cruelty or the expense of war, but nothing short of the moral regeneration of mankind will bring about the reign of peace." At the same time, he continued, pacifism does not mean passivity, and it was incumbent upon the United States, "the first moral superpower in the world," to mobilize an educational and cultural campaign to promote peace and call for disarmament.[28]

Later that year and during the following year, the journal published a series of articles expressing opposition to the war. In May 1915 Maxwell Silver, a seminarian at HUC and the older brother of the renowned Zionist leader Rabbi Abba Hillel Silver, attacked the "new false prophets," who, he claimed, called for suspending the old morality of the prophets and replacing it with a new morality in the spirit of Nietzsche, according to which the purpose of life was not the development of moral character but realization of the will to power and the accumulation of power. When the values of the Nietzschean archetypical "overhuman" (*Übermensch*)—vitality, strength, and cruelty—supplanted the values of humility, compassion, and mutual support, "the aim of the nation is not to work for the spiritual advancement of humanity through spiritual accomplishment and peace, but . . . rather to work for its own material aggrandizement, and this by brutal force."[29]

Silver concluded by calling for the renewal of the true spirit of prophecy, in the cosmopolitan spirit of the German philosopher Johann Gottlieb Fichte, which taught humanity to "seek peace and pursue it."

This last reference to a biblical verse ostensibly promoted by a German philosopher attests to the amalgamation of German thought and Reform Judaism at the time, most specifically at HUC. Silver further called for international cooperation by peaceful means for the sake of Germany and the entire world.[30]

The board's editorial piece in that year's June issue reflects the general crisis of values in Europe as a result of the war. Christianity, the board wrote, had failed in its effort to provide a foundation for peace in the spirit of the promise conveyed by the biblical verse "Glory to God in the highest, and on earth peace, good will toward men" (Luke 2:14). The horrific war had defied the Christian ideal of peace on Earth; hence Europeans had lost their spiritual sense of security. This necessitated the imperative of the hour: The people had to stand on their own and lead the way to a new spirituality, whose power would be akin to the force of life itself. "From the pulpit of the Jew must go forth the cry of Judaism's principle of life for men and nations: Justice and Peace."[31]

In addition to articles opposing the war, *HUC Monthly* also devoted space to promoting the war. In November 1915, before the United States entered the conflict, Kaufmann Kohler, a leading ideologue of the American Reform movement, penned "The Views and Principles of American Reform Judaism and Its Outlook in These Critical Times." Kohler was then president of HUC, and the article, consisting of the full text of his September 25, 1915, speech marking the opening of the school year, advocated war as the necessary means to ushering in a new world order of prophetic justice and peace.[32]

Kohler began by comparing the current crisis with the period of Isaiah, who prophesized during the era when the Kingdom of Israel had fallen to the Assyrians and Judea also came under threat. In that time, "confusion and discord reigned throughout Judea. War and famine struck terror in the hearts of people and ruler. The world seemed out of joint. Man had lost faith in God and the future." Yet only the prophet, "soaring above the valley of woes and tears" and countering those who claimed that humanity was sinking into an abyss of blood and destruction, had called out "*emanu El*" ("God is with us"), preserving the seed of existence and the tree of life in the face of adversity and rivalry.[33]

Kohler also held Christianity to account: "The religion of love which for fifteen hundred years claims to have dominion over the largest part of the world has given evidence of its utter hollowness and hypocrisy, of its complete inefficiency and insecurity." What ruled the world at the moment was not heavenly peace, but hellish hate. The response required rebuilding the world on new foundations, which Kohler located in the just and honest religion of the Jewish prophets, "the only basic principle of ethics, individual and social, national and international ... for which the innermost spirit of humanity longs."[34]

To Kohler, this transformation of the world could not take place through peace associations or the Hague Tribunal (the Permanent Court of Arbitration founded by the Hague Peace Conference in 1899); nor could it be based on any form of compromise with the forces of evil. World history is the world's court, "Die Weltgeschichte ist das Weltgericht," he avowed, citing German poet and philosopher Friedrich Schiller, even if "this might sound harsh to certain sentimentalists."[35] That is, for Kohler history had to run its course in demonstration of God's will, outlined by the prophets, without the preventive intervention of sentimental pacifists (including the likes of his aforementioned students).

Thus, Kohler advanced, support for the war was imperative, in the name of liberty. Cyrus, he said, as well as Alexander the Great, Napoleon, and Abraham Lincoln, "the world's greatest warriors have ever been messengers of God's justice, harbingers of great liberty." This war was an opportunity to break the chains of enslaved nations and religions, including Judaism, which was in peril in the Russian territories. Further, he claimed, the war was an opportunity to eradicate the forces of evil, which included not only nationalism and militarism but also greed and selfish materialism—all to be replaced by the (supposedly) fair and just rule of Germany. Drawing on that week's haftarah (a short reading from the Prophets following the reading from the Torah on Shabbat, with that week's falling during Sukkot's intermediate days and taken from the book of Ezekiel, which describes the war of Armageddon that heralds the coming of the Messiah), Kohler insisted that the terrible upheavals of civilization unleashed by the war were actually "catastrophes that are finally to usher in a new heaven and a new earth!"[36]

Taken in their entirety, the articles published in the Reform seminary journal reflected two largely oppositional schools of thought. The first, voiced primarily by faculty but also some students, promulgated overt pacifism rooted in the conception of Judaism as a religion of peace and justice that by its very nature opposed war. The second school of thought, articulated by Kohler, was nationalist and messianic. War was not to be ruled out; it was a necessary process for the eradication of evil and a harbinger of the utopian era of the Messiah when liberty and justice would prevail. The two perspectives shared a sense of the theological urgency of the current moment and the prophetic calling it demanded, albeit with different interpretations on how this calling should be interpreted.

As such, one could interpret the Mission Theology of the Jewish people in the context of war in one of two ways: as a doctrine of pacifism, or as an eschatological doctrine in which Jews are the bearers of faith in God and humanity, until such time as the victory of good over evil is assured.

These articles also attested to the influence of German culture and reflected the German origins of Reform Judaism. The theories of the aforementioned Schiller as well as Fichte, the founding philosopher of German Idealism, for example, were perceived in a positive light, as representing the moral ideal inherent in German culture. Kohler, in particular, did not criticize or blame Germany for the outbreak of war. In contrast, he maligned Russia, an ally of France and Britain (and later of the United States) and an adversary of Germany and the Axis powers, as "the opposer of the Jews and the arch-fiend of humanity."[37]

His criticism of Russia was consistent with the Reform movement's historical position up to that time: Germany was the birthplace of the liberties granted to Jews, whereas Eastern European countries had a long history of Jewish oppression. Yet Kohler's eschatological messianic view, in which destruction precedes a glorious end-time era, was not at all typical of Reform Judaism, whose generally positivist messianic worldview espoused the gradual triumph of progress and morality.[38] Kohler, it may be argued, likely felt the need to also address the crisis that had befallen Reform Judaism's optimistic theology of progress in light of the unrelenting horrors of the war, and conceivably the overall affinity for Germany as well.

In sum, World War I placed the American Reform movement in a state of crisis. At the root of Reform ideology was a strong bond with German culture, and many of the leading Reform rabbis came from Germany.[39] As long as the United States refrained from entering the war, the American Reform movement could accommodate a pacifist interpretation of Mission Theology in the spirit of universal justice, and even a pro-German apologia that hailed German war efforts as carrying the torch of Enlightenment and high culture and also potentially liberating the downtrodden Jews of Russia. Once the United States joined the fighting, however, the movement had to align itself with the increasingly nationalistic American public and voice public support for the war effort.

The Variants of Magnes's Pacifism

American Reform Jewry's divided principles vis-à-vis the war shed further light on the tense relationship between Magnes's pacifism and Reform's prowar stance. Because Magnes viewed Reform Judaism's Mission Theology as a religious imperative embodying Jewry's pacifist mission among the nations, he refused to prioritize the practical concern of the negative impact opposition to the war would have on the Jewish community, especially given that the German background of some of its leaders had already made the community a target of suspicion. Magnes himself was investigated by the Department of Justice in May 1917, after officials were informed that Magnes kept to himself on the train and talked to no one. In December 1918, deputy attorney general of New York City Alfred Becker reported to the press that Magnes had connections with German agents during the war and had tried to get Mexico involved. Magnes considered pursuing a libel case but decided against it, having been convinced that the hysteria of the time was against him.[40]

Nevertheless, when Magnes spoke to non-Jewish crowds he was more cautious, and his public lectures during this period, which appear in the 1923 compilation *War-time Addresses*, were characterized by restraint. Most of his speeches during these years were not delivered before Jewish audiences but, in the context of the People's Council of America for Democracy and Peace, before general American audiences opposed to the war. As such, those speeches could not—and did not—present an explicitly Jewish position. Moreover, he was aware that as he was the highest-ranking Jewish representative on the Council,[41] his remarks would have ramifications for the image of Jews in American society. Furthermore, even his speeches before Jewish antiwar audiences comprising mainly secularized socialists tended to downplay the religious aspect of pacifism.

In this light, Magnes's journal entry of October 2, 1917, bearing the heading "Jews and Pacifism" deserves careful analysis, given that he wrote it for himself, and not for public consumption.[42] There he offered three main analyses: (1) a response to the argument that his pacifism misrepresented American Jewry's attitude toward the war and fostered antisemitism; (2) a theological analysis of Judaism's pacifist roots, which in his view had been authentically preserved by East European Jewry, including East European immigrants to America; (3) a discussion of the best means to deal with the official representatives of American Jewry, and particularly those in the Reform movement, who supported the war or did not oppose it.

As Magnes understood it, his pacifism was not the product of a shift in the Jewish position, but in fact a return to a more deeply rooted position closer to the original foundation of Judaism. "I am convinced," he wrote, "that I have not misrepresented the attitude of the Jews. On the contrary, I am sustained constantly by the knowledge that what I have said and done has been out of the very heart and soul of the Jewish people." He found support for his position in what he saw as a spontaneous and unreserved opposition to this war on the part of the Jewish "masses." In his view, these masses, of East European heritage, were the keepers of the flame of the living Jewish tradition, and as such they opposed the war regardless of whether they were religiously observant, radical, young, old, intellectual, or illiterate.[43]

According to Magnes, the root of the masses' opposition to the war was both historical and theological. Historically, the Jews were an ancient people who, over the centuries, had seen empires rise and fall, cities turned to rubble, and had themselves often fallen prey to the sword of various armies. This long-term view enabled Jews to grasp the folly, madness, and thirst for blood entailed in war. Among authentic Jews, therefore, war triggered a spontaneous, emotional, and near-primitive opposition grounded in the subconscious rather than reason. Theologically, Magnes argued, Jews were sick of the strife "between Jacob and Esau, between Israel and Edom, between Judah and Rome." The Jewish outlook, rooted in the Holy Scriptures, was that "blood is the life" (Deut. 12:23). The fact that in Judaism animal sacrifice replaced earlier pagan human sacrifice attested to Judaism's primordial opposition to bloodshed. Rabbinic literature, which glorified Jacob and condemned Esau, added another layer to the biblical opposition. Magnes also cited from the book of Zechariah (4:6): "Not by might and not by power but by my spirit, saith the Lord," and, drawing on Exodus (19:6)—"and ye shall be unto Me a kingdom of priests, and a holy nation"—argued that the priests' role was to guard the truth and pursue peace.[44]

The citation from Exodus is noteworthy because by then this verse had often served to describe the Reform conception of the Jewish mission. Thus Magnes was already drawing a connection between Jewish pacifism and Israel's mission among the nations—that is, Mission Theology.[45]

In the same journal entry Magnes linked Reform Judaism's Mission Theology directly with opposition to the war:

> The spiritual "mission" of the Jews to the nations, as formulated by the early 19th century Reform Jewish scholars and teachers, is a revolutionary doctrine: Israel, the international people retaining its identity in order to aid the world in achieving justice and peace. But this revolutionary doctrine was in the hands of petty, bourgeois priests and merchants who used it in order to make Israel safe and sane among the nations. Whatever of the revolutionary mission has been carried out by Jews has been in the hands of those religionists who know nothing of a "mission"; or in the hands of those masses who were outside of the "church" [Reform Judaism] and who slaved and toiled for a living.... What a mockery of the "mission" that in a crisis, in a time of war and of death, the preachers of the "mission" should either be silent or become high priests of the patriotic cult![46]

Two main insights emerge from this. First, Magnes understood pacifism as an inseparable part of the Reform religious outlook: He saw the pursuit of justice and peace as *the* objective of Reform Judaism. Second, he blamed the failure of American Jewry to adopt a pacifist policy during the war on its officials, who had become "high priests of the patriotic cult," rather than on Reform's basic ideology, which in his view accorded with his pacifist efforts. Third, Magnes pointed out the irony: The (largely secular) Jewish radicals and socialists who had opposed the war, and not the Reform rabbinical establishment, had carried out the pacifist "revolutionary mission" of Judaism! Regardless of whether they realized it themselves, these Jews, including Magnes himself, were properly actualizing Reform Judaism's Mission Theology. "What a hopeless feeling as to the future," he concluded, "had there been no Jews to give voice to the dictates of the Jewish spirit!"[47]

And thus, another irony: Despite being drawn to tradition as a tool for revival of the American Jewish spirit, the Reform concept of morality was the basis of Magnes's pacifism. In this sense, the historian Evelyn Wilcock argues, Magnes remained a Reform Jew despite himself.[48]

The Jewish Masses as True Reformers

These journal notes can be seen as the backdrop to Magnes's December 29, 1917, speech, delivered before a Jewish audience of the People's Relief Committee (one of the three American Jewish aid organizations that would later merge to form the American Jewish Joint Distribution Committee, or JDC), pronouncing the Jewish people's mission and decrying Reform's failure of leadership at the time of war. The Jewish people, he argued, had known many cataclysms and had learned in the course of their history that whatever their material fortune, their "real life is in life of the spirit." Reform Judaism, he asserted, "has proven to be bankrupt. For over 100 years past, its one cardinal doctrine has been the universality of Israel, Israel's mission to the nations [based on] the noble message of that Prophet Isaiah of the Fatherhood of God and the Brotherhood of Man." Yet precisely at a time when this prophetic message was most needed, Reform Judaism had stopped preaching of its chosen mission—"*Atta bechartanu* [You chose us], *Am segulah*, the chosen, the peculiar people"—and thus had "failed to justify the very principle of its existence." To be a chosen people, Magnes insisted, meant to preach a revolutionary doctrine, which in turn required revolutionaries; so too "the carrying on of a mission required missionaries." Yet not a "single spokesman" for Reform Judaism had "lifted up his voice in these perilous days on behalf of the revolutionary Jewish idea of the Fatherhood of God and the Brotherhood of Man."

While understanding some of the "practical advantages of this attitude of the Western Jewish Church" (meaning Reform Judaism) and having "no quarrel with them for their practical attitude," Magnes stated, "I merely contest their claim to being the bearers of the living Jewish spirit." He added:

> I have never realized so truly as now and since the war that the bearer and preacher of that mission is not the Western Jewish Church, but rather the masses of the living Jewish people, who are still under the influence of the living Jewish tradition. The present-day spiritual loyalties of the masses of the living Jewish people have made me realize more deeply than ever that the Jewish mission, as a spiritual force, expresses itself not through ecclesiastic forms alone, but through all the ways and hopes of life—religious, moral, artistic, political, social—of a living people. The only standard by which any event in Jewish life is worth being measured is: Does this event aid the Jewish people in carrying on the living Jewish tradition? In the face of such tests and such ideals, the arrogant threats of anti-Semitism, recently made by both Jews and non-Jews against the Jewish people of America, fade into their real insignificance. Every sacrifice is worth while if it give expression to the living Jewish tradition of the living Jewish people. Nothing is worth while if it be merely for the sake of saving our own skins.[49]

Thus Magnes adopted the concept of the Reform mission, but argued that the movement had failed in this essential regard because its leaders lacked the revolutionary will for its realization. By contrast, Jewish socialists who were not visibly religious were expressing authentic Jewish spirituality: the genuine Mission Theology of Reform Judaism. Religious or not, the Jewish masses, bearers of the living Jewish tradition in all its manifestations, were the true missionaries of Judaism to the nations.

Here we see the radicalism of Magnes's position, which demanded absolute commitment to the (his) Jewish spiritual vision, while overlooking such practical considerations as "the arrogant threats of antisemitism" and being willing to pay any price, for "every sacrifice is worth while if it give expression to the living Jewish tradition of the living Jewish people."[50] Also noteworthy is his choice of "the Fatherhood of God and the Brotherhood of Man"—a phrase with distinctly

Christian elements, used as well by members of the Social Gospel with whom Magnes was in contact.[51] In this sense, Magnes's Reform outlook syncretized Jewish ideology with similar Christian concepts.

In his demand that Reform institutions and rabbis adopt a pacifist interpretation of Mission Theology, Magnes overlooked other possible interpretations of the relationship between Judaism's mission to the world and the opposition to war. For example, Reform rabbi Abba Hillel Silver, later a prominent American Zionist leader, avowed, in response to a pacifist manifesto circulated in the wake of the war by Reform rabbi and pacifist Abraham Cronbach, that he could not sign it because he was not a pacifist and had never believed in pacifism. "Just what is ... Jewish about it?," queried Silver in a letter to Cronbach on January 11, 1924. "Judaism believes in organizing social life so as to make war less probable ... [while] pacifism is a program of apocalyptic visionaries, of Buddhists, ascetics and such sects as mold themselves on the Messianic program of primitive Christianity. Judaism is prophetic, and the Prophets were never pacifists."[52]

Thus Magnes's concept of pacifism as necessarily following from Reform Mission Theology was not the only view among the movement's rabbis. In this respect Magnes's position was closer to that of Hermann Cohen, whose moral outlook did not recognize the individual other than as a representative of humanity as a whole, with the state serving as the arena in which morality is actualized.[53]

After the War

After the war ended Magnes found himself alienated from the American Jewish community, with no viable channels for action within the community or via American Zionism. He continued to hold, and act on, views that were considered politically radical. For example, he called for the provision of humanitarian aid to Russia and openly called for the release of Eugene Debs, the Socialist Party candidate for U.S. president who had been sentenced to prison for undermining the government's conscription efforts, in accordance with the Sedition Act of 1918 that extended upon the Espionage Act of 1917.[54] In his November 1921 article in *Debs Freedom Monthly*, a magazine dedicated to Debs's release, Magnes claimed Debs "is the one authentic Saint whom American life has produced. It is not the first time in the spiritual life of mankind that a saint is stoned and martyred." For Magnes, Debs's sainthood was due to his willingness to maintain spiritual freedom during the war, without being "seduced into acquiescence."[55]

At the same time, Magnes's religious quest intensified after the war. In a January 8, 1919, letter, Magnes shared his concerns with fellow socialist Morris Hillquit. "Beside those substantive things ... I am concerned—and how can one not be?—by those things that are not substantive, like the state of the world, and the state of my soul and the souls of others."[56]

This sentiment was typical of the postwar years. The political changes and terrible suffering that ensued from the war and its aftermath made it difficult for faith leaders across the religious spectrum to sustain any enlightened, rational, and optimistic religious outlook. In the postwar issues of *HUC Monthly* a postrational theological discourse emerged. The leading article of December 1917, "The Next Step in Jewish Theology," by future rabbi Lee Levinger, called for reintegrating into Jewish religious life such irrational elements as emotion, desire, and the aspiration to comprehend what is normally unfathomable—in other words, mysticism.[57]

Magnes shared these postwar spiritual sentiments. On May 5, 1920, he drafted a proposal to establish a group of Jewish intellectuals of different types, with different outlooks, to discuss the Jewish question and other questions of the day. Aiming to revive Jewish discourse in part by freeing it from "autocratic" and "reactionary" forces, Magnes invited three types of people to this group: (1) "Jews who, in the arts, literature, religion, sciences, philosophy, scholarship ... express themselves consciously as Jews"; (2) "Jews of intellectual and spiritual distinction whose word has, in general, no conscious Jewish motive, but in whom the Jewish 'soul' may be expressing itself, perhaps in unknown ways"; (3) "Jews (others, perhaps, as well?) of intellectual and spiritual distinction, in whom the Jewish 'soul' is not operative, but who desire to become interested objectively in the creative work of the Jewish people." He further identified three types of "minds and manners of expression" to include in the group—artistic, scientific, and religious.[58] Although he managed to assemble a preliminary group, which included Mordecai Kaplan, among others, it did not progress much beyond the initial organizational phase because genuine interest was lacking. Magnes's second attempt to convene a similar group about a year later also failed.[59]

The period following World War I was a major turning point in Magnes's religious and spiritual quest. Large sectors of society were experiencing crises of faith and the aspiration to find a new theology and novel modes of religious expression in light of religion's failure to deal with the war. While for Magnes the pursuit of an authentic and activist spirituality was part of an ongoing religious quest that characterized his entire life and motivated his political activity as well,[60] in this period at least Magnes's quest was consistent with the spirit of the times—a religious reckoning in the wake of prolonged and seemingly pointless warfare. Even so, his endorsement of religious pacifism would eventually not stand the test of time, and with the tragic annihilation of the Jews of Europe in World War II, Magnes would painfully renounce his pacifism.

Yet there were also practical ramifications to Magnes's pacifist stance. Leaders in the Jewish establishment, from which he was already estranged, were not keen to offer him a position in the United States, fearing his radical reputation would jeopardize the community in the era of postwar "Red Scares." Magnes himself was keen to leave the United States, attesting to his friend from his Berlin days Gotthold Weil that "I need to get away as badly as Palestine soil needed water."[61]

On May 20, 1922, he would embark, with his family, on a planned mission to Eastern Europe on the JDC's behalf. On November 2 they would arrive in Palestine for what was initially planned to be a temporary excursion with no clear goal or end, and he would soon assume the mission of establishing the Hebrew University of Jerusalem.

PART 2

"For the Sake of Zion"

Promoting Binationalism in Palestine

5

The High Holy Days in Jerusalem

In October 1922 Magnes and his family immigrated to Palestine. The "ascent" to Israel, aliyah, entailed for Magnes a complete change in lifestyle and led him to reassess his life and spiritual outlook, as did the reality that for some ten months after immigrating, he had held no formal position.[1]

His inactivity was mostly self-imposed—he had resolved to disengage from Jewish public life and reinvigorate himself spiritually. He vowed to come to Jerusalem "without in any way being a leader, redeemer, savior, or anything else like that . . . I should like to sit upon the Torah and the *avodah* [literally, 'work,' in this context, 'prayer']."[2] Yet, ever the mercurial organizational entrepreneur, he quickly found himself immersed in the first attempt to construct a "Western" synagogue in Jerusalem.

A Western Synagogue in Jerusalem

A few months after his arrival, with the assistance of like-minded expats from German, British, and American Reform and Conservative congregations, Magnes embarked on establishing a modern synagogue in Jerusalem. Unlike the vast majority of Jerusalemites, he and the other

"Westerners" felt comfortable with modernized forms of prayer. While they were emotionally drawn to Sephardic and Hasidic practices, they could not come to terms with the lack of decorum, the raucous prayers, and little if any congregational participation in the service—all the more so in Ashkenazi services of the time. Henrietta Szold described their situation as that of "spiritual homesickness."[3]

Szold, who had arrived in Jerusalem in 1920, had initiated an informal Conservative-like Shabbat service held at the home of poetess Jessie Sampter in which worshipers were "reading from the Mosaic lesson, the prophetical portion, and studying Jeremiah," but the initiative did not pick up steam. Upon these modest beginnings, Magnes wanted to build a new congregation.[4]

Magnes envisioned not just a synagogue but a Jewish center in Jerusalem, fashioned in a similar vein to the efforts of Mordecai Kaplan and Stephen Wise in New York. Magnes believed that Judaism pervaded all Jewish activity. He hoped that a Jewish center, rather than a synagogue, might serve as a means of attracting those alienated from traditional Judaism back to religion. "Here, if anywhere," he proclaimed, "the Temple will have to be approached through many a vestibule, and a Jewish center might do great things for religious life."

Magnes appealed for funds to his supporters in the United States, including banker Felix Warburg; the influential president of the American Jewish Committee (and Magnes's brother-in-law) Louis Marshall; and brothers Arthur and Irving Lehman, the former a banker and philanthropist and the latter the director of the Jewish Welfare Board.[5] Yet (as we shall see), before the funding was secured, the congregation would wither away.

Magnes and his partners proceeded in planning and holding High Holiday services, later dubbed "lively" by Magnes. Magnes was the Torah reader, and the British attorney general Norman Bentwich read the haftarah (portion from the Prophets). Sir Herbert Samuel, British high commissioner for Palestine, also attended the 1923 Yom Kippur service, during which both Magnes and Bentwich preached. A few days after the holidays, Magnes formulated the "General Principles" and "Regulations for the Service" for the *hevra* (prayer group). Historian Naomi Cohen claims that these statements drew from the input of the entire group, but Magnes was the dominant influence.[6]

The General Principles were Magnes's attempt to strike a balance between the desire to reform the services and congregational life, driven by the more progressive nature of the Western expats, and the more traditional demands of the Jerusalem environment. The first principle stipulated "Respect for, and as far as possible, adherence to the Jewish tradition as to religious services. The *Chevra* will however give its own emphasis to this or that part of the service." Here, Cohen points out, the committee struck down Magnes's original draft suggesting that "the Chevra, when occasion arises, use the traditional material and refashion it, or give it an emphasis acceptable to modern men and women." Initially, gender equality was declared: the fifth principle called for "The complete equality of the sexes. This is to be expressed as far as possible within the tradition, but also in ways the tradition has not provided for." Yet the committee's appended "Regulations for the Service" watered down this decisive egalitarianism, stating that "Women shall be able for participation in all parts of the service on the same conditions as men," while also calling for separate seating—albeit without the *mechitzah* (physical barrier) employed by the Orthodox. The seventh principle, which Cohen attributes specifically to Magnes, stipulated that "The *Chevra* will endeavor to point out the present day implications of the teachings of social justice and human brotherhood as inculcated by the Torah, the Prophets and the history of the Jewish people." All in all, Cohen concludes: "The principles and regulations bore the stamp of a Reform rabbi turned Conservative, who ventured beyond the typically moderate Conservative practice."[7]

At the end of the "Regulations," Magnes appended a note designed to protect the independence of the group, probably from the Orthodox rabbinate, citing that "A *Chevra* is a membership society organized primarily to meet the needs of the membership. . . . [It] organizes for a specific purpose, gets a membership, and goes ahead without asking too many questions of persons outside the membership."[8] Nonetheless, in time the official Orthodox rabbinate would play a role in the undoing of the *hevra*.

At the time, another small group was also seeking a "modern" synagogue in Jerusalem. Its organizer was Louis Lober, a young American then residing in Jerusalem who worked as a government clerk. His group was both keen to join forces with the Magnes initiative, which was engaging Jews of a higher public profile, and offer a shared modern service, but he was opposed to many of the religious reforms Magnes and his colleagues had spearheaded. Eventually, after the *hevra* turned down the Lober group on account of their refusal to accept egalitarian services, the Lober group, by then named Congregation Yeshurun, approached Chief Rabbi Abraham Isaac Kook to acquire a second Torah scroll, which was required for High Holiday services. The more moderate service modifications Congregation Yeshurun proposed, such as congregational singing and reading the Torah in Sephardic pronunciation, resonated with the modern Hebrew sensibilities of the Yishuv (the Jewish population in Palestine predating the Zionist movement) and were more easily accommodated by traditional Jerusalem circles than the more radical reforms suggested by Magnes's *hevra*. Impressed by their plans to attract youth, Kook provided Congregation Yeshurun with a Torah scroll from his own *Aron Kodesh* (Holy Ark). Within a month Yeshurun had more than a hundred people joining their Shabbat services—including Magnes himself, and also Henrietta Szold, who attended regularly, although she protested being seated behind a *mechitzah*. Magnes even joined the Yeshurun board, although he did not remain there for long.[9]

Magnes was clearly unwilling to take on the struggle of continuing his group's services against the backdrop of Orthodox opposition. "Tell Bentwich," he wrote in his journal, "I think we must give up all ideas of 'reforms' in the Prayer Book and Services, because neither he nor I will stay to fight for them, and it will not do to quarrel over little things."[10]

The finer details of how the *hevra* was dissolved remain obscure, and their lack of resolve vis-à-vis the more Orthodox option offered by Congregation Yeshurun begs clarification. It seems that Magnes, in line also with his abstention at the time from explicit political activity (up until 1929, as described in chapter 6), opted to avoid confrontation while still adapting to the Yishuv environment. Additionally, he might have felt he lacked the support needed to push back against the unexpected resistance. Cohen claims that, ultimately, progressive Judaism was an American product alien to the Yishuv. It mirrored a society where the conditions for popular acceptance were totally different than those in the Jewish homeland.

In other journal entries at the time, Magnes described the dilemmas and difficulties involved in founding the synagogue as a continuation of his efforts to reconcile East and West. "All the time," wrote Magnes, "I have fought to be identified with 'Eastern' Jews. But here in Jerusalem the term 'Western' does take on a meaning that it would not have in Poland.... Moreover, in Zion a Jew ought to be himself, whatever he is—so I used to think. Zion is the place for differentiation—so I used to think, and so it is in theory. In practice it is a different thing, and 'Western' in relation to the synagogue is about as abhorrent to the Jerusalemites as Reform is to the Orthodox."[11]

These remarks reflect the importance Magnes ascribed to the individual Jewish identity that is true to itself, and to the acceptance of this identity—be it "Eastern" or "Western"—as part of the collective. His expectation, as he described it, was that Zion would be the place where a multifaceted Jewish identity would emerge and all who came would actualize their authentic Jewish uniqueness. But this aspiration clashed with a reality characterized by intra-community strife. As he discovered, Jerusalem's Old Yishuv strongly opposed the Western liturgical style and efforts to combine men's and women's prayer sections. It appears that although Magnes was aware of Orthodox Judaism's negative perception of Reform Judaism, he did not expect that this would also be the case in Palestine, the utopian Land of Zion.

Reflections on the High Holidays

Life in Palestine inspired renewed religious sensitivity and provoked a painful search for the experience of unconditional faith. Most of Magnes's personal writing through the rest of his life would reveal religious doubt and anguish.[12]

In a September 1923 journal entry, on the eve of Rosh Hashanah, Magnes penned a soul-searching account of his religious deliberations. By this time, the forty-five-year-old Magnes had the spiritual maturity to assess his views thoroughly as well as retroactively. All of this combined to become a key moment in the evolution of his religious consciousness.

In the journal entry, Magnes compared the inability to know God with the ability to know man: "Books and life are full of man. War, politics, man's greed and brutality, his capacity for nobility, the motives that guide him and his hopes, ambitions, his ugliness and beauty—a person can get a very fair notion of man, and his knowledge of man increases with the years. The essence of man's soul remains a mystery and can never be probed to its very depths, but it is possible from history, from literature, and our own experience to gain a working-picture of him."[13] It seems (despite his apparent failure to anticipate the objections to his Western synagogue scheme, possibly colored by his rosy expectations of Jerusalem) Magnes believed he had some understanding of the world of man, and of politics as part of this world.

He continued:

> But the Divinity: the older I get, the less I seem to know and understand about it—Him. Oh, I have the deepest of emotions. I am moved (as are but very few of the people I know, so I think) by the mystery of life, by its depth, by simple loves and friendships, by the bravery of

weak persons, by sacrifice, by beauty and music, by sincere worship, public and private, or when persons kneel in a church, particularly uneducated and simple people. In a hassidic *klausel* [small synagogue] I am caught up in the rhythm of worship and sometimes the dark and ancient beginnings of being seem to come nearer. But God, the Father, the Comforter, the Quickener of the Dead, the Creator of the World and the soul of man, the Redeemer of mankind? Oh, how I understand all of this, and feel most of it from time to time, and how I want (and need) it all![14]

Here Magnes describes a turbulent emotional world and feelings of awe that evoke a sense of sanctity. His experience of religious awe was, in his own assessment, unusual. The concept of the "numinous," as defined by philosopher of religion Rudolf Otto, often designated by the Latin phrase "*Mysterium tremendum et fascinans*" (fearful and fascinating mystery), corresponds with these feelings, and one can find congruence between them and some of the numinous moments as Otto outlines them: wholly other, majesty, awe.[15] Magnes's remarks also evince Hasidic elements, particularly in the great importance he attributes to the faith of the simple person and the act of worship.[16] In his description of God ("the Father, the Comforter, the Quickener of the Dead, the Creator of the World and the soul of man, the Redeemer of mankind"), Magnes expresses his desire to translate this abstract sense of sanctity into a more formal religious language, using the formula of prayer that enables one to address God the Being and relate to Him. But such a translation, as the following passage reveals, was beyond his reach:

> But there is never abandon, there is always mental reservation (sometimes more, sometimes less, sometimes bordering upon disbelief, at others merging comfortably with belief). Yes, I can even (at times) come to philosophic conclusions or to the logical necessity of the Godhead (as they call it), on the need in life for absolutes, for *the*

Absolute. But I am never free of doubt, and at times doubt is the major force (at times belief is). I have no doubt that many a preacher and "religious" person is in a similar quandary, and it is no wonder that so many throw themselves into social work and make that the substitute for "religion." Of course, it's part of religion—everything in life is. But that is not *belief*, belief in God, a living force, be He near or far, an active force in individual life and in the redemption of mankind.[17]

Magnes had reservations about the true path of faith, about the belief in a living God as an active force in history. Given the perplexity of modern times with respect to God, Magnes felt many religious believers and preachers faced a quandary similar to his own. But rather than address the theological and experiential difficulty, he argued, many of the religious leaders and adherents had turned to social work as a substitute for religion, and "that is no active *religious* force." Another option, authoritarian religion, offered a blessing and comfort "for those whom doubt crushes," but "that's the kind I can't (my mind can't, my makeup can't) accept. My religion has to be free and voluntary and flowing and capable of abandon if it is to mean sincere and creative prayer. I can sing with abandon, and I can sometimes *davven* [pray] with abandon (what a great thing *davvening* is), but that is not belief grounded in mind, in the whole being."[18]

In discussing his own crisis of faith, Magnes was essentially pointing out the crisis of faith of modern man, whose polite agnostic belief in the divinity does not serve him as a barrier against doubt or as an active creative force; at the same time, however, he cannot accept the original traditional authority of religion. Against this background, Magnes's awe at the act of worship is all the more striking. Bentwich, his first biographer and a friend, attests, "In his later years in Jerusalem he attended a small and devout congregation of the Orthodox section which prayed in a private house. There he felt at home."[19]

This hints to the more traditional inclination occasionally demonstrated by Magnes, dating back to his aforementioned fascination with the Ostjuden prayer in Berlin and his visits to the makeshift Hasidic shuls of the Lower East Side, and evidenced by the above journal entry evoking his deep yearning for a spiritual prayer experience. Perhaps this can also explain his somewhat surprising decision to "jump ship" from the *hevra* to Congregation Yeshurun, avowing also to have his sons bar mitzvahed there,[20] against the grain of his Reform upbringing and commitment.

In the same journal entry Magnes went on to address the tension between a pseudo-prophetic call to action based on religion and his own doubts about the source of such a calling, doubts grounded in the inability to validate God's existence by looking at the world and at history. This tension permeated his religious outlook. As Magnes wrote:

> For some it [awareness of God] may mean quietism—calm, serenity despite the ills of humanity, of life. For others it is a message to do, to battle for the Lord, to save men, to redeem life in justice and truth and mercy and beauty and brotherhood and fellowship. Sometimes I feel this call to action, to help redeem. But is that from "Divinity"? Divinity has never appeared to me to tell me. May it not be sheer humanity, great human pity and love? "To justify the ways of God to man"—what a noble undertaking—difficult, painful, but when done by eager, honest souls and minds, how glorious, and pathetic, and encouraging![21]

Thus Magnes imagined two ways in which awareness of God could manifest in man—either as quietism, which inspired serenity but also passivity;[22] or as a call to action, "to do battle for the Lord." Magnes attested that he sometimes felt this call to action, but at the same time he harbored doubts about its origin—was it a divine power addressing man "from above" or the soul of man speaking to him? The phrase "To justify the ways of God to man," borrowed from the seventeenth-century epos

Paradise Lost, where it defined Milton's aim in his composition,[23] bore for Magnes the problem of theodicy that preoccupied him in the 1920s.

Historian Matthew Silver, who has analyzed this journal entry, points to a contradiction between Magnes's statement that the older he gets the less he knows and understands about God and his assertion that he is a very religious person.[24] According to Silver, Magnes's crisis of faith led him to approach "the sanctity of secular affairs" with the view that the search for unity is to be realized not in the religious sphere but through radical political activity. He therefore posits that Magnes's political activism was an alternative to the religious sphere.

I posit a different argument: In my view, Magnes's political activism was the actualization of religious ideas and conceptions, and his motivation to take action in fact stemmed from an internal religious process. From this perspective, what seems initially like a contradiction was in fact the manifestation of a religious quest that, as we shall see, eventually became a "theological quest" that also had political implications.

Personal Religion

Magnes was, in the words of Jewish scholar and his contemporary Gershom Scholem, a "nineteenth-century man,"[25] and his first intellectual habitat was indeed late nineteenth-century America. Philosopher and psychologist William James was a prominent figure in this arena, both in relation to the question of faith in the modern era and the matter of American pragmatism.

The question of faith is at the heart of James's essay "The Will to Believe," published in 1896, when Magnes was a rabbinical student at Hebrew Union College. At the basis of James's analysis is a distinction between "live hypotheses" and "dead hypotheses." Given the scientific, rationalist, positivist outlook prevalent at the time, which rejected religious belief, he argued that "Pascal's wager"—we should opt for belief rather than nonbelief because the infinite gains we can expect in the event that God does exist outweigh the losses of believing if there is no God—is a "dead hypothesis" that cannot be taken seriously. He proposed a fundamentally agnostic alternative: calling for humanity to cast doubt on our ability to know the truth as a possible means to realizing the existence of God. He therefore advised that one suspend the search for God's existence, letting it remain an open question.[26] He termed his human-centered approach "personal religion," and defined it as "the feelings, acts, and experiences of individual men in their solitude, so far as they apprehend themselves to stand in relation to whatever they may consider the divine."[27]

Personal emotion (rather than analytic dogma) also played a major role in Magnes's religious outlook. The inner struggle between the will to believe, on the one hand, and agnostic doubt, on the other, would be a central theme throughout his life. In the same aforementioned journal entry, Magnes described his religious view that although it is not possible to achieve awareness of God, the quest must continue:

> I am a deeply "religious" man, but Divinity is hazy and vague to me, not always active in me. I may be a religious man, but I am not a religious leader. An understanding of God is what is lacking within me. I doubt Him and question Him—His ways, His aloofness, the sufferings He causes man, the uncertainty of life, the blackness of death. When I read a statement like that of Bertrand Russell in the booklet I picked up yesterday: "I hope that every kind of religious belief will die out.... I regard it as belonging to the infancy of human reason, and to a stage of development which we are now outgrowing,"[28] I have greatly mixed feelings. I do not at all hope religious belief will die out. I hope we shall learn more of God—if there is God; more of the soul, of the creative power in life and in the universe. We *are* in the infancy of human reason, and maybe for that reason we know so little of God, of that Great Fact outside the self, outside of, beyond man—be that Fact, that Power (or those Powers) evil, or good, or just non-moral.[29]

Here Magnes revealed his doubts about being a religious leader in light of his uncertainty about God. In a later paragraph he would propose a model of leadership that embodied this doubt: "Is it perhaps the function of a 'religious' teacher in these uncertain days, to lay his soul bare before the admiring and scoffing gaze of the multitude, in order that the racked and storm tossed of the times may serve as so much clay in the hands of a master potter of tomorrow?"[30] The sentence "I hope we shall learn more of God—if there is God" succinctly expressed his fundamental, paradoxical struggle to hold onto God amid his basic doubt about God's existence.

Magnes continued:

> Yet on the other hand, all the rest of our knowledge is outgrowing our "religious" knowledge, i.e., knowledge—*real* not merely abstruse knowledge—of "God." The passion to make a better, cleaner, more beautiful world is, so it would appear, deeper and more real—i.e., giving rise to action—in those who are not "religious" than in the confessedly "religious." We are learning more about the material side of life, more about astronomy and abstract sciences than about philosophy and theology. The philosophy and theology we learn seem to revolve in the same radius. Where are the extensions of our knowledge, that is, our living knowledge of Divinity? Certainly, if measured only by the "pure light" of cold "reason," Divinity, to say the least, can be (and has been) as easily disproved as proved.... Oh, I desire God, with all my heart. But does that make Him real, does that give Him existence, actuality outside of me? Or, does He exist only in the desire, in the human heart? Do we, then, worship a desire, pray to the human heart?[31]

Here Magnes confronted the paradox he regarded as symbolic of the crisis of religion: Those who do not profess to be religious are actually the ones striving to promote the values he identifies with religion and divinity, and in particular pacifism and socialism. This observation is supplemented by a sense of what may be termed an "epistemological crisis" with respect to God, especially in light of the rapid scientific progress at the time, contributing to Magnes's perplexity regarding the question of God's existence and action on His behalf. Indeed, Magnes pointed out that even James's approach to belief, viewing the existence of God as neither provable nor disprovable, did not answer his query. "God is to be recognized by his works?" Magnes asked, then answered: "Which of his works? A composite picture of Him taken from the beauty and ugliness of nature and of man would hardly be flattering to omnipotence and omniscience. God is the suffering, not omnipotent, not omniscient Being of William James ... requiring the help of man in order to save the world of man which He has made?" He addressed James's doctrine directly: "I held this theory once, too, thinking it fitted in best as a working hypothesis with the realities of life. But do you pray to an hypothesis? How do they know such a half-God exists? Has he appeared to them?" The anguish of Magnes's religious quest is visibly evident. "There is no reason," he concluded, "to accept this being as more *real* than the God of the Fathers, simply because on that hypothesis some of the imperfections of life are better explained away."[32]

King of the Jews: Between the Religious and the Political

After examining the question of belief, Magnes gradually shifted to the practical political sphere. Referring to Christian theology, Magnes pointed out the futility of engaging in political activity without incorporating the religious element. Political salvation, tied in Magnes's thought to a just social order, was insufficient in the absence of a spiritual response to the anguish of human existence:

> But some of those early Jews and Christians were right about one thing: they wanted not a political messiah (King of the Jews) alone, they wanted the religious, the spiritual messiah as well. And if we

were to get our just social order, and its abolition of poverty (which is a far way off), we would still be *m'vakshe adonai* [seekers after God]; we would still be in need of conquering human suffering and death; we would still be in need of approaching closer and closer to the sources of creation, of creative power.[33]

Here Magnes finds even the best political solution inadequate: Messianic redemption must include not just social justice and equality but spiritual elements as well. One also sees the roots of Magnes's criticism of political Zionism for its focus on a speedy outcome (statehood)—which also had a basis in the writings of Ahad Ha'am and resembled the views of Martin Buber (see chapter 10).[34]

Magnes continued:

I *am* religious in that I want God, yet my platform would not be "religious" in that I have not found Him; "religious" in that I am searching for Him, want Him brought nearer by those who think they know Him and understand Him, yet not "religious" in that He should also be discussed, and questioned, perhaps demolished, by those who think they have not proven Him? Can *I* say as much as this publicly, I who have been a preacher of religion; I who feel myself to be "religious"; I who am willing to subscribe to the doctrine: "God above the State, God above Everything"; I who believe that leadership should be in the hands only of those who are certain and feel they know the way? And yet could I say less than this? Could I, knowing myself as I am, preach the sanctity of life and the search for justice, for truth, for beauty, for the new City of God,[35] and yet conceal my religious uncertainties? Or is it perhaps the function of a "religious" teacher in these uncertain days, to lay his soul bare before the admiring and scoffing gaze of the multitude, in order that the racked and storm tossed of the times may serve as so much clay in the hands of a master potter of tomorrow?[36]

One sees the beginnings of Magnes's theological quest in proposing that a religious teacher reveal his uncertainties so that they may serve as "clay in the hands of the master potter of tomorrow." This precursory statement indicates an appreciation of his religious struggle as having value for future generations, who would be able to transform the crisis of modern faith into new religious values. Eventually this idea would lead him on a path of perpetual religious seeking, navigating the challenges presented by the unfolding of history. The search for answers amid uncertainty would become the point of departure for his religious quest, and Magnes would come to view the overt recognition of this process as a desirable approach for modern religious leaders. Finally, Magnes delineated his order of priorities between the religious and the political by saying he accepted the doctrine of "God above the State, God above Everything."

In essence, Magnes's preoccupation with the fundamental questions of religion—the existence of God and the justification of God's deeds in the world—was the expression of a personal (and what would often turn out to be futile) quest to know God. His quest was consistent with the spirit of James's concept of personal religion, which was salient in the United States during the same years the foundational elements of his own outlook began to take shape. At the same time, his journal reveals that, from the outset, political elements entwined with his personal quest. Against this background one can understand why Magnes was drawn to the teachings of Ahad Ha'am, which called for a revival of Jewish culture on the basis of ancient traditions, without committing to the problem of God's existence or the justification of divine deeds.

6

Hebrew University and Brit Shalom

Magnes's involvement in the founding and management of the Hebrew University of Jerusalem, officially inaugurated in April 1925, was the crowning achievement of his work in Palestine during the 1920s and the basis for his authoritative public status. His successful management of the Hebrew University during its early years stemmed in large part from his personal contacts among American Jewish leaders and business tycoons of German heritage, in particular those who knew him from his days as a rabbi at Temple Emanu-El—Jacob Schiff, Felix Warburg, and of course Louis Marshall. Magnes served as the university's chancellor and managing director until 1935, and therefore had almost unlimited authority. A university report of that year notes that more than two-thirds of its revenues came from America.

Nevertheless, the Hebrew University's first decade was marked by strong, persistent tension between Chancellor Magnes and the Board of Governors chairman Chaim Weizmann as well as the Academic Council chairman, renowned physicist Albert Einstein. This went beyond the regular strife of institutional politics: their respective visions for the university differed. Magnes envisioned a university for the Jewish people, with its centerpiece the Institute of Jewish Studies and the humanities at large, whereas both Weizmann and Einstein prioritized the sciences. Weizmann also supported the practical requirements of the Yishuv, promoting such disciplines as agriculture. Finally, Weizmann removed Magnes from the chancellor post in 1935 and appointed him to the symbolic and practically powerless position of university president.[1]

Magnes had a very clear concept of what the university should be: both a center of learning and organized thought and a foundation for the cultural and spiritual revival of Judaism. In a letter to Ahad Ha'am's biographer, the Zionist British intellectual Leon Simon, Magnes wrote that the great task of Judaism—to build a moral society in the spirit of Israel's prophets—could be advanced with the help of the Hebrew University in Zion.[2]

Indeed, Magnes regarded the founding of the Hebrew University as an extension of Ahad Ha'am's vision. In a December 22, 1924, speech marking the inauguration of its Institute of Jewish Studies, in the presence of the British high commissioner Herbert Samuel, Magnes proclaimed: "We had expected today to be honoured by the presence of the man who has been the teacher of our generation, Ahad Ha'am. He has been waiting the coming of this day all his life. May he who healeth the sick of His People Israel vouchsafe his renewed strength of body and mind."[3]

Next, Magnes set out his view that the university would play a vital role in providing answers to the spiritual questions of the generation: "There is a hunger but not for bread, thirsting but not for water. We live in a great historic epoch, perhaps a decisive epoch for humanity. A host of questions agitate out hearts without let-up and press for clear answers from Judaism, if Judaism is to serve us as a teacher and guide, either as a religion, ethic theory or philosophy of life." For Magnes, the study of the Torah was vital to answering that spiritual thirst. "It is altogether impossible," he proclaimed, "that Torah should remain a disembodied substance without connection with life." "Torah will go forth from Zion," he added, "and the word of God from Jerusalem."[4]

Magnes went on to outline his vision of the university's role in shaping relations between Israel and the nations:

> Judaism has numberless points of contact with the nations of history and with the most varied views of life in every age and almost in every place. It is the function of our scholars to explain in what way and to what degree Judaism has hitherto succeeded in absorbing what humanity had to offer without endangering our existence or our specific genius. Not here Judaism, there humanity, but rather a fusion of the two into an harmonious whole—an enriched and enlarged humanity. It is within our purpose to reverse the social process of a century past: Not assimilation amongst the people, but the absorption into Judaism of mankind's spiritual treasures, insofar as the law of the Jewish soul permits this. . . . True to ourselves, we want to absorb and work over in our own way that humanity has to give to us. Perhaps then we may be able the better to give humanity a larger portion of our own soul. We want the Jewish spiritual view of life to be deepened and broadened, so that it may help broaden and deepen the spiritual life of humanity. We want to save mankind.[5]

The spirit of Ahad Ha'am is evident in Magnes's words. To Ahad Ha'am the spirit of the nation served as the main foundation of Judaism, for which religion was only a cover.[6] Consequently, Magnes argued, the university must integrate the soul of the Jewish people with the gift of humanity and take part in the spiritual life of humanity as a whole.

Also discernible in Magnes's remarks was his affinity for the conception of the Jewish mission and purpose—namely, to disseminate the spiritual gospel throughout all of humanity. Indeed, he viewed the particular cultural process of establishing a Jewish cultural center as a means to expanding and enriching the spiritual life of humanity as a whole. This notion—that the particular should serve the general—would also guide his later political activity.

On November 1, 1926, at the official opening of the academic year, Chancellor Magnes presented to the convened students, faculty, and other guests his outlook, according to which the Hebrew University would in actual fact serve as a university for Jewry as a whole, integrating spiritual and practical demands. The Jews, he stated, are inclined to seek a purpose even in their spiritual life; when a young man begins studying at a yeshiva (religious college), for example, he wants to know whether he will become a rabbi or a teacher. "Every university must be closely connected with life," he concluded. "But it is the duty of our University, the University of the People of Israel, to show that we have a purpose that is even higher than the practical—Torah, learning for its own sake."[7]

About a year later, in a October 12, 1927, speech before the university's American Committee at New York's Biltmore Hotel, he offered an anecdote to illustrate the concept of a university that can also influence the entire world. A Harvard University scholar had been invited to the Hebrew University to deliver a lecture on early Christianity: "When he began to talk on his theme," Magnes recounted, "tears trickled down his cheeks.... 'To think,' he said, 'here I have all my life been devoting myself to the study of these sources that came out of Palestine, and here I was at this University, and as I began to talk I looked out of the window of your building and lo, below me was the temple place, the place where your temple and mine once stood.'"[8]

These remarks highlight the religious passion with which Magnes viewed the university. One might go so far as to claim that Magnes was drawing a connection between the university of his vision and the Temple Mount. (Not so incidentally, one of the first biographies of Magnes was titled *Boneh Mikdash Me'at*, literally, "Builder of a Small Temple.")[9]

In concluding his speech, Magnes invoked the language of the prophet Ezekiel: "If it can mean that much to others, is it not reasonable that it can mean equally as much for us, and are we not sure that it will mean much more, that it will give us new spirit and new mind, as the prophet said a new heart, new courage and inspiration to carry on this great tradition of our people and make it, not a tradition that is merely carrying on something obsolete, but a tradition that is more than worthy of its mighty Hebraic source?"[10]

The Founding of Brit Shalom

The Fourteenth Zionist Congress of August 1925 witnessed the ascension of the Revisionist Party (founded and led by Vladimir Jabotinsky), who called for the immediate establishment of a Jewish state utilizing both diplomacy and brute force. Responding to Jabotinsky before the congress, the Zionist leader and anthropologist Arthur Ruppin proclaimed: "Palestine will be a state of two peoples. . . . I hold the view that it is possible to unite the life aspirations of both nations and establish in Palestine a community in which both peoples will work together for the economic and cultural development of the land in full equality, without the superiority of one or the suppression of the other."[11]

Two month earlier, in June 1925, a group of Jewish activists had convened at Ruppin's home in Jerusalem to discuss alternatives to Jewish politics in Palestine. On March 1926 they established the Jerusalem-based association Brit Shalom (Covenant of Peace) to rectify the Zionist position toward the Arab inhabitants of Palestine—specifically to "pave the way towards an understanding between Jews and Arabs, towards coexistence in Palestine based on full equality of the political rights of two nations with broad autonomy." Among Brit Shalom's early members were Hugo Bergman; agronomist Chaim Margaliot Kalvarisky; Zionist leader Jacob Tahon; director of education of the Jewish Agency Schools in Palestine, Joseph Lurie; philosopher and historian Hans Kohn, and Gershom Scholem.[12]

According to historian Adi Gordon, the association's registered members, never more than a few dozen, fell into two camps: those motivated primarily by considerations of political reality, especially the urgency of resolving the Arab problem in Palestine in light of such post–World War I political developments as the emergence of Arab nationalism; and those motivated primarily by ideological, moral, or religious considerations, who viewed the Arab question as the touchstone of Zionism. Ultimately, Brit Shalom would never achieve significant political success, lacking both popular appeal and political clout in Jewish Palestine as well as substantial partners on the Arab side. The organization disbanded in 1933. Yet it continues to be a resource for scholarship, among other reasons because of the relevance of the political issues addressed.[13]

Magnes and Brit Shalom

Historian Hedva Ben-Israel points to the incongruence of Magnes being the person identified "most completely and consistently" with the ideology of Brit Shalom, even though he was never actually a member.[14] Indeed, many researchers have explored the question of why Magnes never officially joined Brit Shalom, as well as the question of his influence on its positions and activities. Arthur Goren ascribes the fact that Magnes never officially joined the association to his criticism of its tactical rather than ideological support for pacifism.[15] Ben-Israel stresses the leadership role of Arthur Ruppin, who Magnes perceived as a tactical rather than truly pacifist supporter of binationalism (Ruppin indeed withdrew from Brit Shalom in 1927).[16] Historian Daniel Kotzin suggests a more pragmatic consideration: Because of his experience with the American Jewish community and its reaction to his pacifism during World War I, Magnes did not wish to engage in political activity that could result in his exclusion from any formal and vital discussions concerning Jewish Palestine.[17]

Notably, Magnes's decision not to become an official member of Brit Shalom did not mean he was uninvolved in the group's activities. Goren reports that Magnes often attended meetings, contributed to the formulation of the group's draft political declarations before they were published, and assisted in securing funding for its periodical *Sheifoteinu* (Our aspirations).[18] Additionally, Brit Shalom members

Hugo Bergman and Ernst Simon, colleagues of Magnes at the Hebrew University, informed him regularly about the association's meetings and activities and sought his advice and assistance.[19] During this time Magnes also solidified ties with Bergman, Kohn, and Scholem, and in fact tried to persuade Bergman and Kohn to withdraw from Brit Shalom and establish an association that would strive for peace with the Arabs on the basis of Jewish pacifism.[20]

The Central European Circle and the Influence of Ahad Ha'am

Most of Brit Shalom's prominent members had come to Jerusalem from Central Europe to hold academic positions at the Hebrew University's Jewish Studies Institute. The political positions of the Central European circle were grounded in and guided by ideological concepts, particularly, as we will see, the organic-developmental conception and faith in absolute values.[21] While it is possible to assess the ideological congruence and points of dispute between Magnes and this circle on the basis of these concepts, given the vast mix of intellectual influences on members of this circle and their own diversity, any such analysis cannot encompass the full complexity of the multiple points of view.

That said, the first and foremost point of congruence between the Central European circle and Magnes was their affinity for the theories of Ahad Ha'am. Many within this circle regarded themselves as his disciples, and his theories found expression within Brit Shalom in two ways. The first was a refusal to ignore the "Arab problem," in contrast to the position of most of the Yishuv's leaders at the time, including Ben-Gurion, who hoped to overcome Arab resistance to Zionism through the economic benefits it was expected to provide them.[22] The second related to the question of Jewish nationalism.

Ahad Ha'am's conception of Jewish nationalism underlay the support for binationalism among Brit Shalom's Central European members. The founders of political Zionism (prioritizing Jewish political rights and eventually statehood in Palestine), including Herzl, formulated their concept of Jewish nationalism in the aftermath of what they viewed as the failure of emancipation to foster the integration of Jews into European societies. Ahad Ha'am's concept of nationalism, in contrast, stemmed from concerns about the *success* of emancipation, which he feared could lead to cultural assimilation and the loss of the Jewish people's unique character. The Jews' exit from the ghetto had coincided with the development of modern nationalism, into which the religious, ethnic, and national uniqueness of Judaism was being absorbed. Ahad Ha'am regarded this two-fold process as a threat to Jewish identity and therefore to Jewry's inner strength. In the absence of a national sense of self that encompassed all of a Jew's personal sense of self—which in Ahad Ha'am's analysis described the Diaspora—the continued existence of the people was imperiled. The solution, as Ahad Ha'am saw it, was to establish a "spiritual center" in Palestine, which would be the focal point of collective Jewish identity. Politically, this would be a small society without international political status of consequence that could exist in Palestine without having to concern itself with superpower conflicts.[23] Ahad Ha'am thus left an intellectual legacy to the Central European circle of this preference for organic cultural development "under the radar" of concrete international politics as an antithetical vision to the goal of political sovereignty championed by political Zionism. Binationalism coincided with the organic vision.

The Central European circle's reliance on Ahad Ha'am was generally comparable with Magnes's approach. As discussed, Magnes regarded himself as a follower and disciple of Ahad Ha'am and shared the latter's concept of a spiritual center, which found expression in the founding of the Hebrew University. Likewise, Magnes shared the view of Ahad Ha'am and Brit Shalom members that the test of Zionism lay in its attitude toward the Arabs. In a February 6, 1930, letter to Stephen Wise, Magnes wrote: "For me this is not so much the Arab question as it is the Jewish question. What is the nature and essence of Jewish nationalism? Is it like the nationalism of all the nations? The answer is given by our attitude towards the Arabs, so that the Arab question is not only of the utmost practical importance; it is also the touchstone and test of our Judaism."[24] (For more on Magnes's view of the moral trial the Arab presence in Palestine presented to Zionism, see chapter 9.)

Magnes also shared a concern about founding a state that would be dependent on the mercy of world superpowers, especially after the Balfour Declaration called for a "national home for the Jewish people" in 1917 and the League of Nations granted the British Mandate for Palestine in 1919. In a November 18, 1929, address marking the opening of the school year, he referred directly to Ahad Ha'am and called for leadership, on both Arab and Jewish sides, that could formulate ideals and live by them:

> Have there been any [Arab] leaders who ... know what it means when one talks of Palestine as not an Arab land and not a Jewish land, but as an international land, as a land sui generis, as a land that is even more important to mankind than it can be to its own inhabitants? Is there a [Italian revolutionary leader, Giuseppe] Mazzini or an Ahad Ha'am among them to formulate and live and teach their ideals? ... If the only way of establishing the Jewish National Home is upon the bayonets of some Empire, our whole enterprise is not worthwhile, and it is better that the Eternal People that have outlived many a mighty empire should possess its soul in patience and plan and wait.[25]

From the outset, Magnes, like American Zionists in general, had made the necessary adjustments to circumvent the lack of a religious element in Ahad Ha'am's teachings while at the same time embracing his spiritual and cultural doctrine. Magnes as well as Buber and other members of the Central European circle did not share Ahad Ha'am's marginalization of religion. For them the revival of Judaism constituted a religious revival and, as such, rested on the Jewish religion. It followed that religion was not merely a tool in service of the national "desire to exist"; rather, it was what granted Jewish nationalism its validity. As

Bergman explained: "Zionism is not here to take over from religion. . . . On the contrary, through Zionism religion will regain its original strength of ancient times."²⁶

Morality and Politics

The Central European Brit Shalom members and Magnes also shared similar positions about the relationship between the moral and the political, essentially subjugating political realism to often-utopian moral considerations. A direct product of this was the group's aspiration, in Bergman's words, that "Judaism's political [in the sense of statehood] moral perspectives leave their mark on the way of life in the Land [of Israel]." In political terms, this meant opposition to the moral injustice of majority rule over the minority population in the name of the "sanctified egoism" of national statehood. Their moral and political outlook was influenced by the thought of German Jewish philosopher Hermann Cohen, who viewed the state as the realm in which ethics must be actualized, and the prophets as those who had shifted morality's center of gravity from the individual to society and the state. Philosopher and educator Ernst Simon supplemented this position regarding the supremacy of the moral over the political with more pragmatic arguments about the dangers inherent in severing the two. In 1973 Simon cited the example of the German people to illustrate how it was possible "to squander a moral and spiritual legacy within just a few generations."²⁷

Magnes was, in fact, the more loyal disciple of Ahad Ha'am in terms of following his concept of absolute morality—namely, the "governance by absolute justice for all of creation"—that Ahad Ha'am attributes to the teachings of the prophets. This concept of morality manifested in Magnes's all-inclusive public opposition to World War I, a stance he consistently maintained, regardless of pragmatic considerations, even after the United States joined the war effort. Another expression of this perspective can be seen in his aforementioned 1929 speech, when Magnes affirmed: "It is one of the great civilizing tasks of the

Jewish people to try to enter the promised land, not in the Joshua way, but bringing peace and culture, hard work and sacrifice and love, and a determination to nothing that cannot be justified before the conscience of the world."[28] This contrasts with Buber's concept of a "boundary line," which calls for defining the true moral objective on the basis of dialogue between the ethical ideal and the political "reality on the ground," and by reaching a compromise between efforts to achieve the maximal good and minimization of the bad to the extent possible.[29]

Another point of confluence between the Central European circle and Magnes was their conception of religious socialism. For the Central European circle, historian Shalom Ratzabi says, "The elements of their Zionist worldview can be understood as a coherent doctrine based on their approach to religious socialism, and not necessarily on the reality on the ground in Palestine." Combining the teachings of Aaron David Gordon, Buber, and Gustav Landauer with the theories of religious socialists such as John Haynes Holmes and Leonhard Ragaz, theirs was not a revolutionary class-based socialism but a utopian socialism aspiring to establish a new Jewish society on the basis of justice, mutual cooperation, and equality.[30] For Magnes, of course, such a socialism coincided with his own blend, which relied heavily on moral imperatives.

Buber had an important influence on the Central Europeans, dating back to his "Three Speeches on Judaism" delivered at the Bar Kochba club in Prague between 1909 and 1911, which formulated a form of Zionism to which they could subscribe. Buber adapted the spirit of Zionism to the most fashionable moods in Europe at the time—anti-intellectualism and neo-mysticism—and opened the Central Europeans to a Jewish nationalism based on these prevailing moods. Bergman described these lectures as "the cornerstone for a new world outlook"; Hans Kohn called them a "turning point for all my views."[31]

At the same time, Buber's cooperation with Magnes deepened after Buber immigrated to Palestine in 1938, and especially after the two men partnered in founding Ichud, the organization that succeeded

Brit Shalom in promoting binationalism in Palestine, in 1942.[32] Buber, more profoundly versed in the modern European Jewish discourse of the time, was able to contextualize Magnes's pragmatic vision in more historical and theoretical terms. Yet when it came to presenting the ideas to policy makers and broader crowds, Buber played second fiddle to Magnes, who was by far a superior public speaker, as best demonstrated in their joint appearance before the Anglo-American Committee of Inquiry in 1946 (see chapter 14).

The Prophetic Imperative

There is another possible reason Magnes never joined Brit Shalom. His political activity was driven, among other factors, by his identification with the image of the prophet and the call to create a prophetic form of politics. Magnes's mode of operation resembled the conduct of a prophet who suppresses his prophecy until there is an actual "call" to action. He thus shifted between cultural, community-based organizational work (such as his organizational efforts in founding the Hebrew University)—in line with Ahad Ha'am's archetypal analysis of the *Kohen* (high priest) as a practical religious executive—and his engagement in "prophetic" politics, characterized by a firm belief in the righteousness of the political path and a willingness to adhere to the truth at any cost. The peak moments of his prophetic political activity were his opposition to World War I (1917), his mobilization on behalf of the concept of binationalism with the publication of his pamphlet *Like All the Nations?* (1929), and his efforts to promote binationalism following the Biltmore Program (1942). In between these peak moments, his notion of politics remained buried, and on the spectrum between doubt and belief that was so central to Magnes, religious doubt outweighed political belief. Drawing on this analysis, when Brit Shalom was most active, Magnes's belief was at a nadir and his doubt quite strong. This analysis does not rule out the practical considerations that may have influenced Magnes's decisions, but instead points to another, deeper factor that guided his conduct.

In summary, Magnes's involvement in founding the Hebrew University attests to the influence of Ahad Ha'am's teachings on his thought and actions. Adam Ha'am's ideals helped shape Magnes's religious passion for the university as well as his vision for its character, essence, and role worldwide. To Magnes, the Hebrew University was a cultural center for the Jewish people that was meant to help build a moral society in the spirit of the prophets of Israel. In line with Ahad Ha'am's worldview and with Reform Mission Theology, the university was to consolidate the Jewish identity and spirit of the nation while simultaneously looking to the outside world to influence and be influenced by it. Magnes's call to establish a university for the sake of Torah (in the sense of Scripture as well as study) combined the principles of academic freedom with ties to Jewish tradition, and particularly the moral prophetic tradition.

As regards Brit Shalom, a great deal of overlap existed between Magnes's perspective and the ideological outlook of its Central European members. Yet there were also differences—grounded in the American foundation underlying Magnes's political and religious outlook. This foundation was multifaceted, consisting of the Mission Theology of Reform Judaism and its political implications in the Zionist context; the absence of an organic national outlook, as such an outlook would have been inconsistent with the development of American civil-political nationalism; the positivist American belief in science and progress; a developed democratic culture that believed in the power of political institutions and constitutional contracts to establish a just society; and American pragmatism. The next chapters address these facets.

7

The Prophetic Model

Magnes's personal writings, from the time he began serving as a Reform rabbi,[1] reveal persistent doubts about the possibility of his forming a genuine bond with God or witnessing the existence of God in the world. If, as suggested in this book, Magnes's political views stemmed from his religious worldview, then the question naturally arises: How did his religious doubts shape the course of his political activity? Below are a number of possibilities.

Scholem, Magnes, and the "Jeremiah Complex"

One of the interesting insights about Magnes comes from the Jewish scholar Gershom Scholem, who as a member of Brit Shalom partnered with Magnes in his political activity, albeit with reservations. In his autobiography, *From Berlin to Jerusalem*, Scholem writes that Magnes had a complex personality: Great charm and a naturally majestic bearing largely obscured his inner turmoil, which Scholem reportedly pondered over the course of more than twenty years. His opinion of Magnes vacillated between what he described as deep admiration for his vision, integrity, and untiring effort, and criticism of him. Furthermore, to Scholem, Magnes was constantly torn between seeking what was best for the Zionist enterprise in Palestine, on the one hand, and his own conscience, on the other. This very religious man struggled with his reservations and doubts about the ways of God; in private conversations he repeatedly stressed his personal experience of "the eclipse of God." The tragedy of Magnes, according to Scholem, was that he failed to discern the motion of history's pendulum—that is, how World War II, the annihilation of European Jewry, and the dismantling of the British Empire swayed history toward a Jewish state. Therefore, his vision remained self-contained, disengaged from surrounding historical and ideological developments.[2]

For Scholem, Magnes's emotional and personal state was a "Jeremiah Complex"—Jeremiah the Prophet representing for Magnes the supreme image of the Jew who knows the price of missionary isolation.[3] This Jeremiah of old had prophesized the Babylonians' destruction of the First Temple in Jerusalem on account of the Judean people, who had committed moral sins and strayed off the path of God: "I will deliver all Judah into the hands of the king of Babylon; he will exile them to Babylon or put them to the sword" (Jer. 20:4). When Jeremiah called the people and leadership to repent, and entreated the king of Judea, Zedekiah, to appease the Babylonian king, Nebuchadnezzar, rather than revolt against him, Zedekiah threw Jeremiah into a cistern instead; then, in 586 BCE, the Babylonians conquered Jerusalem and razed the Temple to the ground. In a similar vein, following Scholem's classification, Magnes consistently stressed the moral requirements presented by the Arab presence in Palestine, and warned against independent Jewish statehood.

Magnes as Modern Jeremiah

Other Jewish and Christian friends likewise saw Magnes as a kind of modern Jeremiah. For example, in a May 1945 letter to Magnes, James Marshall, the son of Magnes's brother-in-law Louis Marshall, wrote, "We have all admired you more than you can ever know. Like Jeremiah of old, you have warned your people at a time of danger, and like Jeremiah, your words have been spurned."[4] Writing of his experience visiting Palestine in February 1929, when Magnes, his friend from the antiwar movement in America, helped introduce him to the country, the Protestant minister John Haynes Holmes observed that Zionism's success or failure had to be understood not in material terms, but in higher spiritual terms: the raison d'être of the Zionist enterprise. The Jews had returned to Zion not to accumulate property and power, but to actualize an ideal, to realize a dream. Theirs was the inner spiritual drive of sacrifice for the sake of a vision of justice and peace on earth—the very vision of the prophets Isaiah and Jeremiah. Earthly success was actually the enemy of such a vision, since the conditions it created annulled the spiritual ideal. Thus, external success would lead to internal failure.[5]

In one passage Holmes compared Magnes to a prophet, and specifically to Jeremiah:

> I regard it as a scandal of the first order that so many of the Jews of this country should now be baying like wolves on Magnes's track. My God, is it possible that the Jews of today, after all their centuries of tragic history, can't recognize one of their own prophets when he rises among them? . . . It is my humble opinion that Magnes is the greatest prophetic spirit in the world of Jewry today. He ranks in my mind with Jeremiah—I can't think of anything but the story of Jeremiah when I think of Magnes at this hour. My prayer is that the Jews are not going to rend Magnes today as they did Jeremiah yesterday.[6]

Here Holmes was also alluding to the fact that, like Jeremiah of old, Magnes encountered fierce opposition once he began to publicly express his political views. His speeches at the opening of the academic year were occasionally disrupted, mostly by members of "Brit HaBiryonim" (the Strongmen Alliance) associated with the Revisionist Party. Mainstream Zionist leaders like Menachem Ussishkin forcefully insisted that Magnes check his politics at the door when addressing academic crowds, and Hebrew newspapers in Palestine demanded Magnes's resignation.[7]

Another description likening Magnes to Jeremiah appeared in an article by Samuel Ralph Harlow, a clergyman and Christian missionary to the Neat East with the American Board of Commissioners for Foreign Missions. Published in the magazine *The Christian Century* on June 17, 1931, under the title "Jeremiah Returns to Jerusalem," the article, written after Harlow's visit to Jerusalem during which he interviewed Magnes, contains numerous references to Magnes as a prophet in—and even surpassing—the image of Jeremiah.

Harlow opens by saying: "One of the most inspiring hours of my life was spent recently on Mount Scopus in the company of Judah L. Magnes, chancellor of the Hebrew University. Here is a man through whom the prophets of Israel have found a voice. In him Jeremiah lives again."[8] Harlow then compares the conditions in Palestine to the conditions that prevailed when the Kingdom of Babylon stormed the gates of Jerusalem prior to the destruction of the First Temple, of contending forces and party strife. He compares "nationalistic Zionism"—that is, political Zionism in general, and more specifically the Revisionist Party—to the "militaristic party" of Zedekiah; the Arabs to the Egyptians; and Britain to the Babylon of Nebuchadnezzar. The "imperialism, nationalism, the war spirit" embodied in Babylon, Zedekiah, and Egypt represented the internal and external forces confronting Magnes in Palestine. Magnes— "through him the voice of Jeremiah can once again be heard in the streets of Jerusalem"—had tried to curtail these forces, suggesting binationalism as a moral (and implicitly God-endorsed) political option.[9]

Harlow goes even further: "Again and again my thoughts turned to Jeremiah, and to One greater than Jeremiah. The chancellor of the Hebrew University would be the last to call himself a Christian, but I dare assert that in Jerusalem today, there is no leader of whose life and attitude one can discover more of that quality of human kindness and divine passion which characterized Jesus, than in this son of Israel.

'Christ-like' is the best definition I can give of his character."[10] Similarly, in his autobiography, the New York Jewish Socialist Party leader Morris Hillquit portrays Magnes as a disciple of Jesus: "This Jewish rabbi was one of the very few divines who took the spirit of the teachings of Christ seriously. He abhorred the brutality and inhumanity of war on the battle fields and the spirit of despotism and intolerance at home. He was sincere and courageous, and he threw himself into the fight headlong and in utter disregard of the admonitions of his shocked parishioners and patrons."[11] The Christian American federal judge Joseph Hutcheson Jr. also compared Magnes with the image of Jesus (see below).

Presumably Magnes's friends' perceptions of him as a Jeremiah figure and Magnes's self-perception were mutually reinforcing, for Magnes deeply identified with the prophet. In November 1929, after "going public" with his program of binationalism in the wake of the August 1929 Western Wall riots, he wrote in his journal:

> My cardinal belief has been in the Jewish people as the carrier-vessel of ideas, of a spiritual tradition. If you object, and say that we have had a Joshua as well as a Jeremiah, I answer that, whereas there is a Joshua within each of us, nevertheless, the main stream of our tradition has been that of the Jeremiahs. I feel myself to be one of the Jeremiahs, to be the heir of the servant of God, of that tradition which tried during political subjection to spiritualize life and to teach a loathing of force.[12]

Asking "Why does Magnes identify with Jeremiah, a prophet who speaks with King Zedekiah mainly about politics, not moral exhortations?," the novelist Hadara Lazar answers that, for Magnes, the substance of Jeremiah's words mattered less than his unyielding stand against the establishment, which she associates with the ethos of the West and nineteenth-century California, where Magnes grew up.[13] "Jeremiah was his lodestar," states Magnes's first biographer Bentwich, referring to the 1929 publication of Magnes's political platform.[14] Reflecting on the various references to Magnes as Jeremiah following the publication of "Like all

The Prophetic Model 111

the Nations?," historian Matthew Silver writes that Magnes "encouraged, or at least permitted, exaggerated comparisons between himself and the Prophet Jeremiah."[15] It follows that Magnes's 1929 decision to make his political views public and actively promote binationalism was perceived both by others and himself as a "jeremiad."

Priest or Prophet?

Historian Arthur Goren offers an interesting analysis of Magnes as prophet. He claims that despite the image of Magnes as complex and ambivalent, one still finds coherence and consistency in his inner life. Ultimately, according to Goren, until his final days, Magnes remained a rabbi in the tradition of American Reform Judaism, strongly committed to prophetic ideals (see below). The centrality of Ahad Ha'am's teachings for Magnes would seem to bolster this view. Ahad Ha'am, Goren asserts, provided the "credo" for Magnes's prophetic leadership.[16]

Ahad Ha'am's influence on Magnes stems also from the image of the prophet in the writings of Ahad Ha'am as he presents it in two essays, "Priest and Prophet" (1893) and "Moses" (1904). In "Priest and Prophet," Ahad Ha'am writes:

> The fundamental idea of the Hebrew Prophets was the universal dominion of absolute justice.... These Prophets of Righteousness transcended in spirit political and national boundaries, and preached the gospel of justice and charity for the whole human race. Yet they remained true to their people Israel.... Their national ideal was not "a kingdom of Priests," but "would that all the people of the Lord were Prophets." They wished the whole people to be a primal force, a force making for Righteousness, in the general life of humanity, just as they were themselves in its own particular national life.[17]

In "Moses," Ahad Ha'am identifies two fundamental qualities of the prophet—as a "man of truth" and as an "extremist." Yet, as claimed by Goren, Magnes's journals attest to his ongoing anguish as he attempted to translate prophetic ideals into political reality—an impossible task according to Ahad Ha'am's analysis, because inasmuch as the prophet cannot shut his eyes to the faults of the world, he also cannot mend the world as he sees fit. In Ahad Ha'am's paradigm, the priest's task is to confront reality and to mediate between contending forces. Of necessity, he must compromise.[18]

This tension between "priest" and "prophet"—between the practical man of the community and the charismatic leader, between the appointed administrator and the preacher who is accountable to no one—was a central factor in Magnes's life and one he was never able to resolve or alleviate. Ahad Ha'am's teachings thus provided Magnes with more than a model for political action: The image of the "priest" infused Magnes with practical sensibility in his academic administration and political organizing, while the mythical "prophet" depicted by Ahad Ha'am offered him a figure with whom to identify and model over the course of his life.

In the pattern of Magnes's political activity one can discern the model of a prophet who cannot suppress his prophecy. For example, Magnes cited the verse "For Zion's sake will I not hold My peace, and for Jerusalem's sake I will not rest" (Isa. 62:1) to explain why he chose not to remain an observer on the sidelines, focused mainly on the university and cultural affairs, and, to the contrary, became involved in the political affairs of Palestine.[19] This prophetic model, whose roots trace back to Reform Judaism in Germany and later in the United States, underscores the prophet's firm stance on moral principles, even in opposition to his own community. This is the prototype of a man who acts alone, which suited Magnes's character, and, as his partner in promoting binationalism, German-Jewish philosopher Martin Buber, pointed out, it merged with the model of American civil disobedience.[20]

Magnes's quasi-prophetic self-perception also provoked criticism. In May 1922 Mordecai Kaplan wrote of Magnes:

He possesses traits which in another age might have led to his gathering around him a band of ardent disciples and he would have gone down in Jewish history as a Jewish seer.... The only way to be effective as a prophet nowadays... is to suffer martyrdom, like the Sinn Feines [*sic*], IWW [Industrial Workers of the World] leaders, and the pacifists who are languishing in the prisons years after the armistice has been concluded. But to have [philanthropist Felix] Warburg praise you as a delightful fellow, and to be in a position to throw off all responsibilities and go travelling and observing the world is not compatible with the martyrdom that we usually expect from the prophets.[21]

Philosopher and educator Akiva Ernst Simon, Magnes's colleague in the association Ichud, also objected to the attempt, especially after his death, to idolize Magnes as a prophet: "He was not a prophet, but a man of deep crises and strong contradictions."[22]

The Prophetic Foundations of American Reform Judaism

The biblical books and figures of the prophets play a major part in Reform Jewish thought, particularly in the "Classical" Reform Judaism of the United States, which peaked in 1885 with the Pittsburgh Platform's declaration of principles. Modernity came to dictate the agenda of Classical Reform Judaism. The Judaism of ancient times was seen as primitive, and the Pittsburgh Platform, in accordance with the principles of nineteenth-century German biblical commentary, even described the Torah as "reflecting the primitive ideas of its own age." Classical Reform Judaism asserted that morality and social justice—rather than belief, law, or ritual—constituted the essence of Judaism, in the spirit of the prophet Micah: "He has told you, O man, what is good, And what the Lord requires of you: Only to do justice, And to love goodness, And to walk modestly with your God" (Mic. 6:8). For this reason Reform Judaism came to be known as "Prophetic Judaism."[23]

One of the prominent Reform thinkers who emphasized the teachings of the prophets was the British Jewish scholar Claude Montefiore, who posited that if Moses was the founder of Judaism, then the prophets may be seen as "second founders." In Liberal Judaism (as Reform Judaism was known in Britain), according to Montefiore, the Ark of the Covenant in a synagogue should house not the scrolls of the Torah but the books of the prophets Amos, Hosea, and Isaiah.[24]

Reform Judaism perceived prophecy as the highest level Judaism could attain in its aspiration to reach divine truth, and as embodying the perfect expression of awareness of God's supranational transcendence and the universality of Israel's role in disseminating divine truth. In a 1915 lecture, Rabbi Julian Morgenstern, later the president of Hebrew Union College, stated that Reform Jews are in effect returning to the concepts of revelation and religion as the prophets perceived them, reinterpreting the entire Jewish history, from beginning to end, in the same spirit in which they were interpreted by the prophets.[25]

Another expression of the Reform concept of prophecy, which both differs from and has similarities to Magnes's conception, appears in the writings of American Zionist leader Rabbi Abba Hillel Silver. On the face of it, there is a vast difference between Magnes and Silver in terms of ideological and political outlooks as well as style of action. Silver did not share Magnes's view that Reform Judaism's Mission Theology should result in pacifism. Moreover, Silver supported the establishment of a Jewish state in Palestine and endeavored to promote this aim through engaging with Zionist institutions (even though at times he clashed with them) as well as exploiting his leverage as an American Jewish leader.[26] Magnes, on the other hand, strongly opposed political Zionism, and his style of action corresponded much more closely to the image of the prophet who challenges the establishment.

Nonetheless, historian Ofer Shiff finds prophetic elements and affinity for the prophets' teachings in Silver's self-perception. From the time of his youth, Silver regarded himself to be a faithful student of these teachings and as destined to play the part of a prophet not only for his own people but for American society and humanity as a whole. His passion for biblical prophecy as symbolic of Judaism's essence, and for the prophets as symbolizing the Jewish leader's calling, were part of the Reform legacy that shaped his education. This passion informed his decision, at the very beginning of his career, to write his doctoral dissertation on prophetic and messianic conceptions as they developed among the Israelites. Shiff also discerns signs of Silver's willingness to go against the flow and stand up to those in power in the second phase of his life as a Jewish leader. Before the founding of Israel, which Silver worked hard to advance, his political activity had a distinctly pragmatic dimension. After the declaration of statehood and his exclusion from Zionist politics by Ben-Gurion (who wanted to cement the leadership role of Israel vis-à-vis the Jewish Diaspora), Silver shifted his focus back to the universal dimension, arguing that the importance and centrality of the State of Israel should be expressed through its transformation into an intermediate stage and means toward the realization of universalist values. Such a process corresponded with Silver's conception of Jewish nationalism as a temporary phenomenon that had to be actualized in order to move beyond it toward a more universal vision.[27] This was consistent with Magnes, who wrote in his journal in March 1924, "Many things predispose [a Jew] to universalism—his prophets, his wanderings, his experiences—but he has a much harder job [than the American] overcoming his nationalism. The only Jew who can really overcome it is the Jew who feels himself firmly rooted in the Jewish nation, for whom there is not the slightest possibility that he can be anything else than a Jew. Such a Jew can become a genuinely tolerant universalist."[28]

Magnes's views on prophecy constituted a core element of his own self-perception and others' perception of him. His concept of prophecy rested first and foremost on American Reform Jewish precepts, which emphasized the role of the prophets and the universal, moral dimension of their teachings. In addition, his outlook echoed the teachings of Ahad Ha'am, who juxtaposed the figures of the priest and the prophet as representatives of different modes of thought and action, between which Magnes found himself torn. His motivation for engaging in political activity was grounded in a quasi-prophetic drive, and he saw himself as called to action despite his own efforts to refrain from involvement and suppress his prophecy, as demonstrated by his choice not to join Brit Shalom in its formative years. In light of his political isolation in Jewish Palestine and the gathering clouds of war in Europe and later in Palestine, his prophetic drive took the form of the tragic figure of Jeremiah, preaching alone against the supposedly imminent danger of Jewish nationalism, rather than the more positive image of Isaiah, who put forward a vision of universal cooperation resulting from national self-realization.[29]

Magnes and Barthian Dialectical Theology

In a March 1928 journal entry, Magnes discussed an article in the *Christian Century* on the doctrine of the Swiss Protestant theologian Karl Barth, applying it to himself and the Zionist enterprise. The article had been authored by the American Protestant clergyman and academic Douglas Horton, the first person to translate Barth's interpretation of the Epistle to the Romans (*Der Römerbrief*) from German to English.[30] At the time, Magnes had yet to engage in serious political activity within Palestine, and this entry therefore provides a useful point of reference for gauging the evolution of his motivation to become politically active as well as the centrality of the religious dimension in this context. Notably, Magnes, who was then chancellor of the Hebrew University and in direct contact with the Central European intellectuals of Brit Shalom, was drawing inspiration not from Jewish sources or modern Jewish philosophy, but from Christian theology via American mediation—an indication that Magnes may have privileged sources connected to his American roots for inspiration. His journal entry opened as follows:

> I evidently slapped my knees while finishing an article on the theology of Karl Barth. Beatie [Beatrice, Magnes's wife] asked me why, and I said I could not tell her. "Was it because of the past?" No. "Because

of questions like that of peace?" "Hardly. It is because of present agonies of which I hardly speak." "But I must know of them." "It is because I am sometimes tortured with the need of an infinite God." "You sleep well. Perhaps you could stay up all the night and tell me about it." "That's it. I don't know how to tell about it. Strange that I should be such a thing as a university administrator." "But if you were not that, then what?" "If I were altogether free and honest, and were to follow the glimmer of the gleam that I sometimes have, I would be a Voice, perhaps in the wilderness. My father's father, and my mother's grandfather talk to me and I do not listen enough."[31]

This passage reveals the depth of Magnes's personal preoccupation with the question of God's existence. Indeed, in his later years he would claim that the need for an infinite God was the main problem that had preoccupied him throughout his lifetime. In a letter of October 24, 1941, for example, he wrote to Gershom Scholem about his interest in Kabbalah, stating that perhaps it stemmed from a basic deficiency on his own part: the lack of any ability, or possibly of any right, to communication with the Heavens.

In the above-cited journal entry Magnes also expressed his understanding of prophetic revelation, that "glimmer of the gleam of a voice" as heard by Isaiah (40:3): "A voice calls: In the wilderness, clear the way of the Lord!" The final sentence in this passage hints at his affinity for Hasidic concepts, through the figures of his grandfather and his mother's grandfather who speak to him, perhaps in a dream. Conceivably, Ahad Ha'am was a source of his reference to the desert. In the aforementioned seminal essay on leadership, "Moses" (1904), Ahad Ha'am wrote about the Prophet Moses:

> That is a price which he will not pay even for the redemption of his people. If there is no way but through enchantments, then let the redemption be achieved by others, and let him alone in his spotless truth, alone in the wilderness.... But it is not easy for the Prophet to

remain in the wilderness. The burning fire which has just roused all his spiritual forces to action has not yet been quelled; it will give him no rest till he find some way to carry out his thought.[32]

Considering how important Ahad Ha'am was to him, Magnes was presumably aware of this allusion to the tension between the feeling of ideological loneliness and spiritual doubt, on the one hand, and public political action, on the other.

Later in this journal entry, drawing on Horton's article, Magnes explained Barth's theology, which he understood as follows:

> There is no way to God. But there is a way from God to us. Man needs God, seeks him, but the search is futile. If man thinks he has found Him it is a Dead Sea apple in his hands—nothingness, farther and farther away. But let a man open himself to receive God's influence upon him. That seems to be the essence of the article I was reading. The first part is true. The second has a glimmering of truth for me.[33]

Thus Magnes found truth in this description of the futility of man's search for God, and only a glimmer of truth in the more merciful aspect of Barth's theory, that which leaves an opening for God to reach man.

Barth's dialectical theology stemmed predominantly from the crisis that befell Christian theology in the aftermath of World War I, which had exposed the helplessness of religious institutions in face of the power of unbridled nationalism, not to mention the cooperation of religious institutions with that power. Unlike liberal theology, which assimilates religion into human culture and renders it devoid of absolute value, or natural theology, which claims that human reason can draw inferences about God from the world, Barth's dialectical theology removes the image and revelation of God from the realm of human understanding and claims that religious belief only works in one direction—from God to man.[34]

Barth's essay on the Epistle of the Romans and the dialectical theology he then formulated were a response to a phenomenon that had begun in the late nineteenth century and peaked during the crisis of values resulting from World War I. This period was characterized by a decline in the power of religion and particularly of liberal, humanist Christian theology, which, much like Reform Judaism at the time of its origin in Germany and later in its formative years in the United States, viewed religion mainly as an expression of supreme morality.[35] The liberal interpretation of religion sparked a debate as to whether this was a secular, fundamentally nonreligious interpretation. Barth proposed a theological alternative: The world of God was "completely different" from the human world, with no points of contact between these two worlds.[36]

Magnes's religious outlook shared with Barth a critique of liberal theology, which ambitiously (and also heretically) placed man and his eventually limited capacity of human morality at the center of the universe. In the Jewish world, this theology was reflected in the Reform movement, which idolized human morality while disregarding the consequences of effectively removing God from the primary role in the universe. And, like Barth, Magnes aspired to reinstate God, that "glimmer of the gleam" of an "infinite God," at the center at the expense of man, although the question of God's existence remained for him a matter of uncertainty.

His efforts in this regard stemmed from his conservative religious perspective relative to the liberalism of his Reform Jewish environment and from his spiritual dissatisfaction with the diminution of the religious experience within this environment. Since Magnes had opposed World War I for pacifist reasons and harshly criticized religion for placing itself at the service of nationalism, he naturally shared Barth and others' postwar sense of suspicion toward religious outlooks that had not aimed to thwart the war. Nor is it surprising that the article on Barth's approach resonated with Magnes. Further in his journal entry he cites Barth (via Barth's English translator Douglas Horton): "The paradox, once more, is our refuge: let a man realize at once his infinite need for finding God, and the infinite futility of his search, and in the clash of these two infinities within his soul, the God of the infinity will be adumbrated, but only adumbrated." Magnes interpreted the ethical paradox as a willingness to take moral action in the name of the quest for God, despite knowing from the outset that this quest is destined to fail.[37] This, I believe, is the basis of his own theological quest (to which I will return), whereby the search for God is in fact a recognition of the Divine.

The Zionist Paradox after Barth

Next, Magnes applied this theological outlook to the political arena of Zionism in Palestine, writing:

> To whom, to what, our highest loyalties? The State, the family, the nation, the Land—all of this important but all of it imperfect. Loyalty to the spirit—if we only dared say "God"—the only really worthy loyalty.... What gives the more perfect freedom—retaining American citizenship or sharing the lot of those with Palestinian [citizenship]? And sharing this lot, trying to rise above it, while being a pawn in the hands of neither British imperialism nor Arab nationalism, but a pawn, if that it be, of Jewish religion—the higher loyalty. The war has shown the hollowness of Church, School and State. Real loyalty can only be rendered the Spirit. But Spirit is vague. If one only had a real God![38]

Here Magnes voices hope that his political activity will be faithful to what he regards as the loftiest possible point of reference—namely, the spirit, or God. His aspiration to be an instrument in the service of the highest loyalty—the Jewish religion—can be seen as motivating his political activity. But this aspiration came up against the barrier posed by Barth's theology as he himself sensed it—that is, the inability to touch this vague spirit. Magnes's desire to work politically in the service of the supreme Jewish religious values, juxtaposed alongside his uncertainty about God's existence, constituted a core, irresolvable tension haunting Magnes throughout his life.

The Prophetic Model

Next, Magnes explicitly applied Barth's outlook to his own political efforts in the Zionist context. In light of the eventual fate of Magnes's plan of binationalism—ending in vain once the State of Israel was established in 1948, just prior to his death—this is a near-prophetic passage: "The Zionist paradox (after Barth): to seek the fullness of Judaism zealously, with the conclusion foregone that this cannot be found; to join the Palestine movement, to live in Palestine with the conviction that one day (now!) this will have been proved to be illusory and almost barren. This is not discovering Judaism, but it is, after all, acknowledging it."[39]

Magnes here paraphrased the maxim offered earlier by Barth to apply to the case of Zionism. According to that maxim, even though man's search for God is eventually proven futile, that search in and of itself is a necessary act of recognizing God's existence and man's dependence on the Divine. In similar vein, Magnes sought the full actualization of Judaism, and searched for the "fullness of Judaism," specifically in Zionism. The search, he himself knew, was doomed to end in failure—but failure of a "sacred" nature, as it embodied the recognition of God.

What was the "fullness of Judaism" as Magnes understood it? For Magnes, I believe, fullness of Judaism meant a world in which Jewish nationalism was realized, while at the same time absolute morality reigned. Here, Magnes expressed, as had Ahad Ha'am, the inability to bridge between the moral sphere of social justice and egalitarianism he perceived as central to Judaism and its political realization as manifested in Zionism in Palestine, which was promoting an arrangement that excluded the Arabs from political equality. Forefather of modern sociology Max Weber, noting the gap between the ethical and the political, holds that a political entity that is fully bound by ethical demands is unsustainable, whether one adopts—in accordance with his famous distinction—a deontological "ethic of conviction" (that is, of justly motivated action) or a consequentialist "ethic of responsibility": "No ethics in the world can dodge the fact that in numerous instances the attainment of 'good' ends is bound to the fact that one must be willing to pay the price of using morally dubious means or at least dangerous ones—and facing the possibility or even the probability of evil ramifications. From no ethics in the world can it be concluded when and to what extent the ethically good purpose 'justifies' the ethically dangerous means and ramifications."[40]

Nonetheless, Magnes sought to bridge the gap described by Weber and implement Zionism in a political framework fully committed to morality. He would not relinquish any moral high ground in the process; for him, the means were just as important as the ends. As such, the ethical justifications offered by the Zionist establishment for inevitably impure political actions vis-à-vis the Arabs were not to be sanctioned. In this sense Magnes also differed from Buber, who was willing to accept some derogation from ethical demands (see chapter 10).

Yet even Magnes was realistic enough to know that the chances of implementing his binational plan (which would be published in detail within two years) were slim. Correspondingly, his concept of God as forever unattainable accorded with his unattainable political plan and its inevitable failure. This understanding challenges the historiography that tends to regard Magnes as naïve for believing that his political efforts just might succeed.

In Magnes's religious experience it was not possible to communicate with God; indeed, the face of God remained eclipsed to him. In this sense Magnes differs from the prophets he aspired to imitate. Yet for him this eclipse did not prevent moral political action; in fact, it necessitated such action, because political action in itself represented the effort, to borrow Barth's imagery, to row toward the shores of God in a sea that belongs to God, even if it is not possible to reach those shores.

Political action itself was a recognition of God. Consequently, it was obligatory to engage in moral political activity "against all odds"— including promoting binationalism in the 1940s, when any willingness in Jewish Palestine to accommodate such positions, let alone take them seriously, had all but dissipated.

And so, Magnes took political action in the form of a binational platform integrating the political touchstones of the America he knew: pragmatism, democracy, and nationalism.

And even though he lacked the prophet's religious conviction, he resembled Jeremiah—risking isolation by speaking truth to power.

8

Nationalism and Binationalism

Magnes was suspicious of nationalism in general, largely because of World War I and its catastrophic consequences for Europe. Regarding Jewish nationalism, however, and binationalism in particular, he had a complex stance, different than that of binationalist supporters such as Martin Buber or Hugo Bergman, because of the American foundations of his political worldview. This chapter examines the salient characteristics of American political thought and how they manifested in Magnes's political outlook.

American Pragmatism

American pragmatism was a notable characteristic of Magnes's political thought. Although the theory of pragmatism as it is known today emerged in the late nineteenth century, the instrumentalist foundations of American thought were evident even earlier. In his 1835 magnum opus, *Democracy in America*, French diplomat and writer Alexis de Tocqueville ascribed the pragmatic approach as inherent in American society and the democratic social order. As his chapter titled "Why the Americans Apply Themselves to the Practice of the Sciences Rather Than to the Theory" explained: "Equality develops the desire in each man to judge everything by himself; it gives him in all things a taste for the tangible and real and a contempt for traditions and forms." But, de Tocqueville noted, this scientific utilitarianism comes at the expense of theoretical development: "In America the purely practical part of the sciences is cultivated admirably, and people attend carefully to the theoretical portion immediately necessary to application; in this way the Americans display a mind that is always clear, free, original, and fertile; but there is almost no one in the United States who gives himself over to the essentially theoretical and abstract portion of human knowledge."[1]

According to American academic Louis Menand, four philosophers contributed to the concept of pragmatism as it developed in American philosophy: William James, Charles Sanders Peirce, Oliver Wendell Holmes, and John Dewey. Menand considered history a core element of this process, in particular the lessons of the American Civil War, which produced a more skeptical approach in matters of religion, politics, culture, and society in general. In addition, he identified pragmatism as a core concept in twentieth-century American thought.[2]

Pragmatism as viewed by James is particularly relevant in light of his influence on Magnes, and because his thinking embodied both pragmatism and the religious experience. At the basis of James's definition of pragmatism is the "principle of pragmatism," from which it follows that faith manifests in action and thought and derives its significance from its practical consequences.[3] A direct outcome of this definition is a skeptical attitude toward deterministic or metaphysical truths (such as the ontological, that is, the actual, existence of God), given that truth becomes a product of human action. Even though this approach renders certainty impossible, in that there is no certain truth "out there" to be perceived or understood, it is important to understand that for James, pragmatism was not meant to refute faith, but rather to protect it in the context of a scientific and overly materialistic era. Toward this end, James shifted religious belief from the realm of knowledge to the realm of concreteness and experience: a more pragmatic standard.[4]

Historian Daniel Kotzin notes that William James seems to have influenced Magnes's thinking about the politics of governance. In *A Pluralistic Universe* (1909), a book of his lectures on pluralism, James, who valued diversity, upheld as an example of pluralism a "federal republic," which allows for difference because "something is self-governed and absent and unreduced to unity," in contrast to "an empire or kingdom." Students of James, like Jewish philosopher Horace Kallen, later applied his theory to American life. Magnes, who previously demonstrated an appreciation of James's writings, may have also been influenced by James's philosophy of pluralism. Indeed, as Kallen would do later, Magnes incorporated James's image of a republic into his discussions about cultural pluralism.[5]

American pragmatism also entailed a certain stance toward politics. According to scholar John Shook, pragmatism is basically an empirical theory about intelligent learning in communities that produce real knowledge: knowledge of both nature and society. The pragmatists defended a close relationship between learning and democracy, viewing public democracy as the best form of government invented to date. Pragmatism additionally proposed a finer form of public democracy, with more citizen participation than mere voting. Furthermore, democracy had the ability to produce social knowledge.[6]

American pragmatism played a large role in Magnes's approach to Zionism. In his book *Like All the Nations?* (1930), Magnes presented a model of an egalitarian pluralistic democracy based on American governmental structures. The influence of pragmatism is evident in two ways: He emphasized that the system of government in itself can serve as an educational means to promoting democracy, and that experience should guide Arab-Jewish relations. He argued that, initially, new egalitarian political institutions should be established, which would facilitate daily contact between citizens; this experience of self-government would then teach both Jews and Arabs to transcend their narrow national interests.[7] In effect, his efforts to apply American democratic ideals to the realization of Zionism was an Americanization of the discourse about the future of the Land of Israel.

For Magnes, religious sentiments were intertwined with a practical approach to politics and daily life, which included optimism and a tendency to rely on dialogue and compromise. "He was a man of action," writes historian Hedva Ben-Israel, "the type of political leader who aspired to infuse spiritual and moral inspiration into a movement whose long-term aims were spiritual—mending the world—while the means of achieving them were practical and political." According to her, all of his activity and writing can be classified either as preaching in praise of long-term spiritual and moral aims or as proposals for practical approaches to a resolution of the problem of Jews and Arabs—with the aim of creating the practical political conditions for realization of the spiritual aims.[8]

Magnes eschewed impractical messianic outlooks and regarded even political Zionism as such a trend. His spiritual quest, like that of James, was characterized by tension between the logical and the experiential. James dealt at length with the religious experience and simultaneously helped found the pragmatic school of thought in the United States. Likewise, despite the distinctly spiritual dimension of Magnes's political thinking, he sought practical solutions.

Magnes's thought can seem contradictory. On the one hand, he was the pragmatic American, wanting to accomplish change through practical action. In the spirit of American pragmatism, he believed in the power of political systems to ultimately influence both perceptions of truth and the actual political and social realities of Jewish-Arab relations in Palestine. At the same, he was religiously inspired to take prophetic and moral political action, even with his faltering religious convictions. Like Buber, Magnes believed only politics based on moral and prophetic principles would stand the test of time and look beyond immediate and utilitarian considerations that would eventually prove shortsighted. He was aware that the binationalism he espoused was highly unlikely to be achieved—but it had to be done for God, his distant God, regardless.

Magnes and American Political Thinking

Historian Yehoshua Arieli, drawing on German historian Friedrich Meinecke's distinction between *Kulturnationen* (culture-defined nations) and *Staatsnationen* (state-defined nations), characterizes the United States as a manifestation of civil nationalism, where identity is expressed through modes of political and social organization. Citizenship is the only criterion for membership in the national society, and national loyalty means both loyalty to the Constitution and accepting the American way of life, which is defined in terms of ideals and norms claimed to be universally valid. This interpretation of American nationalism, despite its paradoxical nature, has had an exceptional power of cohesiveness. The very structure of American society—its multiethnic and multireligious composition, its federal form of government, and its regional loyalties—requires a national consciousness based on universal values. The fact that the birth of the American nation and its political sovereignty were achieved by means of universal concepts is what granted these ideals and norms unique importance in American history.[9]

These universalist American values were at the root of Magnes's political thinking. At the same time, the universalism propounded by Magnes and other American Reform thinkers such as Abba Hillel Silver was more complicated than the general American version. The universalism of American Reform Judaism combined theological and political universalism. Theological universalism, which rests primarily on the teachings of the prophets, is the foundation of Mission Theology, which holds that the Jewish mission is to spread ethical monotheism and the belief in God throughout the world. But this theological outlook developed against the background of the American political infrastructure. Thus, American political universalism provided the soil in which the seeds of a new American Reform movement sprouted once Reform arrived from Germany in the mid-nineteenth century. Rather than revealing the theological roots of the political, as in my argument regarding Magnes's theological politics, this contextual understanding reveals the political roots of the theological.

Yet the mutual influence of the theological and the political is ultimately a dialectical process. My argument is that the characteristics of American national consciousness and political thinking had a formative influence on Magnes, and remained strongly influential even after he left the United States for Palestine. Twenty years after emigrating, for example, in a 1941 diary entry under the heading "The constituents that make up my being," he wrote:

> I am *politically* an American. . . . By "politically" I mean that the American (and English) tradition of democracy has had a great influence upon me—the political institutions of voting and parliamentary government; free speech, and a free press; freedom of religious conviction and worship; the idea of the equality of all men, black and white, great and small; the possibility of men of all races and origins and creeds living together cooperatively; the feeling of individual responsibility for the welfare of the community, for the proper and honest working of the democracy.[10]

This was Magnes's interpretation of the fundamental elements of the American political worldview that shaped his outlook, although later in this entry he also voiced criticism of the shortcomings of the American system in terms of its distribution of wealth and resources.[11]

Magnes's political identity also embraced other aspects of American political activity. As we saw earlier in another context, in a letter to Magnes on the occasion of his sixtieth birthday, Buber wrote, "May you enjoy the hidden blessing in this quality of yours, which has become so rare: the courage of civil disobedience." As Mendes-Flohr points out, although the letter itself was in German, Buber inserted the term "civil disobedience" in English to underscore Magnes's affinity for Henry David Thoreau. Buber drew inspiration from Magnes's efforts to translate Thoreau's ethics into a Zionist context and establish a truly just society in Zion.[12]

Thus far examinations of Magnes have tended to overstate the individualistic aspects of his view and understate the fact that this individualism was actually grounded in American political tradition, which ascribes much weight to political institutions and to the capacity to bridge political divides on the basis of these institutions and a shared constitutionalism.[13] This tradition underpinned Magnes's perception of binationalism as an institutional mechanism that, by virtue of its capacity to regulate the experience of political coexistence over time, also had the capacity to promote cultural and political equality. This view of political institutions set Magnes apart from his more anarchist associates in Ichud, and in particular from Buber.

A People with National Elements

In the aftermath of World War I, European intellectuals, including Jewish thinkers such as Martin Buber and Franz Rosenzweig, began to reconsider the question of nationalism.[14] Around this time, on April 21, 1919, Magnes was invited to deliver an address at a conference of the American Academy of Political and Social Science in Philadelphia. The subject of his address was "The Rights of the Jews as a Nation." Considering the scientific context of this conference, one may view it as a representative statement of the theoretical foundation of Magnes's thoughts on nationality and nationalism in the specific context of the Jewish people.

First Magnes presented what he regarded as the American doctrine of nationalism: namely, that all nations have a right to life, liberty, and the pursuit of happiness. "But," he continued, "many nations, either because of their own aggression or the aggression of others, have found and still find that this right is questioned." Consequently, small nations are at the mercy of large nations. But, fortunately for small nations, "since the aims of the present war have been formulated, the big nations say that they have less inclination than before to dispute the rights of small nations." Aside from the political and economic interests at the basis of this inclination, there was, according to Magnes, another reason: The big nations may instinctively feel that small nations, even if they are "deficient in mechanical efficiency or backward in politics," have "distinctive qualities of spirit, the loss of which would be a loss to the spiritual treasures of mankind."[15]

Magnes's assumption that large nations view small nations as having a unique spiritual quality deserves further attention. This is a fundamentally utopian assumption, which presupposes that the good of the world plays a central part in states' deliberations. Moreover, it does not accord with Magnes's critique of the political agreements reached after World War I or with his criticism of the Balfour Declaration, which stipulated British support for the establishment of a "national home for the Jewish people" in Palestine as an attempt to actualize British imperialism.[16] Nonetheless, his address contains an implicit pluralistic political outlook in its emphasis on the importance of nations' diversity and the unique value of each member of the world's nations.

After discussing the ideal positive attitude toward small nations, Magnes turned to the issue of Jewish nationalism. He proposed a very loose definition of the concept of nation: "any considerable group who regard themselves as a nation as they themselves define the term." In his view, the overwhelming majority of Jews, though not all, regarded themselves as part of the Jewish nation. Yet they also feared the political consequences of being defined as a nation, particularly as the concept of a nation was "so bound up with the conception of political allegiance to the state" that their loyalty to the state could be subject to doubt. It might therefore be preferable to regard the Jews not as a nation but as a "people" with "national elements." These elements, according to Magnes, included the following: belonging to the "same race," not in the sense of purity or a mystical quality, but simply because over the centuries the Jews had married among themselves; a distinctive language, Hebrew, which created "an impressive bond of unity among Jews"; a common history and awareness of a common past; the Jewish religion, which "in addition to the highest concepts of a universal character," embodied several "national" characteristics, including liturgy, traditions, ceremonies, holidays, literature, aspirations, and a religious life; and a culture "with many of the aspects of the national cultures of other 'nations.'"[17]

Thus, according to Magnes, Jews already had so many distinctly national elements, if they had a land and a government of their own, they "would be regarded as a full-fledged 'nation' by everyone using the term."[18] This raises the question of whether they have a right to lay claim to a territory and government of their own. The answer, according to Magnes, must be "peculiar," as the Jews are a "peculiar people": It is yes and no. Jews can be found in differently sized communities in almost every country, and the state's attitude toward its minorities varies by country. In countries with large concentrations of Jews, such as Poland and Lithuania, Jews have a right to be recognized as a nation and a nationality (and particularly in "the democracy of Russia" which would "no doubt" recognize Jewish national rights, in Magnes's view).[19] On the other hand, in the United States, which recognizes only individual rights rather than the rights of nations, nationalities, races, or peoples, the collective rights of the Jews can only be cultural and spiritual, and not political whatsoever. Regarding a territory or government, according to Magnes, "the nearest approach ... can be had, if at all, in Palestine, ... the Jews' old home, the repeopling of which has ever been one of the national aspirations of the Jews." This did not mean that all Jews must necessarily settle there, or that a Jewish state or government should be established. "It means merely that those Jews who think they can serve their own people and the world best by contributing their energies to the creation in Palestine of a Jewish Centre for the Jewish people should be given every opportunity to do so."[20]

An analysis of Magnes's address reveals the American foundations of his concept of nationalism. His definition of a nation's or a people's rights—life, liberty, and the pursuit of happiness—is taken directly from the American Declaration of Independence.[21] This is a distinctly liberal definition, as it derives collective rights from individual rights. Moreover, size is a key issue in terms of nationhood, and Magnes evidently believed he had to prove that a nation as small as the Jewish nation had a right to be recognized as such.

The question, then, is how this perception affected Magnes's assessment of a national presence in a territory as small as Palestine. In my view, Magnes's American background probably caused him to doubt the feasibility of a national enterprise in such a small territory, and this background was one of the factors that led him to propose the fundamentally confederative solution of binationalism.

In addressing the question of Jewish nationalism, Magnes listed the national elements of the Jewish people but refrained from defining the Jews as a "nation," because implicit in such a definition, as he saw it, was the danger that Jews would be branded as having dual loyalties. He preferred the definition of a "people" with "national elements."

In the broader context of theories on the development of Jewish nationalism, Magnes's perspective is comparable to the view that regards Jewish nationalism as predating the modern era. Jewish philosopher Hans Kohn, for instance, identifies three characteristics of Jewish nationalism in ancient times: the concept of the Chosen People, which is based on its covenant with God; the historical consciousness, first crystallized in the Land of Israel, which enabled the Israelites to establish a collective memory that served as a basis for nationality; and the concept of a national mission, which even in its more universal forms as promoted by the prophets preserved Israel's centrality within the universal framework.[22] British historical sociologist Anthony Smith, too, emphasizes the religious aspects of Jewish nationalism, particularly the belief that the Jews are a chosen people and that their continued existence is vital, and he found evidence of these aspects in the Zionism of the labor movement as well. According to Smith's primordial conception, the significance of believing in "chosenness" in the case of Zionism and other forms of modern nationalism is its creation of a sense of continuity and distinction dating back to ancient times and of uniqueness among the many alienated and oppressed peoples. Because "we" are ancient as well as unique, the thinking goes, we have "within ourselves" the capacity to renew ourselves, if only we return, in the true spirit of nationalism, to our spiritual roots.[23]

In his address Magnes describes the Jewish people as endowed with all the characteristics of a nation except two—a national territory and self-government. His examination of the question of self-government explicitly circumvents the Balfour Declaration, issued two years earlier, and its enthusiastic reception by the Zionist movement and in the Yishuv, as he had strong reservations about aspirations of self-government, which the declaration apparently supported. His affinity for cultural Zionism is evident in his focus on cultural and spiritual renewal in the context of returning to the Land of Israel, which he regarded as part of a fundamentally universal process that would benefit not only the Jewish people but the entire world. Magnes's examination of various Jewish communities was also central to his reasoning: Because the Jews were scattered across different countries, the deciding factor in realizing their national rights was the attitude of the host country to collective versus individual rights. This set the United States apart, as its Jewish community had no aspirations of self-determination, in contrast to the European Jewish communities in which Zionism was taking hold. By drawing this distinction Magnes was able to rationalize the general aspiration of American Zionists to neutralize the sovereign dimension of Jewish self-determination.

To sum up Magnes's attitude to nationalism generally and Jewish nationalism specifically, it is safe to say that despite his fundamental suspicion of nationalism, which was itself a response to World War I, he recognized the existence of a Jewish nation and the consequent—albeit qualified—possibility of implementing a national territorial claim. He qualified his recognition of the Jewish nation because he sought, on the one hand, to defend non-national Jewish existence in the United States, and, on the other hand, to ensure the legitimacy of the Zionist enterprise

Nationalism and Binationalism

in Palestine and support alternatives, perhaps even territorial ones, for the large Jewish communities of Eastern Europe. In this context he underscored spiritual and cultural aspects of Jewish nationalism and opposed the rejection of diaspora life.

In terms of theories about Jewish nationalism and nationalism generally, considering the unique role that Magnes attributed to religion in preserving the Jewish nation, his outlook can certainly be classified among the primordial and essentialist approaches to nationalism—that is, it does not coincide with the modernist conceptions of later theorists Ernest Gellner and Eric Hobsbawm, who argued that nationalism is a modern construction and its link with the past is invented or imagined. Rather, Magnes perceived Jewish nationalism as relying on the ancient collective roots of the Jewish people.[24] Yet he qualified the nationalist claim to physical, territorial actualization by recognizing the multitude of the Jewish people's population centers, a recognition that enabled him to overcome political Zionism's "rejection of the Diaspora" and excessive particularism in favor of a universal mission of justice.

Universalism and Nationalism

The relationship between universalism and nationalism is central to Magnes's unique politico-religious outlook, since universalism is at the basis of the Reform Jewish worldview (and, as we saw above, the American national worldview), while nationalism, a core concept of both his Zionism and his conception of binationalism, is by definition particular. In this sense one may view Magnes's concept of binationalism as an effort to bridge the tension between the particular and the universal, which in the view of many American Zionists, and Reform Jews specifically, was inherent to Zionism as a movement for the realization of a Jewish national identity.

Magnes addressed this question in March 1924 in a journal entry labeled "Universalism and Nationalism." He began by stating that "after you have rooted yourself in your nation you can overcome nationalism—not before." Everyone belongs to some people, he continued, "even the most universalistic and denationalized amongst us.... Every man speaks the language of his mother and loves his home, has a given physique, and is influenced in a thousand ways by his heredity and his history."[25] Thus, for Magnes, nationalism was something one needed to overcome.

In contrast to his 1919 address, in which he felt the need to defend the legitimacy of Jewish nationalism within an environment that cast doubt on it, here he revealed his own doubts. For Magnes, the ultimate aim was universalism, and national realization was an interim stage. This position was characteristic of American Zionism, which even interpreted Herzl's political Zionism as consistent with the view that nationalism is an interim stage that ultimately leads to the universal actualization of Jewish nationalism, alongside its actualization in the Jewish homeland in Palestine.[26]

As an example Magnes described how his partner in pacifist activism, the radical economist Scott Nearing, an American, had undergone a natural transition from nationalism to universalism, "growing up out of his roots normally like a firmly rooted tree." He then returned to the issue of Jewish nationalism and universalism:

> With a Jew this is different. Many things predispose him to universalism—his prophets, his wanderings, his experiences—but he has a much harder job overcoming his nationalism. The only Jew who can really overcome it is the Jew who feels himself firmly rooted in the Jewish nation, for whom there is not the slightest possibility that he can be anything else than a Jew. Such a Jew can become a genuinely tolerant universalist. He cannot give himself up, and he can therefore forget himself in higher things.[27]

Magnes pointed to the inherent tension between the universalism that is part of the essence of Judaism—in terms of both its prophetic doctrines and its historical experience—and the particularism embodied in Zionism by virtue of its nature as a concept to be realized at the national political level. Rootedness in the national Jewish soil in the Land of Israel was, for Magnes, the solution that would enable the Jew to become a genuinely tolerant universalist. In his view, being uprooted was what made it difficult for Jews to overcome their nationalism, and therefore the particular realization of nationalism was a precondition for universalism. At the same time, rootedness did not necessarily require the establishment of a national state.

Here too we see a similarity between Magnes's position and that of another American Reform rabbi, Abba Hillel Silver—and again despite their distinctly different styles of activity. Silver did not view Zionism as an end in itself; rather, he saw nationalism as "a scaffold of sorts, whose role is to elevate the believing Jew to a higher level of skeptical relativistic faith so that he may, as in the days of the prophets, devote himself to his universal purpose." In a 1929 article, published as part of a collection in memory of Herzl, Silver wrote, "Nationalism is a means, not an end. . . . After its national life is secured, Israel must push on to the frontiers of the new world—the world of internationalism, of economic freedom, of brotherhood, and of peace. It must resume the burden of its Messianic career."[28]

At the basis of the conceptual proximity between Silver and Magnes lies the theopolitical paradox of American Zionism, which, I believe, they sought to resolve in a similar way. The prophetic universalism of Reform Judaism, undoubtedly the dominant stream of American Judaism during the first half of the twentieth century, was distinctly at odds with Zionist particularism. For American Reform Jews, overcoming this contradiction entailed two strategies: first, the prioritization of Ahad Ha'am's Zionism over that of Herzl's; and second, as illustrated by Magnes and Silver, the subordination of national particularism to universalism through the conception of nationalism as a preliminary step toward realization of a universal vision.

Further in his journal entry, Magnes addressed Reform Judaism and the shortcomings of its approach to universalism:

> The doctrine of the Reform Jews was universalism. Who can quarrel with the doctrine? It is the doctrine of the prophets, of human brotherhood, of the merging of nations and races and peoples into a spiritual synthesis. But while preaching this doctrine they were all the while trying to escape from their Judaism, their Jewish fundamental selves. They made this doctrine an excuse for abandoning their selves, instead of growing into this doctrine with their feet firmly planted on the Jewish earth. The result? They uprooted much of their wholesome, vital *Volkstum* [nationality] and proved themselves false to the very doctrine of universalism they preached. For the most part they remained part-Jews, and in every country became chauvinistic and superpatriotic. Universalism as a mere excuse to become something your comfort or your social standing demands is a spurious universalism.[29]

Magnes was, of course, overtly critical of Reform Judaism, but here we have an insight into the deeper roots of his critique. He was not opposed to Reform universalism. On the contrary, he identified with it and saw it as a worthy ideal. But in his view, it was necessary to consolidate a Jewish sense of identity as a precondition for achieving such universalism. As such, a universalism not rooted in particularism was a spurious universalism that led to overcompensation in the forms of "chauvinism" and "superpatriotism." The Reform movement's patriotic stance during World War I may be seen as such a form of overcompensation. Magnes went on to criticize the Reform establishment in the United States for its instrumentalist universalism, which he saw as serving the aim of successfully embedding itself in the American arena.

Magnes's remarks indicate that he recognized the concepts of nationalism that derived from organic evolutionary theories. The organic developmental conception of nationalism constituted one of the ideological foundations of the Central European circle within Brit Shalom. At the basis of this conception was an affinity for Johann Gottfried von Herder and Johann Gottlieb Fichte's school of thought on German nationalism, understood as a movement for cultural and historical revival (rather than solely a political movement) that exalted the special history and traditions of the nation.[30] Magnes's familiarity with the concept of organic nationalism likely stemmed from his years of study in Germany, but his use of the term *Volkstum* can also be taken as evidence of the influence of the Central European circle. The journal entries cited here were written in March 1924 when Magnes was already serving as chancellor of the Hebrew University and was in contact with Brit Shalom. Alternatively, Magnes's familiarity with these concepts might be attributable to Buber, whose works he had begun to read in 1921.[31] Whatever the case, Magnes had likely been exposed to non-American sources of influence, whether during his studies in Germany or after arriving in Palestine through his contacts with the Central European circle of Brit Shalom.

Also evident in Magnes's remarks is his sense of affinity for "the land," which he was developing around this time. His references in this entry to being "deeply rooted in the Jewish soil" and "firmly planted on the Jewish earth" echo Second Aliyah pioneer Aaron David Gordon's worldview, at the heart of which was an affinity for and a call to return to the Land of Israel. Magnes had probably been exposed to Gordon's views on *kibush ha'avoda* ("conquest of labor"—a slogan and program that advocated the Jews' return to manual and agricultural work) by 1921, through his American Po'alei Zion contacts,[32] but there is no evidence that the two ever corresponded directly.

In my assessment, immigrating to Palestine reinforced Magnes's sense of a bond to the land and the place; he experienced a sense of enchantment that had some measure of Orientalist and even mystical aspects.[33] Magnes had been deeply impressed by the pioneering

Jewish laborers the very first time he visited Palestine, in 1907, when the Zionist activist and land purchaser Yehoshua Hankin served as his guide. According to Bentwich, "to mark his kinship with the pioneers," Magnes grew a beard during his 1907 and 1912 visits. After visiting Jewish farms he wrote: "I catch myself regarding the landscape, the people and the life as though I had lived all my days among them."[34]

Further in his journal entry Magnes explains why Jews were pulling away from the universalist vision:

> Two kinds of Jews can become universalists: the Jew who knows and thinks so little of himself as a Jew that he can in very truth say he is no Jew but an internationalist, universalist ... and the Jew who has so thoroughly grounded himself in his Judaism that his universalism becomes the development and crown of his Judaism. Many a Jew of the latter type is himself predisposed to this higher attitude [universalism], but he is afraid that his people is not strong enough nationally to bear this development.[35]

Despite his use of the third person, Magnes might have been directing these remarks primarily to himself. Possibly he was trying to grant meaning to his immigration to Palestine as a move that connected him to the "soil of the Jewish nation" and consolidated his claim to a higher universalism because he was now more deeply rooted. In this way Magnes was differentiating himself, on the one hand, from the spurious universalism he ascribed to the Reform movement and, on the other hand, from the particular, chauvinistic nationalism he encountered in the Yishuv, which did not regard itself as subordinate in any way to a universal vision.

Magnes attributed excessive nationalism to a weak self-perception. Key to overcoming this weakness was to embed oneself in the land and cultivate physicality in Palestine,[36] while also relying on the strength of a flourishing diaspora Jewry devoted to universal humanistic ideals. Magnes's vision was fundamentally an attempt to create harmony between the Land of Israel and the Diaspora:

General rule: so to act as though the Jews were strong and not weaklings. So to act as though Zion were already rebuilt and were sending her messengers out into the world of man. Zion will be rebuilt; she is already rebuilt in our minds and souls. Therefore with our feet in the soil of our Judaism let us seek our brethren of all peoples. Fear for the Jews or fear of others cannot be our guiding force, only confidence in Jewish strength and belief in great human ideals.[37]

After transitioning from universalism to national particularism, Magnes returned to the universal vision and the search for "brethren of all peoples." His call to rebuild confidence in Jewish strength is reminiscent of the Zionist sentiment in the Yishuv to which he was now exposed, as well as American optimism and self-reliance. He concluded his remarks with a humanist call for a return to the "belief in great human ideals"—a call that accords with Mendes-Flohr's analysis, which proposes that Magnes be viewed as the embodiment of "a new Jewish humanism, a humanism of civic courage and moral responsibility."[38]

Jewish Nationalisms: Comparing Magnes to Dubnow and Cohen

It is interesting to compare Magnes's conception of nationalism with parallel conceptions of Jewish nationalism. There are discernible similarities, for example, between Magnes's outlook and Russian Jewish historian and ideologue Simon Dubnow's "Diaspora Nationalism." Dubnow, utilizing Hegelian terminology, proclaimed that every nation was a primordial entity that developed linearly in three phases: racial-tribal, territorial-political, and spiritual-cultural. Evolving from one stage to the next indicated the vitality of a nation. Reaching the third phase depended on a nation's ability to maintain its cultural heritage. In that third phase, the nation would exist in its supreme manifestation, removed from territorial affiliations or statehood. As the endpoint of this global process, all nations would become nonterritorial and scattered across the earth. The eventual diasporization of all peoples was therefore an inevitable process.[39]

Dubnow's observation in 1898 (in the second of a series of "letters" published in the Russian Jewish paper *Voskhod* between 1897 and 1907) that the Jewish nation was currently in the third, "spiritual-cultural," phase of nationhood is reminiscent of Magnes's Reform universalism and his view of Jewish nationalism as a temporary phase on the path toward a universalist messianic vision. The Jewish Diaspora, accordingly, was not a curse but a historical necessity and an existential state that proved the Diaspora's vitality.[40]

The various archives of Magnes's writings do not indicate that he ever corresponded with Dubnow, or directly addressed Dubnow's outlook in his speeches or writings.[41] The most likely reason was Magnes's strong affinity for Ahad Ha'am. While Ahad Ha'am and Dubnow shared certain views—a sense of rupture from the Jewish past, a need to define strategies for national survival, a selective application of the past to serve the needs of the present and the (essentially secularized) future[42]—they differed on the application of Jewish nationalism. Against Dubnow, Ahad Ha'am insisted that the national self cannot be sustained on historical literature alone; respect for the past does not in itself justify the nation's continued existence and potential suffering. He was pessimistic about long-term Jewish existence in the Diaspora, and rejected Dubnow's vision of Jewish national autonomy in the Diaspora as unrealistic and insufficient to secure Jewish cultural continuity and adaptation to modernity; instead he called for a cultural center in Palestine.[43] In the debate between Ahad Ha'am and Dubnow on the nature of Jewish nationality, Magnes, who saw himself as a genuine Ahad Ha'am disciple, sided with Ahad Ha'am.

It would appear that the Dubnow and Magnes shared a common goal, yet differed in terms of their reading of the historical moment. Magnes's approach to Jewish nationalism shifted following several key events: World War I, his immigration to Palestine, and the growth of political Zionism. World War I and the nationally based violence it begat intensified his suspicion of nationalism generally. His immigration to Palestine then changed his perspective on Jewish nationalism in the context of the Diaspora: He was no longer part of the Diaspora, but rather of the settlement in Palestine, and this reversal compelled him from that point on to emphasize not the vital role of Palestine but instead that of the Diaspora, specifically in the face of what he saw as the "chauvinistic" nationalism of the Yishuv. Thus (as described in chapter 5), his vision of the Hebrew University of Jerusalem incorporated a role for the Diaspora, in hopes of shoring up a more universalist horizon for the nationalistically prone Yishuv. Only in the mid-1940s, on the eve of the founding of the state and in light of his reservations about the violence associated with political Zionism, did Magnes draw closer to Dubnow's views and effectively pull away from Jewish nationalism in favor of a return to the scholarly Jewish existence that could exist in the Diaspora as well.

There were also conceptual similarities between Magnes and the neo-Kantian Jewish philosopher Hermann Cohen. The influence of Cohen's thought on Reform Judaism in Germany, and later in the United States, is particularly evident in the arena of ethical monotheism. For Cohen, as for the early Reformer thinkers, ethical monotheism was the heart of Judaism. God is not one just in the numerical sense but also in God's apartness from nature. God exists as the ground and goal of morality, without which moral aspirations are illusionary. For Cohen's ethical monotheism, God is the idea and the ideal that sustain creation and morality. The early Reformer thinkers applied his thought to confine holiness to the moral realm, and to conclude that Jewish ritual derived its significance only from its capacity to serve as the symbol of moral values.[44]

Magnes's and Cohen's approaches to the moral demands placed on society are also comparable. Cohen viewed the state as the arena in which ethics are to be realized, and the prophets as those who had shifted the moral center of gravity from the individual to society and the state. This view is reminiscent of Magnes's prophetic self-identification and motivation and his demand that Jewish statehood in Palestine only be realized if it meets the moral requirement of granting democratic rights to the Arabs of Palestine. Additionally, Cohen advocated separating Jewish nationalism, which he considered fundamentally religious, from its political realization in the form of statehood. Ultimately this was the reason he opposed Zionism: The isolation of the Jewish nation in its own state, as political Zionism proposed, clashed with the messianic universalist ideal.[45] By the last years of his life Cohen did speak of the Jews as a "nationality," yet that nationality existed to bear a religious message of universal importance for humanity.[46]

Magnes shared this universal vision, but early on he saw nationalism as a means that could serve this vision. Over the 1930s, as the Yishuv grew, and with it isolationist Jewish nationalism, the universalist vision became more central for Magnes and his doubts about nationalism deepened. Thus his attitude toward nationalism depended on the extent to which it could serve universalism as a scaffold of sorts—something that seemed increasingly less likely in the 1940s, especially after the 1942 publication of the Biltmore Declaration, which effectively endorsed Jewish statehood.

To repeat one of his favorite Latin phrases, Magnes was sui generis (unique) in Jewish Palestine. He was practically the only participant of American origin in the political and intellectual discourse on Arab-Jewish relations and the future of the Zionist project in the Land of Israel. His American upbringing and education played a key role in his political thought and, as we see in chapter 9, in his formulation of a binational position. Inspired by the political philosophy of pragmatism, a deep commitment to democracy, and the American model of civic nationalism, Magnes propounded an alternative to European-based perceptions of Jewish nationalism, both in the excessively particular and "chauvinistic" form of political Zionism and the sometimes impractical and excessively idealistic formulations of the Brit Shalom European circle.

Magnes struggled to reconcile the assets and liabilities of modern Jewish nationalism. Even as he harbored a deep distrust of nationalism following World War I, he endorsed Zionism and the right of Jewish self-realization as "a people with national elements." After his immigration to Palestine, he developed a more "organic" conception of nationalism, perceiving it as essential in the eventual realization of authentic universalism—the pinnacle of his Reform ethical monotheism. Eventually, he believed, binationalism would emerge and enable national self-realization, while maintaining the moral higher ground demanded by Jewish ethics, thus preserving the balance between particular and universal elements of Jewish collective existence.

9

Binationalism as Theological Politics

Magnes was not the first to articulate and adopt binationalism as a position in response to the "Arab problem." The seeds of this approach to the resolution of Arab-Jewish relations were evident in the Zionist movement as early as 1911 in the writings of Hugo Bergman. Later advocates of this approach included fellow members of the student union Bar Kochba, Hans Kohn, and Prague-born journalist and editor Robert Weltsch, all of whom had despaired of the idea of Jewish nationalism in a multinational Central European context and shifted the focus of their political and Zionist activism to Palestine.[1] In time, these three would be among the co-founders of Brit Shalom, which Magnes, as noted, never officially joined.

As for nationalism and the political structures Magnes envisioned, the environment in which his thinking developed was decidedly different from that of his associates in Brit Shalom and the Ichud, and from European thinking generally. The American concept of nationalism differed in its very essence from the Central European one, and especially from the German conceptualization that shaped the thinking of the Central European members of Brit Shalom. American nationalism was not ethnic but rather civic: It stemmed from a sense of belonging to a shared political entity. Accordingly, I examine Magnes's binationalism in light of both the American conceptualization of nationalism and his religious worldview.

Another important thread in this discussion is the evolution of the idea of binationalism in both Central Europe and the Yishuv after World War I. Shalom Ratzabi's comprehensive analysis of the intellectual origins of the Central European circle within Brit Shalom points to their concept of Judaism and their critique of European nationalism that emerged after World War I. According to historian Dimitri Shumsky, the evolving conceptualization of binationalism in the thinking of Bergman, Kohn, and the Prague circle stemmed from the uniquely Czechoslovak environment of binationalism and bilingualism. Similarly, Martin Buber, who had been active in Brit Shalom in Germany, and from 1942 was a partner in political activism with Magnes in Ichud, cultivated his own concept of binationalism, which was intertwined with his overall dialogical thinking and conception of theopolitics.[2]

In addition to these thinkers, a number of organizations in the Yishuv—including HaShomer HaTza'ir (a socialist Zionist youth movement that established kibbutzim in Palestine and in 1946 became a political party), the League for Jewish-Arab Rapprochement and Cooperation (an umbrella organization, hereinafter "the League"), and for a while Hadassah as well—supported binationalism as a solution.[3] HaShomer HaTza'ir, writes historian Meir Hazan, "visibly worked on cultivating the foundations of shared living with the Arabs at the local level, alongside an unwillingness to concede on [the question of] a Jewish majority. This duality derived from its members' aspiration of using humanitarian and socialist ideals with Zionist actualization. HaShomer HaTza'ir adopted a moderate stance on the use of force, fiercely opposed division of the country, and sided with binationalism as a solution."[4] The League, established in the summer of 1939, was an umbrella organization of sorts, uniting groups and individuals who supported a solution based on compromise with the Arab community.

These groups included representatives of Kedma Mizraha ("Forward to the East," an Orientalist [i.e., encouraging familiarity with and ties to "the Orient"] group in favor of binationalism, headed by agronomist Haim Margolis-Kalvarisky), HaShomer HaTza'ir, and "refugees" from Brit Shalom, who, in time, together with Magnes, would establish the organization Ichud. Magnes himself did not join the League, because of his strained relations with the leadership of the Jewish Agency. The League lacked any organizational or ideological cohesion; nor did it offer any genuine plan of action.[5] Also worth noting is Hadassah's work in relation to the Arab question and, later, binationalism as an alternative. The prominent figures in this regard were Henrietta Szold and Rose Jacobs, also a founding member and former president of Hadassah, whose efforts reflected U.S. Jewry's special sensitivities regarding Arab rights in the context of the Zionist enterprise and democracy as a dimension of life in the Yishuv. Their engagement with the issue of binationalism would come later, when they established the Committee for the Study of Arab-Jewish Relations in late 1941. Their efforts dovetailed somewhat with Ichud's activities, yet they shared the American Zionist outlook that initially neither viewed the Arabs as a nation nor recognized the dialectical processes that contributed to the formation of Arab nationalism in parallel to the emergence of Zionism.[6]

Like All the Nations?

Magnes's essay *Like All the Nations?* was published in 1929 as a bound pamphlet in Hebrew and English. The essay marked a turning point in his political activity in Palestine, for until that point Magnes had refrained from any such open engagement in the Yishuv. As this is the main essay in which Magnes methodically laid out his action plan and explained the logic behind his concrete program for binationalism, its theological and political elements deserve close analysis.

The Western Wall riots of August 1929, which sparked genuine shock both in the Yishuv and among American Jews, drove Magnes to publish the essay.⁷ "I had been an onlooker at Zionist politics," he wrote, "and I have seen things done and left undone which it was hard to pass by in silence. . . . I had thought that by devoting myself single-mindedly to the building up of the Hebrew University as a center of learning and of inspiration, in the idea of which I believed throughout a generation, it would be possible to leave politics to others."⁸ His description of this political tension, between silence and speech, between leaving politics to others and reengagement, brings to mind the religious tension Magnes experienced between subduing the prophetic voice and sounding it. "Recent events," he continued,

> have made me realize again, all too clearly, what I should have preferred to forget, that, after all, politics means lives and all too often, too, the determination of moral, social and even religious issues. It was for that reason that I concluded, not without conflict with myself, that it would be necessary for me, as it should for all of us in these critical times, to contribute my share, whatever it was worth, to the political discussion. I found this the more imperative because the official attitude on the Arab question appeared to me either stiff-necked or vague.⁹

Politics, according to Magnes, is the arena in which social, moral, and even religious decisions take shape, and as such it was necessary—absolutely necessary in fact—to participate. In terms of the prophetic motif, note Magnes's use of the term "stiff-necked," which comes from the verse "The Lord further said to Moses, 'I see that this is a stiff-necked people'" (Num. 32:9), in which God is speaking to Moses about the People of Israel having turned their back on the Divine in favor of the golden calf. This passage also evokes the sense of a prophet calling upon his people to repent.

Fundamental Rights, the State, and the Majority

At the outset of *Like All the Nations?*, Magnes described his political outlook. The political debate in Palestine, he argued, centers on the "searching question... as to what we want here. What is our Zionism? What does Palestine mean for us?" The answer, for Magnes, rested on three pillars: immigration, settlement on the land, and Hebrew life and culture. "If you can guarantee these for me," Magnes continued, "I should be willing to yield the Jewish 'State' and the Jewish 'majority,' and on the other hand I would agree to a Legislative Assembly together with a democratic political regime so carefully planned and worked out that the above three fundamentals could not be infringed." Not only was Magnes willing to pay the price of conceding the state, but he also believed, as he would later argue, that this price would ensure calm and mutual understanding.

It follows that, for Magnes, neither the "state" nor the "majority" was the essence of the Zionist endeavor to establish a collective Jewish presence in the Land of Israel. The state and the majority were at most means—and impractical means at that time, in Magnes's view—to ensuring the three fundamental rights: of immigration, settlement on the land, and Hebrew culture.[10] These remarks echo Ahad Ha'am's teachings as well as a later article by Martin Buber, "A Majority or Multitude?" from 1944.[11] Notably, Magnes explicitly referred to democracy as the preferred political vision for the country.

Magnes went on to forecast, based on statistical calculations of demographic growth and the absorption capacity in Palestine, that it would take more than one full generation until the territory was filled to capacity (in his view, the country could accommodate roughly two million Arabs and one million Jews at most). This led him to pose the question, "Why not, therefore, let us try to work out a program for a generation, and let the generation after take care of its own problems? If we could do this, we should perhaps be talking less in abstractions, and even though we differed in our philosophies, all of us ought to be able to work together with a will."[12]

As for the aspirations for a Jewish majority, he wrote, "It is pleasing to have such dreams as to the future. But surely no serious practical policy can be built up upon them, and it is a practical policy for the next 10–20–30 years we were after." Further on in the pamphlet he noted, "The situation of the Fellaheen [Arab villagers, usually in the service of other landowners] is one of the cardinal problems of the country. Here is a field for a great constructive program in which both Jews and Arabs should combine."[13] All of these remarks point to the pragmatism at the heart of Magnes's outlook, his preference for the particular over the abstract, and his search for a near-term solution, the foreseeable results of which could provide the basis for a broader agreement in the future.

Building on American Pillars

Magnes presented a plan that would make it possible, through a constitution, to protect Jewish interests beyond Arab legislative authority: "But who is to determine the economic capacity of the country and in what manner? This cannot surely be left simply to a legislative body with an Arab majority, and it is therefore necessary not only to reserve the question of immigration constitutionally as being beyond the province of the legislative to interfere with, but also to become clear as to the machinery that will actually determine the economic capacity of the country." Later he specified: "If a political regime can be worked out either through a constitution or through a treaty or in some other binding and international way, that can safeguard the three rights above outlined, then I am heartily in favor of including within this regime, but by no means as the whole of it, a Legislative Assembly."[14]

In formulating binationalism as a solution, the role of the constitution as Magnes conceived it was to safeguard principles and values that existed beyond the sphere of democratic decision making. Reliance on a constitution is, of course, characteristic of the American political outlook, but here Magnes was using the concept of a constitution in a unique way: adapting it to binationalism as a mechanism for establishing a supra-democratic political order. "Nor need the political forms adopted ape dogmatically or mechanically those of other lands," Magnes continued. "But a beginning has to be made all along the line from the municipalities through the Legislative Assembly and such other legislative and executive organs of government as are required and devised.... The life of this unhappy country will be much saner and much less hysterical the sooner its population can exercise its political energies in legitimate and practical and constructive ways."[15]

These remarks provide further evidence of Magnes's pragmatic political outlook, which held that the people's very experience with democracy would actualize a more balanced political life in Palestine. In his view, practical experience—in democracy, in this case—would be the key factor in achieving the desired outcome. The initial stances of the parties largely did not matter; rather, the political means were front and center.

He continued:

There are of course dangers in all political and in all democratic institutions. I have no illusions about the magnitude of the difficulties here. But it is of much greater danger to let the old sore rankle and form into an abscess again. The best excuse both for home and for foreign consumption that the extremist now has, is the truth, namely, that the people have no share in their own government. I suppose no experiment in democracy was ever made except that there was controversy between those who said that the people were not "ripe" and those who said, trust the people and thus make them ripe.[16]

Here Magnes voiced some reservation about implementing democracy in the Yishuv, given the problems that might ensue. The main difficulty, of course, was the Arab majority and the concern that, through democratic means, the Arabs would be able to impose their will on the Jewish community of Palestine. Nonetheless, in the name of justice—to address charges about residents not participating in their own governance—and in the name of pragmatism, which aimed to foster political equality through experience, he argued in favor of establishing a democratic system in Palestine.

Binationalism as Theological Politics

This is the American political aspect of Magnes's thought, which in combination with the Reform religious dimension consolidated the concept of binationalism as both a moral and pragmatic alternative. In calling for a democratic system, one of the pillars of the American political worldview, Magnes had to properly address questions about the legitimacy of delaying the implementation of democracy in Palestine. Meanwhile, many of the American Zionist leaders who pondered these questions were willing to delay democracy's implementation in Palestine for tactical reasons, until the emergence of a Jewish majority.

A meeting to address this question took place in New York in 1929 with the participation of Reverend John Haynes Holmes, Magnes's partner in advocating pacifism during World War I, who now shared his vision of binationalism; philanthropists Nathan and Lena Straus; Zionist leader Judge Julian Mack; and Stephen Wise. Holmes, who had visited Palestine, supported the implementation of democracy. Mack and Wise, on the other hand, while denying the claim that American Zionists sought to delay the implementation of democracy until Palestine had a Jewish majority, actually insisted that the Jews be afforded every opportunity to grow numerically before democracy was implemented.[17]

The Yishuv, for its part, was less preoccupied with this question. Its political culture, which included elements from the tradition of the Jewish *kehillah* (community) in the Diaspora, and from the major secular ideologies of the nineteenth century—liberalism, socialism, and nationalism—combined democratic traditions with nondemocratic ones. Liberal democracy was not among the structural conceptual foundations of socialist Zionism, and its actualization was secondary in importance to the realization of the vision of national revival and the creation of a new and just society. Thus, for example, Berl Katznelson was able to claim that "there exist aims, objectives, and values the achievement of which permits undermining [formal democracy]."[18]

Magnes, with implied reservations, proposed a concrete political solution based explicitly on the American political system:

> I am no expert in political science, nor have I the responsibility of having to decide as to the practicability or workability of this or any other proposal for the new governmental structure.... If, however, I may interject a personal predilection in this connection it would be for the creation of two Houses, the Lower Chamber elected by the whole population, which would give a large Arab majority, and an Upper Chamber, to be elected or appointed upon the basis of the equality of the three nationalities, Jewish, Arab, British. This is similar to the United States where the Senate is composed of two representatives of each State of the Union, large or small, populous or sparsely peopled, thereby expressing the equal rights of the states constituting the Union, whereas the House of Representatives represents the individuals of the population as individuals.[19]

Magnes viewed a political system based on representative rather than numeric equality (which he later termed "political parity" and "numerical parity") as the foundation on which to actualize the concept of binationalism justly.

The explicit and unmistakable influence of the American political outlook evident here—for example, democratic rule, pragmatism, and the belief that a constitution can provide the basis for restraining self-centered interests (in this instance, each people's aspiration to its own distinct form of national self-realization)—is supplemented by the aforementioned belief that political institutions can ensure fairness, whether through their educational value or thanks to the accumulated practical experience they enable. Again, at the basis of this belief, it is posited here, lies American pragmatism.

Absolute Morality and Elements of Christianity

Magnes's essay also addressed the relation between politics and morality:

> It is right in morals—insofar as political forms have anything to do with morals at all—that the people of this and every other country should have a voice in their own government; and it is not possible,

even if it were desirable, to maintain the present status quo.... The Jewish conscience will not bear this for long. It must recognize, sooner, rather than later and from good will rather than through compulsion, that the inhabitants of this country, both Arabs and Jews, have not only the right but the duty to participate, in equitable and practical ways, in the government of their common Homeland.[20]

These words allude, once again, to the tension between Magnes's self-aware pragmatism and the moral-prophetic aspect of his thinking. On the one hand, he casts doubt on the possibility of a correlation between political order and morality, in a manner reminiscent of Max Weber's *Politics as a Vocation* (1919), of which Magnes was presumably aware, given the essay's importance and the attention it received.[21] On the other hand, he claims that Jewish conscience dictates that political governance be based on principles of justice.

Above all, Magnes's words reveal yet again the American pillars of his thinking—the view that democratic rule is a moral imperative that "must" be recognized. Magnes's rhetoric generally tended to emphasize the obligatory dimension and absolute nature of morality (which as noted are also evident in Ahad Ha'am's moral outlook). As events unfolded, however, his assumption that the Jewish conscience would not tolerate the continued existence of a nondemocratic system would fail the test of reality of life in the Yishuv, which did not prioritize democratic rule, even within the Jewish community itself.

Now, however, the Western Wall riots—the context in which Magnes wrote *Like All the Nations?*—compelled him to address these issues directly:

I am asked, must we do that now? My answer is: Yes, now, and the pity is that we did not do it before Hebron and Safed. Now, because it is right that it be done, and the sooner the right thing is done the better, practically speaking, all around. We must pay bitterly for our fault of not having proposed and done this long since. The blame rests on each of us. Mea culpa.... We must face this problem, not because of the pogroms but despite them, not as a result of violence, not because of pressure from without but because of spiritual pressure from within ourselves.[22]

Here Magnes chose to repeat, not political arguments, but the moral imperative of addressing the Arab problem "because of spiritual pressure from within ourselves." The Christian dimension is quite salient here, through the general tone of guilt and repentance, specifically the Latin phrase mea culpa, which Magnes borrowed from the Catholic practice of confession. His use of this phrase is particularly interesting given that American Reform Judaism's syncretism with Christianity manifested mostly through Protestantism, whereas confession is a Catholic sacrament rejected by Protestants.

He continued:

And with those men—Arab and English—who are directly or indirectly responsible for the shedding of the innocent blood of our brothers and sisters? Yes—if necessary for our brothers' and sisters' sake, and for the peace of Zion—even with them. Israel's question always is, and whether we want it or not, always will be: Are my own hands clean of blood? Not, are his hands clean? Have I done him wrong? Not, has he done me wrong? That he has done us wrong we know, and resent, and suffer from in our own flesh and blood.[23]

Here Magnes was drawing on the biblical verse about the required ritual of *Egla Arufa* (literally, "broken-necked calf") should a body of a murder victim be discovered in an unpopulated area within the Land of Israel; accordingly: "And they shall make this declaration: 'Our hands did not shed this blood, nor did our eyes see it done'" (Deut. 21:7). In line with his pacifist religious outlook, Magnes ratifies the Jewish theological commitment to self-reflection to prevent bloodshed, even in the face of aggression and violence.

Ultimately, Magnes was asserting the same absolute moral imperative: placing the Jewish duty of moral self-conduct ahead of political interests. At the same time, one can also discern Christian elements in Magnes's rationale, which places the question "Have I done him wrong?" ahead of the question "Has he done me wrong?"—or, in the historical context of the 1929 riots, prioritizes Jewish moral soul-searching over criticism of Arab violence. A similar approach is evident in the description of Christ's crucifixion according to the book of Matthew, in which Pontius Pilate "washed his hands before the crowd, saying, 'I am innocent of this man's blood; see to it yourselves.' Then the people as a whole answered, 'His blood be on us and on our children!'" (Matt. 27:24–25).

Similar themes are evident as well in Buber's reaction to the 1929 riots. He wrote: "There has emerged a situation in Palestine whereby we do not live, not in any fundamental sense, with the Arabs, but rather by their side. The result is that [we] do not live together but side-by-side; that our 'enemies' have turned *next* into *against*. If we were truly ready to live together . . . the recent events would not have happened."[24]

Magnes's own concept of absolute morality was likely rooted in two sources. For one, the values of German idealism, and more specifically philosopher Immanuel Kant's categorical imperative claiming that an action is moral only if it can be applied as a universal law, had directly infused German Reform Judaism and, subsequently, the American Reform movement.[25] German idealism had also influenced members of the Central European circle of Brit Shalom, who aspired to subordinate social and political action to the dictates of absolute and eternal moral and religious concepts.

At the same time, Magnes saw himself as a disciple of Ahad Ha'am, whose approach to Zionism aimed at solving "the Jewish problem" (developing a modern Jewish identity that authentically derived from Jewish culture and ideas), rather than the Herzlian "problem of the Jews" (the failure of Emancipation and the inevitability of antisemitism). For Ahad Ha'am, according to Hermann Cohen, the significance of Judaism lay in "tirelessly searching for ways to realize the absolute and unconditional values of justice."[26]

The Sanctity of the Land and the Concept of Binationalism

Another concept of a theopolitical nature that comes to the fore in *Like All the Nations?* is that of the sanctity of the land, from which certain political implications follow.[27] "If the theory advanced in these pages be true," Magnes wrote, then "the Holy Land is no place for an Arab National State or Government, but for a bi-national country with a Mandate as nearly permanent as possible held by Great Britain from the League of Nations."[28]

This was the embryonic articulation of a core argument Magnes would later reassert in his testimony before the Anglo-American Committee in March 1946—namely, that the sanctity of the land made it an unsuitable location for the implementation of separatist nationalism, whether Jewish or Arab. Magnes continued: "This simple Jew who has come to the Holy Land with clean hands and a pure heart is of more importance to me than all my pride and honour, and all my political calculations and theories. What matters to me is that he and I and our People get a chance to live and to work here, and to make the Holy Land and the Holy City sacred again through our labor and our life."[29]

One can discern two spiritual tendencies in Magnes's thinking: his affinity for the "simple Jew"—which contained Hasidic elements alongside Magnes's romanticization and idealization—and the view that through living and working in Palestine (and in this case, actually in Jerusalem) the land would become sacred once again.

There are also two sides to Magnes's remarks about the sanctity of the land: the bond to the land itself and its veneration, an approach reminiscent of Aaron David Gordon's outlook, and also of Rav Kook's; and the concept—shared by Ahad Ha'am and Buber—that the spiritual supersedes the earthly, and that the sanctity of the land is not a given but, rather, requires human labor in order to re-consecrate it:[30]

Binationalism as Theological Politics

> What is Palestine to us? It is the Land of Israel, our Holy Land. It is holy for us in a practical and a mystic sense. Its holiness attracts our old and our young, the religious and the non-religious from far away places, and they want to work its soil, and build up an ethical community, and thereby make the land still more sacred. Its very landscape and color help every child and simple man among us to understand our classic literature and our history. It helps us as through no other means to bare our very soul, to get down deep into the sources of our being.[31]

The land thus possessed a twofold sanctity. Its hidden, mystical dimension allowed one to delve into one's very soul. Yet at the same time, its consecration required moral political action—which, Magnes insisted, meant the realization of binationalism.

"People, Torah, Land," an "International National Unit," and the Democratic Imperative

"It is a fact that cannot be denied," Magnes wrote, "that the Jewish People has and can have no other historical center than the Land of Israel." He described the Jewish practice "of hundreds, now almost thousands of years" of praying three times a day toward Jerusalem. "And, quite frankly," he asked, "has been such a yearning known to history as the century long yearning of Israel for this sacred soil?"

Even as Magnes acknowledged the unique nature of the Jewish people's bond with their land, he avowed that this sacredness did not award the people a unique political status that overrode democratic considerations: "Let us grant therefore the peculiar and profound and exceptional connection of this Jewish People sui generis. But is this a sufficient reason to withhold a Legislative Assembly until the Jews become at least as numerous as the Arabs?"[32]

This point deserves further theopolitical contextualization. Magnes accepted arguments about the singularity of the Jewish people and its historically unique (religious) longing for the land. Nevertheless, the uniqueness of the people and of its relation to the land does not, for Magnes, "exempt" the Jewish people from the precepts of a fair and just political order, which is of religious value in and of itself.

The centrality of the American political tradition as conceptualized in Magnes's theopolitical outlook is discernible in the way he laid out his argument. Democracy receives precedence here at the expense of the theological and realpolitik considerations invoked by others in the Yishuv and the American Zionist movement in order to postpone discussing democracy until the land had a Jewish majority. "Whether through temperament or other circumstances, I do not at all believe, and I think the facts are all against believing that without Palestine the Jewish People is dying out or is doomed to destruction. On the contrary it is growing stronger; and what is more, it should grow stronger, for Palestine without communities in the Dispersion would be bereft of much of its significance as a spiritual center for the Judaism of the world."[33]

Here Magnes reiterated his consistent stance that Jewish life in Palestine should not be viewed as the key to the redemption of the Jewish people. What is more, he reversed his earlier formula (examined in chapter 2) whereby the Diaspora was to be seen as dependent on the center in Palestine: Now the center in Palestine was dependent on life in the Diaspora. This reversal is arguably a direct result of his having relocated from America to Palestine, where convincing the Yishuv of the Diaspora's essentiality, rather than the reverse, was the clear imperative.

Magnes went on to rank the three fundamental elements of Jewish life:

> To me it seems that there are three chief elements in Jewish life, in the following order of importance. The living Jewish People . . . ; the Torah, in the broadest sense of this term, i.e., all our literature and documents and history, is also the great religious and ethical and social ideals the Torah contains for use and development in the present and the future; and third, the Land of Israel. My view is that the People and the Torah can exist and be creative as they have existed and have been creative

without the Land; that however the land is one of the chief means, is not the chief means, of revivifying and deepening the People and the Torah.... The living Jewish People is primary. It is the living carrier and vessel of Judaism, the Jewish spirit. It has used even its Exile for spreading light and learning. Palestine can help this people to understand itself, to give an account of itself, to an intensification of its culture, a deepening of its philosophy, a renewal of its religion. Palestine can help this people perform its great ethical mission as a national-international entity. But this eternal and far-flung People does not need a Jewish State for the purpose of maintaining its very existence.[34]

Alongside Ahad Ha'am's and Gordon's paths—*spirit-people-land* and *land-people-spirit*, respectively—Magnes proposed a third approach to realization of the Zionist vision: *people-Torah-land*. This position had elements unique to the "diasporic" vision of Zionism: It placed the people, and relations with diaspora communities and Jewish centers outside of Israel, at the center.[35] At the basis of this outlook was Magnes's organic concept of the "People"—reflected here and elsewhere in his frequent reference to the "living" Jewish people. In line with the German concept of *volk* (ethnic nationalism), Magnes viewed the "people" as a social organism that operates as dictated by its nature, like any living creature in nature.[36] Similarly, one sees hints of Magnes's dynamic concept of Torah—blending the Reform concept of the historicism of the Torah and the Reconstructionist trope of his contemporary Mordecai Kaplan—that contains the keys to future transformations, which in turn must be approached anew in accordance with the spirit of the times.

It is worth dwelling on Magnes's claim that "Palestine can help this People perform its great ethical mission as a national-international entity." This statement may be seen as containing the essence of Magnes's theopolitical worldview: "Palestine" ("Eretz Israel" in the Hebrew version)—as a political entity, as will become apparent—is presented here as having the role of helping the people realize its potential mission, which is a religious and moral one, while the political structure by which to implement the mission is a national-international entity. This paradoxical framing embodies the tension between the particular and the universal, which, it is argued here, was central to Magnes's political theology. Earlier the discussion considered one possible solution to this tension: namely, viewing nationalism as an interim and inevitable stage on the path to the universal vision. Here another alternative is implied: a political entity that is simultaneously national and international, particular and universal.

The messianic dimension of this alternative also deserves mention. On the one hand, Magnes was relinquishing the notion of gradual development, shifting from the particular to the universal ideal, a notion that accords with Reform Judaism's messianic outlook. On the other hand, the call for a national-international entity, despite its pragmatic aim, can actually be seen as messianic in and of itself, in the sense of the attempt to realize an intrinsically idealistic postulation.

At this point, Magnes stressed the singularity of the Jewish people worldwide: "The Jewish community throughout the world is a wondrous and paradoxical organism. It participates in the life of many nations, yet in spite of numberless predictions in the past and the present, it is not absorbed by them. It is patriotic in every land, yet it is international, cosmopolitan." As such, "Palestine cannot 'solve the Jewish problem' of the Jewish people. Wherever there are Jews there is the Jewish problem. It is part of the Jewish destiny to face this problem and make it mean something of good for mankind."

Magnes concluded by stressing the necessity of diaspora relations with Palestine, which he identified as "the center of this organism but by no means all of it. The Dispersion and Palestine are both required for the fullest development of the Jewish People. This peculiar People cannot be content with either. This sui generis organism which we call the Jewish People has need of these all-embracing, complicated forms—an intensive center and a great periphery." Magnes derived political implications from the context of Jewish-Arab relations: "It is in derogation of the actual importance of the living Jewish People and of Judaism to place them on one side of the scale and have it balanced by the relatively unimportant Arab community of Palestine. The true parallels and balancing forces are Jews and Judaism on the one side, and the Arab peoples and even all of Islam on the other." In this case, he argued, the context was constructive: "In this way you get a truer perspective of the whole and you increase the significance of Palestine as being that point where in this new day Judaism meets Islam again throughout all its confines, as once they met centuries back to the ultimate enrichment of human culture."[37]

Thus, Magnes prioritized the religious over the national, a fundamental principle of his theopolitical worldview. Magnes asserted that he was personally willing to accept the doctrine of "God above the State, God above Everything" (see chapter 5). He also depicted the encounter between Jews and Arabs in Palestine not as a meeting of the Jewish and Arab communities, but rather as the coming together of Judaism and Islam. This anticipated encounter rested on a utopian perception of past cooperation between Judaism and Islam, which he expected to reemerge. In fact, as his testimony before the Anglo-American Committee (discussed in chapter 10) illustrates, his proposed solution encompassed the possibility of a "land sacred to three religions" whose inhabitants would be regarded as proxies of their religion. At the same time, Magnes paid no attention to the religious aspect of relations between Jews and Muslims, nor to the tension between these groups that had erupted into the Western Wall riots—his very reason for writing this tract in the first place.[38]

As we've seen, theopolitical elements underpinned Magnes's early conceptualization of binationalism. As he systematically laid out his political theory in *Like All the Nations?*, he built into the structure of his arguments the religious foundations of his political perspectives. Among these one may discern universalist Reform principles and the salience of absolute justice as borrowed from Ahad Ha'am, with roots in American

Reform Judaism. In addition, he ascribed to the land a sanctity beyond its essentialist and mystical elements: primarily, sanctity would unfold as the outcome of human labor on the land. This pronouncement spoke to the use of political objectives as tools in service of sacred ones. His political impetus was modeled on prophetic motivation, and on a sense of religious duty that underpinned political activity.

Indeed, Magnes infused his political perspective with a variety of religious elements. At its center was an American Reform ideology that ascribed great importance to ethics and drew on prophetic theory. Alongside, one sees more traditional stances, Hasidic perspectives, and even hints of the Christian tendency to prioritize the moral to the extent of conceding the political, demonstrated by his "mea culpa" rationalization of the political endeavor of binationalism.

Additionally, certain distinctly political aspects of the American dimension of his identity—a commitment to democracy, pragmatism, and trust in political institutions and the political order itself—underlie his theopolitical perspective. These characteristics do not merely exist alongside the religious dimension; rather, they are among the factors that shaped it, through a dialectical process. For example, Magnes's universalism is, admittedly, infused with American Reform universalism; however, American Reform universalism itself is to a large extent the product of political universalism in the overall American context.

In effect, the concept of binationalism Magnes proposed in 1929 in *Like All the Nations?* combined American political elements with a fundamentally Reform approach that subordinated the political to the moral ideal, while also being subject to other religious influences. This unconventional construct speaks to the particularist-universalist tension behind Magnes's concept of nationalism, particularly his view of the Jewish people as a "national-international entity." Moreover, as we shall see, the very juxtaposition of this alternative against another theopolitical alternative—the "Joshua method"—attests to and exposes the concealed political theology of the supposedly secular Yishuv.

10

Magnes and the Theopolitics of Buber

Buber's concept of theopolitics also provides important insight into Magnes's political theology.[1] As we will see, the applicability of theopolitics to Magnes's worldview derives mainly from the core element common to the thinking of both Magnes and Buber: the concept of prophetic politics.

Buber and Magnes on "Theopolitics"

Martin Buber was best known for his philosophy of I-Thou dialogue, his studies on Hasidism, and his call for a Jewish spiritual renaissance. To his vexation, however, his political activism received relatively little resonance and was typically seen as detached from his overall Jewish philosophy.

Buber had joined the Zionist movement in 1898. He promoted Zionism through his writings and speeches, exemplified by three famous lectures he delivered between 1909 and 1911 at the Bar Kochba student union in Prague. In 1921 he became involved with World Zionist Congress politics. At the Twelfth Zionist Congress in Carlsbad, representing the German offshoot of the Labor Zionist HaPo'el HaTza'ir party, Buber presented a suggested resolution on the so-called Arab Question, proclaiming:

Our national desire to renew the life of the people of Israel in their ancient homeland... is not aimed against any other people. As we enter the sphere of world history once more, and become once more the standard bearers of our own fate, the Jewish people, who have constituted a persecuted minority in all the countries of the world for two thousand years, reject with abhorrence the methods of nationalistic domination, under which they themselves have so long suffered. We do not aspire to return to the land of Israel with which we have inseparable historical and spiritual ties in order to suppress another people or to dominate them.[2]

Buber's proposed resolution was then passed on to a committee for final wording. There it encountered significant opposition and political maneuverings—dilutions and distortions to the extent that Buber felt the committee version bore no resemblance to his own. This provoked him to withdraw from direct political engagement.[3] He subsequently developed the comprehensive theory he termed "theopolitics."[4]

In his introduction to *Bein Am LeArtso* (Between a people and its land), his 1945 discussion of the theology of Jewish nationalism, Buber laid out the foundations for what he called theopolitics. Zionism, he posited, was not a national doctrine in the regular sense of the term, as it was not named after a particular people or nation but rather after a sacred place—Zion. He pointed to the unique triangular relationship linking God, the People of Israel, and the Land of Israel. God had sanctified both the people and the land, in the sense that both were dedicated to worshipping God. This sanctity, however, did not exist a priori; the people had to repeatedly earn it anew by devoting their deeds and endeavors to God, particularly in the context of the land.[5] Paraphrasing a theory later posited by Modern Orthodoxy forefather Rabbi Joseph Ber Soloveitchik, one might say that this covenant did not represent a *brit goral* (covenant with fate) but a *brit ye'ud* (covenant with destiny), the outcome of which would be an ongoing messianic realization of God's will on earth.[6]

In sum, for Buber, the holiness of the People of Israel and the Land of Israel was not inherent to either; it derived from both the land (having been divinely chosen) and the people (also divinely chosen, and from their covenant with God). Buber's theopolitics, accordingly, called for the implementation and actualization of the people's "chosenness" and the covenant, and a simultaneous reestablishment of the sanctity of the Land of Israel.[7]

In Buber's theopolitical outlook, the prophets had a central role—namely, to promote realization of what he believed to be the supreme political ideal: the "Kingdom of Heaven," by which he meant affirmation of the "absolute kingship of God."[8] The prophets voiced God's expectation that the people realize their destiny in their own land. Their role involved a perpetual struggle with the kings, God's "reluctant representatives," who did not view it as their duty to realize the Kingdom of Heaven on earth. Whereas the kings aspired to have their kingdoms become "like all the nations" (normalization), the prophets embodied theopolitical realism, which did not accommodate a religious faith devoid of the call to realize the political ideal of the Kingdom of God.[9]

This representation of the prophets' role is key to understanding Magnes's prophetic self-perception. He viewed himself as duty-bound to confront the Yishuv in the name of the theopolitical ideal of the Kingdom of Heaven, and he invoked the phrase "Kingdom of Heaven" repeatedly throughout his writing, especially during the 1940s. Moreover, he himself regarded his adopted position as theopolitical realism—that is, as choosing to subordinate the Jews' long-term political aims to Jewish religious and moral imperatives.

It is also quite evident from Magnes's 1929 pamphlet, *Like All the Nations?*, that his ideal did not involve the political normalization of the Jewish people, but rather its formation into a society committed to actualizing the Jewish principles of justice and morality. As Magnes put it: "Palestine is of such moment to us, that it is capable of giving us much even though our community here be poor and small. I do not want it to be poor and small. But poor and small and faithful to Judaism, rather than large and powerful like all the nations."[10] Self-actualization at the political and state levels, according to Magnes, comes after actualization of the principles of justice and morality, and depends upon their implementation.

Buber and Magnes on Political Organization, Morality, and Nationalism

One way to demonstrate the singularity of Magnes's binationalism as a theopolitical position is to juxtapose it with that of Buber, his partner in promoting the concept of binationalism within the framework of Ichud's activities. As we will see, because their conceptions of political organization, morality, and nationalism differed, Magnes and Buber ultimately held different conceptions of binationalism as a solution.

Differences on Political Organization

The starting points for both men's engagement in questions of political order in Palestine differed fundamentally. Buber was essentially an anarchist in both his religious and political views. He shared an anarchist vision with Second Aliyah pioneer Aaron David Gordon—a vision based, on the one hand, on a renewal of the authentic bond between the people and the land, and on the other, on a rejection of the nation-state and a strong mistrust of politics.[11] Magnes, however, despite his emphasis on personal liberty and his affinity for such thinkers as Emerson and Thoreau, did not view himself as an anarchist, as illustrated by the profound spiritual confusion he felt in the aftermath of a 1939 conversation with Gershom Scholem about the authority of the Torah. Although neither Magnes nor Scholem accepted the Torah's teachings as absolutely authoritative, Magnes had reservations about Scholem's view that this position represented "anarchism."[12] Magnes upheld his pragmatic belief in political institutions and in their capacity to create conditions for mutual understanding on the bases of experience and practice. As such, his defiance aimed at optimizing rather than replacing the system.

Differences on Morality in Politics

Another area in which Magnes and Buber somewhat differed relates to the correspondence between politics and morality. For Magnes, in keeping with Ahad Ha'am's concept of complete spiritual actualization and with Reform ethical monotheism, the moral perspective was categorically determinative of the political. This outlook, manifesting in Magnes's ongoing inclination to forego Jewish interests in Palestine if a moral price tag was attached, would lead Jewish philosopher and educator Ernst Simon to describe Magnes as a Jewish extremist and historian Yoram Nimrod to assert that Magnes possessed "that narrowmindedness unique to fanatic preachers."[13]

Buber, on the other hand, presented a softer conception of the moral imperative—the aforementioned "boundary-line" perspective. On the boundary line, specifically in the political context, Mendes-Flohr writes, "The line as it exists in the shared space marks the maximal degree of self-actualization possible with the minimal extent of damage and injustice to the other."[14]

Differences on Nationalism

Magnes and Buber did find common ground in their general suspicions of nationalism. Magnes viewed nationalism as "chauvinism" and "idolatry," while for Buber it represented a "new idol" that had to be shattered, for example, through binationalism.[15] At the practical level, Buber's outlook was comparable to the views of both Magnes and Abba Hillel Silver, all of them recognizing the need to actualize Jewish nationalism as a temporary phase.

Magnes's and Buber's conceptions of nationalism, however, took shape under different geopolitical and intellectual circumstances. Magnes's fundamentally American nationalism, based on civil rather than ethnic nationality, resulted in a "weak" sense of nationalism that did not link Jewish cultural self-realization with national actualization. Buber, on the other hand, saw the people as an organic entity that would become a nation when it identified what made it unique and took action to preserve that uniqueness. At that point, Buber believed, national sentiments were inevitable, but in excess they turned into extreme nationalism, a danger to both Judaism and humankind. Nevertheless, nationalism could be moderated when it recognized the nation made a commitment to universalism, and only then was it justifiable.[16] In an open letter published in August 1916 in *Der Jude* (a Jewish German periodical founded by Buber), in response to Jewish German philosopher Hermann Cohen's criticism of Zionism as betraying Judaism's "messianic idea" of being "a light unto the nations," Buber proclaimed: "The struggle for a Jewish communal existence in Palestine is a supranational one. . . . We do not want Palestine for the Jews; we want it for the realization of Judaism."[17]

Magnes and Buber on Binationalism

Because of their divergent conceptions about political organization, nationalism, and morality, Magnes and Buber held different conceptions of binationalism as a solution. For Magnes it was the absolute symmetric solution to the Jewish-Arab problem in Palestine. An American in his political thinking, despite his romanticization of the pioneers upon his arrival in Palestine, Magnes did not ascribe due importance to the primordial elements of Jewish nationalism undergirding the Zionist enterprise for political self-actualization. Instead, he regarded binationalism as a fair solution that could be realized through the gradual implementation of democracy and the establishment of suitable political institutions.

Buber, on the other hand, was not fully committed to binationalism in itself as a solution: "This plan [for a binational state]," he wrote, "is merely the temporary adaptation of our path to the current historical situation—it is not necessarily the path itself."[18] According to Mendes-Flohr, Buber's support for binationalism was always more of a strictly heuristic suggestion, an attempt to nurture and guide thinking. The driving force behind Buber's Zionism was the pursuit of his own theopolitical vision: the fulfillment of the sacred bond between the people, God, and the land, which demanded a moral commitment from the people. The Arab presence in Palestine was, in Buber's eyes, Zionism's moral test, but he himself was unable to fully realize his vision of an I-Thou relationship with the Arab leaders in his midst. Once he moved to Palestine in 1938, Buber did not establish any meaningful relations with Arab intellectuals or politicians, although it should also be pointed out that during the Arab Revolt of 1936–39 Jewish-Arab connections were severely curtailed. Magnes, conversely, forged direct ties with Arab dignitaries and often met with members of the Arab community. Until 1938 he resided in an Arab neighborhood near the Old City's Damascus Gate in Jerusalem, and, according to various accounts, he made an effort to learn Arabic.[19]

Another possible reason that Buber was not fully committed to binationalism as an aim in itself could be that it did not correspond with the concept of mythical revival that was central to his thinking. In 1913 in the second of his three lectures on Zionism at the Prague Bar Kochba club, "Myth in Judaism," he refused to accept the dichotomy between myth and monotheism, asserting instead that myth, defined as "a story of divine events perceived by the senses," played a key role in preserving the vitality of religious experience.[20] Jewish holy writings and canonical literature do not contain any myths that readily correlate with binationalism as a vision.

Yet despite these differences, one must not overlook what Magnes's and Buber's approaches share—namely, the moral and prophetic dimension of political engagement. For Buber, as for Magnes, the moral teachings of Israel's prophets served as the foundation for political activity, and these held supremacy over utilitarian considerations of separatist Jewish politics. Both men viewed the moral imperative as the main impetus for political participation because—whether it stemmed from the unique bond between the People of Israel, God, and the land (for Buber), or from universal moral principles (for Magnes)—it was, in their view, the foundation underpinning long-term theopolitical realism. Thus, the gradual, organic development of a cultural and religious center, which in time would become the political center of a model society, was, for them, preferable to political achievements that relied on the superpowers' bayonets,[21] such conquests being transient and inconsistent with the people's moral mission. In adopting this approach, Buber and Magnes were in effect continuing in the path of Ahad Ha'am.

The Jeremiah versus the Joshua Method

As Magnes saw it, the Bible presented two opposing theopolitical approaches applicable to the Zionist endeavor in his own day: the prophet Jeremiah's peaceful path, with which he identified, and Joshua's path of conquest, which, even if justifiable at that time, was no longer suitable. For Magnes, the Joshua warrior method had in fact evolved historically into the Jeremiah path of peace. In a September 7, 1929, letter to Chaim Weizmann, Magnes explained: "The question is, do we want to conquer Palestine now as Joshua did in his day—with fire and sword? Or do we want to take cognizance of Jewish religious development since Joshua—our Prophets, Psalmists and Rabbis, and repeat the words: 'Not by might, and not by violence, but by my spirit, saith the Lord.'"[22]

While his critics insisted, "The history of all conquest and colonization shows [that] the only possible hope of success is by the Joshua method," Magnes did not accept this approach or consider it feasible. As he countered in *Like All the Nations?*: "At least I do not believe it, and I know that plain Jews everywhere, and the plain Jews who have come here to live and work, do not believe it. But if it be so, the Jewish People, thank God, will never be successful conquerors and colonizers. Neither the hostile world nor their own soul will let them."[23]

He expressed this same view in a November 24, 1929, article in the *New York Times*: "It is one of the great civilizing tasks before the Jewish people to try and enter the Promised Land, not in the Joshua way, but bringing peace and culture, hard work and sacrifice, and a determination to do nothing that cannot be justified before the conscience of the world."[24]

Similarly, a journal entry reads:

> My cardinal belief has been in the Jewish people as the carrier-vessel of ideas, of a spiritual tradition. If you object, and say that we have had a Joshua as well as a Jeremiah, I answer that, whereas there is a Joshua within each of us, nevertheless, the main stream of our tradition has been that of the Jeremiahs. I feel myself to be one of the Jeremiahs, to be the heir of the servant of God, of that tradition which tried during political subjection to spiritualize life and to teach a loathing of force.[25]

In Magnes's view, external as well as internal factors would prevent realization of the "Joshua method." Internally, as he outlined in *Like All the Nations?*, "The Jewish consciousness will not bear this [the status quo] for long. It must recognize, sooner rather than later and from good will rather than through compulsion, that the inhabitants of this country, both Arabs and Jews, have not only the right but the duty to participate, in equitable and practical ways, in the government of their common Homeland."[26] Externally, his lack of trust in the politics of imperialism (demonstrated, for one, by the suspicions he raised regarding the 1917 Balfour Declaration) meant that Magnes did not believe realizing Jewish sovereignty was sustainable. Thus he differed from mainstream political Zionists like David Ben-Gurion.

Interestingly, Ben-Gurion drew precisely the opposite conclusions from Jeremiah's teachings. During a special biblical study group meeting on the book of Jeremiah convened in Sdeh Boker (the president's residence) on the occasion of his birthday, Ben-Gurion stated:

> In my childhood I studied the Hebrew Scriptures and read the poems of [notable Hebrew poet of the Jewish Enlightenment movement] Judah Leib Gordon. And when I read the sad and wonderful poem "King Zedekiah in Prison," I was wholeheartedly in favor of Gordon and against Jeremiah. Only after I immigrated to the Land . . . And read the Scriptures here did I understand and know that justice lay with those who prophesied admonishment. The first time I saw what we can expect here was when I worked in [the agricultural colony of] Sejera, and during Passover 1909 two friends of mine were murdered by Arabs . . . for no fault of their own, because of the Arab custom of blood vengeance. Only then did I understand what we can expect and what we must do in this Land.[27]

In stark contrast to Magnes, Ben-Gurion drew from Jeremiah the message not of resistance to war but rather preparedness for it.

For Magnes, however, the issue rested on a moral imperative: if the Jeremiah path (as he understood it) was not followed, then there was no reason to continue the Zionist enterprise in Palestine. Returning to his 1929 letter to Weizmann:

> The question is, do we want to conquer Palestine now as Joshua did in his day—with fire and sword? Or do we want to take cognizance of Jewish religious development since Joshua—our Prophets, Psalmists and Rabbis, and repeat the words: "Not by might, and not by violence, but by my spirit, saith the Lord." The question is, can any country be entered, colonized, and built up pacifistically, and can we Jews do that in the Holy Land? If we can not (and I do not say that we can rise to these heights), I for my part have lost half my interest in the enterprise. If we can not even attempt this, I should much rather see this eternal people without such a "National Home," with the wanderer's staff in hand and forming new ghettos among the peoples of the world.[28]

Thus, as Magnes saw it, the world had evolved religiously and morally since the time of Joshua, and this transition included—first and foremost and in keeping with the Reform Jewish worldview—the element of prophecy. The very essence of politics, according to Magnes, lay in the effort to realize the prophetic imperative, and this imperative, or at least the effort to actualize it, was for him absolute by nature. National self-actualization that did not entail realization of the moral imperative was null and void, and like his mentor Ahad Ha'am, Magnes preferred to forgo it altogether.

The Reform concept of the Diaspora as destiny surfaced again in the aforementioned November 24, 1929, editorial in the *New York Times*. Magnes wrote: "The Joshua method is not the way for us of entering the Promised Land. The retention of bayonets in the land against the will of the majority of the population is repugnant to men of good will, and the Eternal People should rather continue its long wait than attempt to establish a Home in the Holy Land, except on terms of understanding and peace."[29]

The fact that Magnes examined a political position contrary to his own using theopolitical concepts deserves explication. Although the association of political Zionism with the book of Joshua was not unique to Magnes,[30] the conceptualization of political Zionism—Zionism that relies on force to achieve its aim—as the "Joshua method" points to his theopolitical frame of reference, in which mythical biblical figures provide a foundation for concrete political action. Here Magnes was to some extent following in the path of Ahad Ha'am, who viewed the concept of a spiritual center as an opportunity to create a small, politically insignificant state that would be able to exist without having to worry about superpower rivalries.

In a 1923 lecture delivered in Jerusalem, Magnes voiced concern over the replacement of Jewish culture in the prophetic spirit of Isaiah with the culture of "Brit HaBiryonim" (the "Covenant of Thugs"—a clandestine faction of the Revisionist Zionist movement).[31] Once again he was compelled to address a political theology that clashed with his own and drew on other sources: "Will the Jews here in their efforts to create a political organism become devotees of brute force and militarism as were some of the later Hasmoneans, and will they, like the Edomite Herod, become the obedient servants of economic and militaristic imperialism? Is it among the possibilities that some day it may become political treason for someone sincerely to repeat in the streets of Jerusalem Isaiah's teaching that swords are to be beaten into ploughshares and men are to learn war no more?"[32]

Here Magnes aligned himself with Isaiah rather than Jeremiah, Isaiah representing a more optimistic and constructive conception of prophecy compared with Jeremiah's prophecies of destruction. He penned these remarks shortly after immigrating to Palestine, and perhaps he initially hoped for more positive relations with the ruling authorities, the Yishuv leadership and the Jewish Agency, who held a constructive vision suggesting eventual cooperation with the Arabs of Palestine for economic or other practical reasons. Yet, as historian Joseph Heller points out: "The model of the Prophet Isaiah, who apparently conducts a successful dialogue with the king of Israel, did not work out [for Magnes], and the model [Magnes] adopted instead was that of the Prophet Jeremiah, who, unable to establish a successful dialogue, was in confrontation with the authorities of the time."[33]

Theological Politics

In short, Magnes's religiosity played a major part in compelling him toward political action. His theological politics offered a specific political solution—binationalism—conceived on the basis of his religious worldview. His efforts to resolve the tension between the religious-moral dimension and American pragmatism accorded with Buber's conception of theopolitics, which entailed "adopting a concrete and 'messianic' policy simultaneously."[34]

Notably, theopolitical concepts also infused the seemingly secular discourse of the Yishuv's main institutions and leaders. Historian David Ohana, for example, argues that Ben-Gurion's messianic outlook was a secular political theology aimed at reformulating the purpose of the Israeli concept of *mamlakhtiyut* (literally, "statehood," or sovereignty, and often referred to as "statism"),[35] which in turn was built on reconceptualizing the Israeli notion of statehood built on Zionist ideology. Ben-Gurion, the argument follows, maintained a theopolitical worldview that regarded redemption as a historical process that takes place in stages, not as the end of history.[36] Israeli historian Anita Shapira holds that even though the labor movement in Palestine inherited two antireligious traditions—the Haskalah (Jewish Enlightenment) and socialism—for the movement's members, rejection of religious authority did not entail severing themselves from Jewish culture, despite its fundamentally religious nature.[37]

The friendship of Magnes and Buber had evolved during a decade of persistent efforts by Magnes, beginning in 1929 and coming to fruition with Buber's 1938 appointment as a professor of the "Philosophy of Society" at the Hebrew University of Jerusalem, and during their joint political activity on behalf of Ichud in the early 1940s (see chapter 14). Albeit articulated differently because of their differing views on morality, nationalism, and political organization, Magnes and Buber shared in common a prophetic orientation for the Jewish politics of Palestine.

For Magnes, having Buber as a ally appears to have added intellectual authority to his more passionate and sometimes crude form of prophetic politics, inspired by his more personal sense of prophetic identification. In the years that followed his 1929 endorsement of the moralistic Jeremiah model at the expense of the overly nationalistic "Joshua method," Magnes was to struggle with the difficulties of realizing prophetic politics in Palestine.

As for Buber, in a 1947 article for an issue of Ichud's publication *Be'ayot* dedicated to Magnes, he wrote that Magnes and Ichud "have made it possible for me to work politically once more within the context and in the name of a political group without sacrificing truth. . . . I feel that in this we are brothers."[38] Thus it was thanks to Magnes that Buber's Zionist political activity came full circle.

11

Faith and Skepticism in the Binational Cause

After publishing *Like All the Nations?*, Magnes made his first attempts to become involved in the political life of the Yishuv. What transpired was a foreshadowing of things to come—both with his own mode of operation and the Yishuv leadership's opposition to his efforts.

Early Forays

On October 27, 1929, the *New York Times* correspondent in Jerusalem, Joseph Levy, showed Magnes the details of a plan for Jewish-Arab rapprochement drafted by John Philby, a former official of the British governorate in Transjordan, scheduled to be published in the newspaper. Granting political self-representation of "all elements" in Palestine on the basis of their numbers, the Philby plan called upon the Jewish population to relinquish its "dream" of "political domination."[1] Magnes was not immediately impressed with the plan on account of Philby's endorsement of Arab nationalism, but he sympathized with the motive behind the plan and perceived it as an opening for possible Jewish-Arab cooperation.

Magnes met with the Zionist leadership on November 4 and 5, 1929, to discuss the plan's possibilities, but Yishuv leaders were uninterested in pursuing it further. Some objected to Magnes's own concessionism in the wake of the Arab riots. Eventually, however, Ben-Gurion, fearing the British would institute a legislative council that would favor the Arabs, did offer a suggestion of his own: two separate national cantons that would join together under a federal government and the high commissioner.[2]

Magnes decided to proceed by himself. In the November 24, 1929, edition of the *New York Times*, responding to the reportage of the Philby plan published in that same edition, Magnes endorsed the suggested plan with one major revision of his own: that it "grants also what has heretofore been resolutely contested, that 'freedom of immigration, subject to the capacity of the country to absorb immigrants might be stipulated as a condition precedent to the establishment of such a [Arab-Jewish] government.'" Notably, the Philby plan had stipulated that the Jewish community remain a permanent minority in Palestine (a proviso evidently formulated by the Supreme Muslim Council, the highest Muslim authority in Mandatory Palestine, headed by the mufti).[3] Magnes's efforts infuriated Weizmann, who argued, with intended irony, that the Arabs would now believe that negotiations were to be conducted with figures such as Magnes, rather than "extremists" such as Jabotinsky or Weizmann himself.[4]

Ben-Gurion, however, considered Magnes's influence among non-Zionist circles in the United States. A potential rift between the Palestine and American groups might splinter the unifying role of the Jewish Agency and jeopardize American philanthropic support to the Yishuv. Meanwhile, the Jewish Agency was grappling with how to respond to the 1929 riots. And so, Ben-Gurion offered a more calculated response. His June 29, 1930, cable to Jewish Agency members in London warned: "Given the debate that is taking place in the Political Committee, you are aware of the differences of opinion between the 'Americans' and the Administration on the Arab question. This dispute could turn into a serious conflict. [The Jewish-American philanthropist Felix] Warburg wrote to Weizmann that he was thinking of withdrawing because he disagreed with [Weizmann's] politics on Arab issues. It is clear that Magnes has had an influence on him." Later Ben-Gurion proposed that Labor Zionism leader Berl Katznelson meet with Magnes frequently in order "to prevent him from taking destructive measures." He added that Weizmann had "acted unwisely in fiercely attacking M. [Magnes] in the Political Committee. I had commented to him, before he spoke, about the loss that would result from incitement against M., and Weitzmann agreed with me, and opened his remarks with the desired tone. But as his words flowed, he grew angry and made some harsh accusations that could create division between us and the American group."[5]

In the United States, Jewish leaders' reactions to Magnes's activities were mixed, but in light of the confusion American Jews were feeling after the violent Arab riots of 1929, which shattered their hopes of a peaceful endgame to the Zionist project in Palestine, those who objected to Magnes's activities had the upper hand. The "Brandeis Group," originally formed around the leadership of Justice Louis Brandeis, regarded Magnes's action as "irresponsible" to say the least: He was presuming to negotiate permanent concessions in Palestine on behalf of all the Jews when the Brandeis Group endorsed the longer waiting game of Jewish politics in Palestine, determined to build Yishuv infrastructure and wait out the crisis. Particularly fierce criticism came from Stephen Wise, who, in a letter to American Zionist leader Richard Gottheil stated, "The kindest construction to put upon it is that [he] was mad. Among the other possible constructions ... is ... that he was treasonable." The Zionist Organization of America (ZOA) issued an official announcement describing Magnes as a "pacifist in panic" and asserting that his efforts were horribly timed (in light of the violent assault on the Yishuv), demonstrated disrespect, lacked judgment, and posed a danger to the future of Jewish settlement in Palestine. American Zionist leader Louis Lipsky defended Magnes's freedom of speech but derided his diplomatic efforts as childish and misguided.

On the other hand, Magnes enjoyed support from Warburg, a leader of the non-Zionist camp in the Jewish Agency, as well as the backing of Hadassah, an organization traditionally favoring Jewish-Arab cooperation in Palestine. Irma Lindheim, ZOA vice president and Hadassah president, argued that the Brandeis Group's response revealed "anti-Arab" and "Revisionist" views, and although she approached Brandeis directly to discuss the issue, he refused to meet with her.[6]

Strong reactions to Magnes's attempted negotiation continued, both in Palestine and elsewhere. Young Revisionists, who endorsed Jabotinsky's "Iron Wall," stating that the Arabs in Palestine would not agree to a Jewish majority and the Yishuv needed to push forward with settlement regardless, disrupted Magnes's March 23, 1931, speech in New York, tossing stink bombs into the auditorium and brawling with more liberal audience members. In February 1932 a group of young nationalists led by Revisionist leader Abba Ahimeir stormed the Hebrew University during an inauguration ceremony for an International Peace Studies research chairmanship, bringing the ceremony to a halt with their charges that the university should instead establish a chairmanship for Security Studies. Magnes, then chancellor of the university, was forced to summon the police, and the demonstrators were arrested.[7]

From the Failure of Brit Shalom to the Image of Jeremiah

In early 1930 Brit Shalom issued its first action plan following the 1929 riots. There are discernible similarities between this proposal—to which Magnes, as a nonmember, was not a signatory—and Magnes's own position as articulated in *Like All the Nations?* Magnes would have undoubtedly welcomed the association's declaration that Palestine "need not be a Jewish state or an Arab state, but rather a binational state in which the Jewish and Arab residents have equal civil, political, and social rights." He would also almost certainly have supported many of the proposal's practical provisions, such as the equal inclusion of Jews and Arabs across the various ranks of governing institutions. At the same time, for Magnes the problem was fundamentally political; he ascribed only secondary importance to other tenets in the proposal addressing economic issues (raising the prosperity level of Arab farmers and workers by directing Jewish economic activity to the whole of the country) and education (development of two independent school systems, with each group studying the language, culture, and history of the other).[8] And whereas the Brit Shalom proposal stressed the egalitarian nature of binationalism and that the load should be equally shouldered on both sides, Magnes assigned greater responsibility for building trust and goodwill between the sides to the Jews, whom, he believed, were experienced in "the ways of the world."

During a Brit Shalom meeting in January 1932, Magnes reiterated his commitment to binationalism, basing his argument on his own as well as his rivals' analyses of religious factors. He admitted that it was not possible to remove the messianic elements from the Jewish soul, but he rejected the integration of religious messianism into politics. He reasserted his claim that Palestine should be both Jewish and Arab, in light of the presence of two peoples with rights and ultimately because the land was sacred to three religions.

In the early 1930s Magnes discovered the extent of political and practical obstacles he would have to confront in promoting binationalism. He was failing in his efforts to persuade both the Jewish Yishuv leadership and Arab leaders in Palestine to move forward with his plans. An August 1931 meeting with Haim Arlozorov, head of the Jewish Agency's Political Department, for example, left him "deeply disappointed." Although Arlozorov acknowledged the existence of Arab nationalism, he did not, in Magnes's words, see "the Arab problem as *the* problem"—and, in fact, insisted that the Jews had an opportunity to become the majority in Palestine. Magnes was similarly disheartened by his meetings with Arab leaders. He had pinned great hopes on Assistant Attorney General of Palestine Musa Alami, and even tried (unsuccessfully) to secure Alami's appointment to the Board of Directors of the Palestine

Faith, Skepticism in the Binational Cause

Economic Corporation, a company established by non-Zionist American Jews for investment in Palestine. In the summer of 1931 Alami arranged for Magnes to meet in Geneva with Shakib Arslan and Ihsan al-Jibri, close associates of Mufti Amin al-Husseini, the most prominent Muslim leader in Palestine. During the meeting, the two demanded concessions from the Zionist leadership, such as a cessation of immigration and land purchases, yet demonstrated no willingness to accept any constitutional arrangements for the Yishuv that would protect the rights of both national groups.

Magnes came away from these encounters with the sense that perhaps Weizmann had been correct in claiming that direct negotiations with the Arabs were destined to fail. He decided to try a different approach: promoting his ideas through British Mandatory authorities. In an August 1931 meeting with High Commissioner Sir John Chancellor, Magnes posed the argument that the "key to a possible understanding between Jew and Arab lay in the field of constitutional development," but the high commissioner demonstrated little interest in this proposal. His appeal to the British high commissioner speaks to Magnes's growing sense of despair after trying to advance binationalism with the peoples who would be most affected by it.[9]

Brit Shalom's failure to promote binationalism in the Yishuv and its subsequent dissolution in 1933, effectively annulling the binational option, as well as Magnes's own inability to effectuate any change whatsoever in Yishuv policy during the early 1930s, fed Magnes's growing doubts. No longer certain his binationalism plan was feasible, he increasingly identified with the prophet Jeremiah, the political prophet who had ultimately failed to convince the kingdom of Judah to mend its ways, was jailed, and then banished to a land of ruin.

This affinity was evident in his October 26, 1931, remarks on the occasion of the opening of the Hebrew University academic year. His speech was marked by references to the prophet. It is impossible not to be moved by Jeremiah's story, Magnes avowed. He characterized the prophet as an "enlightened figure." He found it thrilling that Jeremiah had been born in nearby Anathoth, adjacent to Mount Scopus, site of the Hebrew University, which he "exalted" as the mountain of both Jeremiah and Moses, prophets who had suffered the pain of their people, and hence "the people who had been resurrected should be full of knowledge, as water fills the sea, full of faith as the prophets." Among his audience was Arlozorov, who recognized the religious sources of Magnes's thinking and subsequently observed that it had been a "unique combination of kindhearted humanity, lofty ideas, and Reform Judaism."[10]

The Years of Arab Uprising and Marginalization of Binationalism

In the years preceding the Arab uprising of 1936–39, Magnes changed the nature of his political activity, as illustrated most markedly by his joining efforts with Ben-Gurion. Ben-Gurion had reached out to him for assistance in 1934 after Ben-Gurion's meeting with Arab nationalist and politician Musa Alami earlier that year had left him uncertain as to the latter's position. Later that year, Magnes arranged for Ben-Gurion to meet Awni Abd al-Hadi, and in 1936 he orchestrated a meeting of Ben-Gurion and Moshe Shertok (later, Sharett), head of the Jewish Agency Political Department, with Alami and Christian diplomat and Arab nationalist George Antonius.[11]

Ultimately, however, these meetings did not bear any real fruit. The extent of Ben-Gurion's openness to negotiations with Arab leaders was almost certainly based on tactical internal politics rather than on strategic interest in seeking common ground. Presumably he believed he could use Magnes to serve his own maximalist policy. In his memoirs he wrote that Magnes "could be useful—when he was of assistance to me ... but I would never leave negotiations to him, because on his own he would cause damage, and I told him so more than once, completely in friendship, without making him angry. I intentionally kept him close to me at all times so that he would not act on his own." Eventually, in early 1937, Ben-Gurion effectively severed his ties with Magnes, not because of his negotiating skills but because of his overall philosophy, which in Ben-Gurion's view would pave the way to "assimilation and adaptation to Arab life."[12]

During these years Magnes was involved in two additional initiatives to promote Jewish-Arab constitutional arrangements. In the autumn of 1937, he learned that senior Arab leaders—through the mediation of Albert Hyamson, a former British official in Palestine, and Colonel Stewart Newcombe, a founder of the Arab Information Office in London—had apparently endorsed a set of proposals for Arab-Jewish relations in Palestine. The plan called for an independent Palestinian state following a transition period wherein Jews and Arabs participated more in the administration of the British Mandatory government. Every citizen would have "equal and complete political and civil rights," and both national groups would have "autonomy" over "communal matters." Additionally, the Jewish population in Palestine would be limited to less than 50 percent of the total population for the limited term of the agreement. Magnes made an effort to promote the Hyamson-Newcombe plan among the Zionist leadership as well as the British—a process that once again, as with Philby nearly a decade earlier, exposed how vulnerable he was to deception and misdirection in negotiations. Ben-Gurion and Sharett were skeptical that senior Arab leaders had approved the plan, suspecting that in fact the entire initiative was an effort to undermine the Partition Plan—in other words, any publicity surrounding Zionist interest in alternative plans would jeopardize partition. In the complex political maneuvering that followed, the Zionist leadership endorsed Magnes's role in promoting the program but insisted that the option to eventually create a Jewish state should be left open. Eventually it turned out that the Arab leadership had never approved of the plan in the first place, and the suggestion was scrapped.[13]

A few months later, in early 1938, Magnes joined noted farmer and writer Moshe Smilansky, industrialist Pinhas Rutenberg, engineer and businessman Moshe Novomeysky, and Palestine Supreme Court judge Gad Frumkin in founding Kvutzat HaHamisha (the Committee of Five). The group continued the previous practice of promoting a Jewish-Arab agreement without the official involvement or endorsement of the Zionist leadership, yet with a willingness to make what were considered far-reaching concessions in the areas of immigration and land acquisition. Jewish immigration would be limited to 30,000 per year, based on a demographic projection that, at the end of a ten-year period, with immigration included, Arabs would make up 60 percent of the population and Jews the remaining 40 percent. Furthermore, Jews would commit to purchasing no more than 75 percent of the land of each Arab farmer and to providing funds and technical assistance to develop the land retained by the Arab farmer. However, like earlier, similar initiatives, there was no sufficient political clout on either side and the suggestion faded away.[14]

A few years earlier, in the mid-1930s, Magnes had stopped speaking explicitly about binationalism,[15] which might lead one to question the strength of his commitment to it as a solution. More likely, I think, Magnes's silence on the issue was tactical. His previous attempts to promote binationalism on his own had ended in failure. Subsequently, following the publication of his political vision of binationalism in 1930, he happened upon what he saw as an opportunity, through Ben-Gurion, to promote cooperation between the Yishuv leadership and Arab leaders. Under these circumstances, and in light of the implied as well as explicit criticism voiced against him—that his declared support for binationalism was undermining potential negotiations—Magnes agreed to tone down his statements and make way for official negotiations. But by 1936—once it became apparent, especially in light of the Arab uprising and its repercussions, that this opportunity would not yield results—Magnes returned to his previous position, that of the prophet who stands up to the ruling establishment, and reasserted his full support for binationalism.

His engagement in political activity reinforced his desire for a frame of reference that could address the religious needs of the hour. In 1936 he led an initiative to found Mehapsei Adonai (Seekers of God), an association dedicated to religious pacifism. Magnes expected the association's members to accept the position that there was no such thing as a just war, and that human salvation could be achieved without war, even if it required sacrificing the people's political liberty for the sake of God.[16] The religious association did not materialize, but this perspective illustrates how his call for binationalism was driven in large part by his longing to prevent war at any cost—even by sacrificing the political liberty and self-realization of the Jewish Yishuv in Palestine.

Zionism as False Messianism, and the Reassertion of Binationalism

Magnes's speech before the Jewish Agency Executive Committee in August 1937 marked the end of his cooperation with the Yishuv leadership under Ben-Gurion and revealed the depth of his political isolation. His speech was disrupted by bursts of laughter from the audience, most of whom were delegates of the Twentieth Zionist Congress, and a direct interruption by Ben-Gurion himself, interjecting to ask Magnes whether he had come to Palestine with Arab consent.

At the same time, this isolation enabled him to raise binationalism yet again, on his own terms, as a matter for discussion. Magnes was opposed to the Partition Plan, which suggested separate political entities in Palestine, because, he argued, it would inevitably lead to war with the Arabs. He called upon those assembled to support a binational state as well as Palestinian emigration from Palestine to Transjordan and other Arab countries. But even his partner in the recent past (and in the near future) Moshe Smilansky countered that he was placing the cart before the horse: Binationalism needed to develop gradually rather than be imposed by political agreement from above.[17]

In addressing the Council of the Jewish Agency that met in Zurich in August 1937 during the twentieth Zionist Congress, Magnes provided another window into how his religious conception of Zionism had changed in conjunction with the Yishuv's development and political Zionism's consolidation:

> We know what happened when Sabbatai Zevi called upon the Jewish communities of the world to pack their belongings and be prepared to proceed to the Promised Land. When the call of the false Messiah proved to be a delusion, we all know of the catastrophe that followed. What I fear is that these tens and hundreds of thousands of our brothers and sisters who are in the lands of oppression and who have heard this message from here have believed that in the course of a short time the Jewish State will open its arms, as Rachel opened her arms to her returning children, and they will find that there is room but for few and not for many.[18]

Magnes believed that Zionism without a solution based on mutual Jewish-Arab understanding was analogous to trying to address the political dimension without the religious and moral dimensions, which in his view amounted to false messianism. He was not alone in this regard: Natan Hofshi, likewise a member of Brit Shalom and later of Ichud, also argued that false messianism was the root of the problem: "[medieval false messiah, David] Alroie, Shabtai Zvi, false prophets of all sorts ... are we not approaching such a situation?"[19]

Magnes's reference to Shabtai Zvi reflects theological aspects of his own frame of thought. At the same time, his administrative post at the university exposed him to academic discourse in Jewish history and thought that resonated with his own theopolitical thinking and statements. In 1937 Gershom Scholem published his seminal article "Mitzva HaBa'a BeAvira" (Redemption through sin), which legitimized and to some extent vindicated the otherwise heretical Sabbatean movement. The public uproar that followed, within as well as beyond the university, caused Magnes to start thinking about the Zionist movement in Sabbatean terms—that is, as false messianism.

Also noteworthy in this context was the vast gulf between Reform Jewish thought—which focused on personal, communal, and political morality—and an antinomistic, anarchist moral outlook such as that of the Sabbatean movement, which regarded violations of moral law as opportunities to draw closer to God's presence and the messianic state. In Nietzschean terms this state was considered sited "beyond the good and evil" of simple morality; in Kabbalistic terms it was situated in the *Torah DeAtzilut* (Torah of Emanation), which lay beyond the *Torah DeBriyah* (Torah of Creation) Moses gave to Israel.[20]

HaOl and the Theology of the Quest

The story of the founding of the association HaOl (the Yoke) sheds light on the connections between Magnes's religious position and his political activism. The establishment of HaOl by Magnes in 1939 represented a continuation of his efforts to address the theological questions that weighed on him, expanding the discussion to include potential colleagues. His first attempt to form an intellectual association of a religious nature had been in New York in the 1920s: He'd tried but failed to establish a group to explore matters of the "soul." Three more failed attempts to establish associations of a religious nature in Palestine preceded his founding of HaOl. These groups were Kehillah Shel Mosar Dati Ivri (The Community for Religious Hebrew Morality, 1932), the aforementioned Mehapsei Adonai (Seekers of God, 1936), and Mevakshei Paneikha (Seekers for Thy Presence, January 1939).[21]

HaOl's members included Martin Buber, Hugo Bergman, historian Yitzhak Baer, German Jewish educator and religious philosopher Ernst Simon, and Gershom Scholem. The association's name came from the phrase "the yoke of the Kingdom of Heaven," and its uniting principle was formulated as a rhetorical question: "Are we the Jews merely a persecuted people seeking mercy, or do we have a message that we wish to deliver or realize? Are we aware of the yoke that our Father placed on us?"[22] A year before the association's founding, Magnes wrote a journal entry stressing the tragic aspect of the yoke, asserting that it was incumbent upon him to believe in the God of Israel, even if he cursed Him because of the yoke He had placed on the Jews.[23]

The association discussed abstract theological issues, such as messianic politics, and its political activity consisted mainly of writing two open letters to Mahatma Gandhi, which Magnes and Buber published jointly in response to Gandhi's criticism of Zionism and claim that German Jewry could apply nonviolent civil resistance. Both men were outraged that the Indian leader could suggest that Jews should resort to passive resistance to the Nazis. Magnes rhetorically asked Gandhi for practical advice for German Jews: "How can Jews in Germany offer civil resistance? The slightest sign of resistance means killing or concentration camps."[24]

The differences between Magnes's and Buber's positions vis-à-vis the Zionist enterprise come to light if we examine certain developments that much preceded the establishment of HaOl. In January 1929 Magnes enlisted the support of Bergman and Hans Kohn, former members of the Prague circle who saw themselves as Buber's disciples, to found a religious association that would confront the interlocking social, political, and religious problems facing the Jewish people, most specifically in Palestine. They in turn sent their mentor Buber a fifty-page draft plan, authored by Magnes, for the establishment of a religious-political association—what would become HaOl. In the draft Magnes described his aspiration for peace with the Arabs as something that, rather than stemming from tactical considerations of realpolitik, had emerged from a worldview regarding the meaning and purpose of life.[25] Buber's response illustrates the gaps between his and Magnes's views, thus arguably revealing what is unique in Magnes's position relative to the Central European circle of Brit Shalom.

First, in terms of similarities between their positions, the third point in Magnes's draft was, according to Buber, "most accurate." Magnes had written: "[Members of the Association] are social radicals in the sense that they want to realize here and now the social ideals of law and righteousness that the prophets of Israel advocated. They see very little connection between the current structure of society and these ideals, and therefore, they strive, each in his own way, to align their fate with that of the "masses," or "workers," the fate of downtrodden and oppressed people."[26]

It is easy to understand why this sentence spoke to Buber, as it is in line with the theology of religious socialism that emerged in twentieth-century Europe and of which Buber was a prominent advocate. As previously observed, Magnes's socialism was closer in spirit to Hermann Cohen's ethical socialism and to the Social Gospel movement than to a radical socialism that sought to overturn the existing social order.

Although Magnes and Buber shared an affinity for prophetic teachings, there were discernible differences in their conceptions of prophecy itself. Magnes's starting point, shaped by his Reform background, centered on the moral foundation of the prophets' actions in challenging the ruling authorities. For his part, Buber perceived the prophet as the charismatic leader of a model religious, organic, autonomous, and, to some extent, anarchist community.[27] As such, Buber's fundamental stance on political institutions was based on an anarchist outlook. By contrast, Magnes espoused radical positions but was not fundamentally an anarchist: "We did not know [Magnes] as a revolutionary," Scholem later wrote, "and I doubt that he was ever a revolutionary, but we knew him as a radical, and this is rare in our day, as revolutions are in danger of losing their call for freedom."[28] His American pragmatism and drive to engage with the political imperatives of the hour prevented him from adopting a fully anarchist outlook.[29]

The introduction to Magnes's proposed plan, when compared with the alternative proposed by Buber, illustrates the essentially religious nature of Magnes's worldview and the gap between his outlook and that of Buber and other association members. Here, Magnes:

[Members of the Association] are united in their search for the intellectual basis of faith and in their efforts to live according to the mandate of the "God within" each one of us. This does not necessarily mean declaring faith in a Supreme Being. What we refer to is an obligation as regards religious issues and an honest, vital quest for the answers to these questions. Social values such as family, nation, people, state, religious community, and status are in their eyes of secondary importance relative to that which is absolute, to the absolute ethical or metaphysical values that must serve as the true determining and guiding forces in life.[30]

Buber offered a different formulation:

[The members of the Association] are united in the conviction that faith, not any particular faith but the believing sensibility or attitude, is the genuine ground of human life. By the believing attitude they mean that man strives to obtain an immediate relation to the truth of existence not merely through intellect or feeling, but through his entire being. Such a sensibility can not only be constituted by the inwardness of one's soul: it must manifest itself in the entire fullness of personal and communal life, in which the individual participates.[31]

Two points in relation to the association's theological foundation stand out, and they shed a great deal of light on Magnes's outlook. The first is the individualistic conception of the Divine, as expressed in his reference to the God within each one of us. This formulation, consistent with his concept of a personal God, recalled William James's approach and reflected facets of American individualism.[32] Apparently this view did not sit well with Buber, who underscored that the religious sensitivity to which he alluded must express itself not only inwardly, within oneself, but also through the entire experience of being and thus through communal life as well.[33] Here one sees Magnes's individualistic American worldview, as opposed to the more collective—and in this sense more European—outlook presented by Buber.

The second and arguably more significant point refers to what may be termed the "theology of quest," which Magnes viewed as the pinnacle of religious endeavor. Magnes replaced the commonplace basis of faith—namely, "the assertion of a belief in a supreme being"—with a "living and honest quest" for the answer to the question of God's existence and presence in the world.

The concept of a quest had surfaced even earlier in Magnes's life. In his plan for the association Mevakshei Paneicha, Magnes stipulated that it would comprise people who seek to know God, most of whom "have not found the path . . . and who knows if they ever will find it. Nonetheless, the deepest and most burning aspiration in their life is the search for this path."[34] This sense of a quest was also embodied in the association's name, Mevakshei Paneicha (Seekers of Your Presence), and in Magnes's use of a similar phrase, Mevakshei Adonai, in his journal entry of Rosh Hashanah 1923: "And if we were to get our just social order, and its abolition of poverty (which is a far way off), we would still be *m'vakshe adonai* [seekers after God]; we would still be in need of conquering human suffering and death; we would still be in need of approaching closer and closer to the sources of creation, of creative power."[35] The concept of religious search additionally appeared in Magnes's journal entry exploring Karl Barth's philosophy of the perpetual yet fruitless quest after God (see chapter 7)—Magnes concluding from Barth's thinking that the search itself embodied the glory of human activity on earth. In both instances Magnes presented the very quest for God as the sacred mission assigned to humanity, even when it did not necessarily lead to awareness of the Divine.[36]

Buber, by contrast, had a very different view of faith. Even after the Holocaust, Buber was capable of conceptualizing faith as existing by virtue of the dualistic nature of the I-Thou relationship with the eternal "Thou"—a relationship whose realization stemmed from the validity of the faith in it.[37] In other words, for Buber (and for HaOl leader Bergman, too), faith did not necessarily entail suffering.

And so it was that HaOl, too, was short-lived, and did not see out the end of the year. Its intellectual concerns were superseded by the urgent political issues facing the Jewish people at the start of World War II, and HaOl's celebration of pacifism was rendered irrelevant. At the end of the day, HaOl did not provide the answers Magnes was seeking to his religious and political deliberations.[38] His commitment to political action was stronger than that of his friends and associates, and the engagement in theoretical and theological issues that characterized HaOl's activities—especially the problem of political anarchism, which did not correlate comfortably with Magnes's American pragmatism— was a source of great vexation for him. On the spectrum between theory and action, Magnes was closer than his associates to the activist end of the spectrum—and, of course, he would play this role again, driving to establish the organization Ichud following the release of the Biltmore Program in May 1942.

PART 3

"The Eclipse of God"

War, Holocaust, and the Founding of the State

12

Existential Theology and Moral Politics

The final decade of Magnes's life was characterized by two salient trends. First was his increased engagement with religious challenges in the face of World War II and the Holocaust of European Jewry. He delved ever deeper into theological questions: the eclipse of God, God's possible existence, how one might see the hand of God in the workings of the world—and consequently what action was required of humankind.

The second trend involved the gradual consolidation of his critique of political nationalism, to the point of rejecting nationalism altogether. That rejection, in turn, led to a singular effort to define Jewish nationalism in nonpolitical—that is, religious—terms. Further, it reinforced his promotion of an alternative solution: a binational confederation based on the American political model.

The 1940s saw Magnes being steadily excluded from the Yishuv's political discourse. Calls for the establishment of a national Jewish state were increasing amid overall disillusionment with the possibility of a solution rooted in cooperation with the Arabs. Magnes's declining political status, the erosion of his base of support among American Jews, and mounting financial as well as other support for the Yishuv among U.S. Zionists minimized any concerns Yishuv leaders might have had about possibly sabotaging relations with Magnes' close contacts: non-Zionist American philanthropists who rejected political Zionism but found the binational cause appealing.[1] In a January 8, 1943, letter to British Zionist Blanche Dugdale, Chaim Weizmann wrote, "People here are always frightened that if Magnes is thrown out of the University the financial support will not be forthcoming. This is a mistake."[2]

Magnes's political activism during this decade centered on Ichud, which he had cofounded with Martin Buber in 1942 in response to the Biltmore Declaration's call for the establishment of a Jewish commonwealth in Palestine. Through Ichud, Magnes collaborated with various former members of Brit Shalom, including most notably Buber, who had headed the Brit Shalom branch in Germany. Their most visible cooperative political undertaking was their joint testimony advocating a binational solution for Palestine before the Anglo-American Committee in 1946.

As Magnes's religious doubts steadily increased through the 1940s, he retreated from the moral vision of pacifism—and saw that very retreat as a religious conversion of sorts. His activism during the 1930s had been characterized, at least intermittently, by a proactive sense of prophecy through which he called for morally driven change and believed in the possibility of change. Conversely, his growing religious doubts, in combination with his political exclusion from channels of influence in the Yishuv, reflected a transition to a tragic model of activism, characterized by a sense of operating "against all odds." So it was that he met with U.S. president Truman in May 1948, on the eve of Israel's Declaration of Independence, in a last-ditch effort to prevent the founding of the state (see chapter 14).[3]

Abandonment of Pacifism

The Jewish philosopher and educator Ernst Simon, a contemporary of Magnes, identified three major "crises" that characterized Magnes's life: the transition from Reform to Conservative Judaism; the need to overcome the tension between "unity" and "separation" in Zionism (that is, the tension between universalism and particularism); and the relinquishment of pacifism, which he himself viewed as a religious conversion.[4] On October 29, 1939, in a speech marking the start of the Hebrew University's academic year—Magnes's main platform for speaking out on public issues in those years—Magnes stated:

> I shall say something which it is hard to say. When I support this war, as unhappily I do, I know that thus I am in conscious rebellion against the divine command, "Thou shalt not kill." I have not the steadfastness, as once I thought I had, to fulfill this divine command under any and all circumstances. It is a terrible thing to realise that what one thought was part of one's religion is subject to change because of what a single man can do. Citizenship can be changed, the place of a man's home, his friends, his interests, his social and political ideals. But when a man speaks of his religion, he speaks of his God, of that Absolute which gives life substance and meaning. It is for our sins that we are thus punished. God has hidden His face from us. We must now bend the knee and beg forgiveness.[5]

Magnes felt that he had been driven to renounce pacifism, thereby defying God's word. Unwittingly or not, he was invoking the spiritually Christian call to "bend the knee and beg forgiveness."

Christian theology had left an impact on Magnes's thinking, even if he was unaware of it. According to Magnes biographer Norman Bentwich, "The moral of the Gospels was the moral of the Hebrew prophets. In original Christianity, as in Judaism, the aim was the Kingdom of Heaven on earth." Indeed, Bentwich proclaims that Magnes's critics found his political concepts too Christian, whereas Christians regarded him as "a true Christian in spirit." Yet Magnes was conscious of the differences and refused to accept the Christian concept of redemption as part of the world to come: "The religious genius of [the Jews'] race and tradition cannot recognize as real a religion about another world."[6]

Existential Theology and Moral Politics

At the heart of the Hebrew University speech excerpt is Magnes's view that his own abandonment of pacifism was a direct consequence of God's face being hidden from him. His loss of religious pacifism was interwoven with the ongoing eclipse of God as he experienced it. In the next section I examine the concealment of God's face in Magnes's thinking and consider the political implications that followed from it.

The Eclipse of God

One of the dominant themes in Magnes's religious world was his experience of the concealment of God's face. His religious worldview was a historical one, in that he sought signs of God's work as it had manifested in the annals of human history. The problem of *evil*, however, gave him no rest. For Magnes, according to Bentwich, "The supreme religious problem that baffled him to the end of his days was how to reconcile the existence of the one God making for righteousness with all the gigantic, intolerable evil in the world." He cites a psalm of sorts found among Magnes's testamentary papers, which he describes as "an agonized call to the Deity": "How can you hide your face from me? How ignorant of you I am. How I doubt you, yet how I yearn to see your face. How grateful I would be for a sure sign of your presence. How I would like to open my mouth and heart to commune with you. But I dare not honestly. The mystery behind the veil. How humble I was. If one could but hear the voice."[7]

Magnes's impression of the concealment of God's face is also evident in a brief correspondence, on Hebrew University notepaper, with Gershom Scholem. (The two men's correspondence spanned years.) On October 24, 1941, for example, Magnes wrote to Scholem: "The problem remains: how much we, that is, you and I and our friends and this generation, can receive from the power and the substance of the Kabbalah in one form or another. Maybe my interest stems from a fundamental deficit of mine: the absence of any ability, and perhaps I should say right, to Kabbalistic or any other communication with the

Divine."⁸ He reiterated these sentiments in later notes to Scholem as well, and on January 15, 1947, wrote to the son of his late brother-in-law Louis Marshall, James Marshall:

> [American journalist] Louis Fischer, in his book, which I have just seen, talks about me in an altogether extravagant way. He says that "my constant companions are God and the common people." That indeed would be my great inspiration; but I must say that I have very little companionship, if any, with God. When I see people who believe that they are on some intimate terms with Him, I envy them and wonder if it is true. I find that He turned His face away from me many years ago. That has been for me probably the most fundamental problem of my life.⁹

Hugo Bergman also offered a thorough analysis of Magnes's conception of the eclipse of God. Bergman's article, "On the Eclipse of God and the Radiance of Divine Light," published in the 1947 issue of Ichud's journal, *Be'ayot* (Issues), dedicated to Magnes's seventieth birthday, opened with the following observations:

> Since the day the riots began in Israel, J. L. Magnes, as president of the university, has stood at his lectern annually, as the academic year opens, and spoken to the students, the instructors, the Yishuv, the world. And each year, as the riots have increased, so too these speeches have increasingly contained a tone of reproach toward the heavens. "Why do You eclipse Your face?" The words varied each year, becoming stronger, more urgent, and more demanding of a reply and a remedy, but the question remains in his heart and his language. Why? Why? I remember one year, toward the end of the war, when the feared riots had already become a certainty, how Magnes reiterated his eternal question, and the speaker's expression and voice told the audience more than the words themselves: this was a true act of rebellion toward the heavens. At that moment the speaker

seemed to resemble those heroes of Israel who had genuinely dared hold the Holy One Blessed Be He to account. "Why dost Thou hide Thy face?"[10]

Bergman proceeded to propose a theoretical approach to the concept of "the eclipse of God"—"this impenetrable issue that so preoccupies Magnes." Prefacing the discussion, he avowed: "I make the fundamental assumption that there is no eclipse of God on the part of the Holy One Blessed Be He."[11] Then he laid out his own theory: The eclipse of God actually occurs in the human realm. In his view, "When You hid Your face, I was terrified" (Ps. 30:8) can only have been "directed at us, at man," who was given "the authority and the possibility" to block "the channels through which Divine Lights flows." To him, what is demanded of humankind is the very opposite—"a reorientation of one hundred and eighty degrees"—redirecting one's gaze inward, away from the external world in which God is seemingly absent. "The great revolutionary instrument" for making this shift was prayer—not public prayer, but individual prayer. Drawing on Jewish philosopher Franz Rosenzweig, Bergman asserted that prayer itself, and the individual's ability to pray, are what revives the bond between the individual and God, and "God does not eclipse His face for the person who prays."[12]

Magnes's friend Bergman thereby presented prayer as the means to salvation from doubts about God's existence. Magnes would have known Bergman's thinking, and Magnes too allowed for the power of prayer to create a sense of closeness to God and release from doubt. In a Hasidic synagogue, he described "being caught up in the rhythm of worship and sometimes the dark and ancient beginnings of being seem to come nearer."[13] At the same time—and this is a recurring theme for Magnes—prayer was not enough. To reiterate Magnes: "How I would like to open my mouth and heart to commune with you. But I dare not honestly. The mystery behind the veil. How humble I was. If one could but hear the voice."[14]

Magnes did—clandestinely—pray with a devout Hasidic congregation in Jerusalem.[15] Yet this prayer, too, did not provide Magnes with a satisfactory answer to the question of doubt. After a visit to the Western Wall following the 1929 riots, he wrote in a journal entry:

> This is the one place for me where the sincerity of the worshipers seems beyond question.... It is the one place where sometimes I feel as though I were one with All Israel in its prayers and its devotions. But before a blank wall! So far and no further. The wall cannot be scaled. It is too high—pious men and women bore nails through the interstices. They put petition papers through the apertures. Perhaps God will read and hear. The shouts of the prayers are fervent, the body vibrates and sways at the [prayer] *Shema*, all fingers are on the eyes, and the [last word] *Ehad* is long-drawn. But the Lord God—is He behind these high walls? Is He anywhere? And if He is, does He hear? Can the walls be scaled, or is this boring of little holes as far as we can get? The pathetic pastime of pious women?[16]

As I see it, during the 1940s Magnes underwent a theological transition of an existential nature that culminated with a decision to "choose life" and leave the question of God's existence unanswered. The thoughts Magnes recorded at the Western Wall make it difficult to accept the hypothesis that he could undergo such a theological transition solely through the power of prayer, as Bergman proposed. Furthermore, the weakness of Bergman's argument lies in his starting point, that "there is no eclipse of God on the part of the Holy One Blessed Be He." Magnes was familiar with the view that apparent concealment of God's face was in fact evidence of the human inability to perceive the Divine's abundance—as his speech "For Thy Sake We Are Killed All Day Long" (below) demonstrates—and he rejected it. In many ways Magnes's interpretation is bolder and more unusual because, after the Holocaust, Jewish theology could no longer fully accept the fundamental assumption posited by Bergman, which dismissed any possibility that God was hiding the Divine face and instead placed sole responsibility on man's limited perception of Divine will. Post-Shoah, Jewish theology needed other alternatives.[17]

The "Tragic Man" as Political Theology

Magnes's struggle with "the eclipse of God"—which he described as possibly the most fundamental problem of his life—can also be seen as influencing his political outlook and activity.

Here, arguably, the French philosopher and sociologist of Jewish origin Lucien Goldmann's model of the "tragic man," found in his book *The Hidden God*, is applicable to Magnes.[18] What makes this model apt is its linkage of the theological concept of God being hidden with a paradigm of political action based on a purely moral foundation.

At the basis of the tragic worldview suggested by Goldmann is the sense that God has intentionally abandoned humankind, that "the primary characteristic of existence manifests in a negative theology, that is, in the impression that God has abandoned the world." This differs from atheism, because God still exists, but has left the world without guidance. Because of this impression, the individual reaches a state of despair that can only be overcome through a rebellion of sorts that involves trying to create a new world subject to absolutist moral guidelines in the sense of "all or nothing." This rebellion takes the form of trailblazing activity directed at changing history—and also involving self-sacrifice. At the same time, the rebellion is never completed. The individual remains in a perpetual state of struggle between being determined to act decisively and feeling committed to leading a moral life. This struggle is a source of tremendous torment because one can never be certain of the best path to one's aims, and examining the best course of action invariably entails agonizing deliberations.[19]

Historian Ofer Nordheimer Nur proposes the "tragic worldview" paradigm as a tool to examine the Socialist-Zionist and Marxist-oriented youth movement, kibbutz movement, and political party HaShomer

HaTza'ir, founded in Galicia in 1913. Magnes was never associated with the movement, but one might argue that the movement and Magnes shared a significant theological starting point—the sense of God's absence from the world. Although for HaShomer HaTza'ir members this impression was more acute and focused, with Nietzschean roots,[20] compared with Magnes's more ambivalent and agnostic perspective, over time Magnes's sense of God's absence intensified, in tandem with historical events—especially World War I and, even more acutely, World War II. Moreover, Magnes himself recognized that he was uncompromising in his political pursuits and that their outcome was likely to be tragic: "If one wants to achieve, one must compromise," he wrote in his journal, adding that "if one wants to be true, give up ambition to achieve concretely."[21]

Activism based on soul-searching was another characteristic common to Magnes and HaShomer HaTza'ir members. "In the life of Magnes two strains of endeavor were in constant competition," according to Bentwich, "the man of action" and "the rabbi, the teacher, concerned to arouse the conscience of the people."[22] To Scholem, Magnes was in a state of perpetual dissonance, torn between wanting what was best for the Yishuv and the Zionist enterprise in Palestine and his own conscience-driven deliberations.[23]

Magnes was aware of his own soul-searching tendencies and their religious aspects. On January 5, 1944, he wrote to Scholem, "Knowledge of the word of God is, in my view, admittedly a fundamental and important question, but a secondary one. The main issue is whether the word of God is even present. I reach affirmative awareness through the *'vicissitudes of God'* and the preponderance of evidence, from before the time of Moses, through all the prophets up to the last of the righteous men."[24]

Magnes's political activism, resting on an absolutist, uncompromising moral perspective combined with one practical and indispensable solution—binationalism—also accords with the tragic model. Both

Magnes and HaShomer HaTza'ir focused on binationalism, a fundamentally utopian theory,[25] as a solution. Furthermore, the HaShomer HaTza'ir movement interpreted immigration to Palestine as a groundbreaking act that took place against all odds, and this interpretation applies to Magnes as well. His own act of immigrating to Palestine was exceptional in the context of U.S. Jewry and American Zionism, and it simultaneously embodied other core components of the tragic model: the decisive, trailblazing action directed at changing history and the self-sacrifice.

At the same time, one should use caution in fully applying the tragic paradigm to Magnes. First, the rejection of God at the basis of the tragic paradigm as presented by Goldmann and Nordheimer Nur is absolute, with near-gnostic themes criticizing the cruel God who has duplicitously abandoned the world.[26] For Magnes, however, despite fierce doubts and a sense of reproach toward God, his Sisyphean struggle to achieve awareness of God's presence in the world was unrelenting. He never gave up on God, even if he never found Him. Second, Nordheimer Nur's starting point is sociological, in the sense that he examines the tragic experience as characteristic of a social group of declining status whose members seek to break the barriers in their path.[27] Magnes's situation differed in that his efforts were those of a single individual and his mode of action drew on American individualism. Moreover, his American pragmatism and practical outlook moderated the more romantic and tragic European mindset that characterized Goldmann's model.

In sum, the contribution of the "tragic man" model lies in the methodical explanation it offers for the correlation between the eclipse of God, a fundamental pillar of Magnes's conception of God, and his political activism, which was based on absolute morality and predestined to fail. This model complements that of the aforementioned prophetic mode of activity, in which the prophet shifts between withdrawing into himself and taking determined action when he can no longer "suppress his prophecy." The prophetic model aptly describes Magnes's proactive efforts during the 1930s, when there was still some hope of actualizing the concept of binationalism, whereas the tragic model more accurately expresses Magnes's efforts during the 1940s, as his religious doubts grew stronger in the face of World War II and the slaughter of European Jewry.

"For Thy Sake Are We Killed All Day Long?"
—A Theology of Existential Choice

Magnes's speech of November 1, 1944, marking the start of the Hebrew University's academic year, is almost certainly the most comprehensive and methodical theological essay he composed.[28] In a chapter devoted to Magnes in his book *Faith and Reason*, Bergman places the spotlight on this speech, taking it as a testament of Magnes's religious thinking, which according to him involved radically overcoming pessimism through faith.[29] Scholar Paul Mendes-Flohr believes that this same speech might be the first theological analysis of the Holocaust by a Jewish thinker to posit that, even though it is Sisyphean, the search for meaning through historical manifestations of God must continue.[30]

Magnes opened by reading from a document he had received, during a rescue effort in Istanbul, in his capacity as chairman of the Middle East Advisory Committee of the Joint Distribution Committee (also known as the Joint). As the Joint expanded its sphere of activities, Palestine became a center of regional operations, and Magnes participated in many of the organization's rescue operations—including the delivery of packages to Jews in the Soviet Union, transport of a thousand Polish Jewish children to Palestine through Tehran, efforts to save Hungarian Jewry, and postwar aid for the Jews of Greece. The document from which Magnes read aloud was a detailed report by two Jews who had fled the extermination camp at Auschwitz in April 1944—a report he subsequently conveyed to the Joint in New York, in July 1944, with the request that it be publicized as widely as possible.[31] By late 1942 information about the extermination camps in Europe had already reached the United States and the Yishuv, but this report was one of the first detailed accounts of the gas chambers and the Birkenau operation in particular to reach the West.³² After apologizing to the audience for quoting from "so harrowing a statement," Magnes read an excerpt detailing the works of the gas chambers. He then posed the theological question that troubled him most in light of these revelations: "In all of human history there has never been anything like this either in extent or in the methods employed. Even now, as proofs continue to pile up, our minds prefer to reject the truth." He continued:

> Is it possible that this can happen under God's heaven? I must raise this question, even though I have no adequate answer. It gives millions of men no rest. The world today faces many fateful problems, but none so momentous as this. Is there a living God for whom all this has meaning? Is there design and purpose? Or, is the universe ruled by a blind, unmoral force, by some *deus absconditus*, who created the world and is no longer interested in its fate—withdrawn, asleep, or gloating over the writhing of his creatures upon the earth? I try to evade this question, and cannot. "And it was in my heart as a burning fire shut up in my bones, and I was weary with forbearing, and I could not" (Jer. 20:9).³³

The key concept in Magnes's remarks—Deus absconditus—is taken from the Vulgate, a late fourth-century Latin translation of the Bible,³⁴ which renders Isaiah 45:15 as "vere tu es Deus absconditus Deus Israhel" (You are indeed a God who concealed Himself, O God of Israel, who brings victory!). The term also appears in Martin Luther's theology. What troubled Luther, according to scholar Steven Paulson, was "not so much that God cannot be seen ... but that God actually and actively hides. God hides in order not to be found where humans want to find God. But God also hides in order to be found where God wills to be found."³⁵ The concept is also present in the seventeenth-century French philosopher Blaise Pascal's *Pensées* (a collection of philosophical fragments), in Thought 194:

> If this religion claimed to have a clear view of God, and to possess it openly and unveiled, then to say that we see nothing in the world which manifests him with this clearness would be to assail it. But since on the contrary it affirms that men are in darkness and estranged from God, that he has hidden himself from their knowledge, that the very name he has given himself in the Scriptures is *Deus absconditus*, ... what advantages it them, when, in their professed neglect of the search after truth, they declare that nothing reveals it to them?[36]

Magnes's use of the phrase Deus absconditus spoke to the eclipse of God that was so central to his religious and political thought. Furthermore, his citation from Jeremiah, "And it was in my heart as a burning fire shut up in my bones, and I was weary with forbearing, and I could not," applies the prophet's withholding of prophecy to his religious torments in the wake of the Holocaust.[37]

Following these impassioned remarks, Magnes proposed a response to the problem of evil—a response he regarded as fundamentally religious. "As with every basic position," he observed, "so this approach involves metaphysical assumptions. Yet our approach is not philosophic, it is religious. Our attitude must also take account of the presuppositions and achievements of science. But it is not scientific, it is religious." Unlike "judgments of philosophy" that were "arrived at through reason, through speculative methods," he explained, the religious approach required "not the rational powers only ... but rather a man's entire being; and the decision must emanate from all the sources and roots of the human soul." He added: "Arriving at a judgment concerning evil and the evil-doer is almost an act of heroism, and as with every such act, choice and decision require all the strength of a man's spirit and not the reasoning faculties alone."[38] Here Magnes was integrating elements of religious existentialism—of a heroic Kierkegaardian "leap of faith" recognizing reason's inability to generate faith—with Hasidic motifs of man choosing God through his "entire being." Even so, for

Magnes the "leap" or choice did not mean overcoming the crisis of faith and coming to truly believe in God's presence; rather, it was an act of choosing life and saying "yes" (in the Nietzschean sense) while leaving open the question of God's existence.[39]

Magnes systematically examined the responses that philosophy and religious thought had provided to date to the question of evil, and rejected their validity in light of the Holocaust. First he considered the idea that evil had to exist in the world, as the absence or negative of good, so that good itself could exist. "In order that the good may have its proper setting," he asked, "is it really in need of this Holocaust of millions of innocents?"[40] He also rejected the contention that "man is purified through suffering, and that through sin and misery the personality is exalted." Such "abominations" could not be what "man requires . . . to discipline his character." Moreover, "the very possibility of such atrocities, the massiveness of the thing, the depravity of its forms, are likely not to lift us to a higher plane of being, but to degrade us." Finally, even if this approach offered a rationale for individual suffering, it most certainly did not justify the "bodily and spiritual agonies of these hundreds of thousands." He asked: "Were their souls exalted when they were led to the place of slaughter, when with towels and soap they were driven into these gas chambers? Rabbi Akiba, so the tradition tells us, prolonged the recital of 'The One' at the terrifying moment when he was martyred. But even his attending angels cried out: 'Is this the Torah and its reward?'"[41]

Magnes went on to refute other theological explanations. In response to the argument, "If we could reach the place of the Most High—the *ens absolutissimum et perfectissimum*—we should perceive that evil only seems to be evil, and that for the Absolute Being there is no room for the distinction which mortals make between good and bad," he countered: "What man of flesh and blood can reach the Absolute? And meanwhile such a formula helps to obscure the boundaries between good and evil." To the Stoics, for whom the world was "all reason" with no place for suffering "except to be mastered as though it did not exist," Magnes retorted that one can no longer hide within an abstract "temple" of reason where "it is all too possible for the spirit to dwell in such tranquility that evil is not real but is mere seeming." As to Quietism, which "would guarantee your peace and which enjoins quiet acceptance of everything going on about you," Magnes conceded that "some of the most moving of the Psalms have arisen out of the spirit," but "encountering it in these awful days, it is difficult not to protest." In response to the "words of our tradition: 'Because of our many sins,'" and the argument that evil is punishment for the sins of "all of us individuals and as a people," Magnes was not averse to acknowledging either the sin of the "first man" or collective sin, but he challenged the proportionality of the present circumstances, for "who can say with a clear conscience that this 'liquidation' of millions of the sons and daughters of Israel is chastisement commensurate with their sins, however heavy these may have been? Is there any proportion here?" As for natural theology, which viewed Nature as a manifestation of God's existence, Magnes responded that despite the beauty and glory of Nature, this approach did not address the question of whether the God of Nature was "a moral God concerned for the life of man."

In fact, "Nature all too often reveals itself as indifferent to man. 'To cause it to rain on the earth where no man is; in the wilderness where there is no man' (Job 38:26)." Analyzing as well the story of Job, from whom God had permitted the angel to take away his wealth, his children, and his physical health, Magnes critiqued Job's personal conception of evil, observing that "at the time when God's blessings were resting upon him individually, might he not have known that all was not right with the world—suffering and sorrow, and cruelty and the torture of the innocent? He did not rise up against his Creator then, or curse his day." After all, he pointed out, "We ourselves, through chance, have not been cast into those gas chambers and furnaces. Does the problem on that account not stare us in the face?" This was not only a question for the individual sufferer; on the contrary, it was relevant because of "the very possibility that what is happening to these myriads and millions *can* happen under heaven."[42]

Two additional aspects of this speech evoked Magnes's religious worldview. The first related to his criticism of the scientific method in its appropriation of the concepts of truth and human morality. While "it is the glory of science to be able to utter objective and sure judgments on all kinds of facts and phenomena," he asserted, "the scientific method refuses to ask questions that cannot be answered."[43] Like the philosopher of pragmatism William James, Magnes believed that moral and religious decisions could not await the assembly of all the factual material. When a scientist refuses even "to produce these ethical and religious questions, much less try to answer them," because "not all the evidence is before him," Magnes charged, "he is in reality deciding against any possibility of an affirmative conclusion." The religious approach, however, "asserts that it is impossible to be a neutral" because "life itself is constantly calling for decisions."[44]

Second, Magnes commented on the unbridgeable gulf between God and man, in the spirit of Isaiah's words: "For my thoughts are not your thoughts, neither are your ways my ways, saith the Lord" (Isa. 55:8). "Yes," Magnes asserted, "the abyss between the Creator and His creatures is immeasurable, terrifying; and it is the very essence of the religious problem to struggle unceasingly with the question: Is it possible to bridge this chasm, dare flesh and blood set foot upon this bridge? If today the answer be yes, tomorrow doubts creep in. Today 'he beholds the light and whence it flows,' tomorrow the eye is without seeing, and there is cloud and thick darkness and the shadow of death. The struggle renews itself within the soul each day, each night."[45] These words echo Magnes's interpretation of Karl Barth's theory—the imperative to row on the sea separating man and God, even though one can never reach the other shore (chapter 7).

Toward the end of his speech Magnes offered the following observations:

> We added that there are manifold possibilities, various alternatives, between which men are called upon to choose. There is the possibility of a kingdom of heaven and that of a kingdom of iniquity and depravity, and we may not content ourselves with formulas, or stand to one side and take up a neutral, a so-called scientific position. . . . And when we finally decide this way or that, this power of decision within us is a very complex substance. It is compounded of all that has happened to us as individuals and as a group. At the moment of decision, it is the course of history streaming through us, and everything we have learned from the great in mind and spirit, from prophets and saints, from philosophers and artists. When we make a fateful choice, all the soul's forces are brought into union at a single focus and all at once.[46]

Magnes demanded that human beings choose a kingdom of heaven over a kingdom of iniquity and depravity. All of an individual's spiritual powers, learned and acquired from others and over the course of history itself, come together at the moment of choice. And all of the main concepts in the development of Jewish thinking, from the conception of the world's creation through the messianic idea, pointed to one choice: "Israel's great decision, which precedes and follows all the rest: the living choice of a living God."[47]

To Magnes, this choice did not involve a revelation or the cultivation of religious awareness, as he himself did not know "*what* the meaning is of this desert of thick darkness that shuts us in." Yet by adopting this religious approach—"the living choice of a living God"—an individual could begin a turn to the "positive" direction, the direction of "Yes" in response to the question of the meaning of life:

> But by means of this religious approach I find myself facing in the positive direction, and not the reverse. It is as though two men were

together standing on a narrow, obscure path. This path is the pessimism common to both. Then someone turns with all his might in the direction of No, and then he remains standing, while the other turns with all his might in the direction of Yes—yes, there *is* a meaning to all this.

Thus turned, this man cannot stand still. He has started on a long and weary road. He wants with all his will to be among those who seek the Face and pursue righteousness. But from that man God hides His Face. An opaque screen holds him asunder from the living God. For all his trying to come nearer and to touch the outer fringe, he cannot. It will not be given him to appear before the presence, to hear the voice, or to understand the meaning of these massacrings, this wanton butchery. Yet he can do no other than to persist in his quest to the last, to keep on inquiring, struggling, challenging. He will not be granted tranquillity [sic] of soul. But if it be given him to renew the forces of his being day by day and constantly to be among the seekers, the rebellious—that is the crown of his life and the height of his desire.[48]

For Magnes, experiencing the concealment of God's face meant confronting an existential decision in which one had to choose the (immanent) alternative of the kingdom of heaven on earth over the gnostic alternative that viewed the world as the kingdom of wickedness and the rule of evil. The choice of "Yes" did not necessarily lead to knowledge of God. "God hides His Face" from the individual, who has remained among those "seekers" over the course of history who could not attain awareness of God, because for Magnes "to appear before the presence" and "to hear the voice" went hand-in-hand with understanding "the meaning of these massacrings." Both were impossible endeavors. Still, by engaging in constant struggle toward an eternal quest, by relinquishing the possibility of tranquility while constantly renewing one's spiritual forces so as to remain among "the seekers, the rebellious," one could reach the height of human existence.⁴⁹ The search itself continually renewed the seeker's strength throughout the impossible journey to behold God's manifestation in the world.

In his quest for God, Magnes sought a solution in human history—that is, through the manifestation of God's deeds in the world. Correspondingly, one may view his continuing efforts to advance binationalism as a political solution—even though it never gained traction—as demonstrating his persistence in the face of the Sisyphean task of seeking God in the world. For Magnes, his refusal to abandon a binational solution that would historically attest to God's existence in the world, in that it would be a just solution for a just God, was akin to refusing to relinquish the possibility of experiencing God's presence.

This perspective—the presence of God revealed through the pursuit of a political alternative that could be expected to validate His existence, were it implemented—is important in explaining Magnes's stubborn persistence in promoting binationalism even when politically all hope seemed lost. Just as he was unable to abandon God even though he never found Him, so too was he unable to abandon binationalism as a solution—a solution that would prove God's existence—even if it never had a chance of actually succeeding. As Mendes-Flohr well observed, for Magnes, political action grounded in moral deliberations was ultimately an act of religious faith.⁵⁰

13

Religion Overrides Nationalism

Among Magnes's personal papers one finds two documents from the 1940s that reveal his inclination to return to religion at the expense of Jewish nationalism. Both are notes for planned lectures: the first titled "The Religious Role of the Land of Israel" (1941, never delivered) and the second examining Baruch Spinoza's *Theological-Political Treatise* (1947, delivered at the Hebrew University). The two sets of lecture notes embody another stage in the evolution of Magnes's approach to religion and nationalism—a religious turning point, from which the ideals of Jewish study and Jewish Scripture took precedence over national aspirations.

"The Religious Role of the Land of Israel"

In April 1941 Magnes was invited to deliver a lecture before Emet VeEmunah, the first Conservative congregation in Israel (founded in 1936) on "The Religious Role of the Land of Israel."[1] Accepting the invitation, Magnes began preparing notes for the lecture, but in December 1941 he informed the Jerusalem-based congregation's Rabbi Dr. Yaakov David Wilhelm that in retrospect he had to decline the opportunity, because the more he thought about it, the more certain he became that he lacked "the spiritual authority to speak publicly on this important and fundamental issue."[2] Nevertheless, his draft lecture notes provide a comprehensive summary of his outlook and the historical, developmental analysis underpinning it.

Responses to Modernity

"The relation between religion and nationalism," Magnes began, "is not absolute in Judaism, but rather changes from one period to another in accordance with the historical circumstances. As a rule, Judaism should not be viewed as a crystallized mass but as a living creature. And in order to reconfigure it, we must consider the historical setting in which we find ourselves. This point is clearly illustrated by two movements from the modern era: Reform Judaism and Zionism."[3]

To Magnes, Reform Judaism and Zionism were Judaism's two main responses to modernity. Reform Judaism, he held, was a response to two processes: first, religious tolerance, developed in the intellectual sphere toward the end of the eighteenth century, in which social morality was essentially based on a logical, natural religion common to all; and second, the movement for civil equality in the political sphere. Reform Judaism, as the Jewish response to these developments, "tend[ed] to emphasize the universal principles of Judaism and downplay or reject the national aspect. As a consequence, it has led to assimilation. But first it met the needs of the hour, in that it opened the gates to civil equality and education."[4] Thus, Magnes considered Reform Judaism to be an appropriate response for its time, but he also regarded its universalism as excessive and a source of assimilation. This had been his position since the early twentieth century, when he first began critiquing the Reform movement.

As to Zionism, he considered it a response to subsequent, late nineteenth-century developments in the intellectual and political spheres: the shift away from religion and toward science, the rise of nationalism, and increased antisemitism. Judaism had responded in the form of Zionism, which "emphasizes nationalism and completely neglects religion. A one-sided response, but undoubtedly a necessary one at the time, as a reaction to Reform Judaism and a refuge from assimilation."[5]

Thus, Magnes also perceived of Reform Judaism and Zionism as reciprocal responses to modernity: the first emphasized the religious—which for Magnes meant the universal—at the expense of the particular, whereas the second underscored the particular and the national at the expense of the religious.[6] Both Reform Judaism and Zionism were necessary responses at the time, but their continuing necessity had to be assessed as a function of the time. The sphere of the intellect, he argued, no longer had any absolute moral foundation. Science had failed to live up to the hopes pinned on it, and "nationalism, socialism, and the like resemble idolatries—that is, they godify part of existence, and by doing so, awaken other opposing deities (another people's nationalism, fascism, etc.)." From these had followed other manifestations of idolatry, among them dictatorial decision making and the obliteration of the individual, whose will becomes subject to a collective ideology. "Even Zionism," he added, "was tainted by a measure of such idolatry."[7]

The Idolatry of Political Zionism

By Magnes's theopolitical analysis, the major ideologies, such as nationalism and socialism, were "idolatries" because, he argued, they sanctified only part of the foundation of existence. On the eve of the new State of Israel's first academic year of 1948, which coincided with the Jewish New Year, Magnes wrote to the new rector of the Hebrew University, historian and legal scholar Simcha Assaf:

> Why have our people and our land suffered destruction time and again? The answer of the prophets and sages of Israel has been: Idolatry, the worship of idols, our prostrating ourselves before the works of our own hands and before the hosts of the heavens. In the course of the generations, the idols change their forms. Among the more important

tasks before each generation is to point to the idols which pretend to be God almighty, and before which mankind are expected to bend the knee and to sacrifice their most precious offerings, their sons and daughters. Today the world stands trembling and fearful on the brink of Gehennah, the new world war—Heaven protect us. Among the idols of our own day, we find militarism and totalitarianism, that is, the exalting of the army above everything else, and the exalting of the state above every other social form.[8]

As he argued in essay notes from the same period, Zionism, rooted in nationalism, was one such form of idolatry: "The idea of the state has taken over the vast majority of Jewry. . . . We are all guilty—including the American Jews who remained silent. . . . The sanctification of these means has made it so that it is difficult to be a Jew among one's people. . . . It will bring about our ruin. This is the final moment."[9]

Magnes saw similarities between his own era and the Second Temple era. Both political Zionism and the Hasmonean dynasty faced political and religious threats: the addiction to power and the lure of false messianism. In his August 1937 speech before the Jewish Agency Executive (see chapter 11), he had compared Zionism to the false messianism of Shabtai Zvi, whose call for the Jews to pack their belongings in preparation for immigrating to the Land of Israel turned out to be both illusory and disastrous for the Jewish people.[10] He said: "What I fear is that these tens and hundreds of thousands of our brothers and sisters who are in the lands of oppression and who have heard this message from here have believed that in the course of a short time the Jewish State will open its arms, as Rachel opened her arms to her returning children, and they will find that there is room but for few and not for many."[11]

"The Return to Religion"

Given Magnes's analysis pointing not to greater Jewish nationalism but to an opposing historical trend—that of the world gradually transforming into one state—he viewed the necessary solution as a return to religion at the expense of nationalism: "The return to religion, and perhaps also its dissemination among the nations, has become our order of the hour.... Political nationalism will be reduced to a secondary aim; our nationalism will be essentially religious, as in the time of the Second Temple. What does it mean to be a Jew? Not race, not land, but rather a life of Torah. In contrast to [the claims of] Reform Judaism and political Zionism—there is no nationalism without religion, and there is no religion without nationalism."[12]

Thus, according to Magnes, both Reform Judaism and Zionism had failed in their efforts to separate nationalism from religion. The former relinquished nationalism, whereas the latter abandoned religion. Their actual separation, however, was in his view impossible. He proposed instead a religious—but not political—model of nationalism. It would be centered on a life of Torah, even at the expense of the communal dimension of nationalism and the land itself—that is, at the expense of national political self-actualization.

Implications for the Diaspora and Palestine

This approach had implications for both the Diaspora and Palestine. To date, Magnes wrote, the Diaspora had been seen as doomed to fail, and efforts had been made to save a few people and funds. But now "we must call on every Jew to preserve his religion and educate his son in the ways of Judaism, with the education of the old as well as the young an aim in itself. Indeed, it is difficult to be a Jew in the Diaspora, and therefore anyone who can should immigrate to the Land of Israel."[13]

In Palestine, "a minimal level of communal self-rule should be maintained as a means; but the calls for full political independence are unnecessary."[14] In effect, Magnes called for the return to a traditional religious community that would preserve itself through education and could survive in the Diaspora as well; at the same time, he saw in

Palestine the possibility of existing on the basis of communal self-rule, without political independence.

In some sense Magnes was returning to Ahad Ha'am's concept of a national center, though with notable differences. Apparently Magnes was not relying on the concept of a revival of Jewish culture but rather on a more essentially religious conception of two communities existing simultaneously, without any political governance, in both Palestine and the Diaspora. Nationalism, in this context, was a tool for the preservation of religion.

Magnes went on to voice pessimism about Judaism's survival in the Diaspora. The rise of the "great ideologies"—nationalism, socialism, fascism, and the like—would increase the pressure on Jews to assimilate. In countries with large concentrations of Jews, Judaism would have to fight or assimilate. The solution lay in Judaism and Christianity cooperating against these "idolatries":

> It therefore seems to me that in the Diaspora Judaism will either have to enlist supporters among the nations, or join forces with Christianity against the common enemy. In any event Judaism should be viewed as a religion that is not intended solely for the People of Israel; and the question arises as to the relation between the national religion, which we are certainly bound to preserve, and the universal religion. The question is somewhat beyond us; nevertheless, we will never be whole within ourselves unless we know how to answer it.[15]

Here again one sees Magnes's affinity for Christianity as well as Reform Mission Theology, which ascribes to Judaism a universal mission.

In sum, as an alternative to the political conception of nationalism, Magnes proposed a return to a religious nationalism based on and united by the study of Torah, and from which morality and political activity derived. Such a national entity required some measure of communal autonomy, but the national-cultural community of learners did not necessarily have to be a political entity.

Religiously, Magnes came up against the tension between the universal characteristics that he believed underpinned religion ("the fundamental principles of our religion are universal and the world needs them") and recognition of the vital importance of preserving a national character so as to ensure the survival and transmission of the religion. This tension between the singular and the universal was in fact a theopolitical tension between particularist, national religion (which, as noted, was in danger of being overridden by the national aspect) and universal religion, which translated politically into the Jewish mission in the world, without any need for an independent political entity—and such an entity could in fact undercut the mission. As posited earlier, one might view the idea of binationalism as a theopolitical model that aims to overcome this paradoxical tension.

Also notable is the absence of any reference to "Zionism" in Magnes's proposed approach to the interrelationship between nationalism and religion—an absence that illustrates his decreasing reliance on Zionism in articulating his views, in contrast to previous decades, when he sought to defend it: "Some of my friends say that, although I live in Zion, I am not a Zionist at all. I wonder where that ecclesiastic authority as to who is and who is not a Zionist rests."[16]

Influence of Spinoza's *Theological-Political Treatise* (1947)

Building further on the themes explored in his journal in preparation for the 1947 Hebrew University opening address, Magnes examined a political-theological tract by the Dutch Jewish philosopher Baruch Spinoza and reached his own conclusions. His very engagement with this essay is further evidence of his search for the connection between the religious and the political:

> Recently, I briefly reviewed Spinoza's monumental work, *Tractatus Theologico-Politicus*—a book that is full of the Jewish spirit. He reads the prophets of Israel as [conveying] God's word and he believes

in the divine spirit of the Holy Scriptures. And it is only possible to understand the foundations of rationalist ethics on the basis of his faith in inference (that the Torah comes from Heaven, from the mouth of Divinity), of the Israelite prophecy and the Holy Scriptures of the People of Israel.[17]

Magnes was drawing on Spinoza to present the Torah as preceding morality and laying the foundation for a system of ethics. His own return to religion was, in this sense, also a response to the loss of any absolute moral foundation (in his view the prevailing intellectual outlook of the time).

Torah Study as a Basis for Jewish Nationalism

Magnes proceeded to offer a new outlook on nationalism: one that rested on the study of Torah. First he described the centrality of reiterative Torah study in Judaism:

> One area of consensus is that this concept of Torah study is of greater fundamental value for the Israeli public than for any other populace.... If these spiritual aspects become the fundamental qualities of the Israeli character, then undoubtedly there follows the privilege of perpetually returning, day after day through the generations, to the book of prayer, which is the most precious spiritual foundation of all the People of Israel.[18]

Next Magnes presented the three pillars of Judaism as he saw them—religion, morality, and study:

> In these days of great hopes and great dangers at the same time, it is essential to closely review the Torah in the broadest sense of this term. In times of perplexity... we are historically obligated to delve into the sources of our lives and the structural foundations of our society. There [we will find] the guidelines and edicts of Israel's morality, which will provide strong foundations on which to build

the House of Israel in Palestine.... We need to reemphasize that the moral basis of our society lies in the Torah of Israel, the prophecy of Israel, the tradition of Israel. The foundation for all of this is study and knowledge.[19]

His unique typology of religion, morality, and study, while echoing the traditional view expressed in *Pirkei Avot* that the world stands upon three things—Torah, *avodah* (worship), and *gemilut hasadim* (charity)—differs from the Zionist model of people-Torah-land that he himself posited in 1929. What stands out in Magnes's holy trinity is the status granted to morality, which for him derived directly from the Torah and its study, while also standing on its own as one of the three pillars of Judaism. At the same time, Torah study and adherence to the mitzvot (imperative deeds) were inextricably interlinked—further evidence that, in strictly theological terms, Magnes was more of a Conservative Jew than a Reform Jew in his outlook. "Although the Torah exists for its own sake and the *mitzvah* for its own sake, one of the most characteristic qualities of Judaism is their historical integration and the consistent emphasis on Torah and deed in tandem"[20]—by which he meant that learning effectively led to the realization of the deed.

Magnes viewed the return to Jewish learning as the imperative of the hour. Since the Zionist enterprise lacked an adequate moral foundation, a return to religion was the means to reestablish morality as the basis for political action in Palestine. More generally, his remarks convey his continued drawing away from Zionism.

Next, he laid out the theopolitical doctrine he derived from universal morality. Universal morality would follow from the return to Torah and to Jewish study. The democratic and universal character of the Sages' outlook was attributable to biblical passages and the exegesis surrounding them: "A clear indication of the democratic and universal conceptions of Our Sages can be found in the well-known interpretation of the passage about the Torah and the *mitzvot* being the laws 'by the pursuit of which man shall live' [Lev. 18:5]. Not only does man learn them, he also lives his life by them."[21]

The return to religious sources ultimately led Magnes to a political worldview that incorporated distinctly American principles. In the spirit of American individualism, he underscored the religious value the individual would derive from the study of Torah. This was no minor reward. Torah study, Magnes promised, "liberates you, makes you a free man, through your acceptance of the only yoke that leads you from slavery to freedom, the yoke of the Kingdom of Heaven, which makes you a free man amidst the slavery surrounding you."[22]

Peace as a Religious-Political Concept

Near the end of Magnes's notes on Spinoza's essay there appears an interesting comment:

> About the bringing of peace, on the one hand it is written "seek peace and pursue it." [Ps. 34:14]. Efforts by man are necessary in order to bring peace. On the other hand, our Sages believe that peace can only be achieved through Supreme mercy. [The plea] "grant peace" means "a blessing to advance peace." Peace is a religious-political concept, and it is brought about through a partnership between man and the Holy One Blessed Be He.

Here, in effect, Magnes was describing his own political activity as theopolitical, in the sense that it was almost theurgic—a human act intended to invoke the action of God.[23] Thanks to the deeds of those (like himself) who abided by the imperative "seek peace and pursue it," humankind and God become partners in the act of bringing peace to the world.

This chapter, in combination with the previous one, outlines the evolution of Magnes's thought during the 1940s along two tracks—theological and political—and examines the correlation between them. In religious terms, this decade was characterized by a theological shift in Magnes's thinking about faith and doubt. His experience of the eclipse of God took shape during the later years of his political life, concurrent with the interwar period and the Holocaust. All in all, his analysis of the problem of evil, consequent doubts as to God's presence in the world and manifestations in human history, and his theology of the quest led him to propose an essentially existential answer: a Kierkegaard-style "leap of faith" that nonetheless left open the question of God's existence. During the 1940s Magnes continued advocating a positive theology of quest that made the search imperative and awarded it religious value.

Meanwhile, politically, Magnes's skeptical view of nationalism, formed during World War I, only hardened, as illustrated by his testimony before the Anglo-American Committee and his opposition to the Partition Plan. Partition would in fact have accorded with his earlier, more moderate approach, which recognized separatist nationalism as a stage in the realization of Israel's religious mission to the peoples of the world.

I have endeavored here to reconstruct Magnes's views on nationalism in the later period of his life. As previously pointed out, Magnes was not a systematic thinker, and the work here relies on two fragments of notes relating to this topic, during a time when he himself claimed that he did not have the intellectual authority to address the relationship between nationalism and religion. Nevertheless, these fragments reveal some conclusions about this problem, the resolution of which alluded him.

His notes for a speech on Jewish nationalism and religion disclose the dichotomy he was experiencing between these two elements, and the failure of their reconciliation in light of the dramatic shifts of the 1940s: World War II, the full materialization of political Zionism into a statist project symbolized by the 1942 Biltmore Declaration (demanding a Jewish political commonwealth, effectively a state), the Holocaust (harbingering the need of a home for Jewish refugees and cementing the Zionist belief negating Jewish diasporic existence). Eventually,

Magnes chooses a religious form of collectivism over political nationalism, stating his vision that "political nationalism will be downgraded to a minor goal; our nationalism would be essentially religious."[24]

Spinoza's *Theological-Political Treatise* appears to have helped Magnes in developing a conceptual framework that both established Jewish learning as the foundation of Jewish nationality and viewed a return to religion and morality as a precondition for Jewish nationalism's existence as a political entity. Revisiting Spinoza's work triggered in Magnes an attempt to return, perhaps even in the religious sense of repentance, to the original religious sources, to religious study, and consequently, to morality—the coalescing ingredients of Jewish collective existence—at the expense of nationality.

The political implications were effectively a renunciation of political Zionism.

14

The Sacred Land and the Negation of the State

The Anglo-American Committee of Inquiry on Palestine was established in 1946, as a consequence of various policy shifts and political developments. It represented the first cooperative British-American attempt to reach a decision about the future of Palestine, particularly the issues of refugees and displaced persons within Europe and the appropriate political and governing system in Palestine. The Committee received statements from many figures and organizations and heard testimony from numerous witnesses in North America, Britain, Continental Europe, Arab countries, and Palestine. Its conclusions, published in an April 1946 report, included an urgent call to bring 100,000 Jewish refugees to Palestine, revoke the White Paper issued by the British government in 1939 restricting land purchases, reject the exclusive nationalist claims of both Jews and Arabs, and instead issue a recommendation for the continuing development of a cooperative governing framework under the auspices of the British Mandate.

Magnes's testimony before the Committee in March 1946 was probably the high point of his 1940s political activity. He posited a unique theopolitical formula centered on the moral view that Palestine's sanctity to three religions negated any possibility of separate nationalist self-actualization within its borders, and therefore any solution had to be based on binationalism. His decision to present this formula in an arena beyond regular Jewish or Zionist discourse—before an international committee with a political mandate, in fact—deserves examination, as does whether his efforts actually influenced the Committee's conclusions.

The Anglo-American Committee of Inquiry

The Anglo-American Committee, convening during January–March 1946, marked a turning point in the handling of Arab-Jewish affairs. It was the first occasion since 1922, when Britain was granted the Mandate for Palestine, during which its Foreign Office and Colonial Office did not have the exclusive authority to make decisions about Palestine's future. The inclusion of an American voice attested to both the postwar rise of U.S. political power and the decline of the British Empire, which was busy regrouping and preparing to surrender its imperialist dream.[1]

The Committee itself was formed amid a dispute between the Colonial Office under George Henry Hall, which supported some form of partition, and the Foreign Office under Ernest Bevin, which favored a state based on binationalism. Britain's waning status as an empire meant that Bevin had the upper hand. His approach prevailed and remained the policy in practice until early 1948, when the British government began secretly promoting a plan for partition between Arab and Jewish Palestine.[2]

The Committee's mandate was fourfold: (1) to examine the political, economic, and social conditions in Palestine, their effect on Jewish immigration and settlement, and their impact on the Arab population; (2) to examine the postwar conditions of Jews in European countries, the feasibility of rehabilitation that would enable them to live in Europe without discrimination or oppression, and the estimated number of those who would wish to or were being compelled to immigrate to countries outside Europe; (3) to hear the views of Jewish and Arab representatives so as to formulate recommendations for the governments of

Britain and the United States regarding both the interim management of problems in Palestine and a permanent solution; (4) to issue urgent recommendations regarding the problem of Jewish refugees in Europe, with attention to the immigration options available to them.[3]

The issues and scope of the Committee's mandate reflected the growing U.S. influence in the Middle East as well as President Harry Truman's interest in resolving the problem of "displaced persons" (Jewish refugees). His support for Jewish immigration to Palestine stemmed from domestic American concerns in addition to humanitarian considerations. He was aware of the harsh conditions at the displaced persons camps, as well as the high costs of maintaining them. Moreover, surveys conducted between December 1945 and March 1946 indicated that about 80 percent of those Americans who were following the issue supported the Zionist call for immigration to Palestine. On the basis of this data, Truman advised British prime minister Clement Attlee to permit 100,000 Jews to enter Palestine, to ease their suffering and ensure the future peace of Europe. In response, British foreign secretary Bevin initiated the formation of the Committee. On October 6, 1945, the British Foreign Office produced a first draft plan for the establishment of the Anglo-American Committee, and on November 13 the Committee's appointees were announced.[4] There were twelve members—six British and six American—and two co-chairs: U.S. Circuit judge Joseph Hutcheson and British politician and judge John Singleton.

The Committee convened for the first time in Washington on January 4, 1946. While in Washington, the Committee heard testimony from the American Zionist leader Rabbi Stephen S. Wise and the Protestant theologian Reinhold Niebuhr, who testified in support of the Zionist position. The Committee also heard testimony and collected findings in London, at sites across Europe where displaced Jews were concentrated (including Berlin, Poland, Vienna, Italy, and Athens), in Cairo, in Palestine, and later in Beirut, Baghdad, Riyadh, and Amman. In Palestine, over a three-week visit starting on March 6, 1946, the Committee met with prominent figures from the Yishuv (Chaim Weizmann, David Ben-Gurion, and Moshe Sharett), representatives of the Arab community (Awni Abd al-Hadi, who held deliberations with Magnes's 1938 Committee of Five initiative; and Jamal Husseini, secretary of the Muslim Supreme Council in Palestine, who for all practical purposes represented the exiled grand mufti),[5] and local British government officials.

Among the testimonies the Committee heard, only the statements by Magnes and Ichud considered the land's sanctity to three religions and the political implications thereof. The statement by HaShomer HaTza'ir, a kibbutz-settling movement and socialist political party with high stakes in the Zionist enterprise, also called for a binational arrangement based on the principle of nondominance (traces of which are also evident in the Committee's third recommendation) but completely overlooked the holiness of the land, to the extent that religion did not even appear in the list of areas that should come within the purview of specific communal administrations. Avoiding the issue of religion was consistent with HaShomer HaTza'ir's deeply Marxist-influenced worldview.[6]

The Committee released its conclusions on April 20, 1946. The general policy recommendations as well as guidelines for immediate measures included the immigration of 100,000 displaced persons to Palestine (per Truman's call); revocation of the White Paper's restrictions on land sales to Jews; rejection of Zionist claims to Palestine; recognition of the need to develop the land based on Jewish-Arab cooperation under the auspices of the Mandate government; and repudiation of the claim that Jewish immigration to Palestine was the only solution to the Jewish problem. The Committee was also critical of the economic gap between Jews and Arabs and suggested that any efforts to facilitate illegal Jewish immigration or oppose the recommendations be quelled by force.[7]

The Committee's conclusions dashed the hopes of two bodies: the Jewish Agency, which, after initially objecting to the Committee, had hoped that its report would view the possibility of a Jewish state favorably; and the British government, which had seen in the Committee an opportunity to scale back the American figure of 100,000 refugees. The final report, in fact, sparked fury among the British because they believed the United States was endangering British interests while leaving Britain to cope alone with the repercussions of implementing the recommendations—particularly the Arab public's violent response to more Jewish immigration, on the one hand, and the growth of Jewish terrorism by Jewish splinter groups determined to put an end to the British Mandate, on the other. Nevertheless, preserving relations with the United States was the top concern for Britain, and it therefore continued working jointly to address the future of Palestine.

In the meantime, various actors who opposed the Committee's conclusions took steps to hinder the implementation of its recommendations. At Foreign Secretary Bevin's initiative, the British government demanded that the military defense groups of the Yishuv—Haganah, Etzel, and Lehi—be dismantled as a condition for Jewish immigration, clearly a demand the Yishuv would not accept. At the same time, American Jewish leaders, especially co-chair of the American Zionist Emergency Council Rabbi Abba Hillel Silver, maneuvered to ensure Truman's rejection of the Committee's recommendations. First, he took steps to ensure a coordinated a response by American Jewish organizations and the Jewish Agency. He then held negotiations with close associates of the American president and, in effect, dictated the text of the statement Truman issued on April 30, 1946, expressing full support for the immediate immigration of 100,000 Jewish refugees and for revocation of the White Paper restrictions, while also calling for the Committee's recommendations regarding political arrangements in Palestine to be reevaluated at a later time. Two weeks later, while delivering a sermon at his Cleveland Reform congregation, Tifereth Israel, Silver fiercely criticized the report, yet praised President Truman for his responses to its policy recommendations. The significant influence that U.S. Jews, and particularly Silver, had on the American administration is evident here.[8]

Magnes's Testimony before the Committee

On March 14, 1946, Magnes, Martin Buber, and First Aliyah pioneer Moshe Smilansky testified on behalf of the recently established binationalist association Ichud before the Anglo-American Committee of Inquiry.[9] Their ability to appear before the Committee was not self-evident, as the Yishuv was then engaged in a struggle over the right of representation before this body. The Jewish Agency, after settling the internal debate over whether to appear in the first place, sought a united front to present the Jewish demand for statehood before the Committee—but Magnes refused to be silenced. He announced his plan to make his own public statement before the Committee, in addition to the testimony he was submitting on behalf of Ichud. Conversely, the HaShomer HaTza'ir party, which also opposed the Yishuv's position, was content with submitting a written statement to the Committee. Eventually, the Jewish Agency conceded, and these Jewish opposition voices were awarded a hearing.[10]

Buber delivered the opening statement on behalf of Ichud. He stressed the unique bond between people and land that characterized the Jewish people and Eretz Israel, and the centrality of the Jewish concept of messianism—both as the driving force behind the Zionist enterprise and as a vital part of human civilization generally. At the same time, he criticized the view (a misguided one, in his opinion) that a national home for the Jewish people in Palestine necessarily meant a Jewish state, adding that one people's independence should not be acquired at the expense of another people's independence. Moreover, he argued, Jewish immigration should not undermine the political and economic status of the current inhabitants of the land. The Jewish tradition of justice had to be implemented throughout the entire country.[11]

Magnes began his testimony by presenting Ichud's fundamental assumption: that Jewish-Arab cooperation was both vital and possible. The "plain" Jews and Arabs do not want war, he argued, and the Committee should therefore find a constructive and acceptable compromise based on two key principles. The first was "political parity"—meaning that Palestine should be a binational country for two peoples of equal political status. Magnes then spelled out the existing options for implementing binationalism, while noting that this was a progressive American idea, and, furthermore, he presented a detailed plan for the formation of a binational, autonomous Palestine. Magnes's second principle was "numerical parity"—meaning that "Jewish immigration is to be encouraged up to parity with the Arabs." He then examined the technical conditions, such as birth rates and immigration quotas, for maintaining such a demographic balance.[12] Later, during the question-and-answer session, Magnes contended with numerous reservations voiced by Committee members, including questions about support for his views in the Yishuv, the Jewish Agency's position on his plans, deteriorating Jewish-Arab relations, and the difficulties of creating a joint government. Committee member British politician Richard Crossman listed four conditions he believed were necessary for Ichud's plan to be operational: (1) agreement between the political leaders on both sides, (2) a decrease in "nationalistic fervour" on both sides, (3) confidence on each side that the other was willing to "give up its ultimate desires" and would continue doing so, and (4) an administration capable of "the extremely skillful job of conducting this together." Magnes agreed with these conditions in principle but argued that they could be realized gradually. He refrained from criticizing the Yishuv's political leadership—that is, the Jewish Agency.[13]

The "Sanctity of the Land" as a Rejection of Separatist Nationalism

One of Magnes's main arguments was that the land's sanctity for three religions precluded the exclusive realization of either Jewish or Arab nationalism in Palestine. In fact, the very first political action plan he ever published, in *Like All the Nations?*, alluded to this formulation: "The Holy Land is no place for an Arab National State or Government, or for a Jewish National State or Government, but for a bi-national country."[14]

This same theme surfaced repeatedly in Magnes's articles as well, and he would pose similar arguments in his last, nearly desperate attempt—at a meeting with President Truman in early May 1948—to prevent the Partition Plan's implementation and Israel's founding. According to his own journal entry, Magnes had pled, "We must save the Holy City, we must save the Holy Land." In response, Magnes recorded in his diary, Truman had explained:

> Among his dreams had been that the peoples whose life was based more or less upon the same moral code might get to understand one another. Jews had a Mosaic code. The Christians had the same code and the Sermon on the Mount, which really meant, "Do unto others. . . ." The Moslems' moral code was also based on this moral code. He had dreamed that these peoples might get to understand one another better and might help to lift the world from the materialism which was holding the world down to the ground and might destroy it.[15]

Ichud's statement, submitted to the Anglo-American Committee in advance of its representatives' testimony, included the following assertion: "Palestine is not just an Arab land like any other Arab land. For one thing, it is a Holy Land for three monotheistic religions, of which two—Judaism and Christianity—had their origin here, whilst the third, Islam, regards Jerusalem as next in holiness to Mecca and Medinah."[16] During Magnes's oral testimony and the subsequent question-and-answer session as well, the land's sacredness was a salient theme. Indeed, at the very start of his testimony, Magnes stated:

> This is a land *sui generis*, a Holy Land for three monotheistic religions. It is, therefore, not just a Jewish land or just an Arab land. . . . We regard the Arab natural rights and the Jewish historical rights as, under all the circumstances, of equal validity. We look upon Palestine as a bi-national Jewish-Arab land, a common motherland for these

two Semitic peoples who have the privilege of acting as trustees for millions of their co-religionists all over the world. In such a land it is not fitting that one people should dominate the other.[17]

This link between the land's holiness for three religions and the rejection of separatist nationalism—the corresponding illegitimacy of any political dominance in such a religiously significant land—was the main theme of Magnes's testimony. The ensuing solution, proposed by Ichud, alluded to rising above narrow national struggles by invoking the transnational framework of those religions for which the Jewish, Muslim, and Christian peoples sitting in Palestine effectively served as representatives and trustees. Like Magnes's call for binationalism as a remedy to the inherent Jewish tension between separatism and universalism, here this same concept offered an interreligious approach to circumventing nationalism in the name of religious universalism.

The Yishuv's Response to Magnes

The Yishuv categorically rejected Magnes's testimony. On March 27, 1946, novelist Israel Cohen, an editor at the Labor Party (Mapai)–associated newspaper *HaPo'el HaTza'ir*, published an editorial dismissing Magnes as representing "a small cult with little influence" rather than any real community, and asserting that Buber and Magnes had no right to surrender the Jews' exclusive claim to the land in the name of their own "abstract politics." Furthermore, Cohen noted, throughout the inquiry Magnes had consistently dodged the question of his plan's practical feasibility.

Most important was Cohen's claim that Magnes was speaking on behalf of Reform Judaism: "Something has been left out of the Jewish People's prayer book. It is only the distorted historiosophy of [Reform] Mission Theology that interprets the verse about Israel not being 'like all the nations' to mean something spiritually akin to the legend of the eternal Jew." That is, according to Cohen, only assimilated Jews would view the rights of Jews and the rights of Arabs in the land as equally valid. Cohen was attributing Magnes's concept of binationalism to his Reform roots, particularly to Mission Theology and the universalist worldview that did not grant preference to any nation, not even to a political minority in a hostile environment.[18]

Magnes's position did receive support, in a backhanded way, from an unexpected source—the testimony of British historian of Lebanese descent Albert Hourani, who appeared before the Committee about ten days after Magnes. Hourani fiercely attacked Magnes, arguing that he was actually a veiled Zionist who was furthering the cause of political Zionism. As a result, future first premier of Israel David Ben-Gurion refrained from attacking Magnes during Mapai's council meetings, observing that "even Magnes" would not have conditioned Jewish immigration rights on the consent of non-Jews.[19] Subsequently, after British prime minister Clement Attlee dismissed the Committee's conclusions, effectively annulling any chance of a binational solution in Palestine, Zionist Organization (today, World Zionist Organization) president Chaim Weizmann too refrained from attacking Magnes—and, in a personal letter, even expressed agreement with his critique of the excessive "chauvinism" in Jewish education in the Yishuv.[20]

The Impact of Magnes's Statement on the Committee

In contrast to the limited impact that Magnes's and Ichud's theopolitical arguments had in the Yishuv, the interreligious argument as a basis for rejecting separatist nationalism in Palestine—and consequently the call for binationalism—evidently did have some impact on the Committee. Signs of Magnes's influence are discernible in several parts of the Anglo-American Committee's report, especially in its key political recommendation and the accompanying comment. The recommendation reads as follows:

Recommendation No. 3. In order to dispose, once and for all, of the exclusive claims of Jews and Arabs to Palestine, we regard it as essential that a clear statement of the following principles should be made:

    I. That Jew shall not dominate Arab and Arab shall not dominate Jew in Palestine. II. That Palestine shall be neither a Jewish state nor an Arab state. III. That the form of government ultimately to be established, shall, under international guarantees, fully protect and preserve the interests in the Holy Land of Christendom and of the Moslem and Jewish faiths.

Thus Palestine must ultimately become a state which guards the rights and interests of Moslems, Jews and Christians alike; and accords to the inhabitants, as a whole, the fullest measure of self-government, consistent with the three paramount principles set forth above.[21]

The explanatory comment accompanying this recommendation—basically listing its rationales—includes the following argument, taken nearly verbatim from Magnes's statement:

We, therefore, emphatically declare that Palestine is a Holy Land, sacred—to Christian, to Jew and to Moslem alike; and because it is a Holy Land, Palestine is not, and can never become, a land which any race or religion can justly claim as its very own. We further, in the same emphatic way, affirm that the fact that it is the Holy Land, sets Palestine completely apart from other lands, and dedicates it to the precepts and practices of the Brotherhood of Man, not those of narrow nationalism.[22]

The opening words of this comment—stressing the unique sanctity of the land and the geopolitical implications thereof, particularly the fact that it cannot serve as a focus for the realization of national aspirations in the narrow sense—starkly echo Magnes's main argument. Admittedly, the importance of preserving holy places and ensuring their accessibility had already been recognized in the text of the British Mandate

(Article 13) and the conclusions of the 1937 Peel Commission, which identified the holy cities of Bethlehem and Jerusalem as "a sacred trust of civilization." In these early proposals, however, as long as freedom of worship was maintained at the holy sites, the land's sanctity had no bearing on the political solution proffered. The position taken by both Magnes and the Committee—that the sacred nature of the land precluded any exclusive national claim—was unique.[23]

Elsewhere as well, the Committee's report referred to the multireligious nature of Palestine and the implications that followed. The seventh recommendation, for example, in addressing land policy, explicitly stated, "We recommend that the Government should exercise such close supervision over the Holy Places and localities such as the Sea of Galilee and its vicinity as will protect them from desecration and from uses which offend the conscience of religious people, and that such laws as are required for this purpose be enacted forthwith." The comment accompanying this recommendation specifically mentioned "the 'Lido' [beach] with its dancing and swing music" on the shore of the Sea of Galilee, which "offends the sensibilities of many Christian people."[24]

There are similarities to Magnes's testimony in statements by non-Zionist Jewish representatives who appeared before the Committee in Washington, including, notably, Judge Joseph Proskauer on behalf of the American Jewish Committee, and businessman and philanthropist Lessing Rosenwald, head of the American Council for Judaism, the main anti-Zionist organization in the United States. Proskauer argued that the question of Palestine should be referred to the United Nations because the administration of a land containing sites holy to Jews, Muslims, and Christians should be devoid of any conflicts of interest. Rosenwald cautioned that the Jews' claim to exclusivity in Palestine could lead to the emergence of a racial or even theocratic state.[25] Yet both their statements, in the spirit of American Reform Judaism's traditional opposition to Zionism, began by rejecting the view of Judaism as a nationality and insisting on regarding it solely as a religion. This contrasts with Magnes's more complex outlook, which rather than surrender the national element, incorporated it into a religious framework in the model of a binational partnership.

Other testimonies recognized the land's sanctity for one or all of the three monotheistic religions, yet drew different political conclusions. Ben-Gurion's statement, for one, dismissed the view that the Jewish bond to the land was solely a mystical, spiritual connection to the "Zion of Heaven." The love of Zion, Ben-Gurion asserted, had brought 600,000 Jews to the land of Zion: It was real and living. Conversely, Palestinian moderate notable Omar Dajani testified that Palestine was at least as sacred to Christians around the world as was is to Jews, if not more so.[26] Because it was so dear to Christians and Muslims the world over, accepting "Mr. Ben-Gurion's theory of love" would basically mean opening "the gates of our land" to international immigration, clearing the world of Christians, Muslims, and Jews, and settling them in Palestine.[27]

Magnes took the Committee's recommendations as evidence that he had successfully presented his own and Ichud's views.[28] The Committee's core political position—that Palestine should be neither a Jewish state nor an Arab state—was in harmony with Ichud's advocacy of binationalism. On May 1, 1946, the day the recommendations were made public, Magnes issued the announcement: "The Ichud council welcomes the recommendations of the Anglo-American Committee of Inquiry and expresses its hope that the mandatory administration in Palestine proceed without delay toward their implementation. . . . The road is open to Jewish-Arab cooperation in a binational Palestine."[29] Indeed, the report served as validation of their position by a body appointed by two global powers, and Magnes saw it as leverage for the extrication of Ichud from its forced political isolation. Buber, on behalf of Ichud and in an effort to broadcast the association's position worldwide, appealed to Hutcheson, the Committee's American president, to nominate Magnes for the Nobel Peace Prize. Hutcheson turned down the request.[30]

In his foreword to the published version of Ichud's testimony, biographer Norman Bentwich commented that the testimonies of Buber, Magnes, and Smilansky "made a deep impression" and that "it is clear from the recommendations of the Commission that it had an influence on the Report."[31] Historian Joseph Heller has noted that the publication of the Anglo-American Committee's report marked the highlight of Ichud's activities, because even though the Committee did not explicitly recommend binationalism, its conclusion that neither a Jewish state nor an Arab state should be established in Palestine was taken by Ichud members as an endorsement of binationalism.[32]

Further proof of the influence of Ichud's testimony appears in chapter 5 of the Committee's report, "The Jewish Attitude." After reviewing the positions of Mapai and HaShomer HaTza'ir and before considering the Revisionists, the chapter mentions Ichud, which it identifies as "very close" to HaShomer HaTza'ir but "without its socialist ideology."[33] As to Magnes's "small Ichud group," the report describes its importance as "far greater than its numbers," adding that "taken altogether, these Palestinian critics of the Biltmore Program certainly do not exceed at the moment one quarter of the Jewish population in Palestine. But they represent a constructive minority."[34] Thus, in addition to demonstrably overestimating Ichud's political power, the Committee regarded its positions favorably.

Members of the Committee also attested to the positive impression left by Magnes's testimony. According to Magnes and Buber's account of their testimony before the committee, *Arab-Jewish Unity*, Richard Crossman, a British member of Parliament, related to Magnes that he had been told that Magnes is "the only reasonable man in Palestine," and that "when I was listening to you, I began to see why."[35] Although Crossman was inclined to agree with Magnes's call for the immigration of 100,000 refugees, he was concerned about Magnes's proposed political solution because it seemed clear to him that even though these views had no concrete foundation in Palestine's politics, they would resound with a majority of the Committee members. In *Palestine Mission*, Crossman's detailed account of the works of the Anglo-American Committee of Inquiry, he explained: "Maybe twenty-five years ago that was possible; it's too late for it now. . . . [Magnes's] ideas would be all right if all the Jews were as patient and rational as he is; if the Arabs were not certain that the British are on their side; and if Mr. Bevin were able to replace all the key officials in the Middle East by men who believed in the national home and in helping Arabs and Jews to work together. But isn't that just Utopia?"[36]

Notwithstanding his own reservations, Crossman's remarks point to the potential impact left by Magnes's testimony. American Committee member and diplomat James McDonald, later the first U.S. ambassador to the State of Israel, voiced a similar opinion, combining appreciation for Magnes's proposal with reservations about the feasibility of binationalism: "Then came Dr. Magnes, who held his audience almost breathless for more than two hours. His statement was eloquent at times, deeply moving, and showed a moral courage of the very highest kind. His political thesis about a bi-partisan state did great credit to his breadth of understanding, but little, I fear, to his sense of statesmanship, for I don't think it is at all practicable."[37]

Was the religious rationale a central factor in persuading the Committee to reject exclusive Jewish or Arab national self-actualization in Palestine, or did the religious argument cloak, and buttress, a more practical position and calculated political considerations? Did Ichud's promotion of an idealistic moral politics that simultaneously circumvented existing political mechanisms for authorization and operation have an impact on real-world political considerations? The answer appears to be no and that it did not. The processes that drove the Committee's formation and conduct, and the reasons that its recommendations remained on paper, were ultimately a product of the global balance of powers between a rising superpower (the United States) and a declining empire (Britain). Yet within this context, domestic American political factors, such as the weight of the Jewish vote, also had an impact.[38] And, most probably, the American and British governments had actually consolidated their positions even before the Committee was announced.[39]

Judge Hutcheson and the Religious-Political Dimension

In shaping the Committee's conduct and conclusions, the American co-chair, Judge Hutcheson, was almost certainly the most influential participant. He was the highest-ranking member of the delegation with the most decision-making sway, given the shifting global balance of power. That power dynamic was evident in the Committee's work—for example, in its unequivocal acceptance of Truman's call for the immediate immigration of 100,000 refugees. "In the end, it was the leadership of Judge Hutcheson which kept us all together," the American lawyer Bartley Crum, a Committee member, would later report. "He would not permit our initial differences to result in the breakup of the committee into American and British groups. It is not an overstatement to say that had it not been for him, the final report would not have been unanimous. He labored for twelve to sixteen hours a day, drafting proposals and trying to reconcile points of view without yielding on basic principle."[40]

Intriguingly, Hutcheson brought his own religious perspective to the matter at hand. According to Crum, even during the Committee's preparatory sessions in Washington, Hutcheson described himself as an Old Testament Christian,[41] and during the concluding sessions in Lausanne, Switzerland, Hutcheson spelled out a religious context for the Committee members. Several passages from Hutcheson's statement served as a basis for the Committee's final conclusions, including the assertion that neither an Arab state nor a Jewish state should be created in Palestine, and that "the development of the Jewish National Home must go on with the fullest protection to Arab and Christian in that Holy Land, through some form of bi-national arrangement which will protect all interests."[42] Like Ichud in its statement, Hutcheson drew a direct link between Palestine's unique religious character and the need for a binational political framework. Furthermore, among the testimonies that influenced Hutcheson's position, Crum lists the testimony of Judah Leib Magnes.[43]

What, then, if any, influence did Magnes have on Hutcheson by expressing his own religious-political position? Hutcheson's exchange with Magnes during the question-and-answer session reveals an interesting and somewhat puzzling approach to the religious dimension. The full text of Hutcheson's statement, which Ichud published, includes the following remarks: "I would like to preface my questions by saying, Dr. Magnes, I am not ready to assess your proposals, but I am a fairly old man, and I recognise moral power when I see it. I want to say, sir, that I can say in the words of my Leader: 'Behold an Israelite indeed in whom there is no guile.' ... You are not denominated a Christian, but you talk as I should like Christians to act."[44]

Hutcheson's words constituted a striking tribute to Magnes's moral power. Moreover, Hutcheson's reference to a New Testament verse (John 1:47) that quotes Jesus Christ, his stated "Leader," made this an exceptionally powerful religious declaration. And, yet the text, "Behold an Israelite indeed in whom there is no guile," is itself borderline antisemitic, or its implications at the very least offensive toward all those witnesses from the Yishuv who preceded Magnes. Nevertheless, Hutcheson's observation that Magnes spoke as he would wish a Christian to act reveals the tremendous importance he attributed to the religious dimension.

The connection between Hutcheson and Magnes did not elude Buber, who would later invite the judge to take part in a special issue of the Ichud periodical *Be'ayot* in honor of Magnes's seventieth birthday. In his contribution, Hutcheson wrote:

> In my desk I keep a copy of the minutes of the testimonies of Dr. J. L. Magnes, Prof. M. Buber, and Mr. M. Smilansky, who represented the

Sacred Land and Negation of the State 249

association Ichud before the Anglo-American Committee on March 14, 1946.... I will never forget that day. And reading the minutes takes me back to what I felt then, enchanted by the power of the words of Dr. Magnes, the elegance and dignity of his appearance, the deep righteousness of his outlook, which truly compares to that of a messiah. My spirit was exhausted by then, depressed and despairing, after listening to a long series of extremist and hate-filled testimonies; it revived after hearing him. So too now, when the atmosphere is rife with greed-fueled claims and demands that lack any consideration of the other, as the hope for justice fades, my spirit is revitalized with new hope and new vigor each time I remember that day.[45]

The historical records confirm Hutcheson's prominent decision-making role among Committee members, the importance of religion in his worldview, his strong personal impression of Magnes's testimony, and the direct impact of his proposals on the Committee's final report. Ultimately it is difficult to say with certainty whether Magnes's view had an impact on Hutcheson or on the Committee's conclusions, even if the leaders of Ichud believed it did. According to such sources as Crossman's and Crum's books, the Committee's British and American members were mainly basing their actions on realpolitik considerations and attention to the fundamental political positions of the governments they represented.

The testimonies by Magnes and his Ichud associates before the Committee were essentially the swan song of binationalism as a political alternative, and of Magnes's own political activity. In contrast to the first decade of his activism (1929–38), when his political plans seemed at least somewhat promising, and Yishuv leaders, including Ben-Gurion, relied on him to arrange meetings with Arab leaders, the second decade (1939–48) was marked by his marginalization and exclusion from Yishuv political discourse. Following the outbreak of World War II, the destruction of Jewish life in Europe, the resulting refugee problem, and the growing violence on both sides of the Arab-Jewish conflict, the Yishuv had grown weary of binational solutions. While Magnes's testimony did leave a strong impression, and the Committee's report can be read as favoring binationalism, nevertheless, the balance of global geopolitical power, the aftershocks of the Holocaust, and near-total support among American Jews for the Partition Plan and the establishment of Israel ultimately combined to tip the balance in favor of a solution based on Jewish statehood.

15

The Confederation Plan between Hope and Despair

The friendship Magnes formed with the Jewish intellectual Hannah Arendt was among the most influential factors in his life during his later years.

Arendt's first impression of Magnes had been critical. She had read his article "Towards Peace in Palestine" in the January 1943 edition of *Foreign Affairs*, which aimed "to warn of the danger of war between Jews and Arabs, and to offer an alternative based upon a reasonable compromise."[1] The "indispensable prerequisite for a reasonable compromise," wrote Magnes, was "that American moral and political authority be thrown into the balance." He explored three possible models of "Union for Palestine": a binational state in Palestine; an economic and political federation that also included Transjordan, Syria, and Lebanon; and a federation in union with a greater Anglo-American union of the free nations "now laboring to be born out of the ruins of the decaying world."[2] His preference was for a combination of a local federation (binational or including the neighboring states) within a larger, universal, democratic federation. In this, the Jewish people would play a vital role. "The utterance of the prophets of Israel," he concluded, "contain as powerful a revolutionary fragment as mankind has ever known. Until Israel and the nations of mankind succeed in establishing a universal society based upon those ideals, there will continue to be a Jewish problem. That is Israel's destiny."[3]

Although Arendt supported his proposal for an Arab federation, she had serious misgivings about relying on an Anglo-American alliance—in her view, an extension of Weizmann's pro-British policy—to implement it. Eventually, however, she would change her mind about Magnes and Ichud, mainly because of their efforts to promote a genuine political alternative to the Jewish Agency's Biltmore Program, which effectively called for the realization of Jewish statehood, and which she considered dangerous.[4]

The Magnes-Arendt Connection

During a visit to the United States in 1946, Magnes enlisted former supporters to join a new organization of his making, which in time would become the unofficial "Friends of Ichud" in the United States. The group included non-Zionist Jewish-American leader Maurice Hexter, notable psychologist and philosopher Erich Fromm, philosopher and historian Hans Kohn, and lawyer James Marshall. When Magnes arrived in the United States for a subsequent visit in March 1948 (a visit that would last until Magnes's death in October 1948 of heart failure), he and Hannah Arendt corresponded, met, and consulted on one another's political articles, and Arendt came to join Ichud's U.S. political committee. In time Magnes invited her to chair the group, but she declined, claiming that "I lack quite a number of qualities a good chairman must have."[5]

Their relationship lacked intellectual symmetry: Arendt was a more methodical and sophisticated thinker, whereas Magnes was first and foremost an activist. Nonetheless, their conceptual outlooks were similar and there was a reciprocity to their interactions. According to Arendt, Magnes was the inspiration for her 1950 article "Peace or Armistice in the Near East?," which she dedicated to his memory.[6] Like many of his Brit Shalom associates who were thinkers rather than doers, she too was particularly drawn to Magnes because of his drive to action. Her own efforts at political activism had failed: Politics was not her calling, and her intellectual authority could not sustain her political struggles. Furthermore, she was concerned that direct political engagement might undermine her scholarship. In Magnes, though, she saw a model for political activism based on moral authority. "Will you permit me to tell you," she wrote in a Rosh Hashanah greeting just a few weeks before his death, "how grateful I am that the last year brought me into the privilege of knowing you.... Politics in our century is almost a business of despair and I have always been tempted to run away from it. I wanted you to know that your example prevented me from despairing and will prevent me for many years to come."[7]

The mutually enriching friendship the two developed especially informed Magnes's political views. He adopted Arendt's fundamental analysis regarding the decline of nationalism and the emergence of two basic options for political organization—federalism or imperialism—the former being preferable as well as essential for Jewish political self-organization. Magnes's interactions with Arendt may also have bolstered the American aspects of his political outlook. At the time, she herself was undergoing a process of "Americanization" as a new immigrant and becoming acquainted with U.S. political culture and academic discourse.[8]

Rejection of Nationalism in Favor of Federalism

Arendt's rejection of nationalism, articulated most strongly in her 1945 *Menorah Journal* article "Zionism Reconsidered,"[9] rested on the hypothesis that the concept of nationalism was no longer relevant in the global political reality of the mid-twentieth century. In her view, the national movements that had emerged toward the end of the nineteenth century, including Zionism, had originally offered a new and revolutionary form of political organization on the basis of nationality. Yet, since then, national movements had been demonstrably incapable of ensuring their people's sovereignty or of contributing to the general stability of the global political order—and the call for a nation-state had in fact become the root of the evil.[10] Regarding federalism as a solution, she wrote:

> For Jews, however, there is only too little reason for rejoicing in the decline of the national state and of nationalism. We cannot foretell the next steps of human history, but the alternatives seem to be clear. The resurgent problem of how to organize politically will be solved by adopting either the form of empires or the form of federations. The latter would give the Jewish people, together with other small peoples, a reasonably fair chance for survival. The former may not be possible without arousing imperialist passions as a substitute for outdated nationalism, once the motor to set men into action. Heaven help us if that comes to pass.[11]

For the fate of the Jews, therefore, federalism was the more pragmatic and necessary option; relying on the superpowers could mean the end of the Jewish people. This same argument underpinned her critique of Herzl's political Zionism: Reliance on the dominant powers would turn the Jewish state into an alien presence and a source of foreign colonial intervention in the Middle East. Hence, rather than cultivating ties with the superpowers in order to actualize aspirations of nation-statehood, Zionism should invest in building trust and cooperation with the inhabitants of Palestine and its Arab neighbors—precisely as Magnes and Ichud were doing in practice.[12]

Federation or Confederation?

In the 1950 article she dedicated to Magnes, "Peace or Armistice in the Near East?," Arendt explored the concept of a confederation, rather than a federation, as a solution. In contrast to a federal system, which is usually taken to mean "a multiple government in a single state," she noted that "the very term Confederation indicates the existence of two independent political entities." Considering the feasibility of this concept in Palestine, she observed that Magnes's proposal had also drawn support among Arab figures. On November 29, 1947—the day of the UN General Assembly vote on the Partition Plan—for example, Lebanon's envoy to the United Nations, Camille Chamoun, had called for a federal system and "like Dr. Magnes" had cited the U.S. Constitution as a model. The alternative to federalism, Arendt argued, was the continued and devastating "Balkanization" of the region, leading to continuous armed struggles between ethnic groups with conflicting national aspirations.[13]

In the same article Arendt examined a proposal by Magnes published in the October 1948 edition of *Commentary* magazine. A month earlier, *Commentary* had printed "The Future of Arab-Jewish Relations" by Aubrey (Abba) Eban (who would later become Israel's permanent representative to the United Nations), which reported on the troubled history of Arab-Jewish relations in Palestine by squarely placing the blame on Arab violence and lack of political leadership. Endorsing partition as the best applicable option, Eban had proclaimed: "In every field of Arab-Jewish relations, the keynote is the cooperation of equal and separate states—not the imposed union of divergent elements."[14] In response, Magnes's article, "United States of Palestine—A Confederation of Two Independent States," listed several areas that could be handled cooperatively by the two states through "the political center of a possible Confederation," among them foreign affairs, defense, international loans, federal court, and "protection of religious shrines and historical monuments and collections of cultural, artistic, and scientific importance."[15] Jerusalem would be "constituted as a *corpus seperatum*, as an international, demilitarized, neutralized city." The confederation's proposed name was admittedly "somewhat analogous to the name United States of America," Magnes noted, but "the United States of America is a federal structure in which the sovereignty of the individual states is much more limited than would be the case in the

Palestine Confederation." Per Magnes, immigration would remain autonomously regulated until the subject could be "taken up within the framework of the Confederation."[16]

Arendt's arguments surrounding the nonviability of the modern nation-state and the preference for federalism over imperialism merged in Magnes's thinking, given the federalist foundations of American political organization and his own resistance to political dependence on the superpowers (which dated back to the 1917 Balfour Declaration). In 1920 Magnes had written, "The growing imperialism and militarism of the world ... will probably lead to future and more devastating wars. ... We cannot depend on the economic imperialism of the British Empire, nor that of the United States or any other imperialism. The leaders of the Zionist movement undoubtedly see this quite clearly, but they refrain from saying so for fear of offending their sources of political charity. Yet it is precisely for this reason that those residing elsewhere must remind the Jews of the old adage, 'Do not trust philanthropists.'"[17] Not only did the name he choose attest to the American roots of his conceptual framework; he also devoted time during those years to rereading *The Federalist Papers* of James Madison, John Jay, and Alexander Hamilton, because he expected them to be "illuminating for the Palestine Confederation." He also wrote in his October 1948 *Commentary* article, a year into his friendship with Arendt, that "the Constitution-makers of the new Palestine may well use as primary sources both as to terminology and as to substance the American Articles of Confederation of 1777, which because of defects discovered in practice, led to the Constitution of 1787."[18] Thus, Magnes openly and visibly relied on the pillars of the American political system. His friendship with Arendt appears to have had the effect of legitimizing the American influence on his political outlook. This became increasingly evident in his political proposals as his ties with Arendt strengthened.

The concept of a federation, specifically as Magnes understood it, deserves a brief, critical mention. Historian Joseph Heller writes that

Magnes's pragmatic proposal for a Jewish-Arab federal state was fundamentally utopian. Rather than viewing the federal system of organization as one possible way of forming a state, with advantages as well as disadvantages, he regarded the models of Switzerland, Canada, Yugoslavia, and Austria-Hungary as incontrovertible success stories. Yet, as Heller points out, federalism by its very nature necessitates an atmosphere of trust and respect, but Magnes's and Ichud's model of federalism did not take into account the crucial differences between the above examples and the polarized dynamics of nationalism in Palestine.[19]

"The Conscience of the Jewish People"

Magnes, wrote Arendt in "Peace or Armistice in the Near East," published in 1950 in *Review of Politics*, "based his protest on purely humanitarian grounds—and laid himself wide open to the old accusations of quixotic morality in politics where supposedly only advantage and success count." She continued: "In a world like ours, however, ... uncompromising morality has suddenly changed its old function of merely keeping the world together and has become the only medium through which true reality ... can be perceived and planned."[20]

After his death she composed a brief eulogy, "Magnes, the Conscience of the Jewish People," stressing Magnes's morality as a proactive aspect of his character that, despite charges of quixotic, impractical utopianism, actually embodied true political realism. At the same time, it is evident here and elsewhere that Arendt completely overlooked the religious aspect of his character. Given that the issue of Judaism as a faith was not a major focus of her scholarship, one may, with due caution, conclude that she was not a partner to his theological dialogue.[21]

In sum, Magnes's exchanges with Arendt reinforced his rejection of nationalism and resistance to imperialism. In the spirit of her political analysis, he too came to believe that the only possible solution to the situation in Palestine was a binational confederation. Later, his friendship with Arendt—who, after immigrating to the United States, developed a strong admiration for the American political model—further consolidated and validated the American aspects of his political worldview. Arendt's biographer Elisabeth Young-Bruehl notes: "In Winchester, Hannah Arendt became aware that she could dislike American social life while admiring American political life. She formed an opinion she kept for the rest of her life: 'The fundamental contradiction of the country is political freedom coupled with social slavery.'"[22] No longer was Magnes the only American in the Central European intellectual environment of the Hebrew University. He now had a prominent intellectual as a partner, although she had yet to receive the renown associated with her name today.

Conclusion

Toward the end of his life, the American philosopher and psychologist William James received a copy of a doctoral dissertation that meticulously examined and classified the religious characteristics in the body of his work. In response, James wrote to the dissertation's author:

> From the technical point of view you may be proud of your production. I like greatly the objective and dispassionate key in which you keep everything, and the number of subdivisions and articulations which you make give me vertiginous admiration. Nevertheless, the tragic fact remains that I don't feel wounded at all by all that output of ability.... This is splendid philology, but is it live criticism of anyone's *Weltanschauung* [worldview]? . . . Building up an author's meaning out of separate texts leads nowhere, unless you have first grasped his center of vision, by an act of imagination.[1]

This book represents an attempt to capture Judah Leib Magnes's "center of vision"—to find the assumed Archimedean point from which to identify the source of his motivation, and on that basis to reposition him as a historical figure in academic scholarship. For Magnes this center had a religious essence, and his fundamental worldview was a product of Judaism's centrality in his life and his own conceptualization of religion. Magnes repeatedly consulted contemporaries and associates, including Hugo Bergman, Gershom Scholem, Norman Bentwich, and Ernst Simon, about his religious questions. This book has therefore sought to chart the complexities of Magnes's religious understandings of the world and position them at the heart of his worldview, using them as a point of departure to examine his political outlook generally, and his position on binationalism specifically.

The theology of Reform Judaism is manifest not only in the movement's official documents and the writings of its thinkers; it is also the product of existential experience and the expansive social fabric generated by community life and religious practice.[2] Similarly, Magnes's theology was not the perspective of a methodical philosopher or scholar but essentially that of a rabbi called upon to examine Jewish life in practice from the perspective of the religious person, the religious community, and, in time, the Jewish people. The drive of the religious quest in the modern era compelled Magnes on his journey: He sought to embrace the revitalizing power of Reform Judaism as adapted to modernity, while also to overcome what he perceived as Reform's failings, including its spiritual depletion. As a result, Magnes opened himself up to a broad range of religious influences along three principal channels:

> Within the Jewish world—the rational Conservative Judaism of Schechter, as well as a form of Hasidic neo-Orthodoxy that characterized his religious worship and mystical search for the "soul";

> In the surrounding Christian world—the Social Gospel movement and the Quakers, whose religious pacifism resonated for him; and

> In the secular world—early Zionism, radical socialism, and the Jewish as well as non-Jewish pacifism that emerged on the eve of and during World War I, in which he found elements of divinity even in the absence of religious discourse. Such signs of the Divine in the

secular world formed part of his continuous effort to find evidence of God's dynamic presence in history, just as Hasidism seeks to extend the realms of the Divine as far as possible across specific, historical human experiences.

World War I marked a turning point, triggering a religious crisis for Magnes, who was not alone in this regard. The war seemingly defied the optimistic view of human moral development in the spirit of Enlightenment, and invalidated the liberal theology that had prevailed during the latter half of the nineteenth century and the early twentieth century. In the aftermath of World War I, a sense of religious crisis infused Magnes's outlook—as it did for many thinkers within and beyond the Jewish world, including Franz Rosenzweig, Martin Buber, Paul Tillich, Leonhard Ragaz, and Karl Barth, among others. For Magnes it manifested as a theology of quest, a repeated underscoring of the futility of seeking God even though the seeker should never to abandon the search. This is how Magnes explained himself in his personal journal, in a religious confession written shortly after immigrating to Palestine; this is how he understood Barth's dialogical theology; and this is how he approached how to reconcile God's existence with the Holocaust. Driven by the intensity of the eclipse of God as he experienced it, Magnes insisted on the imperative of life and on the search for God.

The tension between Judaism as a religion and Judaism as a nationality lay at the heart of Magnes's theopolitical worldview. Initially, as a Zionist in the United States, he struggled to counter the claim that Jewry represented only a religious community. Rather, he emphasized, the Jewish religion cannot exist without the Jewish people. He regarded Zionism and Jewish nationalism, even when formulated in terms more reminiscent of Ahad Ha'am than Herzl, as the means to revitalizing and renewing the Jewish religion. Over time, however, and against the background of World War I, the tension he felt between nationalism and religion grew, and he became increasingly disillusioned with, and suspicious of, nationalism. His disillusionment is patently evident in his assertion, on the eve of Israeli statehood, that "the ideal of the state has taken over the vast majority of Jewry." This marked the culmination of his retreat from viewing Zionism as essential to Jewish revival and his move toward viewing nationalism as a threat to the moral survival of Judaism and to his aspirations for a model Jewish society in the spirit of Ahad Ha'am and Israel's prophets. In the 1940s, in light of his disillusionment with the political character Zionism had acquired, Magnes proposed reframing Judaism on the basis of three religious pillars: religion, morality and study—nationalism excluded.

The tension Magnes experienced between nationalism and religion was also an expression of tension between nationalism—even in its more universal, less ethnic, American form—and the supranationalism that served as a cornerstone of Reform Judaism's religious worldview. In proposing binationalism as a solution, Magnes sought to bridge the inherent tension between Zionism, essentially a movement aimed at actualizing separatist Jewish nationalism, and the Mission Theology of Reform Judaism, which held that Jews have a calling among the nations. The tension could not be resolved by focusing solely on the particular, because that would mean abandoning the Jews' messianic universal mission. This was the reason Magnes spoke out against statehood on the eve of Israel's founding.

His conceptualization of binationalism, in contrast, resolved for him the tension between Zionism's particularism and the ideal of universalism. Binationalism, for Magnes, incorporated both the particular—that is, the national dimension—and the universal, which constrained nationalism, by placing it in a multinational framework. In this sense, binationalism represented Magnes's attempt to actualize the concept he coined in *Like All the Nations?*—a national-international entity. Furthermore, binationalism, for Magnes, offered a just solution that embodied the temporary nature of Jewish nationalism on the path to a more universal political vision. There is a messianic-political dimension to this outlook, which holds that one should actively pursue the universal vision even in the context of a separatist national framework, and that one should prioritize the teachings of the prophets over political constraints.

Binationalism, as Magnes conceived it, also had distinctly and even overtly American elements. His concept of nationalism was rooted in his American background—a fact that set him apart from the Central European advocates of binationalism among whom he operated. American nationalism, including Magnes's, was not ethnic-cultural but civil-political—that is, it stemmed from a sense of belonging to a common political entity. In turn, Magnes's advocating of binationalism as a solution was shaped by fundamental principles of the American political system, American pragmatism and democracy, and the American experience with federalism. His concept of binationalism presupposed a political structure that, given its inherent institutional capacity to regulate coexistence, could guarantee cultural and political equality. The American principles behind Magnes's outlook are discernable here: Democracy is framed not only as the optimal form of political organization but also as having moral value. In essence, binationalism as posited by Magnes fused his American Jewish religious worldview, which centered on ethical monotheism and Reform Judaism's concept of prophetic justice, with his fundamentally American pragmatic political outlook, which ascribed importance to political institutions and viewed them, and the constitutional system, as foundations for a society regulated by sustainable justice.

Why were neither Magnes nor his views accepted in the Yishuv? Might the religious dimension of his views explain at least in part his outsider status? Addressing this question requires taking into account how his religious thinking was interwoven with his American identity. His American Jewish identity represented an exception to the norm of Yishuv life, and, moreover, his religiosity seemed foreign to the nonreligious ethos of the Yishuv. In the secular atmosphere of the Yishuv, Gershom Scholem noted, Magnes came across as archaic.[3] Paradoxically, despite the American background that he personally associated with a spirit of progress, within the Yishuv's political discourse he was seen as a representative of now-obsolete diaspora notions.

Was Magnes's political program viable? Does examining it from a theopolitical perspective shed new light on the issue? Today there is a tendency, stemming in no small part from the current political mood and underlying events, to reframe the Arab-Jewish conflict as fundamentally religious rather than political. One must, however, take into account religion's weak standing during the first half of the twentieth century, as illustrated by Walter Benjamin's reference, in *On the Concept of History*, to theology, "which as everyone knows is small and ugly and must be kept out of sight."[4] As such, and in particular after World War I, it would have been very difficult to promote a theopolitical discourse aimed at introducing substantial changes in Yishuv politics. This book's presentation of Magnes's concept of binationalism as political theology therefore underscores its lack of persuasiveness in the political arena of the Yishuv rather than highlighting its political validity. The same holds true with respect to the views of Buber and the Central European circle of Brit Shalom.

This book additionally touches on the political theology of the Zionist enterprise as a whole. Interest in this issue has increased with the return of religion to political discourse and the consolidation of explicit political theologies, such as that of religious Zionism generally or of Gush Emunim (Bloc of Faithful—the settlers' movement) in particular, which have been studied extensively. A question that follows is whether there might exist today an explicitly theological alternative to the worldview of religious Zionism. After the Holocaust of European Jewry and subsequent transformations in the Jewish world, there remain two major centers of Jewish life: Israel and North America. An alternative political theology might therefore rest on an American Jewish liberal religious worldview, such as that advanced by Magnes. His case study, as explored in this book, attests to the potential difficulties of introducing such a political theology in Israel.

In closing, it is fitting to add a general observation about using Magnes as a case study to examine the present political discourse surrounding binationalism. As the book underscores, Magnes's political worldview was embedded in his religious worldview. He saw binationalism as a way to restore Jewish values in the face of what he believed was a trend toward letting the national ethos override the Jewish ethos. His solution included two distinct political subunits, which, through mutual relations to be established and supported by their cooperative institutions, would be able to reach a higher plane of coexistence and a more inclusive worldview. In the spirit of Ahad Ha'am's teachings, Magnes's plan referred explicitly to the creation of a Jewish cultural center. For him, binationalism was not a call to create "a state of all its citizens," but rather an attempt to establish a model Jewish society in Palestine based on the principles of prophetic justice. As such, championing Magnes as a harbinger of current binational trends in Israel/Palestine is to some extent misleading.

In his memoir of Magnes, "He Looked Out on Zion from Atop Mount Scopus and Dreamt of Peace," Israeli journalist and peace activist Gabriel Stern recalls a pilgrimage he made years after Magnes's death to the office that had served Magnes when he was president of the Hebrew University. "To be precise," Stern recalls, "I should say that I made an ascent, for the room is in the lofty dome of the building which, in the early days of the University, was the loftiest of them all—the National and University Library, now the Law School—at the highest elevation in the Judean hills surrounding the city of Jerusalem: Mount Scopus." He describes the view Magnes would have witnessed from the seclusion of his study: "To the east I gaze out at the Judean Desert, the Jordan Valley, and the Dead Sea. In the background loom the Mountains of Ammon and Moab, and in the distance, one can see the ancient village of Anatot or Anata, the site of the birthplace of the prophet Jeremiah. They appear just as the late Magnes himself must have seen them."[5]

These words ring a felicitous note in bringing to completion this journey of exploration into the world of Judah Leib Magnes. The attempt to elevate politics to the moral plateau of a Mount Scopus, infused with the prophetic voice of his hero Jeremiah, this was the linchpin of Magnes's spiritual and political quest. As for whether or not his position—prophesizing endless war and struggle unless binationalism was implemented—was realistic, as current affairs stand, the court of history seems to be adjourned.

NOTES

ARCHIVE ABBREVIATIONS

AJA American Jewish Archives, Cincinnati
BAN Bancroft Library, University of California Berkeley
BGA Ben-Gurion Archives, Midreshet Ben-Gurion
CAHJP Central Archive for the History of the Jewish People, Jerusalem
NLI National Library of Israel, Jerusalem

PREFACE

1. Agnon, *Shira*, 103.
2. Magnes, *Dissenter in Zion*, 268–69.
3. Segev, *One Palestine, Complete*, 410–11. For more on al-Sakakini, see Sakakini, *Kaze Ani Rabotai!*
4. From an unpublished essay by Magnes titled "To Arab Friends," April 1942, CAHJP, Magnes Archives, P3/340.

INTRODUCTION

1. Arendt, *The Jewish Writings*, 451–52.
2. Bergman, *Faith and Reason*, 142–43.
3. The role of the chancellor during the Hebrew University's first decade combined administrative and academic responsibilities. As Uri Cohen notes, citing Simcha Assaf, university rector from 1948 to 1950, Magnes effectively ran the university on his own during the first decade, assisted by his friend Max Schlesinger and secretary Ari Even-Zahav. See Cohen, *HaHar VeHagivaa*, 70–73.

4. The term "theopolitical" as used here should be distinguished from the concept of "theopolitics" coined by Martin Buber in 1934, partly in response to Carl Schmitt's charged concept of "political theology." Theopolitics refers to religiously motivated politics, whereas political theology, a far more critical concept, explores the ways in which theological thinking relates to politics and society, viewing even secular politics as subconsciously informed by religious considerations and structures. The term as used here is closer to Buber's concept, although it refers more generally to theological-political analysis.
5. The article was published in 1929 as a booklet in Hebrew and English. See Magnes, *Like All the Nations?*
6. Magnes, *Dissenter in Zion*, 7–8; Kotzin, *Magnes*, 48.
7. See Goren, *New York Jews*, 1–5.
8. Kotzin, *Magnes*, 146–48; Magnes, *War-time Addresses*, 18.
9. Magnes, *Dissenter in Zion*, 431–32.
10. Heller, *MiBrit Shalom Le-Ichud*, 301–5; Magnes, *Dissenter in Zion*, 497–98.
11. Sarna, *American Judaism*, 201.
12. Lazar, *Shisha Yechidim*, 127.
13. From notes taken by Avraham Shapira for Gershom Scholem's autobiography, *From Berlin to Jerusalem*.
14. Myers, *In Search of the Harmonious Jew*; Goren, "Between Priest and Prophet," 57–67.
15. Kotzin, "An Attempt to Americanize the Yishuv."
16. Recent works, representing these respective trends, include Joseph Heller's *From Brit Shalom to Ichud: Judah Leib Magnes and the Struggle for a Binational State* (2003) and Hedva Ben Yisrael's contribution in a collection of articles edited by Adi Gordon, *Brit Shalom and Binational Zionism: The "Arab Question" as a "Jewish Question"* (2009).
17. See, for example, Tal, *Teologia Politit*, 9.
18. Taubes, "Teologiya VeTeoriya Politit," 91–93.
19. Rechnitzer, *Nevua VeHaseder HaMedini HaMushlam*, 21.
20. Binyamini and Hotam, "Likrat Teologiya Bikortit," 193–205.
21. Cavanaugh and Scott, *The Blackwell Companion to Political Theology*, 1–3.

1. THE IMPORTANCE OF BEING EARNEST

1. Rosenbaum, *Cosmopolitans*, 19–21, 67–68. On Stein's reservations regarding the Zionist "daydream," see Will, "Gertrude Stein and Zionism," 437–55.
2. Bentwich, *For Zion's Sake*, 14.
3. Bentwich, *For Zion's Sake*, 22.

4. For the text of the sermon Magnes delivered at age eight, see "Hebrew Sabbath School: Service Held at Shuttuck's Hall this Afternoon," BAN, 709 (Magnes Papers), 1–3.
5. Cited in Rosenbaum, *Cosmopolitans*, 103–4.
6. Rosenbaum, *Cosmopolitans*, 104–5.
7. Kotzin, *Magnes*, 36–37; "Rabbi Magnes Delivers First Sermon," *San Francisco Call*, August 12, 1900, BAN, 709 (Magnes Papers), 1–3.
8. See "Newspaper clippings," August 1900, BAN, 709 (Magnes Papers), 1–3; the name of the newspaper is not mentioned.
9. Rosenbaum, *Cosmopolitans*, 171–72. See also "Report Concerning Suffering Jews in San Francisco Earthquake and Fire," May 7, 1907, BAN, 709 (Magnes Papers), 2–2; "Totally Destroyed," *Emanu-el*, May 18, 1906, CAHJP, P3/392.
10. Rischin, "The Jewish Experience," 41–42.
11. Sarna, *American Judaism*, 132.
12. Kotzin, *Magnes*, 21–25.
13. Kotzin, *Magnes*, 28–29.
14. Kotzin, *Magnes*, 28–29. See also Bentwich, *For Zion's Sake*, 18–20; Magnes, "Palestine—or Death," BAN, 709 (Magnes Papers), 1–4.
15. In contrast, and in accordance with Magnes's argument, the Hebrew University Jewish philosopher Julius Guttmann, a contemporary of Magnes, held that for Gaon, the subject matter of divine revelation was identical with intellect, and any prophetic theories that followed must first meet the intellectual requirements of ethics. See Kotzin, *Magnes*, 34–35; Guttmann, *HaPhilosophia Shel HaYahadut*, 63, 70.
16. Kotzin, *Magnes*, 37–39.
17. Bentwich, *For Zion's Sake*, 27; Kotzin, *Magnes*, 41. Regarding the influence of Frankel's philosophy on Magnes, see Heller, *MiBrit Shalom Le-Ichud*, 35. For more on Frankel, Zunz, and the Breslau seminary, see, for example, Meyer, *Bein Masoret Lekidma*, 105–10.
18. Bentwich, *For Zion's Sake*, 30; Kotzin, *Magnes*, 41–42.
19. Magnes, "Notes on Visit to Grandfather's Grave," August 5, 1922, CAHJP, P3/329.
20. Bentwich, *For Zion's Sake*, 28.
21. Bentwich, *For Zion's Sake*, 28–29; Kotzin, *Magnes*, 40–41; Buber, *Letters*, 529–31.
22. Bloch wrote that he hoped, like Magnes, to attend often and to establish his place there if they would agree to accept him. "Lower East Side Synagogue," *Ernest Bloch Society Bulletin*, no. 7 (1974), BAN, 709 (Magnes Papers), 2–25.
23. Bentwich, *For Zion's Sake*, 29.

24. Sarna, *American Judaism*, 187-91; Schechter, for example, concerned about the integrity of the faith, never taught a course critiquing the biblical scriptures; he argued that before engaging in such a critique, one must study and become familiar with the scriptures themselves. Fine, "Solomon Schechter," 3-24.
25. Kotzin, *Magnes*, 61, 78; Bentwich, *Solomon Schechter*, 206; Friesel, "Zionism in Judaism," 73-74; Magnes, *Dissenter in Zion*, 62.
26. For an updated and comprehensive biography of Marshall, see Silver, *Louis Marshall*.
27. Bentwich, *For Zion's Sake*, 40-41; Kotzin, *Magnes*, 67-71.
28. Magnes, *Dissenter in Zion*, 88.
29. Butler, Wacker, and Balmer, *Religion in American Life*, 68-69.
30. Magnes, *Dissenter in Zion*, 107-8.
31. Magnes, *Dissenter in Zion*, 109-10.
32. Magnes, *Dissenter in Zion*, 111-12. As explained later in this book, there were religious elements in the radicalization Magnes underwent because, in his view, it followed the true doctrine of Reform Judaism, and he regarded the East European Jewish pacifists as emissaries of the authentic Reform doctrine. Ultimately, therefore, the notion of a new movement that would be completely detached from Reform ideology did not accord with Magnes's views, and perhaps his call for Temple Emanu-El and like-minded congregations to become part of an unofficial but nonetheless genuine Reform Judaism should be taken with a grain of salt.
33. For a discussion of this term as Schechter used it, see, for example, Bentwich, *Solomon Schechter*, 37-38; Cohen, *The Birth of Conservative Judaism*, 1-6.
34. "Dr J. L. Magnes Resigns as Associate Rabbi of Temple Emanuel," *American Hebrew*, May 22, 1910.
35. "Schechter: Special Interview for the Jewish Chronicle with Prof. Dr. Schechter," *Jewish Chronicle*, July 8, 1910, BAN, 709 (Magnes Papers), 2-24.
36. Cohen, *The Birth of Conservative Judaism*, 26-43.
37. Magnes to Louis Marshall, August 30, 1915, BAN, 709 (Magnes Papers), 1-12.
38. Goren, *New York Jews*, 1-5; Kotzin, *Magnes*, 103-5.
39. Kotzin, *Magnes*, 106-7.
40. Kotzin, *Magnes*, 107-11, 116, 124.

2. "PALESTINE OR DEATH"

1. The Reform movement underwent an upheaval after Felix Adler abandoned Judaism. Adler was the son of Rabbi Samuel Adler of New York's Temple Emanu-El in New York, one of the leading Reform congregations at the

time, which Magnes would later serve as rabbi. On May 15, 1876, Felix Adler announced his rejection of God and the Jewish religion and inaugurated the Sunday Lecture Movement. These lectures did not entail any ritual, but rather sermons aimed at exploring the history of human inspiration and the ability of music to lift the soul. On February 21, 1877, the New York Society of Ethical Culture was officially founded, with the aim of promoting a universal ethical culture and egalitarian study of the world's religions. Sarna, *American Judaism*, 132; Kraut, *Felix Adler's Emergence out of Judaism*, 181–85.

2. "Palestine—or Death," January 10, 1896, BAN, 709 (Magnes Papers), 1–4.
3. Shiff, *Yehudim Mishtalvim*, 28–29, 34–35.
4. Shiff, *Yehudim Mishtalvim*, 51–54. For the complete text of the platform, see Meyer, *Response to Modernity*, 387–88.
5. Shiff, *Yehudim Mishtalvim*, 16–17.
6. Shiff, *Yehudim Mishtalvim*, 51–54.
7. Greenstein, *Turning Point*.
8. Meyer, *Judaism within Modernity*, 362–77.
9. Sarna, "Converts to Zionism," 223–43.
10. Kotzin, *Magnes*, 38–51; Bentwich, *For Zion's Sake*, 31. For his doctoral dissertation Magnes translated the philosophical essay *A Treatise as to (1) Necessary Existence (2) The Procedure of Things from the Necessary Existence and (3) The Creation of the World* by Joseph Ibn Aknin from Jewish Arabic. The essay aimed to juxtapose Aristotelian philosophy with the Islamic school of Kalam, a scholastic form of Islamic theology. As later demonstrated by Julius Guttmann, professor of Jewish philosophy at the Hebrew University and a contemporary of Magnes, this essay, mistakenly attributed to the medieval Jewish philosopher and poet Joseph ben Judah Ibn Aknin, was in fact authored by Joseph ben Judah of Ceuta, Morocco, a favorite disciple of Maimonides. This treatise is the only philosophical essay by Joseph ben Judah known to have survived to date. Guttmann, *HaPhilosophia Shel HaYahadut*, 174–77.
11. Ratzabi, *Between Zionism and Judaism*, 65–82.
12. Magnes, *Dissenter in Zion*, 9.
13. Magnes, "Herzl's Influence upon Jewish Students in German Universities," *The Maccabean* 7, no. 2, August 1904, 103–5, BAN, 709 (Magnes Papers), 1–4. Later in this article Magnes describes the emergence of a Jewish philosophy of life (*Lebensanschauung*) among German students. This concept—or, more precisely, its absence—would later form the basis of Magnes's critique of American Reform Judaism in his Passover sermon at Temple Emanu-El in 1910.

14. Avineri, *HaRa'ayon HaZioni LiGvanav*, 131-42. Ahad Ha'am further stated: "The true and only foundation of Zionism should be sought only from the second problem, the moral one. . . . A political concept not based on the national culture can lead the people away from its spiritual power and create in it a tendency to seek its 'honor' through physical power and a political government, thus severing its ties with the past and undermining its historical foundation." Ahad Ha'am, *Kol Kitvei Ahad Ha'am*, 135-38.
15. According to Friesel, during the first two decades of the twentieth century the Zionist movement in the United States underwent four identifiable phases. Initially (1897-1904) the Federation of American Zionists was headed by figures such as Richard Gottheil and Jacob de Haas, and the movement was characterized by personal and ideological ties to Herzl and political Zionism. (Richard Gottheil was the son of Gustav Gottheil, whom Sarna identified as one of the first "converts" to Zionism.) Between 1904 and 1910, when the major American Zionist leaders were Harry Friedenwald, Israel Friedlander, and Judah Leib Magnes, the movement adopted Ahad Ha'am's ideas, adapting them to the American Jewish arena. At the time, a visit by Ahad Ha'am to the United States was also planned, although ultimately it did not take place. During Louis Lipsky's leadership of the Zionist Organization of America (ZOA) between 1922 and 1930, the movement was divided between Ahad Ha'am's followers and Lipsky and his supporters, who maintained an independent ideological position. Between 1914 and 1921, Louis Brandeis, ZOA leader from 1916 to 1922, established a new ideological stance, influenced by Kallen's cultural pluralism, which drew the movement away from Ahad Ha'am's positions. See Friesel, "Ahad Ha-Amism," 133-34. Regarding Herzl's influence on Gottheil and other Zionist leaders, and the way in which he adapted his teachings to the needs of American Jewry, see Segev, "European Zionism," 274-91.
16. Kornberg, "At the Crossroads," xvi-xix.
17. See Seltzer, "Ahad Ha-Am and Dubnow," 60-72.
18. Friedlander, *Past and Present*, xi.
19. Quoted in Zipperstein, *Elusive Prophet*, 267-68.
20. Mordecai Kaplan similarly criticized U.S. Reform Jews for not disseminating their ideas in the spirit of Mission Theology, for their passivity and lack of spiritual engagement, and for not having produced thinkers within the movement. See Kaplan, *Judaism as a Civilization*. Magnes and Kaplan were both close associates of Schechter during the first decade of the twentieth century in New York.

21. Cited in Bentwich, *For Zion's Sake*, 35. For the full text of the lecture, see Judah L. Magnes, "The Harmonious Jew," *The American Hebrew*, January 25, 1907.
22. Magnes apparently borrowed this term from Nietzsche, whose hero Zarathustra sought "the one who writes new values on new tables." Nietzsche, *Thus Spoke Zarathustra*, 164. For a discussion of Nietzsche's concept of "transvaluation," see, for example, Mayshar, "Cohen VeNavi," 438–63.
23. Judah L. Magnes, "A Jewish Spiritual Culture," n.p., c. 1911, BAN, 709 (Magnes Papers), 1–4.
24. Judah L. Magnes, "Notes on the Nature of Jewish Nationalism," CAHJP, P3/351. Magnes's aversion to philosophy as a means of addressing questions about life was also evident in a speech he delivered on November 1, 1944, to mark the opening of the Hebrew University's 1944–45 academic school year, "For Thy Sake Are We Killed All the Day Long."
25. See, for example, Schatz-Uffenheimer, *HaHasidut KeMistika*. Schatz-Uffenheimer writes, "Not only is the *hasid* expected to be apathetic to the contempt or 'non-valuation' of society, but he is asked to be suspicious of the open admiration of society, as the latter—which is superficially a positive value, in that he serves as a 'good example'—harms the inner self-valuation of the spirit" (253).
26. Magnes, "Jewish Spiritual Culture."
27. Otto's essay, published in 1917, focuses primarily on a phenomenological analysis of the irrational and its relation to the rational. See Otto, *The Idea of the Holy*, 1–11, and the afterword to the Hebrew edition by Yosef Ben-Shlomo, 182–203.
28. On Rabbi Kook's view of secular Jews and secularization as an essential aspect of the redemption process, see Aran, *Kookism*, 122–38. Nonetheless, according to Aran, "Despite his image, Rabbi Kook was also unable to reduce the religious-secular divide. His pact with the secular was in fact quite limited, superficial, and flimsy, circumscribed in terms of subject matter, and based on mutual misunderstanding. The secular did not delve past overt expressions of the rabbi's doctrine and activities, whereas he from the outset did not accept them as they saw and identified themselves, but instead imposed his own interpretation on them, which he saw as their reality" (132).
29. Magnes, "Jewish Spiritual Culture."
30. Magnes, "Jewish Spiritual Culture."
31. According to Ahad Ha'am, "Judaism seeks to return to its historical base, to lead a life of natural progression, to implement its potential in all areas of human culture, to develop and complete the national assets it has acquired

to date, and thus also to make national culture, the fruit of the labor of a people who lives spiritually, part of the treasure of the human race in the future, as it has done in the past. . . . And then, when the national culture in Palestine reaches such a level, we will be able to rely on it because it will produce people who will be able, at the right time, to create a 'state' there as well—not merely a state of Jews but a truly Jewish state." Ahad Ha'am, *Al Parashat Drachim*, 138.

32. Kornberg, "At the Crossroads," xvi–xix.
33. Greene, *The Jewish Origins*, 74–77.
34. Quoted in Greene, *The Jewish Origins*, 75.
35. Schechter to Magnes, December 22, 1908 [untitled letter], CAHJP, P3/115.
36. Greene, *The Jewish Origins*, 74–75.
37. Horace M. Kallen, "Democracy versus the Melting Pot: A Study of American Nationality," *The Nation*, February 18, 1915, 192–93; February 25, 1915, 217–20.
38. Responding to Kallen's article in a March 1915 letter, the prominent philosopher and educator John Dewey wrote, "I quite agree with your orchestra idea, but upon [the] condition we really get a symphony and not a lot of different instruments playing simultaneously. . . . That each cultural section should maintain its distinctive literary and artistic traditions seems to me most desirable, but in order that it might have more to contribute to others . . . there seems to be an implication of segregation geographical and otherwise." Later that year Dewey wrote, "The dangerous thing is for each factor to isolate itself, to try to live off its past, and then to attempt to impose itself upon other elements, or, at least, to keep itself intact and thus refuse to accept what other cultures have to offer." Cited in Menand, *The Metaphysical Club*, 400–401.
39. Magnes, *Dissenter in Zion*, 101–6.
40. In a June 1914 letter to Chaim Weizmann, Magnes wrote, "The Despair theory of Zionism does not appeal to me. I have not despaired of the Jewish people, and I believe in its eternity even without Palestine." He went on to propose an approach based on reciprocity between Palestine and the Diaspora: "The Jews of the world influence Palestine; Palestine influences the Jews of the world." Cited in Friesel, "Zionism in Judaism," 74.
41. Magnes, *Dissenter in Zion*, 105.
42. For the compete script of the play and an article analyzing it, see Nahshon, *From the Ghetto*, 211–365.
43. Magnes, *Dissenter in Zion*, 106. As we can see, Magnes preceded Kallen by several years in invoking the orchestra metaphor that came to be explicitly associated with Kallen's cultural pluralism and Brandeis's leadership. See

Silver, *Louis Marshall*, 151. In fact, Richard Gottheil, one of the first Zionist leaders in the United States, proposed a similar idea as early as 1900, defining Zionism as "a tremendous yearning to be better Jews in order to be better men." Segev, "European Zionism," 279.

44. Shiff, *Yehudim Mishtalvim*, 83–85.
45. Magnes, *Dissenter in Zion*, 105.
46. Segev, "European Zionism," 275–76.
47. Shiff, *HaTzionut Shel HaMenutsahim*, 8, 401–27. For further discussion of various positions regarding the integration of and tension between Silver's Zionist identity and his Reform identity, see Meyer, *Judaism within Modernity*, 378–402. For a comparison of the Zionist outlooks of Magnes and Wise, see Urofsky, "Two Paths to Zion," 85–97.
48. In 1907 Yitzhak Epstein, a member of the First Aliyah, described Zionism's attitude to the Arab issue as a "hidden question." Gorny, *HaShe'ela HaAravit*, 11.
49. According to Goren, Magnes was a devoted reader of *HaShiloah*, a literary journal in Hebrew edited by Ahad Ha'am, and in his own writings he often referred to the first three volumes of *Al Parashat Drachim*, published between 1895 and 1904. Magnes, *Dissenter in Zion*, 11.
50. According to Ahad Ha'am, "From abroad we are accustomed to believing that the Arabs are all desert savages, like donkeys, who neither see nor understand what goes on around them." But in reality the Arab who resides in the cities of Syria and Palestine, "like all children of Shem, has a sharp intellect and is very cunning.... The Arabs, and especially those in the cities, understand our deeds and our desires in Eretz Israel, but they keep quiet and pretend not to understand, since they do not see our present activities as a threat to their future. Therefore they try to exploit us as well, to extract some benefit from the new visitors as long as they can. Yet they mock us in their hearts." Ahad Ha'am, *Kol Kitvei*, 24.

3. PROPHETIC SOCIALISM, SOCIAL GOSPEL

1. Michels, *A Fire in Their Hearts*, 16–20.
2. Michels, *A Fire in Their Hearts*, 4–6.
3. For a detailed portrait of Chaim Zhitlovsky, see Frankel, *Prophecy and Politics*, 285–87.
4. Quoted in Michels, *A Fire in Their Hearts*, 154.
5. In a 1917 interview, Hillquit stated: "I am a Jew, a Socialist, a Russian, an American, a lawyer, a lecturer.... As a lawyer I have one sort of interest, as a Jew another, as a Socialist—another.... As you see, it is not easy, either for you or me to explain the way a person should act." Pratt, *Morris Hillquit*, 156.

6. Quoted in Pratt, *Morris Hillquit*, 156-57.
7. Magnes to Morris Hillquit, July 23, 1918, Judah L. Magnes Papers, 1912-19, MF-2440, AJA.
8. Landauer, *For Socialism*.
9. Mendes-Flohr, *Kidma VeNaftuleiha*, 289-91; Ratzabi, *Between Zionism and Judaism*, 389-404.
10. Notable in this context is Buber's initial support for World War I and Landauer's criticism of him in this regard. See Mendes-Flohr, *Kidma VeNaftuleiha*, 301-21.
11. Mendes-Flohr, *Kidma VeNaftuleiha*, 289-91, 320-21.
12. See Bergman, *Faith and Reason*, 151.
13. Mendes-Flohr, *Kidma VeNaftuleiha*, 321.
14. White and Hopkins, *The Social Gospel*, xi-xix.
15. Sarna, *American Judaism*, 195.
16. Meyer, *Bein Masoret LeKidma*, 447-48. The Reform rabbis did not propose concrete measures toward these aims.
17. Norman Thomas to Magnes, June 14, 1918, June 27, 1918; Magnes to Norman Thomas, July 1, 1918, MF-2440, AJA. Magnes also expressed reservations about the magazine's subtitle (*A Journal of Christian Thought and Practice*), to which Thomas responded that he viewed the magazine as a means of "calling Christianity to be true to itself," but that did not make it exclusionary or intolerant. There is no further correspondence on this.
18. See Magnes, *Dissenter in Zion*, 431-32. A 2012 book by Norman Thomas's granddaughter Louisa Thomas uses the format of a historical novel to describe Thomas's wartime activities and early work as a congregational minister within New York's Social Gospel movement. See Thomas, *Conscience*. On Thomas's socialism, see Hyfler, *Prophets of the Left*, 121-42.
19. Magnes, *War-time Addresses*, 109-10.
20. Magnes, *War-time Addresses*, 110.
21. For a discussion of Russell's pacifist position during World War I, see Ryan, *Bertrand Russell: A Political Life*, 55-80.
22. Magnes, *War-time Addresses*, 110.
23. Magnes, *War-time Addresses*, 114-15.
24. Magnes, *Dissenter in Zion*, 262.

4. RELIGIOUS MISSION OF PACIFISM

1. BAN, 709 (Magnes Papers), 1-40. For more on Hardy's poem, see Page, *Oxford Reader's Companion to Hardy*, 474.
2. Kazin, *War against War*, 205; Kennedy, *Over Here*, 26-27.

3. Magnes, *War-time Addresses*, 10; Kotzin, *Judah L. Magnes*, 146–48; Hillquit, *Loose Leaves from a Busy Life*, 170–79.
4. Magnes, *War-time Addresses*, 10.
5. Magnes, *War-time Addresses*, 18.
6. Brock, *Pacifism in the United States*, 943–48.
7. For more on the Quakers' pacifist activism during World War I, see Barbour and Frost, *The Quakers*, 247–60.
8. See Kotzin, *Magnes*, 156–58. Gershom Scholem, too, draws a connection between Quaker precepts and Magnes's pacifist radicalism. Scholem, *Devarim BeGo*, 220.
9. See Samuel Ralph Harlow, "Jeremiah Returns to Jerusalem," *The Christian Century*, June 7, 1931.
10. Rockefeller, *The Christian Church—What of Its Future?*, 14.
11. Magnes to John D. Rockefeller Jr., March 15, 1918, and John D. Rockefeller Jr. to Magnes, March 18, 1918, AJA, Judah Leib Magnes Papers 1912–19, MF-2440.
12. Magnes, *War-time Addresses*, 36.
13. Magnes, *War-time Addresses*, 36–37.
14. Magnes, *Dissenter in Zion*, 159.
15. The larger quote is as follows: "Statements of this nature, made in public and in effect to governmental agencies by Jews against Jews, are not unknown in Jewish history. For such statements the Jews have the term *m'sira* [betrayal] and for the persons making such statements, they have the term *mosrim* [informers]. Jewish history is replete with tragedies that have come over the Jewish people because of the activity of Jewish *mosrim*." Magnes, *Dissenter in Zion*, 188.
16. Magnes to Max Heller, March 2, 1911, AJA, Max Heller Papers, MS-33, 4/2. On Max Heller, see Malone, *Rabbi Max Heller*.
17. Abraham Cronbach, a young rabbi at the time, only became an active pacifist after the war. On Cronbach's pacifism, see Wilcock, *Pacifism and the Jews*, 118–32.
18. Kennedy, *Over Here*, 67–68.
19. See Gotthard Deutsch, "Justice to the Enemy: A Lesson in Honest Apologetics," *HUC Monthly* (December 1916): 29–35, AJA, HUC-JIR nearprint, O/10.
20. Meyer, *Hebrew Union College*, 74–76; Dobbert, "The Ordeal of Gotthard Deutsch," 131–32, 136; Deutsch, "Justice to the Enemy," 22–24.
21. Dobbert, "The Ordeal of Gotthard Deutsch," 130.
22. Dobbert, "The Ordeal of Gotthard Deutsch," 130–32, 145–52; Board of Governors Minutes, November 27, 1917, December 11, 1917, December 26, 1917, AJA, MS-5/D-22.

23. Board of Governors Minutes, December 26, 1917, AJA, MS-5/D-22. See also Meyer, *Hebrew Union College*, 80.
24. Magnes to Gotthard Deutsch, June 14, 1916, Gotthard Deutsch Papers, AJA, MS-123, 2/30.
25. For the full text of the declaration in English, see Philipson, *The Reform Movement in Judaism*, 354 (and http://www.zionism-israel.com/hdoc/Philadelphia_Conference_1869.htm). For more on the conference background and its declaration, see Meyer, *Bein Masoret LeKidma*, 289–97.
26. Meyer, *Bein Masoret LeKidma*, 447–48.
27. For more on Magnes's time at Hebrew Union College, see Kotzin, *Magnes*, 21–37.
28. Jacob I. Meyer, "The Assurance of Peace—the Moral Nature of Man," *HUC Monthly* (April 1915): 19–21, AJA, HUC-JIR nearprint, O/9.
29. Maxwell Silver, "False Prophets," *HUC Monthly*, May 1915, 22–24, AJA, HUC-JIR nearprint, O/9. On the importance of Nietzsche's philosophy with respect to the outbreak of war, see Aschheim, *The Nietzsche Legacy*, 128–29. Aschheim observes that the salient belief among Germany's enemies—that Nietzsche was in some way responsible for the outbreak of war and extent of its cruelty—was reflected in the appellation it received: "the Euro-Nietzschean war."
30. Silver, "False Prophets."
31. "Men of the Hour," Editorials, *HUC Monthly* (June 1915): 42–43, AJA, HUC-JIR nearprint, O/9.
32. Kaufmann Kohler, "The Views and Principles of American Reform Judaism and Its Outlook in These Critical Times," *HUC Monthly* (November 1915): 71–75, AJA, HUC-JIR nearprint, O/9.
33. Kohler, "The Views and Principles," 71.
34. Kohler, "The Views and Principles," 71–72.
35. Kohler, "The Views and Principles," 72.
36. Kohler, "The Views and Principles," 72–73.
37. Kohler, "The Views and Principles," 72.
38. Leo Baeck, for example, writes, "The distinctiveness of Judaism, which it passed on to the rest of mankind, is its ethical affirmation of the world: Judaism is the religion of ethical optimism." Baeck, *The Essence of Judaism*, 84. On the Reform conception of messianism as a gradual ethical process, see Baeck, *The Essence of Judaism*, 250–53.
39. For an analysis of the influence of German Jewish identity and German culture generally on Reform Judaism in the United States, see Meyer, *Judaism within Modernity*, 322–44.
40. Kotzin, *Magnes*, 151.

41. Stephen Wise resigned from the council after the United States entered the war. See Magnes, *Dissenter in Zion*, 159.
42. Magnes, *Dissenter in Zion*, 166–62.
43. Magnes, *Dissenter in Zion*, 163.
44. Magnes, *Dissenter in Zion*, 163.
45. Years later this verse was used toward the same end in Reform Judaism's 1997 Miami Platform. Its first article includes the statement: "We believe that the eternal covenant established at Sinai ordained a unique religious purpose for Am Yisrael [the Jewish People]. Medinat Yisrael, the Jewish State, is therefore unlike all other states. Its obligation is to strive towards the attainment of the Jewish people's highest moral ideals to be a *mamlechet kohanim* [a kingdom of priests], a *goy kadosh* [a holy people], and *l'or goyim* [a light unto the nations]." "Reform Judaism & Zionism: A Centenary Platform" ("The Miami Platform"), adopted by the Central Conference of American Rabbis, June 24, 1997, Miami. See https://www.ccarnet.org/rabbinic-voice/platforms/article-reform-judaism-zionism-centenary-platform/.
46. Magnes, *Dissenter in Zion*, 166.
47. Magnes, *Dissenter in Zion*, 166.
48. Wilcock examines the roots of Magnes's pacifism from childhood up to the time of his studies at Hebrew Union College, when, in 1898, he wrote to his parents that the Spanish-American War was "unjust." Magnes expressed shame over the reaction of Rabbi Marcus Friedlander from the congregation of his hometown, Oakland, who identified as one of the "fighting priests." "What a contradiction in terms," wrote Magnes. Wilcock, *Pacifism and the Jews*, 26–27.
49. Magnes, *War-time Addresses*, 96–98.
50. Also evident is Magnes's view of the Jewish People in terms reminiscent of Ahad Ha'am's teachings and of organic developmental concepts. See Ratzabi, "Ishei Merkaz Eropa," 81–83.
51. For example, Washington Gladden, regarded as one of the leading thinkers of the Social Gospel movement, wrote in 1899, "If God is the father of all men, all men are brethren; and there can be but one law for the home and school and shop and factory and market and court and legislative hall. One child of the common father can not enslave another nor exploit another; the strong and the fortunate and the wise can not take advantage of the weak and the crippled and the ignorant, and enrich themselves by spoiling their neighbors; each must care for the welfare of all, and all must minister for the good of each. This is the law of the brotherhood which directly follows from Christ's doctrine of Fatherhood, and which is beginning to be seriously

considered, all over the world, as the only solution of the problems of society." Gladden, "Recent Reconstructions of Theology," 208. For more on Gladden and Social Gospel's influence on the American Reform movement, see Meyer, *Bein Masoret LeKidma*, 330-31.

52. Cited in Charles L. Arian, "Disciples of Aaron: Pacifism in the Reform Rabbinate, 1924-1945" (paper presented to Dr. Jonathan D. Sarna), HUC-JIR, January 1985, AJA, SC-480.
53. See Ratzabi, *Between Zionism and Judaism*, 257-58.
54. For more on the Red Scare in the United States after World War I, see Kennedy, *Over Here*, 287-95.
55. *Debs Freedom Monthly* 1, no. 4 (November 1921): 1, 5, Magnes Archive, BAN, 709 (Magnes Papers), 2-7. Also available at https://www.marxists.org/archive/debs/works/1921/d288d437_1921.pdf.
56. Magnes to Morris Hillquit, January 8, 1919, AJA, Morris Hillquit Papers 1895-1940 (Microfilm), MF-1634.
57. Rabbi Lee Levinger, "The Next Step in Jewish Theology," *HUC Monthly* 4, no. 3 (December 1917): 79-83, AJA, HUC-JIR nearprint, O/11.
58. "Proposal of Judah Magnes," May 5, 1920, BAN, 709 (Magnes Papers), 2/7.
59. Morris R. Cahn to J. L. Magnes, January 29, 1921, BAN 2-7; Ludwig Lewinson to J. L. Magnes, January 28, 1921, BAN, 709 (Magnes Papers), 2-7; Kotzin, *Magnes*, 163.
60. See Bentwich, *For Zion's Sake*, 199-213.
61. Cited in Kotzin, *Magnes*, 167.

5. HIGH HOLY DAYS IN JERUSALEM

1. Kotzin, *Magnes*, 175-80.
2. Kotzin, *Magnes*, 168.
3. Quoted in Cohen, *The Americanization of Zionism*, 98.
4. Cohen, *The Americanization of Zionism*, 99-100. For more on Jessie Sampter, see Hazan, "HaIsha HaChakhama MiGivat Brener," 32-45.
5. Cohen, *The Americanization of Zionism*, 99-100.
6. Cohen, *The Americanization of Zionism*, 100-101.
7. Cohen, *The Americanization of Zionism*, 101-3.
8. Cohen, *The Americanization of Zionism*, 102.
9. Cohen, *The Americanization of Zionism*, 103-6.
10. Quoted in Cohen, *The Americanization of Zionism*, 103, 106.
11. Magnes, *Dissenter in Zion*, 219.
12. Magnes, *Dissenter in Zion*, 205.
13. Magnes, *Dissenter in Zion*, 220.

14. Magnes, *Dissenter in Zion*, 220.
15. Otto, *HaKedusha*, 7-13, 182-203. His distinction between the religious and the numinous accords with the tension between the irrational experience described by Magnes and the attempt to fit it into a rational philosophical framework.
16. Regarding the status of the "simple person" in Hasidism, see Buber, *BePardes HaChasidut*, xxxiv-xxxvi. On the importance of prayer in Hasidism, see Wertheim, *Halakhot VeHalikhot BaChasidut*, 85-90.
17. Magnes, *Dissenter in Zion*, 220 (emphasis in the original).
18. Magnes, *Dissenter in Zion*, 221-22 (emphasis in the original).
19. Bentwich, *For Zion's Sake*, 29.
20. Cohen, *The Americanization of Zionism*, 106.
21. Magnes, *Dissenter in Zion*, 221.
22. Magnes critiques quietism in a November 1944 opening address marking the start of the Hebrew University school year: "It is the attitude of religious Quietism which would guarantee your peace and which enjoins quiet acceptance of everything going on about you.... But encountering it in these awful days, it is difficult not to protest." Magnes, *Addresses by the Chancellor*, 73. On the quietist aspects of Hasidism, see Schatz-Uffenheimer, *HaHasidut KeMistika*, 9-22.
23. Milton's original formulation was "to justifie the ways of God to men" (original spelling). Scholar David Loewenstein argues that Milton's intention, influenced by Arminianism, a Protestant denomination based on the ideas of the theologian Jacobus Arminius, was to pose an alternative to the Calvinist doctrine of predestination: one that embodied the concept of free will. Loewenstein, *Milton*, 26-27.
24. Silver, "Midfus Pa'il LiDfus Savil," 311-14.
25. Scholem, "Adam Chofshi," 207-10.
26. James, *The Will to Believe and Other Essays*, 13-45. For Pascal's argument, see "The Necessity of Wager," in particular, Part III, §233: "Now, what harm will come to you by taking this side? You will be faithful, honest, humble, grateful, generous, a sincere, true friend. Certainly you will not be taken by unhealthy pleasures, by glory and by luxury, but will you not have others? I tell you that as a result you will gain in this life, and that, at each step you take on this road, you will see such a great certainty of gain and so much nothingness in what you risk, that you will at last recognize that you have wagered for something certain and infinite, for which you have given nothing." Pascal, *Pensées*, 214.
27. James, *The Varieties of Religious Experience*, 48.

28. See Russell, *Skeptical Essays*, 146-47. For a discussion of Russell's pacifist stance during World War I, see Ryan, *Bertrand Russell: A Political Life*, 55-80.
29. Magnes, *Dissenter in Zion*, 221-22.
30. Magnes, *Dissenter in Zion*, 225.
31. Magnes, *Dissenter in Zion*, 222-23.
32. Magnes, *Dissenter in Zion*, 223.
33. Magnes, *Dissenter in Zion*, 224.
34. Both Ahad Ha'am and Buber, each at different times, emphasized that political Zionism's focus on immediate statehood prevented the organic development of Jewish culture in Palestine in a manner that would in due time evolve into a "worthy" Jewish state. Ahad Ha'am's essay "Lo Ze HaDerech! [This is not the way!]" is devoted entirely to this question. He states, "It follows from what has been said above that we ought to have made it our first object to bring about a *revival*—to inspire men with a deeper attachment to the national life, and a more ardent desire for the national well-being. By these means we should have aroused the necessary determination, and we should have obtained devoted adherents. No doubt such work is very difficult and takes a long time, not one year or one decade; and, I repeat, it is not to be accomplished by speeches alone, but demands the employment of all means by which men's hearts can be won. Hence it is probable—in fact almost certain—that if we had chosen this method we should not yet have had time to produce concrete results in Palestine itself: lacking the resources necessary to do things well, we should have been too prudent to do things badly. But, on the other side, we should have made strenuous endeavors to train up Jews who would work for their people. We should have striven gradually to extend the empire of our ideal in Jewry, till at last it could find genuine, wholehearted devotees, with all the qualities needed to enable them to work for its practical realization." Buber writes: "National forms without the eternal purpose from which they have arisen signify the end of Israel's specific fruitfulness. The free development of the latent power of the nation without a supreme value to give it purpose and direction does not mean regeneration but the mere sport of a common self-deception behind which spiritual death lurks in ambush." See Ahad Ha'am, *Kol Kitvei*, 11-16. Available also at http://www.zionism-israel.com/hdoc/Achad_haam_not_the_way.htm; Buber, *On Zion: The History of an Idea*, xxi.
35. This is almost certainly a reference to St. Augustine's book *The City of God* and further attests to the influence of Christian sources on Magnes's religious thinking.
36. Magnes, *Dissenter in Zion*, 225.

6. HEBREW UNIVERSITY AND BRIT SHALOM

1. Cohen, *HaHar VeHagivaa*, 70-80. For a detailed discussion of the Magnes-Weizmann-Einstein conflict, see Parzen, "The Magnes-Weizmann-Einstein Controversy," 187-213.
2. Mendes-Flohr, *Kidma VeNaftuleiha*, 317.
3. Magnes, *Addresses by the Chancellor*, 1-2.
4. Magnes, *Addresses by the Chancellor*, 6-7.
5. Magnes, *Addresses by the Chancellor*, 7-8.
6. In the preface to the first edition of *Al Parashat Drachim* [At the crossroads], Ahad Ha'am writes, "That which the personal individual spirit can achieve is not beyond reach for the spirit of a people, and if we look at the histories of various peoples, or even just the history of our own people, we will find many such visions, because of which for long periods of time the spirit of the nation was entirely subservient to a single spiritual foundation that operated through all aspects and ways of life of the people, even those that do not superficially appear to have any connection between it and them, making fundamental changes in them in accordance with its purpose, and none of its inner workings were visible to them or felt in their hearts" (x).
7. Magnes, *Addresses by the Chancellor*, 23.
8. Magnes, *Addresses by the Chancellor*, 47.
9. See Even-Zahav, *J. L. Magnes: Builder of the Hebrew University*.
10. Magnes, *Addresses by the Chancellor*, 47.
11. Garling, "'Kasha Mikol,'" 174.
12. Heller, *MiBrit Shalom Le-Ichud*, 4-11; Zadoff, *MiBerlin LeYerushalaim Wu-VaHazara: Gershom Scholem*, 39.
13. Gordon, *Brit Shalom*, 7-19.
14. Ben-Israel, "Magnes VeBrit Shalom," 111.
15. Magnes, *Dissenter in Zion*, 57.
16. Ben-Israel, "Magnes VeBrit Shalom," 111-12.
17. Kotzin, *Magnes*, 199.
18. Magnes, *Dissenter in Zion*, 57.
19. Ben-Israel, "Magnes VeBrit Shalom," 111. In this author's view, however, Ben-Israel's claim that members of Brit Shalom saw Magnes as their "leader" is probably an overstatement; nor does it accord with the members' intellectual critiques regarding Magnes.
20. Magnes, *Dissenter in Zion*, 198-99.
21. Ratzabi, *Between Zionism and Judaism*, 425.
22. See, for example, Buber, *Eretz LiShnei Amim*, 14-21; Gorny, *HaShe'ela HaAravit*, 78-108.

23. Ratzabi, "Ishei Merkaz Eropa," 162-67.
24. Magnes, *Dissenter in Zion*, 304.
25. Magnes, *Addresses by the Chancellor*, 99-102. Later the approach expressed here regarding the Jewish side would form the basis for collaboration between Magnes and Hannah Arendt.
26. Quoted in Ratzabi, "Ishei Merkaz Eropa," 180-81.
27. Ratzabi, "Ishei Merkaz Eropa," 219-24, 387-91.
28. Magnes, *Addresses by the Chancellor*, 102.
29. Buber, *Eretz LiShnei Amim*, 24-30; Simon, *Kav HaTichum*, 5-6. Regarding this boundary line, Simon writes, "This line has to be redrawn every day. It stretches between the absolute imperative and the limited possibility of implementing it. One may add, in the spirit of Buber, that from this dilemma between the objective validity of the imperative and the relative personal or public possibility of implementing it there emerge two apparent courses of action, only one of which is a true path, which is that of the boundary line" (5). The first path, according to Simon, dispels the tension between the existing and the imperative on the basis of practicality, relinquishing the ethical. In contrast, "the second is a mirage that branches off to a heavenly path, on the one hand, where the absolute imperative in all its sanctity rules, without touching flesh and blood or being touched by them, and an earthly path, on the other hand, where the supposedly 'realistic' political power, be it individual or collective, has grown wild" (6). This passage embodies a critique of the concept of the absolute moral imperative (which is consistent with Magnes's approach) for its potential to lead to a disconnection from political reality because of the inability to have any real influence within this reality, thus abandoning it to other forces.
30. Ratzabi, "Ishei Merkaz Eropa," 321-30, 409.
31. Ratzabi, *Between Zionism and Judaism*, 33-36.
32. The correspondence between Magnes and Buber before 1938 mainly addressed administrative aspects of the effort to bring Buber to Jerusalem to teach at the Hebrew University. See, for example, Buber, *Letters*, 365-66.

7. THE PROPHETIC MODEL

1. See Bentwich, *For Zion's Sake*, 277.
2. Scholem, *From Berlin to Jerusalem*, 218-20.
3. Heller, *MiBrit Shalom Le-Ichud*, 389. While I have not found discussion of a "Jeremiah Complex" elsewhere, there are similarities between what Scholem describes and what is termed the "Cassandra Complex," a metaphor for the fate of Cassandra, daughter of King Priam of Troy. Cassandra had the

gift of prophecy, but because of a curse cast by Apollo, no one believed her warnings. On the tragic prophetic figure of Cassandra in Aeschylus's play *Agamemnon*, see Brault, "Playing the Cassandra," 197–220. See also Buber's comparison between the members of Ichud and a contemporary Cassandra in his 1947 essay "The Binational Approach to Zionism," 178–79.

4. James Marshall to Judah Leib Magnes, May 21, 1947, AJA, MS-157 (James Marshall letters), Box 21, file 9.
5. Holmes, *Palestine To-Day and To-Morrow*, xiv, 242–43.
6. John Haynes Holmes to Jacob Billikopf, December 3, 1929, AJA, SC-1027.
7. Kotzin, *Judah L. Magnes*, 231–32.
8. See Samuel Ralph Harlow, "Jeremiah Returns to Jerusalem," *The Christian Century*, June 7, 1931, https://archive.org/details/jeremiahreturnst00harl/mode/2up.
9. Harlow, "Jeremiah Returns to Jerusalem."
10. Harlow, "Jeremiah Returns to Jerusalem."
11. Hillquit, *Loose Leaves from a Busy Life*, 170.
12. Quoted in Bentwich, *For Zion's Sake*, 179.
13. Lazar, *Shisha Yechidim*, 153.
14. Bentwich, *For Zion's Sake*, 179.
15. Silver, "Midfus Pa'il LiDfus Savil," 315. Silver argues that Magnes encouraged, or at least permitted, an exaggerated comparison between himself and the prophet Jeremiah in periodicals across the world, motivated by his interest in redeeming his image, which had been hurt by publications affiliated with the official Jewish establishment. Silver describes this as a fabricated public relations campaign. The argument presented here, which is consistent with that of Gershom Scholem, is that Magnes's affinity for the image of Jeremiah was an essential part of his self-perception.
16. Goren, "Between Priest and Prophet," 60–66.
17. Ahad Ha'am, *Selected Essays*, 133–35.
18. Goren, "Between Priest and Prophet," 64.
19. In a letter to Weizmann dated September 7, 1929, following riots sparked by events at the Western Wall in August 1929, Magnes wrote, "But I cannot keep silent for Zion's sake in these tragic days, and I want to do what little I can to give voice to the views to which I have been trying hitherto to give expression through work [at the University] alone." Magnes, *Dissenter in Zion*, 297. The phrase "for Zion's sake" is also the title of the first biography of Magnes, authored by Norman Bentwich.
20. Mendes-Flohr, *Kidma VeNaftuleiha*, 316–17.
21. Quoted in Goren, "Between Priest and Prophet," 66–67.

22. Simon cites three major crises in Magnes's life—his transition from Reform to traditional Judaism, the unraveling of his pacifist worldview during World War II, and internal party struggles within the Zionist movement. See Heller, *MiBrit Shalom Le-Ichud*, 389.
23. Sarna, *American Judaism*, 194-95.
24. Cited in Meyer, *Response to Modernity*, 214-15.
25. Cited in Shiff, *Yehudim Mishtalvim*, 100-104.
26. For further information, see Segev, *MiPolitika'im Ethni'im LeManhigim Leumi'im?*, 62-81.
27. Shiff, *HaZionut Shel HaMenutsahim*, 15, 403.
28. See Magnes, *Dissenter in Zion*, 226.
29. For further information, see Heller, *MiBrit Shalom Le-Ichud*, 100-110. See also how philosopher Michael Walzer attributes this political vision to Isaiah. Walzer, *Leumiyut Ve-Universalism*, 8.
30. Douglas Horton, "God Lets Loose Karl Barth," *Christian Century*, February 16, 1928.
31. Magnes, *Dissenter in Zion*, 267-69.
32. Ahad Ha'am, *Selected Essays*, 319.
33. Magnes, *Dissenter in Zion*, 268.
34. See Luz, "HaYesod HaDialekti," 75-89.
35. See Meyer, *Response to Modernity*, 143-44. Regarding the American context, see, for example, Sarna, *American Judaism*, 82-88.
36. Flusser, "LeZichro Shel Karl Bart," 9.
37. Magnes, *Dissenter in Zion*, 268.
38. Magnes, *Dissenter in Zion*, 268.
39. Magnes, *Dissenter in Zion*, 268-69.
40. Weber, *Weber's Rationalism and Modern Society*, 41-42.

8. NATIONALISM AND BINATIONALISM

1. Tocqueville, *Democracy in America*, https://edisciplinas.usp.br/pluginfile.php/4209010/mod_folder/content/0/Tocqueville_Democracy%20in%20america.pdf?forcedownload=1.
2. Menand, *The Metaphysical Club*, x-xii.
3. James, *Pragmatism*, 12-22.
4. James, *Pragmatism*, 27-29. See also Menand, *The Metaphysical Club*, 351-58.
5. Kotzin, *Magnes*, 111.
6. Shook, "Pragmatism, Pluralism and Public Democracy," 11.
7. Kotzin, *Magnes*, 236-37. Historian Matthew Silver also identifies pragmatism as one of the political aspects of Magnes's American heritage, alongside

optimism and reliance on dialogue and compromise. Silver, "Midfus Pa'il LiDfus Savil," 350.
8. Ben-Israel, "Magnes VeBrit Shalom," 113.
9. Arieli, *Historiya VeMetta-Historiya*. However, as political theorist Michael Walzer points out, such citizenship-based nationality was not always universal or available to all, since African Americans, women, and Native Americans were excluded. In addition, this purported universalism has been in perpetual conflict with more homogenous outlooks, and particularly with American "nativism," which "was probably closer in its politics to a Rousseauian republicanism." See Walzer, *What It Means to Be an American*, 30–32.
10. Magnes, *Dissenter in Zion*, 379.
11. Among the characteristics of American political tradition he cited, Magnes listed "the opportunity for criticism and the duty to criticize (for me, particularly) the failure of the American democracy thus far to distribute its wealth and products so that every man may have work and a modest living." Magnes, *Dissenter in Zion*, 379.
12. Mendes-Flohr, *Kidma VeNaftuleiha*, 316–17.
13. According to historian Yehoshua Arieli, "Where society's national unity is based on an ideological contract, embodied in the state's institutional system, the room for ideological and critical deviation by individuals and groups is extremely limited." Arieli, *Historiya VeMetta-Historiya*, 369. On the role of the Constitution in this regard, see Arieli, "The Constitutional Tradition in the United States," in *Historiya VeMetta-Historiya*, 456–83.
14. On the reversal of Buber's attitude to German nationalism during the war, see Mendes-Flohr, *Kidma VeNaftuleiha*, 295–312. Regarding the influence of the war on Rosenzweig's attitude to nationalism and on his thinking generally, see Horwitz, *Franz Rosenzweig*, 44–47, arguing that in contrast to Buber and Hermann Cohen, whose attitude to the war was overtly nationalistic, Rosenzweig was not an enthusiastic supporter, although he also did not oppose the war as, for example, Albert Einstein did.
15. Magnes, *War-time Addresses*, 91–92. Nineteenth-century French scholar Ernest Renan, for example, provided a more complex definition of the modern nation as a body whose members have spiritual feelings of solidarity based on a shared past and a present aspiration to continue working together to achieve "great deeds." See Renan, "What Is a Nation?," 19.
16. For example, in a February 1920 speech in Chicago, Magnes asserted that, after the war, "Peace treaties have been made which for savagery, hypocrisy, ineffectiveness know no equal in history." Magnes, *War-time Addresses*, 89. He regarded the 1921 Washington Conference—which led to a treaty in

which the United States, Japan, Britain, and France agreed to avoid conflict and reduce the arms race in the Pacific Ocean—as a move by "imperialist powers" to exploit China economically. Magnes, *War-time Addresses*, 27; Magnes, *Dissenter in Zion*, 27-28.

17. Magnes, *War-time Addresses*, 92-93.
18. In this context Magnes touched upon an anomaly regarding the concept of a Jewish nation: Jews form a collective ethnic group whose bonds traverse state boundaries. In this sense the Jewish people do not accord, for example, with the concept of nationalism posited by the leading theorist, British Czech philosopher Ernest Gellner, which requires congruence between ethnic borders and state borders. See Gellner, *Nations and Nationalism*, 171-73. Although Jews are indeed a notable example of this phenomenon, they are not unique, given that the imagined unity of the modern nation-state is in perpetual tension with the multicultural identities of its citizens. For more on this discussion, see Rechnitzer, "HaTheologia HaReformit," 73.
19. This is reminiscent of Dubnow's views. Historian Simon Rabinovitch regarded Dubnow as the leading Jewish thinker to have developed a coherent historical, philosophical, and ideological worldview, including the political action plan of "Diaspora Nationalism." Rabinovitch, *Jews and Diaspora Nationalism*, 23-25.
20. Magnes, *War-time Addresses*, 94-95.
21. "We hold these truths to be self-evident, that all men are created equal, that they are endowed by their Creator with certain unalienable Rights, that among these are Life, Liberty and the pursuit of Happiness." See Armitage, *The Declaration of Independence*, 165.
22. See Hastings, *The Construction of Nationhood*, xxviii-xxix. According to Hastings, Kohn further emphasizes the centrality of the Hebrew Bible and the biblical concept of nationalism as contributing factors in the emergence of modern nationalism.
23. Smith, *Chosen Peoples*, 85-94.
24. See Gellner, *Nations and Nationalism*, 134-43, in particular; Hobsbawm, *Nations and Nationalism since 1780*.
25. Magnes, *Dissenter in Zion*, 226.
26. Segev, "European Zionism in the United States," 279.
27. Magnes, *Dissenter in Zion*, 226.
28. Quoted in Shiff, *HaTzionut Shel HaMenutzahim*, 27.
29. Magnes, *Dissenter in Zion*, 227.
30. Ratzabi, "Ishei Merkaz Eropa," 81-83.
31. Kotzin, *Magnes*, 381n89.

32. Kotzin, *Magnes*, 381n89.
33. See Bentwich, *For Zion's Sake*, 58–59.
34. Bentwich, *For Zion's Sake*, 58–59.
35. Magnes, *Dissenter in Zion*, 227.
36. For a detailed discussion of the bodily perception that Zionism promoted, and particularly of Nordau's "muscular Judaism" and its divergence from the traditional "diasporic" Jewish body image, see Gluzman, *HaGuf HaTzioni*.
37. Magnes, *Dissenter in Zion*, 227.
38. Mendes-Flohr, *Kidma VeNaftuleiha*, 316.
39. Silber, "Dubnow," 88–89.
40. See Silber, "Dubnow," 88–90.
41. Kotzin discussed the influence of Dubnow's views on Israel Friedlander, who formed part of the circle that formed around Schechter in New York during the first decade of the twentieth century and included Magnes, Henrietta Szold, and Mordecai Kaplan. Magnes and Friedlander shared outlooks and participated side by side in Zionist activity. Both were members of the Zionist club Achava (Brotherhood) established in New York in 1909 at Magnes's initiative. Kotzin, *Magnes*, 61. For a thorough discussion of the founding of Achava, and particularly of how Friedlander adapted Ahad Ha'am's Zionism to American circumstances by drawing on Dubnow's perspective, see Davis, "Israel Friedlander's Minute Book of the *Achava* Club," 157-213.
42. Weinberg, *Between Tradition and Modernity*, 3–25.
43. Seltzer, "Ahad Ha'am and Dubnow," 60–72.
44. Meyer, *Response to Modernity*, 205–7.
45. Ratzabi, *Between Zionism and Judaism*, 258–59.
46. Meyer, *Response to Modernity*, 206.

9. BINATIONALISM AS THEOLOGICAL POLITICS

1. Shumsky, "MiDu-Leshoniyut LeDu-Leumiyut," xv.
2. Ratzabi, *Between Zionism and Judaism*; Shumsky, "MiDu-Leshoniyut LeDu-Leumiyut."
3. For a complete list of the figures and bodies that supported the concept of binationalism to some degree or in some form, see Hattis, *The Bi-National Idea*.
4. Hazan, *Metinut*, 353.
5. See Heller, *MiBrit Shalom Le-Ichud*, 141–78.
6. Gerber, "Itzuv Leumi, Politika VeMigdar," 65–114.
7. See, for example, Hillel Cohen, *Tarpat*; Naomi Cohen, *The Year after the Riots*, 50–84.

8. Magnes, *Like All the Nations?*, 2.
9. Magnes, *Like All the Nations?*, 2.
10. Magnes, *Like All the Nations?*, 5–6.
11. Buber, *Eretz LiShnei Amim*, 134–37.
12. Magnes, *Like All the Nations?*, 3.
13. Magnes, *Like All the Nations?*, 4.
14. Magnes, *Like All the Nations?*, 4–5.
15. Magnes, *Like All the Nations?*, 5.
16. Magnes, *Like All the Nations?*, 5–6.
17. Medoff, *Zionism and the Arabs*, 1–7.
18. Quoted in Neuberger, "Haim Yesh LeIsrael Masoret Politit Democratit?," 589–92.
19. Magnes, *Like All the Nations?*, 6.
20. Magnes, *Like All the Nations?*, 5.
21. See Weber, *Weber's Rationalism and Modern Society*, 129–98.
22. Magnes, *Like All the Nations?*, 5.
23. Magnes, *Like All the Nations?*, 5.
24. Buber, *Eretz LiShnei Amim*, 88–89.
25. Many Reform Jewish leaders in the United States were of German descent; the cultural and spiritual influences are unmistakable. See Meyer, *Judaism within Modernity*, 323–44.
26. Quoted in Ratzabi, "Ishei Merkaz Eropa," 88.
27. The notion that the sanctity of the land has political implications also appears in Buber's writings, in particular in his essay *Bein Am LeArtso* (1945), and lies at the foundation of his theo-politics, although sanctity has a different meaning for Buber.
28. Magnes, *Like All the Nations?*, 5. Admittedly, "the Holy Land"—as the phrase is used in English—might be a casual reference to Palestine, but as Magnes uses it here and later, it has distinctly religious connotations.
29. Magnes, *Like All the Nations?*, 11.
30. This observation rests on Buber's distinction between two paths to realization of the Zionist vision, with identical elements but different processes: Ahad Ha'am's path follows the sequence spirit-people-land, whereas Gordon's approach is land-people-spirit. Ratzabi, "Bein Am LeArtso," 275.
31. Magnes, *Like All the Nations?*, 7.
32. Magnes, *Like All the Nations?*, 6.
33. Magnes, *Like All the Nations?*, 6.
34. Magnes, *Like All the Nations?*, 6–7.

35. Simon Rabinovitch defines "diaspora nationalism" as a sense of national belonging to a place other than where one is, usually a faraway homeland. In this sense, particularly since Israel's establishment in 1948, Zionism has become the dominant form of Jewish diaspora nationalism. In his view, during the late nineteenth and early twentieth centuries in particular (the relevant period for us), the rise of modern nationalism in its various forms, on the one hand, and the struggle for civil rights and equality, on the other, were at the center of the discourse on Jewish particularism versus Jewish universalism. In the Jewish context, the various forms of diaspora nationalism that have been proposed reflect efforts to preserve, renew, or fortify Jewish nationalism for the sake of survival in the Diaspora. Rabinovitch, *Jews and Diaspora Nationalism*.
36. Ratzabi, "Ishei Merkaz Eropa," 82. See, for example, Magnes's sermons at Temple Emanu-El in March 1910 (chapter 1), and his presentations in December 1917 before the Committee to Support Jewish War Victims and in January 1919 before the Jewish Labor Congress in New York (chapter 3). Thus, Magnes's use of the term "the Jewish people" indicates his acquaintance with the members of Brit Shalom, although one should bear in mind that Magnes had written his doctoral thesis in Germany around the turn-of-the-century (1900–1904), and the German *volk* spirit evidently left its mark at the time.
37. Magnes, *Like All the Nations?*, 7.
38. Regarding the religious dimension, see for example, Cohen, *Tarpat*, 106–54.

10. MAGNES AND THE THEOPOLITICS OF BUBER

1. "Theopolitics" is a term coined by Buber to convey his aversion to the way in which the term "Political Theology" was used by Carl Schmitt. See Brody, *Martin Buber's Theopolitics*, 1–17. For the sake of the discussion here, the terms are practically interchangeable.
2. Buber, *Eretz LiShnei Amim*, 41.
3. Buber, *Eretz LiShnei Amim*, 60–67.
4. Buber's conception of theopolitics was also a response to Carl Schmitt's teachings. On the relevance of Carl Schmitt to this discussion, see, for example, Schmitt, "Carl Schmidt BeIvrit"; Schmidt, "BeTshuva Al Hashe'ela: Mahi Theologia Politit?" For a more detailed discussion in the context of Magnes and the subject of this book, see Barak-Gorodetsky, "Bein Yahadut Nevuit LeDu-Leumiyut," 153–55.
5. Buber, *Bein Am LeArtso*, 7–12.

6. For clarification of Soloveitchik's use of these terms, see, for example, Ratzabi, *Bein Goral LeYeud*, 194–96.
7. Ratzabi, *Anarchizm BeTzion*, 166–67.
8. Mendes-Flohr, *Martin Buber*, 228.
9. Ratzabi, *Anarchizm BeTzion*, 166–78.
10. Magnes, *Like All the Nations?*, 7.
11. Ratzabi, *Anarchizm BeTzion*, 9–12. Buber's anarchism was rooted in his relationship with his mentor Gustav Landauer. On Landauer's anarchism, see Ratzabi, *Anarchizm BeTzion*, 104–5; Landauer, *Ktavim VeMikhtavim*, 7–20.
12. Mendes-Flohr, *Kidma VeNaftuleiha*, 322–23.
13. Heller, *MiBrit Shalom Le-Ichud*, 389; Nimrod, "Chelko Shel Yeudah L. Magnes," 106.
14. Buber, *Eretz LiShnei Amim*, 24–30. Mendes-Flohr, *Kidma VeNaftuleiha*, 11. See also Simon, "HaChinukh LeShalom," 13.
15. See Ratzabi, "HaTanakh KeHistoriya U-KheMitus," 478.
16. Simon, *Kav HaTichum*, 2–4.
17. Quoted in Mendes-Flohr, *Martin Buber*, 115–16.
18. Buber, *Eretz LiShnei Amim*, 179. Mendes-Flohr, *Kidma VeNaftuleiha*, 11. This rather abstract approach to the issue clashed with Magnes's American pragmatism, which regarded binationalism as a serious solution.
19. See, for example, Segev, *Yemei HaKalaniyot*, 333. Magnes had already acquired some mastery of Arabic writing at the start of the century while in Germany, as his doctoral work included translating a text in Jewish Arabic. This does not mean, however, that Magnes refrained from adopting a critical, and even Orientalist, view of the Arabs in Palestine. At one point he remarked, for example, "I can understand a philosophical Arabic text from the Middle Ages more easily than the words of an Arab living in Palestine." See Silver, "MiDfus Pa'il LiDfus Savil," 334.
20. Cited in Ratzabi, "HaTanakh KeHistoriya Wu-KeMitus," 490–94.
21. Magnes, *Dissenter in Zion*, 285.
22. Magnes, *Dissenter in Zion*, 277.
23. Magnes, *Like All the Nations?*, 8.
24. Quoted in Magnes, *Dissenter in Zion*, 285; Bentwich, *For Zion's Sake*, 178.
25. Quoted in Bentwich, *For Zion's Sake*, 179.
26. Magnes, *Like All the Nations?*, 5.
27. Lurie, *Iyunim Besefer Yermiyahu*, 21; Bentwich, *For Zion's Sake*, 179.
28. Quoted in Magnes, *Dissenter in Zion*, 277. Ernest Simon voiced similar concerns: "Palestine"—he writes in his 1952 article "Are We Still Jews?"—"has given us spheres of life that must be sanctified, after they had become

secularized in the Diaspora. A great opportunity is inherent here, and there is no small danger inherent [too]. The opportunity: consecration of the profane, including the state. The danger: desecration of the holy, including faith." He also noted that the "danger was greater than the opportunity." Simon, *Pirkei Chaim*, 193.

29. Quoted in Magnes, *Dissenter in Zion*, 285.
30. Thus, for example, during Passover 1949, poet Natan Alterman released a poem dedicated to Nun, Joshua's father, which draws a clear link between Joshua's conquest and the war of independence. For an in-depth examination of this poem, see Luz, "Talush Haya HaIsh," 147–54.
31. For more on the theopolitical views of Brit HaBiryonim as compared with those of Brit Shalom, see Strasberg-Dayan, "Tzion," 181–93. Strasberg-Dayan claims that the basis of the dispute was the conflict between aspiring to be "like all the nations" versus to be "a light unto the nations" (193).
32. Magnes, "Eretz Israel and the Galut," address delivered in Jerusalem, May 23, 1923. Cited in Magnes, *Dissenter in Zion*, 232. Magnes delivered the address in Hebrew. It was published in *HaPo'el HaTza'ir*, June 8, 1923. He wrote the address in English before translating it. The English version is used here. These remarks are reminiscent of the dispute between Brit Shalom and Brit HaBiryonim to which Strasberg-Dayan refers.
33. Heller, *MiBrit Shalom Le-Ichud*, 394.
34. Ratzabi, *Anarchizm BeTzion*, 175.
35. For an in-depth discussion, see Keidar, "Ben-Gurion's Mamlakhtiyut," 117–33.
36. Ohana, *Mashikhiyut VeMamlakhtiyut*, 1–2.
37. Shapira, "The Religious Motifs," 251–58.
38. Martin Buber, "Truth and Deliverance," *Be'ayot* (July 1947): 189, quoted in Mendes-Flohr, *Martin Buber*, 211.

11. FAITH, SKEPTICISM IN THE BINATIONAL CAUSE

1. Kotzin, *Magnes*, 226.
2. Kotzin, *Magnes*, 227–28.
3. Judah Magnes, "An International Enclave," *New York Times*, November 24, 1929.
4. Kotzin, *Magnes*, 226–30; Heller, *MiBrit Shalom Le-Ichud*, 51–57; Magnes, Kaufman, and Gudman, *The Magnes-Philby Negotiations*, 14–18.
5. Cable to Jewish Agency Board members, London, 3 Tammuz 5690 (June 29, 1930), BGA, item no. 008663.
6. Naomi Cohen, *The Year after the Riots*, 75–83.
7. Hillel Cohen, *Tarpat*, 360.

8. Hattis, *The Binational Idea*, 51–53.
9. Kotzin, *Magnes*, 243–45.
10. Quoted in Heller, *MiBrit Shalom Le-Ichud*, 82.
11. Bentwich, *For Zion's Sake*, 190–91; Kotzin, *Magnes*, 250–52. For a description of these meetings from Ben-Gurion's perspective, see Ben-Gurion, *Pgishot Im Manhigim Aravim*.
12. Quoted in Heller, *MiBrit Shalom Le-Ichud*, 91–92.
13. Magnes, *Dissenter in Zion*, 310–11; Kotzin, *Magnes*, 263–71.
14. Heller, *MiBrit Shalom Le-Ichud*, 91–92.
15. This is also the conclusion reached by Heller, who dates the reappearance of binationalism in Magnes's public statements to 1938. Heller, *MiBrit Shalom Le-Ichud*, 93. By 1937 Magnes had reintroduced binationalism as a solution.
16. Heller, *MiBrit Shalom Le-Ichud*, 92–93. Like Magnes's past projects along these lines, the initiative was short-lived, and the association soon dissolved.
17. Heller, *MiBrit Shalom Le-Ichud*, 92–93; Magnes, *Dissenter in Zion*, 331–33.
18. Quoted in Magnes, *Dissenter in Zion*, 361.
19. Quoted in Heller, *MiBrit Shalom Le-Ichud*, 93.
20. See Scholem, "Mitzva HaBa'a BeAvira." For a recent survey of literature, see Goldish, *The Sabbatean Prophets*.
21. Mendes-Flohr, "The Appeal of the Incorrigible Idealist," 147–48; Hugo Bergman, "J. L. Magnes Seeks His God" [Hebrew], *Haaretz*, October 17, 1949.
22. Mendes-Flohr, "The Appeal of the Incorrigible Idealist," 147–50. Mendes-Flohr also notes that the term "HaOl" is reminiscent of the rabbinic teaching "Take upon yourselves the yoke of the kingdom of Heaven, and strengthen each other in fear of Heaven, and treat each other with lovingkindness" (Sifre Devarim 323:1 on Deut. 32:29). The phrase "the yoke that *Our Father* placed on us" (emphasis added), which echoes the Christian portrayal of God as a father figure, also deserves mention. In addition, according to Noam Zadoff, Scholem, who was not an association member, had only been invited as a guest speaker. See Zadoff, *MiBerlin LeYerushalaim Wu-BaHazara*, 154.
23. Cited in Bentwich, *For Zion's Sake*, 281.
24. Quoted in Kotzin, *Magnes*, 278.
25. Mendes-Flohr, "The Appeal of the Incorrigible Idealist," 145.
26. Quoted in Mendes-Flohr, "The Appeal of the Incorrigible Idealist," 145–46.
27. Scholem, too, presented an anarchist position to members of the association, and feared the reactions. According to Zadoff, this was the first time he articulated his conception of "religious anarchism," which he would reassert in the future as well. For this argument and an analysis of Scholem's worldview, see Zadoff, *MiBerlin LeYerushalaim Wu-BaHazara*.

28. Scholem, "Adam Chofshi," 207.
29. Magnes argued, regarding Scholem, for example, that "according to conventional thinking, the oral Torah is an addendum to the Torah, and according to Scholem it is a release from the written Torah. This was the position of the gospels. This is the nullification of the Torah." Quoted in Zadoff, *MiBerlin LeYerushalaim Wu-BaHazara*, 155.
30. Quoted in Mendes-Flohr, "The Appeal of the Incorrigible Idealist," 146.
31. Quoted in Mendes-Flohr, "The Appeal of the Incorrigible Idealist," 146-47.
32. Matthew Silver, for example, reads all of Magnes's efforts as part of an attempt "to import the model of individualism that is so fundamental to the American mentality." Silver, "MiDfus Pa'il LiDfus Savil," 325.
33. This is distinct from the "absolute or metaphysical values" to which Magnes refers and that, according to Mendes-Flohr, Buber regarded as too superficial. Mendes-Flohr, "The Appeal of the Incorrigible Idealist," 146.
34. Quoted in Mendes-Flohr, "The Appeal of the Incorrigible Idealist," 150.
35. Magnes, *Dissenter in Zion*, 224.
36. Bentwich hits the nail on the head with his observation that Magnes "struggled like Jacob wrestling with the Angel, but did not prevail. Yet the record of his searching and wrestling is itself a religious message." Bentwich, *For the Sake of Zion*, 279.
37. See Buber, *Eclipse of God*, 44-45. For a discussion of Buber's distinction between the "two concepts of faith"—according to which the Jewish faith is akin to "faith in someone, without this faith being sufficiently justifiable," as opposed to the Christian faith, which is akin to "asserting the truth of a certain fact, without the ability to provide sufficient justification"—see Ratzabi, "Mitzvot VeOrthodoxia," 644-45.
38. Mendes-Flohr, "The Appeal of the Incorrigible Idealist," 150.

12. EXISTENTIAL THEOLOGY AND MORAL POLITICS

1. On the weakening of Magnes's American base of support, see Magnes, *Dissenter in Zion*, 370. According to historian Zohar Segev, "The 1930s saw a significant increase in funds raised by Jewish philanthropies and Zionist foundations, a substantial rise in the number of Hadassah's member organizations, and increased enlistment in the Zionist movement as well as greater participation at Zionist events." Segev, "MeShkia VeAd Hadacha," 455-94.
2. Weizmann, *Letters and Papers*, 20:391.
3. See Magnes's notes on this meeting, Magnes, *Dissenter in Zion*, 494-97.
4. Cited in Heller, *MiBrit Shalom Le-Ichud*, 389.

5. Magnes, *In the Perplexity of the Times*, 20–21. The original speech in Hebrew uses the term "We must now bend the knee and beg forgiveness" whereas the later translation is worded "throw ourselves into the dust and try to find forgiveness." The original form has been maintained for the sake of the argument presented. Magnes, *BeMevuchat Hazman*, 16–17.
6. Bentwich, *For Zion's Sake*, 289–90.
7. Bentwich, *For Zion's Sake*, 278, 288.
8. NLI, Gershom Scholem Archives, ARC.1599.1673.
9. For the archival source, see MS-157 (James Marshall Papers), Box 21, file 9, AJA. Bentwich refers to Louis Fischer's *The Great Challenge* (1947), which describes Magnes's constant companions as "God and the common man." Bentwich, *Dissenter in Zion*, 235. Elsewhere Fischer says about Magnes that the precept "Love thy neighbor as thyself" led him to identify with workers, sometimes with Communists, and always with Arabs. Fischer, *Men and Politics*, 244.
10. Bergman, "Al Hastarat HaPanim," 204.
11. Bergman, "Al Hastarat HaPanim," 204.
12. Bergman, "Al Hastarat HaPanim," 204–6. Bergman summarizes the view of Franz Rosenzweig "on whose grave the words 'I am forever with Thee' are engraved" with respect to the link between prayer and what is sought through prayer as follows: "This is not a question of whether the prayer is heard and fulfilled. The prayer itself is its own fulfillment.... The soul prays for what it can pray, and its prayer is answered with the certainty of God's love." Bergman, "Al Hastarat HaPanim," 206.
13. Magnes, *Dissenter in Zion*, 220.
14. Quoted in Bentwich, *For Zion's Sake*, 278.
15. Bentwich, *For Zion's Sake*, 29, 278.
16. Quoted in Bentwich, *For Zion's Sake*, 279–80. The *Shema* is one of the most fundamental acts of speech in Jewish tradition. It reads as follows: "Shema Israel, Adonai Eloheinu, Adonai Echad" (Hear O Israel, the Lord is our God, the Lord is one).
17. There is extensive scholarly research and theoretical literature on the question of Jewish faith and God's existence after the Holocaust. See, for example, Greenberg, "Cloud of Smoke"; Berkovits, *Faith after the Holocaust*; Meir, *Ma'aseh Zikaron*; Jonas, "The Concept of God"; Ben-Pazi, "Mishnato HaDatit," 193–202. On Buber and his concept of the "eclipse of God," see Ratzabi, "Shtei Darkei Emunah"; on a "theology devoid of God," see Nahar, "Haster Panim," 259–62. In another Buber essay, *Shtei Darkhei Emunah*, written during the war and published in 1950, the eclipse of God is not real

in the sense that it does not nullify the relation with God, nor the potential for redemption inherent in this bond. Regarding the verse "You are indeed a God who concealed Himself, O God of Israel, who bring victory!" (Isa. 45:15), Buber writes, "Faith must change during an eclipse of God, in order that one can stay true to God without renouncing reality. The fact that God hides Himself does not diminish that which is nonmediated; by being unmediated He remains the Redeemer, and the contradictions of being become a theophany for Him." Buber, *Shtei Darkhei Emunah*, 169–70. For more on this essay, see Ratzabi, "Shtei Darkei Emunah."

18. Goldmann, *The Hidden God*.
19. Nordheimer Nur, "HaEstetika HaAnarchistit," 36, 40–41.
20. Nordheimer Nur, "HaEstetika HaAnarchistit," 39–40.
21. Quoted in Bentwich, *For Zion's Sake*, 273.
22. Bentwich, *For Zion's Sake*, 277.
23. Cited in Heller, *MiBrit Shalom Le-Ichud*, 390.
24. Quoted in Heller, *MiBrit Shalom Le-Ichud*, 390 (emphasis in original).
25. On binationalism as utopia, Nitzan Lebovic points to the analogy Bergman proposes between the real and metaphorical bridges of Prague and the utopian bridges of Brit Shalom in Palestine. He cites Bergman, "We let Prague into our hearts as the city of bridges, and we learn from it how to try to overcome incidents of loathing. It is probably no coincidence that Bohemian Jews were the bearers of the concept of Brit Shalom. This, it seems to me, is the lesson we will pass on to our descendants." Lebovic, "Philosophiyat HaZman," 149.
26. On the origins of Gnosticism, see Hotam, *Gnosis Moderni VeTzionut*, 43–48.
27. Nordheimer Nur, "HaEstetika HaAnarchistit," 40.
28. The text of the speech was later published as part of the 1946 collection, *In the Perplexity of the Times*.
29. Bergman, *Faith and Reason*, 151.
30. Mendes-Flohr, *Kidma VeNaftuleiha*, 325–26.
31. Magnes, *Dissenter in Zion*, 49–50, 408n6.
32. On the manner in which news of the extermination of European Jewry, including the Riegner telegram, among other documents, reached Jews in the United States, and the Jewish American response, see Medoff, *The Jews Should Keep Quiet*, 102–30; Segev, *The World Jewish Congress*, 23–42. For a comprehensive discussion of how the details of the Holocaust of European Jewry became known to the Yishuv leadership, see Friling, *Hetz BaArafel*.
33. Magnes, *In the Perplexity of the Times*, 65–67.
34. For more on the Vulgate translation, see the introduction by Yosef Or, *Hagigim*, xi.

35. For a discussion of God's absence in Luther's thinking, see Paulson, "Luther on the Hidden God," 363-71; Pascal, *Hagigim*, 363.
36. Pascal, *Hagigim*, 43; English translation from https://oll.libertyfund.org/titles/pascal-the-thoughts-of-blaise-pascal.
37. See also the discussion in the Babylonian Talmud (Sanhedrin 89a) of the punishment bestowed on a prophet who withholds his prophecy, which underpins the argument here presented.
38. Magnes, *In the Perplexity of the Times*, 68-69.
39. For a detailed discussion of Kierkegaard's religious existentialism, see Sagi, *Kirkgor*, 58-64.
40. Magnes, *In the Perplexity of the Times*, 69.
41. Magnes, *In the Perplexity of the Times*, 69.
42. Magnes, *In the Perplexity of the Times*, 69-75.
43. Huxley, *On Living in a Revolution*, 44, cited in Magnes, *In the Perplexity of the Times*, 70.
44. Magnes, *In the Perplexity of the Times*, 71.
45. Magnes, *In the Perplexity of the Times*, 72.
46. Magnes, *In the Perplexity of the Times*, 76.
47. Magnes, *In the Perplexity of the Times*, 76-77.
48. Magnes, *In the Perplexity of the Times*, 77.
49. There are discernible similarities here to Nietzsche's thinking: saying "yes" to the world even in light of eternal recurrence and the impossibility of redemption. This is an affirmative decision to choose life even in the absence of any hope for salvation in this life or for the world—essentially in the absence of God—and such a decision entails constant struggle. See Yovel, *Spinoza VeKofrim Acherim*, 398-402.
50. Mendes-Flohr, "The Appeal of the Incorrigible Idealist," 152.

13. RELIGION OVERRIDES NATIONALISM

1. Ernst Simon was among Emet VeEmunah's prominent members. See Tabory, "Reform and Conservative Judaism," 41-61.
2. Magnes to Wilhelm, December 14, 1941, CAHJP, P3/2773.
3. Magnes, "Dat VeLeumiyut," undated, CAHJP, P3/2773.
4. Magnes, "Dat VeLeumiyut."
5. Magnes, "Dat VeLeumiyut."
6. On the inherent tension between Zionism and Reform Judaism, as well as initial attempts to bridge it, see Meyer, *Judaism within Modernity*, 366-67.
7. Magnes, "Dat VeLeumiyut."

8. Quoted in Stern, "He Looked Out on Zion," 182.
9. Magnes, Notes on an essay by Spinoza, 1947, CAHJP, P3-350.
10. See Magnes, *Dissenter in Zion*, 333-34. Significantly, he made these remarks soon after the publication of Gershom Scholem's first essay on the Sabbatean movement, "Mitzvah HaBa'a BeAvira," first published in the 1937 compilation *Knesset* (in memory of Israel's national poet, Haim Nachman Bialik). The political thinker Hannah Arendt voiced similar opinions, albeit later. In 1946 she wrote: "There is nothing in Herzlian Zionism that could act as a check on this; on the contrary, the utopian and ideological elements with which he injected the new Jewish will to political action are only too likely to lead the Jews out of reality once more—and out of the sphere of political action. I do not know—nor do I even want to know—what would happen to Jews all over the world and to Jewish history in the future should we meet with a catastrophe in Palestine. But the parallels with the Shabbetai Tzevi episode have become terribly close." Arendt, *The Jewish Writings*, 387.
11. Magnes, *Dissenter in Zion*, 334.
12. Magnes, "Dat VeLeumiyut.".
13. Magnes, "Dat VeLeumiyut."
14. Magnes, "Dat VeLeumiyut."
15. Magnes, "Dat VeLeumiyut."
16. Magnes, *Like All the Nations?*, 6.
17. Magnes, Notes on an essay by Spinoza.
18. Magnes, Notes on an essay by Spinoza.
19. Magnes, Notes on an essay by Spinoza.
20. Magnes, Notes on an essay by Spinoza.
21. Magnes, Notes on an essay by Spinoza.
22. Magnes, Notes on an essay by Spinoza. Magnes's use of the term "free man" is interesting, as his contemporary Gershom Scholem used this very phrase to describe Magnes in an essay honoring him on the occasion of his seventieth birthday. See Scholem, "Adam Chofshi," 207-10.
23. For a modern examination of theurgy, see Loberbaum, *In God's Image*, 94-99. Loberbaum differentiates between the scholarship of Gershom Scholem and Yehuda Liebes, both of whom address the mystical and supernatural aspects of theurgy, and the approach adopted by Moshe Idel, who considers adherence to the mitzvot a theurgic act. One may view "theological politics" as another form of theurgic action.
24. Magnes, "Dat VeLeumiyut."

14. SACRED LAND AND NEGATION OF THE STATE

1. On the consolidation of American strategy and the importance it ascribed to the Middle East toward the end of World War II and in its aftermath, see Migdal, *Shifting Sands*, 3–5.
2. Golani, *HaNatziv HaAcharon*, 52–53.
3. *Anglo-American Committee of Inquiry Report*, Preface (unpaginated).
4. Hahn, *Caught in the Middle East*, 32–33.
5. Heller, "Va'adat HaChakira," 273–347.
6. Carlebach, *Va'adat HaChakira*, 692–93. For more on HaShomer HaTza'ir members' critique of religion, see Heller, *MiBrit Shalom Le-Ichud*, 226–30.
7. Segev, *MiPolitika'im Ethni'im LeManhigim Leumi'im*, 220–21.
8. Heller, *MiBrit Shalom Le-Ichud*, 313; Segev, *MiPolitika'im Ethni'im LeManhigim Leumi'im*, 220–22.
9. See Magnes and Buber, *Arab-Jewish Unity*, 95.
10. Heller, "Va'adat HaChakira," 281–88, 302.
11. Magnes and Buber, *Arab-Jewish Unity*, 44–48.
12. Magnes and Buber, *Arab-Jewish Unity*, 49–58.
13. Magnes and Buber, *Arab-Jewish Unity*, 59–76.
14. Magnes, *Like All the Nations?*, 12.
15. Magnes, *Dissenter in Zion*, 495–96.
16. Magnes and Buber, *Arab-Jewish Unity*, 13.
17. Magnes and Buber, *Arab-Jewish Unity*, 49–50.
18. Cohen, quoted in Heller, *MiBrit Shalom Le-Ichud*, 307–8.
19. Heller, *MiBrit Shalom Le-Ichud*, 309–10.
20. Weizmann, *Letters and Papers*, 22:137–38.
21. *Anglo-American Committee of Inquiry Report*, 3.
22. *Anglo-American Committee of Inquiry Report*, 3–4.
23. Carlebach, *Va'adat HaChakira*, 692–93. For more on HaShomer HaTza'ir members' critique of religion, see Heller, *MiBrit Shalom Le-Ichud*, 226–30.
24. *Anglo-American Committee of Inquiry Report*, 7–8.
25. Carlebach, *Va'adat HaChakira*, 101, 113.
26. Omar Dajani was the son of popular moderate Hasan Dajani, who was assassinated on the mufti's order in 1937. Omar probably worked for Jewish Agency Intelligence, and his testimony here might have been aimed at masking his true sentiments. McDonald, *To the Gates of Jerusalem*, 182.
27. Quoted in Carlebach, *Va'adat HaChakira*, 175–76, 331, 463.
28. Heller, *MiBrit Shalom Le-Ichud*, 312–13.
29. "Magnes: The Time Is Right for Cooperation with the Arabs," *Haaretz*, May 2, 1946.

30. Heller, *MiBrit Shalom Le-Ichud*, 314–18.
31. Magnes and Buber, *Arab-Jewish Unity*, 9.
32. Heller, *MiBrit Shalom Le-Ichud*, 312–18.
33. Although no HaShomer HaTza'ir members testified, the Committee did receive the movement's pamphlet, *BiZkhut HaDu-Leumiyut* [In favor of binationalism].
34. *Anglo-American Committee of Inquiry Report*, 27.
35. Magnes and Buber, *Arab-Jewish Unity*, 63.
36. Crossman, *Palestine Mission*, 132–34.
37. McDonald, *To the Gates of Jerusalem*, 157.
38. Segev, *MiPolitika'im Ethni'im LeManhigim Leumi'im*, 258–71.
39. Heller, "Va'adat HaChakira," 276.
40. Crum, *Behind the Silken Curtain*, 265.
41. Crum, *Behind the Silken Curtain*, 5.
42. Crum, *Behind the Silken Curtain*, 268.
43. Crum, *Behind the Silken Curtain*, 269. Elsewhere in his account, Crum again underscores the strong impression left by Magnes's testimony, "particularly" on Judge Hutcheson—a testimony based on many years of living in Palestine and on his American background (253).
44. Magnes and Buber, *Arab-Jewish Unity*, 93–95.
45. Hutcheson, "Ish HaEmunah VeHaOz," 211.

15. CONFEDERATION PLAN BETWEEN HOPE, DESPAIR

1. Magnes, "Towards Peace in Palestine," *Foreign Affairs*, January 1943, 241.
2. Magnes, "Towards Peace in Palestine," 243.
3. Magnes, "Towards Peace in Palestine," 249.
4. Young-Bruehl, *Hannah Arendt*, 225–26.
5. Young-Bruehl, *Hannah Arendt*, 227–30.
6. Arendt, *The Jewish Writings*, 423–50.
7. Quoted in Young-Bruehl, *Hannah Arendt*, 233. Buber had similar observations about Magnes as a force against despairing of politics: "You have granted me a great gift; you made it possible for me to return to political activism … without sacrificing the truth." Buber, *The Letters*, 521–22.
8. See Kielmansegg, Mewes, and Glaser-Schmidt, *Hannah Arendt and Leo Strauss*.
9. Arendt, *The Jewish Writings*, 343–74.
10. Ratzabi, "Shlilat Medinat HaUma," 226.
11. Arendt, *The Jewish Writings*, 371.

12. Ratzabi, "Shlilat Medinat HaUma," 227. See also Arendt, *The Jewish Writings*, 362–64.
13. Arendt, "Peace or Armistice," 78–79.
14. Aubrey S. Eban, "The Future of Arab-Jewish Relations," *Commentary*, September 1948, 199–206, https://www.commentarymagazine.com/articles/aubrey-eban/the-future-of-arab-jewish-relationsthe-key-is-the-cooperation-of-equal-and-separate-states/.
15. Magnes played an important part in the undertaking to save "Diaspora treasures" such as Jewish libraries and archives from the German authorities and bring them to Jerusalem. For a critical examination of these efforts, see Gish, *Ex Libris*, 31–76. The final phrase, "protection of religious shrines and historical monuments and collections of cultural, artistic, and scientific importance," might refer to the Dead Sea Scrolls, as Magnes had participated in their acquisition and transfer to Jerusalem. On his role in this process, see Kalman, *Hebrew Union College*, 3–6.
16. Magnes, *Dissenter in Zion*, 512–14.
17. Quoted in Magnes, "Al Tivtechu BeNedivim," 210.
18. See Magnes, *Dissenter in Zion*, 514–15.
19. Heller, *MiBrit Shalom Le-Ichud*, 392.
20. Arendt, "Peace or Armistice," 77–78.
21. See, for example, the preface by philosopher Jerome Kohn to Arendt, *The Jewish Writings*, arguing that although some Jews might "actualize" their Jewishness through religious creed and beliefs, Arendt was not among them. Arendt, *The Jewish Writings*, xiii. For Arendt's eulogy of Magnes, see Arendt, *The Jewish Writings*, 451–52.
22. Young-Bruehl, *Hannah Arendt*, 166.

CONCLUSION

1. James to Miss S., May 16, 1909, in *The Letters of William James*, cited in Collins, *Interpreting Modern Philosophy*, 401.
2. Amir, "Likrat Hagut," 23–38.
3. Scholem, "Adam Hofshi," 207.
4. Benjamin, "On the Concept of History," 2.
5. Stern, "He Looked Out on Zion," 175–77.

BIBLIOGRAPHY

Agnon, Shmuel Y. *Shira*. [In Hebrew]. Jerusalem: Schocken, 1999.
Ahad Ha'am. *Al Parashat Drachim* [At the crossroads]. Warsaw: Achiasaf, 1902.
——. *Kol Kitvei Ahad Ha'am* [Complete works of Ahad Ha'am]. Tel Aviv: Dvir, 1956.
——. *Selected Essays*. Translated by Leon Simon. Philadelphia: The Jewish Publication Society of America, 1912.
Amir, Yehoyada. "Likrat Hagut Teologit Reformit Be-Israel [Toward Reform theology in Israel]." In *HaYahadut HaReformit: Hagut, Tarbut, Chevra* [Reform Judaism: Thought, culture, society], edited by Avinoam Roznak, 23–50. Jerusalem: Van Leer Institute, 2014.
Anglo-American Committee of Inquiry on Jewish Problems in Palestine and Europe. *Report of the Anglo-American Committee of Inquiry*. London: HMSO, 1946.
Aran, Gideon. *Kookism: Shorsei Gush Emunim, Tarbut HaMitnachalim, Teologiya Tziyonit, Meshichiyut Bezmanenu* [Kookism: The origins of the Bloc of the Faithful, settler culture, Zionist theology, current messianism]. Jerusalem: Carmel, 2013.
Arendt, Hanna. *The Jewish Writings*. New York: Schocken Books, 2007.
Arieli, Yehoshua. *Historiya VeMetta-Historiya* [History and metahistory]. Jerusalem: Mosad Bialik, 2003.
Armitage, David. *The Declaration of Independence: A Global History*. Cambridge MA: Harvard University Press, 2007.
Aschheim, Steven. *The Nietzsche Legacy in Germany*. Berkeley: University of California Press, 1994.

Avineri, Shlomo. *HaRa'ayon HaZioni LiGvanav: Prakim BeToldot HaMachsava HaLeumit HaYehudit* [Varieties of Zionist thought: Chapters in the history of national Jewish thought]. Tel Aviv: Am Oved, 1980.

Baeck, Leo. *The Essence of Judaism*. New York: Schocken, 1948.

Barak-Gorodetsky, David. "Bein Yahadut Nevuit LeDu-Leumiyut: Hana'a Datit VeTeologiya Politit BeOlamo Shel Yehuda Leib Magnes [Between prophetic Judaism and Binationalism: Political theology in the world of Judah Leib Magnes]." PhD diss., University of Haifa, 2016.

Barbour, Hugh, and J. William Frost. *The Quakers*. New York: Greenwood Press, 1988.

Ben-Gurion, David. *Pgishot Im Manhigim Aravim* [Meetings with Arab leaders]. Tel Aviv: Am Oved, 1967.

Ben-Israel, Hedva. "Y. L. Magnes VeBrit Shalom [J. L. Magnes and Brit Shalom]." In *Brit Shalom VeHatzionut HaDuleumit: 'HaShela HaArvit' Ke-Shela Yehudit* [Brit Shalom and Binational Zionism: The 'Arab Question' as a Jewish Question], edited by Adi Gordon, 111–21. Jerusalem: Carmel, 2009.

Benjamin, Walter. "On the Concept of History." In *Walter Benjamin: Selected Writings*, edited by Michael W. Jennings, 389. Cambridge MA: Belknap Press, 2004.

Ben-Pazi, Hanoch. "Mishnato HaDatit Shel Yeshayahu Leibowitz, Ke 'Teologiya Radikalit' SheLeachar HaShoah [The religious doctrine of Yeshayahu Leibowitz as a post-Holocaust 'radical theology']." *Iyun* 57 (April 2008): 193–202.

Bentwich, Norman. *For Zion's Sake: A Biography of Judah L. Magnes, First Chancellor and First President of the Hebrew University of Jerusalem*. Philadelphia: The Jewish Publication Society of America, 1954.

———. *Solomon Schechter: A Biography*. Philadelphia: The Jewish Publication Society of America, 1938.

Bergman, Samuel Hugo. "Al Hastarat HaPanim VeAl HaOra HaElohit" [On the eclipse of God and on the Divine Light]. *Be'ayot: Bama Hadasha LeChayei HaTzibur* 29–30, no. 5 (July 1947): 204–6.

———. *Faith and Reason: An Introduction to Modern Jewish Thought*. Washington DC: B'nai B'rith Hillel Foundations, 1961.

Berkovits, Eliezer. *Faith after the Holocaust*. Hoboken NJ: KTAV, 1973.

Binyamini, Yitzhak, and Yotam Hotam. "Likrat Teologiya Bikortit—Minshar [Toward a critical theology—A manifesto]." *Tabur* 5 (2012): 193–205.

Brault, Pascale-Anne. "Playing the Cassandra: Prophecies of the Feminine in the *Polis* and Beyond." In *Bound by the City: Greek Tragedy, Sexual Difference and the Formation of the Polis*, edited by Denise Eileen McCoskey and Emily Zakin, 197–220. New York: State University of New York Press, 2009.

Brock, Peter. *Pacifism in the United States: From the Colonial Era to the First World War*. Princeton NJ: Princeton University Press, 1968.
Brody, Samuel H. *Martin Buber's Theopolitics*. Bloomington: Indiana University Press, 2018.
Buber, Martin M. *Bein Am LeArtso: Ikarei Toldotav Shel Raayon* [Between a people and its land: The origins of an idea]. Jerusalem: Schocken, 1985.
———. *BePardes HaHasidut: Iyunim BaMachshava VeBeHavaya* [In the orchard of Hasidism: Reflections on its thought and experience]. Tel Aviv: Mosad Bialik, 1945.
———. "The Binational Approach to Zionism." In *Towards Union in Palestine: Essays on Zionism and Arab-Jewish Cooperation*, edited by Martin Buber, Judah Leib Magnes, and Ernst Simon, 7–13. Jerusalem: Ichud Association, 1947.
———. *Eclipse of God: Studies in the Relation between Religion and Philosophy*. New York: Harper and Brothers, 1952.
———. *Eretz LiShnei Amim* [A land of two peoples]. Edited by Paul Mendes-Flohr. Jerusalem: Schocken, 1988.
———. *The Letters of Martin Buber: A Life of Dialogue*. Edited by Nahum Glatzer and Paul Mendes-Flohr. Syracuse NY: Syracuse University Press, 1996.
———. *On Zion: The History of an Idea*. Translated by Stanley Godman. Syracuse NY: Syracuse University Press, 1997.
———. *Shtei Darkhei Emunah* [Two paths of belief]. Tel Aviv: Resling, 2011.
Butler, John, Grant Wacker, and Randall Balmer. *Religion in American Life: A Short History*. Oxford: Oxford University Press, 2011.
Carlebach, Azriel. *Va'adat HaChakira HaAnglo-Amerikayit LeInyanei Eretz-Israel* [The Anglo American Committee of Inquiry on Palestine]. Tel Aviv: Z. Leinman, 1946.
Cavanaugh, William T., and Peter Scott. *The Blackwell Companion to Political Theology*. Malden MA: Blackwell Publishing, 2004.
Cohen, Hillel. *Tarpat: Shnat HaEfes BaSichsuch HaYehudi-Aravi* [1929: Year zero of the Arab-Israeli conflict]. Jerusalem: Keter, 2013.
Cohen, Michael R. *The Birth of Conservative Judaism: Solomon Schechter's Disciples and the Creation of an American Religious Movement*. New York: Columbia University Press, 2012.
Cohen, Naomi W. *The Americanization of Zionism, 1897–1948*. Waltham MA: Brandeis University Press, 2003.
———. *The Year after the Riots: American Responses to the Palestine Crisis of 1929–30*. Detroit MI: Wayne State University Press, 1988.
Cohen, Uri. *HaHar VeHagivaa* [The mountain and the hill]. Tel Aviv: Am Oved, 2007.

Collins, James. *Interpreting Modern Philosophy*. Princeton NJ: Princeton University Press, 1972.

Crossman, Richard H. S. *Palestine Mission: A Personal Record*. New York: Harper and Brothers, 1947.

Crum, Bartley C. *Behind the Silken Curtain*. New York: Simon and Schuster, 1947.

Davis, Moses. "Israel Friedlander's Minute Book of the *Achava* Club (1909-1912)." In *M. M. Kaplan Jubilee*, edited by Moses Davis, 157-214. New York: Jewish Theological Seminary, 1953.

Dobbert, Guido A. "The Ordeal of Gotthard Deutsch." *American Jewish Archives* (1968): 129-55.

Even-Zahav, Ari. *J. L. Magnes: Builder of the Hebrew University*. New York: Jewish Education Committee Press, 1966.

Fine, David J. "Solomon Schechter and the Ambivalence of Jewish Wissenschaft." *Judaism* 46, no. 1 (Winter 1997): 3-24.

Fischer, Louis. *Men and Politics: An Autobiography*. New York: Duell, Sloan and Pearce, 1941.

Flusser, David. "LeZichro Shel Karl Bart [In memory of Karl Barth]." *Ptachim* 9 (June 1969): 9-18.

Frankel, Jonathan. *Prophecy and Politics: Socialism, Nationalism and the Russian Jews, 1862-1917*. New York: Cambridge University Press, 1984.

Friedlander, Israel. *Past and Present: A Collection of Jewish Essays*. Cincinnati OH: Ark Publishing, 1919.

Friesel, Evyatar. "Ahad Ha-Amism in American Zionist Thought." In *At the Crossroads: Essays on Ahad Ha-am*, edited by Jacques Kornberg, 133-41. Albany: State University of New York Press, 1983.

———. "Zionism in Judaism." In *Like All the Nations? The Life and Legacy of Judah L. Magnes*, edited by William M. Brinner and Moses Rischin, 69-81. Albany: State University of New York Press, 1987.

Friling, Tuvya. *Hetz BaArafel: David Ben-Gurion, Hanagat HaYishuv VeNisionot Hatzala BaShoah* [An arrow in the fog: David Ben-Gurion, the Yishuv leadership and rescue attempts during the Holocaust]. Sdeh Boker: HaMerkaz LeMoreshet Ben-Gurion, 1998.

Garling, Nadin. "'Kasha Mikol Nireit Li She'elat HaAravim': Arthur Ruppin Bein Tzionut Maasit LeDuleumiyut BeBrit Shalom ['Most difficult to me seems the Arab Question': Arthur Ruppin between practical Zionism and binationalism in Brit Shalom]." In *Brit Shalom Ve Hatzionut HaDuleumit: "HaShela HaArvit" Ke-Shela Yehudit* [Brit Shalom and binational Zionism: The "Arab Question" as a Jewish question], edited by Adi Gordon, 169-80. Jerusalem: Carmel, 2009.

Gellner, Ernest. *Nations and Nationalism*. Ithaca NY: Cornell University Press, 2008.

Gerber, Vardit. "Itzuv Leumi, Politika VeMigdar: Rose Jacobs VeIrgun Hadassah BaMachatzit HaRishona Shel Ha-Meah HaEsrim [National design, politics and gender: Rose Jacobs and Hadassah in the first half of the twentieth century]." Master's thesis, University of Haifa, 2014.

Gish, Amit. *Ex Libris: Historya Shel Gezel, Shimur VeNichus BaSifriya HaLeumit BeYerushalayim* [Ex Libris: A history of plunder, preservation, and appropriation at the National Library in Jerusalem]. Jerusalem: Van Leer Institute and HaKibbutz HaMeuchad, 2014.

Gladden, Washington. "Recent Reconstructions of Theology." *Homiletic Review* 37, no. 3 (March 1899): 201–8.

Gluzman, Michael. *HaGuf HaTzioni: Leumiyut, Migdar VeMiniyut BaSafrut HaIvrit HaChadasha* [The Zionist body: Nationalism, gender, and sexuality in the new Hebrew literature]. Tel Aviv: HaKibbutz HaMeuchad, 2007.

Golani, Moti. *HaNatziv HaAcharon: Sir Alan Gordon Cunningham 1945–1948* [The last high commissioner: Sir Alan Gordon Cunningham 1945–1948]. Tel Aviv: Am Oved, 2011.

Goldish, Matt. *The Sabbatean Prophets*. Cambridge MA: Harvard University Press, 2004.

Goldmann, Lucien. *The Hidden God: A Study of the Tragic Vision in the Pensées of Pascal and the Tragedies of Racine*. London: Routledge and K. Paul, 1964.

Gordon, Adi, ed. *Brit Shalom VeHatzionut HaDuleumit: "HaShela HaArvit" Ke-Shela Yehudit* [Brit Shalom and binational Zionism: The "Arab Question" as a Jewish question]. Jerusalem: Carmel, 2009.

Goren, Arthur A. "Between Priest and Prophet." In *Like All the Nations? The Life and Legacy of Judah L. Magnes*, edited by William M. Brinner and Moses Rischin, 57–67. Albany: State University of New York Press, 1987.

———. *New York Jews and the Quest for Community: The Kehillah Experiment, 1908–1922*. New York: Columbia University Press, 1970.

Gorny, Yosef. *HaShe'ela HaAravit VeHaBaaya HaYehudit: Zramim Mediniyim-Ideologiyim BaTzionut Beyachasa El HaYeshut HaAravit BeEretz Israel Bashanim 1882–1948*. [The Arab question and the Jewish problem: Political-ideological currents in Zionism in relation to the Arab entity in Palestine in the years 1882–1948]. Tel Aviv: Am Oved, 1986.

Greenberg, Irving. "Cloud of Smoke, Pillar of Fire: Judaism, Christianity and Modernity after the Holocaust." In *Holocaust: Religious and Philosophical Implications*, edited by John K. Ross and Michael Berenbaum, 305–48. St. Paul MN: Paragon House, 1989.

Greene, David. *The Jewish Origins of Cultural Pluralism: The Menorah Association and American Diversity.* Bloomington : Indiana University Press, 2011.

Greenstein, Howard R. *Turning Point: Zionism and Reform Judaism.* Chico CA: Scholars Press, 1981.

Guttmann, Julius. *HaPhilosophia Shel HaYahadut* [Philosophies of Judaism]. Jerusalem: Mosad Bialik, 1951.

Hahn, Peter L. *Caught in the Middle East: U.S. Policy towards the Arab-Israeli Conflict.* Chapel Hill: University of North Carolina Press, 2004.

Hastings, Adrian. *The Construction of Nationhood: Ethnicity, Religion and Nationalism.* Cambridge: Cambridge University Press, 1997.

Hattis, Susan Lee. *The Bi-National Idea in Palestine during Mandatory Times.* Haifa: Shikmona, 1970.

Hazan, Meir. "'HaIsha HaChachama MiGivat Brener': HaMeshoreret Yesha Sampter VeHaKibbutz ['The wise woman from Givat Brener': Poet Jessie Sampter and the kibbutz]." *Zmanim* 130 (Spring 2015): 32-45.

———. *Metinut: HaGisha HaMetuna BeHapoel HaTzair VeBeMapai, 1905-1945* [Moderation: The moderate approach in HaPo'el HaTza'ir and Mapai, 1905-1945]. Tel Aviv: Am Oved, 2009.

Heller, Joseph. *MiBrit Shalom Le-Ichud: Yehuda Leib Magnes VeHaMaavak LeMedina Duleumit* [From Brit Shalom to Ichud: Judah Leib Magnes and the struggle for a binational state]. Jerusalem: Magnes Press, 2004.

———. "Va'adat HaChakira Ha-Anglo Amerikanit 1945-1946 [The Anglo American Committee of Inquiry 1945-1946]." In *Maavak, Mered, Meri: HaMediniyut HaBritit VeHaTziyonit VeHamavak Im Britanya 1941-1948* [Struggle, revolt, rebellion: The British and Zionist policies and the struggle with Britain 1941-1948], edited by Yaakov Shavit, 273-347. Jerusalem: Merkaz Zalman Shazar, 1987.

Hillquit, Morris. *Loose Leaves from a Busy Life.* New York: Macmillan, 1934.

Hobsbawm, Eric J. *Nations and Nationalism since 1780.* Cambridge: Cambridge University Press, 1990.

Holmes, John Haynes. *Palestine To-Day and To-Morrow: A Gentile's Survey of Zionism.* New York: Macmillan, 1929.

Horwitz, Rivka. *Franz Rosenzweig: HaCochav VeHaAdam* [Franz Rosenzweig: The star and the man]. Beersheba: Ben-Gurion University Press, 2010.

Hotam, Yotam. *Gnosis Moderni VeZionut: Mashber HaTarbut, Philosophyat HaChayim VeHagut Leumit Yehudit* [Modern Gnosis and Zionism: The culture crisis, philosophy of life and Jewish national thought]. Jerusalem: Magnes Press, 2007.

Hutcheson, Joseph. "Ish HaEmunah VeHaOz [The man of faith and courage]." *Be'ayot: Bama Hadasha LeChayei HaTzibur* 29-30, no. 5 (July 1947): 211-12.

Huxley, Julian. *On Living in a Revolution*. New York: Harper, 1944.
Hyfler, Robert. *Prophets of the Left: American Socialist Thought in the Twentieth Century*. Westport CT: Greenwood Press, 1984.
James, William. *The Letters of William James*. Boston: Atlantic Monthly Press, 1920.
———. *Pragmatism*. New York: Dover, 1995.
———. *The Varieties of Religious Experience: A Study in Human Nature*. New York: The Modern Library, 1950.
———. *The Will to Believe and Other Essays in Popular Philosophy*. New York: Dover Publications, 1960.
Jonas, Hans. "The Concept of God after Auschwitz: A Jewish Voice." *Journal of Religion* 67, no. 1 (1987): 1–13.
Kalman, Jason. *Hebrew Union College and the Dead Sea Scrolls*. Cincinnati OH: Hebrew Union College Press, 2012.
Kaplan, Mordecai M. *Judaism as a Civilization: Towards a Reconstruction of American-Jewish Life*. Philadelphia: The Jewish Publication Society, 2010.
Kazin, Michael. *War against War: The American Fight for Peace, 1914–1918*. New York: Simon and Schuster, 2017.
Keidar, Nir. "Ben-Gurion's Mamlakhtiyut: Etymological and Theoretical Roots." *Israel Studies* 7, no. 3 (Fall 2002): 117–33.
Kennedy, David M. *Over Here: The First World War and American Society*. Oxford: Oxford University Press, 2004.
Kielmansegg, Peter G., Horst Mewes, and Elisabeth Glaser-Schmidt, eds. *Hannah Arendt and Leo Strauss: German Émigrés and American Political Thought after World War II*. Washington DC; Cambridge: German Historical Institute and Cambridge University Press, 1995.
Kornberg, Jacques. "At the Crossroads: An Introductory Essay." In *At the Crossroads: Essays on Ahad Ha-am*, edited by Jacques Kornberg, xvi–xix. Albany: State University of New York Press, 1983.
Kotzin, Daniel P. "An Attempt to Americanize the Yishuv: Judah L. Magnes in Mandatory Palestine." *Israel Studies* 5, no.1 (2000): 1–23.
———. *Judah L. Magnes: An American Jewish Nonconformist*. Syracuse NY: Syracuse University Press, 2010.
Kraut, Benny. "Felix Adler's Emergence out of Judaism." PhD diss., Brandeis University, 1975.
Landauer, Gustav. *For Socialism*. St. Louis MO: Telos Press, 1978.
———. *Ktavim VeMikhtavim (1900–1919)* [Writings and letters (1900–1919)]. Tel Aviv: Alef, 1982.
Lazar, Hadara. *Sisha Yechidim* [Six singular individuals]. Tel Aviv: HaKibbutz HaMeuchad, 2012.

Lebovic, Nitzan. "Philosophiyat HaZman Shel Hugo Bergman: Bein Geula Le-Brit Shalom [Hugo Bergman's philosophy of time: Between redemption and Brit Shalom.]" In *Brit Shalom Ve Hatzionut HaDuleumit: 'HaShela HaArvit' Ke-Shela Yehudit* [Brit Shalom and binational Zionism: The 'Arab Question' as a Jewish question], edited by Adi Gordon, 149–67. Jerusalem: Carmel, 2009.

Loberbaum, Yair. *In God's Image: Myth, Theology and Law in Classical Judaism.* New York: Cambridge University Press, 2015.

Loewenstein, David. *Milton: Paradise Lost.* Cambridge: Cambridge University Press, 2004.

Lurie, Ben-Tzion, ed. *Chug HaIyun BaTanakh BeBeit Nasi HaMedina.* Vol. 3, *Iyunim BeSefer Yermiyahu* [The Bible study circle at the home of the president of Israel. Vol. 3, Reflections on the Book of Jeremiah]. Jerusalem: HaChevra LeCheker HaMikrah BeIsrael, 1972.

Luz, Ehud. "HaYesod HaDialekti BeKitvei Harav Y.B. Soloveitchik [The dialectical method in the writings of Rabbi J. B. Soloveitchik]." *Daat* 9 (1982): 75–89.

———. "Talush Haya HaIsh VeKmo Michutz LaZman: Mikra BeShnayim MiShirey HaEt Shel Natan Alterman [The man was detached and seemingly outside of time: A reading in two of the time poems by Natan Alterman]." *Dapim LeMechkar BeSafrut* 12 (1999–2000): 147–54.

Magnes, Judah L. *Addresses by the Chancellor of the Hebrew University.* Jerusalem: Hebrew University, 1936.

———. "Al Tivtechu BeNedivim [Do not trust the charitable]." *Be'ayot: Bama Hadasha LeChayei HaTzibur* 29–30, no. 5 (July 1947): 210.

———. *BeMevuchat Hazman* [In the perplexity of the times]. Jerusalem: Hebrew University, 1946.

———. *Dissenter in Zion: From the Writings of Judah L. Magnes.* Edited by Arthur A. Goren. Cambridge MA: Harvard University Press, 1982.

———. *In the Perplexity of the Times.* Jerusalem: Hebrew University, 1946.

———. *Like All the Nations?* Jerusalem: Herod Gate, 1930.

———. *A Treatise as to (1) Necessary Existence (2) The Procedure of Things from the Necessary Existence and (3) The Creation of the World, by Joseph Ibn Aknin.* Berlin: H. Itskowski, 1904.

———. *War-time Addresses: 1917–1921.* New York: Thomas Seltzer, 1923.

Magnes, Judah L., and Martin Buber. *Arab-Jewish Unity: Testimony before the Anglo-American Inquiry Commission for the Ihud (Union) Association.* London: V. Gollancz, 1947.

Magnes, Judah L., Menachem Kaufman, and Mosheh Gudman. *The Magnes-Philby Negotiations, 1929: The Historical Record.* Jerusalem: Magnes Press, 1998.

Malone, Bobbie. *Rabbi Max Heller: Reformer, Zionist, Southerner, 1860–1929*. Tuscaloosa: University of Alabama Press, 2013.
Mayshar, Yoram. "Cohen VeNavi: Shtei Mahapechot HaMusar Shel Nietzsche [Priest and prophet: The two moral revolutions of Nietzsche]." *Iyun* 52 (October 2003): 438–63.
McDonald, James G. *To the Gates of Jerusalem: The Diaries and Papers of James G. McDonald, 1945–1947*. Edited by Norman G. W. Goda, Barbara McDonald Stewart, Sevrin Hochberg, and Richard Brietman. Bloomington: Indiana University Press, 2015.
Medoff, Rafael. *The Jews Should Keep Quiet: Franklin D. Roosevelt, Rabbi Stephen S. Wise, and the Holocaust*. Philadelphia: The Jewish Publication Society, 2019.
———. *Zionism and the Arabs: An American Jewish Dilemma, 1898–1948*. Westport CT: Praeger, 1997.
Meir, Ephraim. *Ma'aseh Zikaron: Chevra, Adam VeElohim Leachar Auschwitz* [An act of remembrance: Society, mankind and God after Auschwitz]. Tel Aviv: Resling, 2006.
Menand, Louis. *The Metaphysical Club: A Story of Ideas in America*. New York: Farrar, Straus and Giroux, 2001.
Mendes-Flohr, Paul R. "The Appeal of the Incorrigible Idealist." In *Like All the Nations? The Life and Legacy of Judah L. Magnes*, edited by William M. Brinner and Moses Rischin, 139–54. Albany: State University of New York Press, 1987.
———. *Kidma VeNaftuleiha: Maavakam Shel Intelectualim Yehudim Im HaMorderna* [Progress and its vicissitudes: Jewish intellectuals' struggle with modernity]. Tel Aviv: Schocken, 2010.
———. *Martin Buber: A Life of Faith and Dissent*. New Haven CT: Yale University Press, 2019.
Metzer, Yaacov. *Hon Leumi* [National capital]. Jerusalem: Yad Itzhak Ben-Zvi, 1979.
Meyer, Michael. *Bein Masoret LeKidma: Toldot HaTnua HaReformit BaYahadut* [Between tradition and progress: The history of the Reform movement in Judaism]. Jerusalem: Merkaz Shazar, 1990.
———. *Hebrew Union College—Jewish Institute of Religion: A Centennial History—1875–1975*. Cincinnati OH: Hebrew Union College Press, 1976.
———. *Judaism within Modernity: Essays on Jewish History and Religion*. Detroit MI: Wayne State University Press, 2001.
———. *Response to Modernity: A History of the Reform Movement in Judaism*. Detroit MI: Wayne State University Press, 1995.
Michels, Tony. *A Fire in Their Hearts: Yiddish Socialists in New York*. Cambridge MA: Harvard University Press, 2005.

Migdal, Joel S. *Shifting Sands: The United States in the Middle East*. New York: Columbia University Press, 2014.

Myers, David N. *In Search of the Harmonious Jew: Judah L. Magnes between East and West*. Berkeley: Judah L. Magnes Museum, 1993.

Nahar, André. "Haster Panim VeDmama BaNevuah [The eclipse of God and silence in prophecy]." *Divrei Ha-Congress HaOlami LeYahadut* (1969): 259–62.

Nahshon, Edna. *From the Ghetto to the Melting Pot: Israel Zangwill's Jewish Plays*. Detroit MI: Wayne State University Press, 2006.

Neuberger, Binyamin. "Haim Yesh LeIsrael Masoret Politit Democratit? [Does Israel have a democratic political tradition?]." *Divrei Ha-Congress HaOlami LeYahadut* (1989): 589–92.

Nietzsche, Friedrich. *Thus Spoke Zarathustra: A Book for All and None*. Translated by Walter Kaufmann. New York: Modern Library, 1995.

Nimrod, Yoram. "Chelko Shel Yeudah L. Magnes BeSikul Tochnit Peel [The role of Judah Leib Magnes in foiling the Peel Plan]." Master's thesis, University of Haifa, 1978.

Nordheimer Nur, Ofer. "HaEstetika HaAnarchistit Shel HaShomer HaTza'ir Beshnot HaEsrim VeTfisat HaOlam HaTragit [An aesthetic of anarchism of HaShomer HaTza'ir in the 1920s and the tragic worldview]." In *Tor HaNeurim: Noar Germani-Yehudi BaIdan HaModerni* [The age of youth: Jewish German youth in the modern era], edited by Yotam Hotam, 33–44. Jerusalem: Magnes Press, 2008.

Ohana, David. *Mashikhiyut VeMamlakhtiyut: Ben-Gurion VeHaIntelektualim: Bein Hazon Medini LeTeologiya Politit* [Messianism and statism: Ben-Gurion and the intellectuals: Between a political vision and political theology]. Beersheba: Ben-Gurion University Press, 2003.

Otto, Rudolf. *HaKedusha: Al haLoRatzionali beIdeat haEl veYahaso laRatzionali*. Translated by Miriam Ron. Afterword by Yoseph Ben-Shlomo. Jerusalem: Carmel, 1999.

———. *The Idea of the Holy*. Oxford: Oxford University Press, 1923.

Page, Norman, ed. *Oxford Reader's Companion to Hardy*. Oxford: Oxford University Press, 2000.

Parzen, Herbert. "The Magnes-Weizmann-Einstein Controversy." *Jewish Social Studies* 32 (1970): 187–213.

Pascal, Blaise. *Hagigim* [Pensées]. Translated by Yosef Ur. Jerusalem: Magnes Press, 1976.

———. *Pensées*. Edited and translated by Roger Ariew. Indianapolis IN: Hackett Publishers, 2005.

Paulson, Steven D. "Luther on the Hidden God." *Word and World* 19 (1999): 363–71.

Philipson, David. *The Reform Movement in Judaism*. New York: Macmillan, 1907.

Pratt, Norma F. *Morris Hillquit: A Political History of an American Jewish Socialist*. Westport CT: Greenwood Press, 1979.

Rabinovitch, Simon, ed. *Jews and Diaspora Nationalism: Writings on Jewish Peoplehood in Europe and the United States*. Waltham MA: Brandeis University Press, 2012.

Ratzabi, Shalom. *Anarchizm BeTzion: Bein Martin Buber LeAharon David Gordon* [Anarchism in Zion: Between Martin Buber and Aharon David Gordon]. Tel Aviv: Am Oved, 2011.

———. "Bein Am LeArtso: Yahid, Uma VeEretz BeHaguto Shel AD Gordon [Between a land and its people: Individual, nation, and land in the thought of A. D. Gordon]." In *Misaviv LaNekuda: Mehkarim Hadashim Al M. Y. Berdichevsky, Y. H. Brener, A. D. Gordon* [Around the dot: New research on M. Y. Berdichevsky, Y. H. Brener, and A. D. Gordon], edited by Avner Holzman, Gideon Katz, Shalom Ratzabi, 275–320. Sdeh Boker: Ben-Gurion Research Institute, 2008.

———. *Bein Goral LeYeud: HaSiach HaTeologi HaYehudi BeArtzot Habrit* [Between fate and destiny: The Jewish theological discourse in the United States]. Tel Aviv: Am Oved, 2003.

———. *Between Zionism and Judaism: The Radical Circle in Brit Shalom, 1925–1933*. Leiden: Brill, 2002.

———. "HaTanakh KeHistoriya Wu-KeMitus: Iyun Mashve BeMekomo Shel HaTanakh BeHagutam HaTzionit Shel David Ben-Gurion VeShel Martin Buber [The Bible as history and myth: A comparative study of the Zionist thought of David Ben-Gurion and Martin Buber]." In *Tarbut, Zikaron VeHistoriya: BeHokara LeAnita Shapira* [Culture, memory, and history: In honor of Anita Shapira], edited by Meir Hazan and Uri Cohen, 471–96. Tel Aviv: Tel Aviv University, 2012.

———. "Ishei Merkaz Eropa BeBrit Shalom: Ideologiya BeMibchan HaMetziut 1925-1948 [East European figures in Brit Shalom: Ideology in the test of time 1925–1948]." PhD diss., Tel Aviv University, 1993.

———. "Mitzvot VeOrthodoxia BeHaguto Shel Martin Buber [Halakhic deeds and Orthodoxy in the thought of Martin Buber]." *Iyunim BeTkumat Israel* 10 (2000): 641–71.

———. "Shlilat Medinat HaUma: Bein Hanna Arendt LeBuber VeIshey Merkaz Eiropa BeBrit Shalom VeIchud [The negation of the nation-state: Between Hanna Arendt and Buber and the Central European circle of Brit Shalom and Ichud]." In *Leumiyut Vemusar: HaSiach HaTzioni VeHaShe'ela HaArvit* [Nationalism and morality: The Zionist discourse and the Arab question], edited by Efrayim Lavie, 213–50. Jerusalem: Carmel, 2014.

———. "Shtei Darkei Emunah: Trumato VeMekomo BaMifaal HaHaguti Shel Martin Buber [Two paths of faith: Its role and place in the intellectual enterprise of Martin Buber]." *Hidushim BeCheker Toldot Yehudei Germaniya VeMerkaz Eiropa* 17, no. 2 (2015): 1–97.

Rechnitzer, Haim O. "HaTheologia HaReformit El Mul HaMifal HaTzioni: Iyun BeMatzaei HaTnua HaReformit [Reform theology vis-à-vis the Zionist enterprise: Reflections on the platforms of the Reform Movement]." In *HaYahadut HaReformit: Hagut, Tarbut, Chevra* [Reform Judaism: Thought, culture, society], edited by Avinoam Roznak, 23–50. Jerusalem: Van Leer Institute, 2014.

———. *Nevua VeHaseder HaMedini HaMushlam: HaTeologiya HaMedinit Shel Leo Strauss* [Prophecy and the perfect political order: The political theology of Leo Strauss]. Jerusalem: Mosad Bialik, 2012.

Renan, Ernst. "What Is a Nation?" In *Nation and Narration*, edited by Homi Bhabba, 8–22. London: Routledge, 1990.

Rischin, Moses. "The Jewish Experience in America: A View from the West." In *Jews of the American West*, edited by Moses Rischin and John Livingston, 26–47. Detroit MI: Wayne State University Press, 1991.

Rockefeller, John D., Jr. *The Christian Church—What of Its Future?* [New York]: Protestant Council, 1918.

Rosenbaum, Fred. *Cosmopolitans: A Social and Cultural History of the Jews of the San Francisco Bay Area*. Berkeley: University of California Press, 2009.

Russell, Bertrand. *Skeptical Essays*. London: George Allen and Unwin, 1960.

Ryan, Alan. *Bertrand Russell: A Political Life*. New York: Oxford University Press, 1981.

Sagi, Avi. *Kirkgor—Dat VeEkzitentsia: HaMasa El HaAni* [Kierkegaard—Religion and existentialism: The journey to the self]. Jerusalem: Mosad Bialik, 1997.

Sakakini, Halil al-. *Kaze Ani Rabotai! MiYomano Shel Halil al-Sakakini* [Such Am I, Oh World! From the diary of Halil al-Sakakini]. Translated by Gideon Shilo. Jerusalem: Keter, 1990.

Sarna, Jonathan D. *American Judaism*. New Haven CT: Yale University Press, 2004.

———. "Converts to Zionism in the American Reform Movement." *Tauber Institute for the Study of European Jewry Series* 30 (1998): 188–203.

Schatz-Uffenheimer, Rivka. *HaHasidut KeMistika* [Hasidism as mysticism]. Jerusalem: Magnes Press, 1968.

Schmidt, Christoph. "BeTshuva Al Hashe'ela: Mahi Theologia Politit [In response to the question: What is political theology?]." In *HaElohim Lo Yealem Dom: HaModerna HaYehudit VeHaTeologiya Hapolitit* [God will not stand still: Jewish Modernity and political theology], edited by Christoph Schmidt and Eli Schonfeld, 18–35. Jerusalem: Van Leer Institute and HaKibbutz HaMeuchad, 2009.

———. "Carl Schmitt BeIvrit? Machsavot Al HaRelevantiyut Shel HaTeologiya Hapolitit LaModerna (HaYehudit) [Carl Schmitt in Hebrew? Thoughts on the relevance of political theology to (Jewish) modernity]." In *HaElohim Lo Yealem Dom: HaModerna HaYehudit VeHaTeologiya Hapolitit* [God will not stand still: Jewish modernity and political theology], edited by Christoph Schmidt and Eli Schonfeld, 7–17. Jerusalem: Van Leer Institute and HaKibbutz HaMeuchad, 2009.

Scholem, Gershom. "Adam Hofshi [A free man]." *Be'ayot: Bama Hadasha LeChayei HaTzibur* 29–30, no. 5 (July 1947): 207–10.

———. *Devarim BeGo: Pirkei Morasha VeTchiya* [Explications and implication: Essays on Jewish heritage and renaissance]. Tel Aviv: Am Oved, 1976.

———. *From Berlin to Jerusalem: Memories of My Youth*. New York: Schocken Books, 1980.

———. "Mitzva HaBa'a BeAvira: LeHavanat HaShabtaut [Fulfillment by transgression: Toward an understanding of Sabbatianism]." *Knesset* 2 (1937): 9–67.

Segev, Tom. *One Palestine, Complete: Jews and Arabs under the British Mandate*. New York: Macmillan, 2000.

———. *Yemei HaKalaniyot: Eretz Israel BeTkufat HaMandat* [The days of the anemones: Palestine during the mandate]. Jerusalem: Keter, 1999.

Segev, Zohar. "European Zionism in the United States: The Americanization of Herzl's Doctrine by American Zionist Leaders—Case Studies." *Modern Judaism* 26, no. 3 (2006): 274–91.

———. "MeShkia VeAd Hadacha: Chaim Weizmann, Artzot Habrit VeHaTzionut HaAmerikait BeShnot HaArbaim [From downfall to ousting: Chaim Weizmann, the US and American Zionism in the 1940s]." In *Weizmann Manhig HaTzionut* [Weizmann the leader of Zionism], edited by Uri Cohen and Meir Hazan, 455–94. Jerusalem: Merkaz Shazar, 2016.

———. *MiPolitika'im Ethni'im LeManhigim Leumi'im: HaHanhaga HaTzionit-Americanit, HaShoah VeHakamat Medinat Israel* [From ethnic politicians to national leaders: The American-Zionist leadership, the Holocaust and the founding of the State of Israel.] Sdeh Boker: Ben-Gurion Research Institute, 2008.

———. *The World Jewish Congress during the Holocaust: Between Activism and Restraint*. Boston: Walter De Gruyter, 2014.

Seltzer, Robert. "Ahad Ha-Am and Dubnow: Friends and Adversaries." In *At the Crossroads: Essay on Ahad Ha-am*, edited by Jacques Kornberg, 60–72. Albany: State University of New York Press, 1983.

Shapira, Anita. "The Religious Motifs of the Labor Movement." *Tauber Institute for the Study of European Jewry Series* 30 (1998): 251–72.

Shiff, Ofer. *HaZionut Shel HaMenutzahim: HaMasa Shel Abba Hillel Silver El Me'ever LaLeumiyut* [The Zionism of the defeated: Abba Hillel Silver's journey beyond nationalism]. Tel Aviv: Resling, 2010.

———. *Yehudim Mishtalvim: Universalism Reformi Amerikani Mul Tzionut, Antishemiut VeShoa* [Integrating Jews: Reform Zionist universalism vis-à-vis Zionism, antisemitism, and the Holocaust]. Tel Aviv: Am Oved, 2001.

Shook, John R. "Pragmatism, Pluralism and Public Democracy." *Revue Française D'études Américaines* 124 (2010-2): 11–28.

Shumsky, Dimitry. "MiDu-Leshoniyut LeDu-Leumiyut: Yahadut Tzecho-Germanit, Tzionei Prag VeReshito Shel HaRaayon HaDuleumi BaTzionut 1900–1930 [From bilingualism to binationalism: The Czecho-German Jewry, the Prague Zionists and the origins of the binational idea in Zionism, 1900–1930]." PhD diss., University of Haifa, 2005.

Silber, Marcus. "Dubnow: Raayon HaLeumiyut HaDiasporit VeTfuzato [Dubnow: The idea of diasporic nationalism and its dispersion]." *Iyunim BeTkumat Israel* 15 (2005): 83–101.

Silver, Matthew M. *Louis Marshall and the Rise of Jewish Ethnicity in America*. Syracuse NY: Syracuse University Press, 2013.

———. "MiDfus Pa'il LiDfus Savil: Peilut Tzionit Americanit BeEretz Israel BeTkufat HaMandat [From active to passive patterns: American Zionist activity in Mandatory Palestine]." PhD diss., The Hebrew University in Jerusalem, 1999.

Simon, Ernst A. "HaChinukh LeShalom BeItot Milchama [Educating for peace in times of war]." In *HaZkhut LeChanekh, HaChova LeChanekh* [The right to educate, the duty to educate], edited by Ernst Simon, 7–20. Tel Aviv: Sifriyat Poalim, 1983.

———. *Kav HaTichum: Leumiyut, Tzionut VeHaSichsuch HaYehudi-Aravi BeMishnat Mordechai Martin Buber WuBePeilutu* [The boundary line: Nationalism, Zionism and the Jewish-Arab conflict in the thought and action of Mordecai Martin Buber]. Givat-Haviva: The Center for Arab Studies, 1973.

———. *Pirkei Haim: Binyan Betokh Chorban* [Chapters of life: Construction amid destruction]. Tel Aviv: Sifriyat Poalim, 1987.

Smith, Anthony D. *Chosen Peoples: Sacred Sources of National Identity*. Oxford: Oxford University Press, 2003.

Stern, Gabriel. "He Looked Out on Zion from Atop Mount Scopus and Dreamt of Peace: A Memoir." In *Like All the Nations? The Life and Legacy of Judah L. Magnes*, edited by William M. Brinner and Moses Rischin, 175–86. Albany: State University of New York Press, 1987.

Strasberg-Dayan, Sarah. "Tzion: Malchut Shamayin O Malchut Israel? Bein Brit Shalom le-Brit HaBiryonim [Zion: The Kingdom of Heaven or the Kingdom of Israel? Between Brit Shalom and 'The Covenant of Thugs']." In *Brit Shalom Ve Hatzionut HaDuleumit: "HaShela HaArvit" Ke-Shela Yehudit* [Brit Shalom and binational Zionism: The "Arab Question" as a Jewish Question], edited by Adi Gordon, 181–94. Jerusalem: Carmel, 2009.

Tabory, Ephraim. "Reform and Conservative Judaism in Israel: A Social and Religious Profile." *American Jewish Year Book* 83 (1983): 41–61.

Tal, Uriel. *Teologia Politit Ve HaRaych HaShlishi*. Introduction by Paul Mendes-Flohr. Tel Aviv: Sifriyat Poalim, 1991.

Taubes, Jacob. "Teologiya VeTeoriya Politit [Theology and political theory]." Translated by Yaniv Farkash. *Tchelet* 44 (2011): 90–102.

Thomas, Louisa. *Conscience: Two Soldiers, Two Pacifists, One Family: A Test of Will and Faith in World War I*. New York: Penguin Press, 2011.

Tocqueville, Alexis de. *Democracy in America*. Translated by Harvey C. Mansfield and Delba Winthrop. Chicago: University of Chicago Press, 2012.

Urofsky, Melvin. "Two Paths to Zion: Magnes and Stephen S. Wise." In *Like All the Nations? The Life and Legacy of Judah L. Magnes*, edited by William M. Brinner and Moses Rischin, 85–97. Albany: State University of New York Press, 1987.

Walzer, Michael. *Leumiyut Ve-Universalism* [Nationalism and universalism]. Jerusalem: Shalem, 2009.

———. *What It Means to Be an American: Essays on the American Experience*. New York: Marsilio, 1992.

Weber, Max. *Weber's Rationalism and Modern Society: New Translations on Politics, Bureaucracy, and Social Stratification*. Translated by Tony Waters and Dagmar Waters. London: Palgrave Macmillan, 2015.

Weinberg, David H. *Between Tradition and Modernity: Haim Zhitlowski, Simon Dubnow, Ahad Ha-Am and the Shaping of Modern Jewish Identity*. New York: Holmes & Meier, 1996.

Weizmann, Chaim. *The Letters and Papers of Chaim Weizmann*. 23 volumes. New Brunswick NJ and Jerusalem: Transaction Books and Israel Universities Press, 1968–80.

Wertheim, Aharon. *Halachot VeHalichot BeHasidut* [Halakha and the ways of Hasidism]. Jerusalem: Mosad Harav Kuk, 2003.

White, Ronald C., and C. Howard Hopkins. *The Social Gospel: Religion and Reform in Changing America*. Philadelphia: Temple University Press, 1976.

Wilcock, Evelyn. *Pacifism and the Jews: Studies of Twentieth Century Pacifists*. Gloucestershire, UK: Hawthorn Press, 1994.

Will, Barbara. "'Gertrude Stein and Zionism." *Modern Fiction Studies* 51, no. 2 (Summer 2005): 437–55.

Young-Bruehl, Elisabeth. *Hannah Arendt: For Love of the World*. New Haven CT: Yale University Press, 1982.
Yovel, Yirmiyahu. *Spinoza VeKofrim Acherim* [Spinoza and other heretics]. Tel Aviv: Sifriyat Poalim, 1988.
Zadoff, Noam. *MiBerlin LeYerushalaim Wu-VaHazara: Gershom Scholem Bein Israel VeGermaniya* [From Berlin to Jerusalem and back: Gershom Scholem between Israel and Germany]. Jerusalem: Kovner Center and Carmel Publishing, 2015.
Zipperstein, Steven J. *Elusive Prophet: Ahad Ha'am and the Origins of Zionism*. Berkeley: University of California Press, 1993.

INDEX

Abd al-Hadi, Awni, 187, 236
Adler, Felix, 27, 272n1
Adler, Samuel, 272n1
Agnon, Shmuel Yosef, ix, 269n1
Ahad Ha'am: and American Zionism, 27, 274n15, 291n41; and the Arabs, 277n50; and Brit Shalom, 99–100; and Buber, 159, 284n34; and diaspora, 27, 100; and Dubnow, 143; harmonious Jew, 28; and Hebrew language, xv; a Jewish state, 26, 158, 275n31; Magnes and, 38, 90–91, 94–95, 101–2, 112–13, 116, 118–19, 122, 143, 151, 156, 164, 171, 177, 222, 263–64, 267, 277n42; moral outlook, 27, 102, 171, 274n14; on nationalism, 99–100, 222, 263; and the prophets, 102, 104–5, 112–13, 118; and Reform Judaism, 28, 105; and religion, 28–29; spirit of the nation, 26–27, 33, 95, 105, 285n6; spirit-people-land, 162, 292n30. *See* Zionism
Alami, Musa, 185–87
Alexander the Great, 64
American Council for Judaism, 244

American Declaration of Independence, 133, 290n21
americanization: of American Jewry, 6, 40; of the Yishuv, 128
American Jewish Committee, 78, 244
anarchism, 170, 197, 294n11, 296n27
Anglo-American Committee of Inquiry, xxii, xxiv, 104, 233–35, 238, 240, 242, 245–47, 303n33
"Arab problem," 36–38, 147, 149–50, 157, 185; "Arab question" and, 98–101, 167, 182
Arendt, Hannah, xix, xxx, 253–60, 269, 286n25, 301n10, 304n12
Arlozorov, Haim, 185, 187
Arslan, Shakib, 186
assimilation, 27, 35, 95, 100, 242; to Arab life, 188; of Jews in America, 6, 11, 21–22, 34; and Reform Judaism, 23, 222–23, 226
Atley, Clement, 235, 242

Baer, Yitzhak, 192
Balfour Declaration, 38, 101, 132, 175, 258

Bar Kochba students' union, 103, 147, 167, 173
Barth, Karl, 117, 119-23, 196, 216, 263
Be'ayot. *See* Ichud (association)
Ben-Gurion, David, xii, 99, 116, 175-76, 179, 182-83, 187-90, 236, 242, 245, 250, 296n11
Bentwich, Norman, 78-80
Bergman, Hugo, xix, xx, 44, 97, 99, 102-3, 125, 147-48, 192-93, 196, 205-7, 211, 262, 298n12, 299n25
Bevin, Ernest, 234, 235, 237, 247
biblical criticism, 12
Bigelow, Herbert, 59
Billikopf, Jacob, 59, 287n6
Biltmore Program, xxiv, 105, 197, 246, 254; or Biltmore Declaration, 145, 202, 231
binationalism: American aspects, 131, 152-55, 160-61, 172, 265, 294n18; Anglo-American committee, 246-47; Arab views on, xi; bridging particular and universal, 24-25, 136-38, 264; and Brit Shalom, 98-100, 185; develops gradually, 190; Jewish-American, xxv, 265; as lost cause, x, 122-23, 128, 219; national-international entity, 264; political platform in 1929 of, xxix, 111, 147-65; as political theology, xxviii, 110, 112, 178, 190, 219, 227, 233-34; Reform roots, 242, 262, 264, 266. *See* Buber, Martin; confederation; HaShomer HaTza'ir
Biram, Arthur, 25
Bloch, Ernst, 10, 11, 271
Bonaparte, Napoleon, 64
Brandeis, Louis, 36, 183-84, 274n15, 276n43; "Brandeis Group," 183
Brit Habiryonim, 109, 177, 295nn31-32
Brit Shalom, xii, xix, 103, 107; Ahad Ha'am's influence on, 99-101;

Central European Circle of, xx, xxix, 29, 40, 99, 117, 140, 147, 193, 266; founding of, 97-98; and Ichud, 149, 202; idealism, 145, 158; Magnes's role in, 98-99, 104-5, 117, 140, 147, 285n19, 293n36; and nationalism, 147-48; political platform, 184-85; utopianism, 299n25. *See* binationalism
Buber, Martin, xix-xx, 90, 101, 123, 151, 192, 263; anarchism, 170-71, Anglo-American Committee testimony, xiv, xxix, 104, 238, 241, 246; on binationalism, 148, 172-74; "boundary line," 103, 171, 286n29; and Brit Shalom, 28, 103-4; on faith, 196, 297n37, 298n17; Hasidism, 10; Ichud, 202, 287n3; I-Thou, 167, 173, 196; immigration to Palestine, 103; *Kingdom of Heaven*, 44, 169; and Magnes, 10, 113, 130, 179-80, 192-95, 249-50, 286n32, 303n7; morality and politics, 171-72; on nationalism, 131, 140, 278n10, 284n34, 289n14; Nobel prize for Magnes, 245; religious socialism, 43, 103; theopolitics, 148, 167-69, 178-79, 270n4, 293n1, 293n4. *See* Ahad Ha'am

Central Conference of American Rabbis (CCAR), 24, 45, 57, 281n45
Chancellor, John, 186
Chevra, 79-80
"chosenness," Jewish, 134, 169
Christianity: early Jews and Christians, 89; Magnes as Jesus Christ in, 111, 249; perceiving Magnes as prophet, 57, 109-11; syncretism with Judaism, 57, 167. *See* pacifism
civil disobedience, 113, 130

322 *Index*

Cohen, Herman, xix, xxviii, 43, 72, 102, 142, 144–45, 158, 289n14
Cohen, Israel, 241–42
Committee for the Study of Arab-Jewish Relations, 149
Committee to Support Jewish War Victims, 293n36
confederation: American articles of 1777, 258; binational, xxx, 201, 256–59; "United States of Palestine," 257
Congregation Yeshurun (Jerusalem), 80–81, 85
conscience: Jewish, 156, 209; Magnes of Jewish People, xix, 259; of the world, 103, 175
Conservative Judaism, 77–79, 221; Magnes's affiliation with, x, xiv, 9, 12–14, 16–18, 20, 37, 120, 202, 229, 262; "Unofficial Reform Judaism" as, xxii, 16, 272
constitution, 105, 129, 131, 152, 155, 186, 188, 257–58, 265, 289n13
conversion, 202–3
Cronbach, Abraham, 72, 279n17
Crossman, Richard, 239, 246–47, 250
Crum, Bartley, 248–49, 303n43
cultural pluralism, 33–34, 36, 127, 274n15, 276n43
Cyrus, 64

Dajani, Hasan, 302n26
Dajani, Omar, 245, 302n26
Debs, Eugene, 39, 51, 72–73
De Haas, Jacob, 274n15
democracy, 40, 52, 124, 127, 130, 145, 149, 151, 153–54, 161, 165, 172, 265, 289n11
Deus absconditus, 212–13
Deutsch, Gotthard, 58–60
Dewey, John, 126, 276n38
diaspora, nationalism, 142, 290n19, 293n35; rejection of, 136

Dubnow, Simon, 27, 142–44, 290n19, 291n41

Eban, Aubrey, 257
eclipse of God, vii, xxix, 108, 123, 201, 204–8, 210, 231, 263, 298n17
Einhorn, David, 23
Einstein, Albert, 93–94, 285n1, 289n14
Emerson, Ralph Waldo, 170
Espionage Act of 1917, 45, 52, 73
ethical monotheism, xx, 27, 30–31, 61, 129, 144, 146, 171, 265
"ethic of conviction," and "ethic of responsibility," 122
Even-Zahav, Ari, 269n3

faith: crisis of, 84, 86, 214; and doubt, 231; after the Holocaust, 298n17; leap of, 213, 231; question of, xxi, 86; in a Supreme Being, 195
federalism, xxi, 255–59, 265; *Federalist Papers*, 258
Felsenthal, Bernard, 24
Fichte, Johann Gottlieb, 62, 140
Frank, Rachel, 3
Frankel, Zecharias, xxiii, 9, 12, 271n17
Friedlander, Israel, 12, 28, 56, 291n41
Friedlander, Marcus, 281n48
Fromm, Erich, 254
Frumkin, Gad, 189

Gandhi, Mahatma, 193
Gaon, Sa'adia, 8, 271n15
Gladden, Washington, 281n51
Goldmann, Lucien, 208, 210
Gordon, Aaron David, xix, 103, 170
Gordon, Judah Leib, 176
Gottheil, Gustav, 274n15
Gottheil, Richard, 24, 183, 274n15
Guggenheim family, 13
Gutmann, Julius, 271n15, 273n10

Index   323

Hadassah, ix, 11, 148-49, 184
Hall, George Henry, 234
Hamilton, Alexander, 258
Hankin, Yehoshua, 141
HaOl (association), 192-93, 196-97, 296n22
Hardy, Thomas, 51, 278n1
Harlow, Samuel Ralph, 110
HaShomer HaTza'ir: binationalism, 148-49, 236, 238, 246, 302n6, 303n33; "tragic man" worldview, 208-10
Hasidism, x, xxii, 6, 10-11, 30, 78, 83, 85, 118, 159, 165, 167, 206-7, 213, 262-63, 283n16
Hasmoneans, 178, 224
Hebrew Union College (HUC), xiv, xxiii, 4-7, 21, 58-63, 73, 86, 115
Hebrew University, Jerusalem, vii, xxix, 9, 74, 110, 117, 150, 184, 223, 227, 260; founding of, 74, 93-94, 99-100, 104; and Jeremiah, 187; Magnes role in xix-xx, xxiii, 140, 267; as spiritual center, 94-96, 105, 144, 150
Heinsheimer, Eduard, 59
Heller, Max, 24, 57, 279n16
Herder, Johann Gottfried, 144
Herzl, Theodor, 25-26, 99, 138, 263, 274n15
Hexter, Maurice, 254
Hillquit, Morris, 41-42, 73, 111, 277n5
Hirsch, Emil, 4, 59
Hochschule (Lehranstalt für die Wissenschaft des Judentums), 25
Hofshi, Natan, 191
Holmes, John Haynes, 57, 103, 109, 126, 154, 287
Holmes, Oliver Wendell, 126
Holocaust, viii, xxix, 196, 199, 201, 207, 211, 213, 231, 251, 263, 266, 298n17, 299n3

Hourani, Albert, 242
humanism, 43, 142
Husseini, Amin al-, 168
Husseini, Jamal, 236
Hutcheson, Joseph, 111, 235, 245, 248-50, 303n43
Hyamson, Albert, 178

Ibn Aknin, Joseph, 273n10
Ichud (association), xii, xix-xx, 286n3; and Anglo-American Committee, xxix, 235, 238, 240, 245-46, 248-50, 253; *Be'ayot* and, 188, 205, 249; founding of, xxiv, 103, 149, 197, 202; "Friends of Ichud" and, 254
idealism, xi-xii, xiv, 28, 46, 65, 145, 158, 163, 247
idolatry, 171, 223-24
imperialism, 45, 55, 110, 121, 132, 175, 178, 234, 255-56, 258-59, 289n16
Isaiah, 45, 55, 63, 70, 109, 115, 117-18, 177-78, 212
Islam, 164, 240

Jacobs, Rose, 149
James, William, 86, 89, 91, 126-28, 195, 216, 261
Jay, John, 258
Jeremiah, xx, xxix, 57, 78; and Ben Gurion, 175-76; jeremiad sermon, 14; "Jeremiah Complex," 107-8, 286n3; and Joshua, 174-75, 179; Magnes as, 108-12, 117, 124, 174-76, 178-79, 186-87, 213, 268, 287n15
Jewish Distribution Committee (JDC), 56, 70, 211
Jewish spiritual culture, 29-31, 33
Jewish Welfare Board, 78
Jewish Labor Congress, 46
"Jewish Soil," 32, 138, 140
Jewish Theological Seminary (JTS), 11-12

Jewish Theological Seminary of Breslau, xxiii, 9, 271n17
Jibri, Ihsan al-, 186
"Joshua method," 103, 111, 165, 174–77, 179, 295n43

Kabbalah, 118, 204
Kallen, Horace, 34, 36, 127, 274n38, 276n43
Kaplan, Mordecai, 11, 74, 78, 112, 162, 274n20
Katznelson, Berl, 154, 183
Kedma Mizraha, 149
the Kehillah, xxiii, 16, 19–20
Kehillah Shel Mosar Dati Ivri, 192
Kierkegaard, Søren, 213, 231
Kingdom of God on Earth, 54
Kingdom of Heaven, 47, 217–18, 230
Klal Israel (Catholic Israel), 12, 17
Kohler, Kaufmann, 4–5, 63–66
Kohn, Hans, 97, 99, 103, 134, 147–48, 193, 254, 290n22
Kook, Isaac Abraham, xix, 31, 90, 159, 275n28
Kvutzat HaHamisha (Committee of Five), 189

Landauer, Gustav, 43, 103, 278n10, 294n11
League for Jewish-Arab Rapprochement and Cooperation, 148–49
League of Nations, 42, 101, 159
Lehman, Arthur and Irving, 78
Leissin, Abraham, 42
Levy, Joseph, 181
liberalism, x, 3–4, 6, 21, 120, 154
Lincoln, Abraham, 64
Lindheim, Irma, 184
Lipsky, Louis, 183, 274n15
Lober, Louis, 80

Mack, Julian, 154
Madison, James, 258
Magnes, Beatrice, 12, 117
Maimonides, 29, 273n10
Margolis-Kalvarisky, Haim, 149
Marshall, George, xxiv
Marshall, James, 108, 205
Marshall, Louis, 13, 19, 59, 78, 93, 108, 205, 254, 272n26
McDonald, James, 247
Mehapsei Adonai, 190, 192
Meinecke, Friedrich, 129
The Melting Pot (Zangwill), 33–34
messianism: eschatological, 66; ethical, 66; existential, 217; political, 128, 185, 193, 264; universal, 5, 23, 48, 90, 138, 143, 145, 163, 172, 264, 280n84; in World War I, 48, 58, 65; Zionism as false, 190–91, 224
Mevakshei Paneikha, 192, 196
Mission Theology, 12, 24, 28, 31, 60–61, 65–72, 105, 115, 129, 226, 241–42, 264, 274n20
Montefiore, Claude, 114–15
Morais, Sabato, 7
Morgenstern, Julian, 115
Muslim Supreme Council in Palestine, 236
mysticism, xxiv, 10, 25, 49, 73, 103, 132, 140, 160, 165, 245, 262, 301n23

nationalism: American, 58, 129, 147, 171, 265; chauvinist, 22, 139, 141, 144–45, 171, 242; culture-defined or state-defined, 129; as idolatry, 171, 223–24; Jewish, 26, 99–101, 103, 122, 125, 132–37, 142–45, 201, 221–32, 263–64, 293n35; and national rights, 133, 135; primordial, 134, 136, 172; as "sanctified egoism," 102; as temporary phase, 115–17. *See* diaspora
national spirit, 27, 139–40, 162, 293n36

Index 325

Nearing, Scott, 137
neo-Orthodoxy, 262
Newcombe, Stuart, 188
Niebuhr, Reinhold, 235
Nietzsche, Friedrich, 36, 54, 62, 192, 209, 214, 275n22, 280n29
Novomeysky, Moshe, 189
numinous, 31, 83, 283n15

orchestra metaphor, 34, 36, 276
Orthodoxy, xxiv, 4-5, 7-8, 10-11, 16, 18, 20, 37, 79-82, 84, 168
Ostjuden, 9, 85
Otto, Rudolph, 31, 83, 275n27, 283n15

pacifism, xxviii, 38-39, 44, 51, 53, 88, 98-99, 115, 154, 197, 202, 281n48; Christian, 53, 55-57; Quaker, 53; Reform, 60-62, 65-67, 72; religious, xxviii, 38, 66, 74, 190, 262; renouncement during WWII, 74, 203-4; socialist, 49
Palestine Economic Corporation, 185-86
Partition Plan, 234, 240; of the land, xi, xxiv, 188, 190, 231, 251, 257
Pascal, Blaise, 212; "Pascal's wager," 86, 283n26
Peirce, Charles Sanders, 126
People's Council of America for Democracy and Peace, xxiii, 41, 45, 52, 59, 67
Philby, John, 181-82, 188
Pittsburgh Platform, 17, 23-24, 61, 114
Plato, xxv, xxvi
"political parity," and "numerical parity," xxiv, 55, 239
positive-historical Judaism, 12
pragmatism, xii, xxi, 20, 62, 86, 105, 124-28, 145, 152-53, 155-56, 165, 178, 194, 197, 210, 216, 265, 288n7, 294n18

the Prague circle, 148, 193, 299n25
prayer, 3, 5, 8, 11, 13, 15, 17, 24, 51, 77-79, 81, 83-85, 109, 206-7, 228, 241, 283n16, 298n12
prophecy: leadership, 112; Magnes perceived as, 108-14; Prophetic Judaism, 44, 114; prophetic politic, xii, 56, 104, 167, 171, 179; teachings of the prophets, 102, 114, 129, 265; withholding of, 213, 300n37
Proskauer, Joseph, 244

Quakers, 53, 262, 279n7
quietism, 85, 215, 283n22

Ragatz, Leonhard, 43, 103, 263
Rauschenbusch, Walter, 44
realpolitik, 43, 161, 193, 250
Red Scare, 74, 282n54
Reform Judaism: classical, xxiv, 22, 114; counter-Reform, 14; of Magnes, x, 7-15, 262, 264; prophetic teaching, 114-17; and World War I, 58-66; and Zionism, x, 17, 22-24, 222-25. *See* Mission Theology; pacifism; universalism
Reinhold, Niebuhr, 235
religious existentialism, 213, 300n39
Rockefeller, John D., 53
Rockefeller, John D., Jr., 53-54
romanticism, 9-10, 12, 42, 159, 172, 210
Rosenwald, Julius, 59
Rosenwald, Lessing, 244
Rosenzweig, Franz, xix, 131, 206, 263, 289n14, 298n12
Ruppin, Arthur, 97-98
Russel, Bertrand, 47, 87, 278n21
Rutenberg, Pinhas, 188

Sabbateanism, xii, 191-92, 196, 301n10
Sakakini, Khalil al-, xi, 269n3

Sampter, Jessie, 78, 282n4
Samuel, Herbert Louis, 78, 94
sanctity of the land, 159–60, 233, 236, 239–41, 292n27
San Francisco earthquake of 1906, 6
Schechter, Solomon, xxii–xxiii, 11–12, 14, 18, 34, 262, 272n24, 272n33, 274n20, 291n41
Schiff, Jacob, 13, 93
Scholem, Gershom, 86, 97, 99, 107–8, 118, 170, 191–92, 194, 204–5, 209, 262, 265, 279n8, 286n3, 287n15, 296n22, 296n27, 297n29, 301n10, 301nn22–23
Schiller, Friedrich, 64–65
Schlesinger, Max, 9, 25, 269
Sharett, Moshe, 187–88, 236
Sheifoteinu, 98
Silver, Abba Hillel, 37, 62, 72, 115–16, 129, 138, 171, 237
Silver, Maxwell, 62–63
Silverman, Joseph, 12–13
Simon, Akiva Ernst, xx, 99, 102, 114, 171, 192, 202, 262, 286n29, 288n22, 294n28, 300n1
Simon, Leon, 94
Singleton, John, 235
Smilansky, Moshe, 188, 190, 238, 246, 249
Social Gospel, xxiii, xxviii, 39, 44–45, 49, 57, 72, 194, 262, 278n18, 281n51
socialism, xxiii–xxiv, 25, 51, 54, 88, 154, 179, 223, 226; American-Jewish, 39–41; ethical, 39, 43, 49, 194; Jewish masses, 47–49; radical, 44, 49–50, 194, 262; religious, xxvii–xxviii, 39–40, 43–44, 46–47, 103, 194; sober view, 49
Soloveitchik, Yosef Dov, 168, 294n6
Spinoza, Baruch, xxvi; *Theological-Political Treatise*, 221, 227, 232
Stein, Gertrud, 3, 270n1

Stern, Gabriel, 267
Strauss, Leo, xxvi
Szold, Henrietta, ix, 11, 78, 80, 149, 291n41

Taubes, Jacob, xxv–xxvi
Temple Emanu-El, xxii, 12–19, 28, 34, 39, 57, 93, 272n1, 272n32, 273n13
theodicy, xxi, 86
theological politics, 129, 178, 301n23
theology: critical, xxvii; dialectical, xxix, 119; liberal, 4, 119–20, 263; political, xxi, xxv–xxviii, 32, 163, 165, 167, 178–79, 208, 266–67, 270n4, 293n1; of quest, 196, 231, 263
theopolitical realism, 169, 174
theurgy, 230, 301n23
Thomas, Norman, 45, 57, 278n17
Thoreau, Henry David, 130, 170
Tillich, Paul, 43, 263
"Tragic Man," 208, 210
Truman, Harry, xxiv, 202, 235, 237, 240

universalism: American, 141; Jewish, 116, 129; of the Jewish Sages, 229; and nationalism, 136–38, 145; and particularism, 46, 142, 203; political, 129, 165; radical, 27, 222; Reform, 22–24, 138–39, 141, 143, 146, 165; theological, 129
utopianism, 49, 65, 82, 102–3, 132, 164, 210, 247, 259, 299n25, 301n10

Verein Jüdischer Studenten, 26
Voorsanger, Jacob, 4–7

Warburg, Felix, 13, 78, 93, 114, 182, 184
Weber, Max, 42, 122–23, 156
Weizmann, Chaim, xii, 93–94, 174, 176, 182–83, 186, 202, 236, 242, 276n40, 285n1, 287n19

Weltsch, Robert, 147
Western Wall riots (1929), xxi, xxiii, 111, 149, 156, 164
Weyl, Walter, 45
Widoma, Poland, 10
Wilde, Oscar, 3
Wilhelm, Yaakov David, 221, 300n2
Wise, Isaac Meir, 4, 7–8
Wise, Stephen, 13, 27, 37, 56, 78, 100, 154, 183, 235, 277n47, 281n41
World Peace Fellowship, 55
World War I, xxi, xxiii, xxvi, 11, 22, 38–39, 41, 43–44, 47–48, 51–54, 66, 74, 97–98, 102, 104, 119–20, 125, 131–32, 135, 139, 143, 146, 148, 154, 209, 231, 262–63, 266, 278n10, 278n21, 279n7

World War II, xi, xxiv, 108, 197, 201, 209, 211, 224, 231, 250, 288n22, 302n1

Yiddish, 9, 14, 40–42

Zangwill, Israel, 33–36
Zhitlovsky, Chaim, 41, 277n3
Zionism: American, 27–28, 34, 36, 72, 137–38, 210; cultural, xii, xxviii, 14, 17, 26, 33, 49, 135; "despair theory" of, 35, 276n40; political, xxviii, 26, 90, 99–100, 110, 115, 128, 136–37, 143–45, 175, 177, 191, 202, 224–25, 231–32, 242, 256, 274n15, 284n34
Zunz, Leopold, 9, 271n17
Zvi, Shabtai, 191, 224

www.ingramcontent.com/pod-product-compliance
Lightning Source LLC
Chambersburg PA
CBHW021832110226
39531CB00026B/200